UPBUILDING DISCOURSES IN VARIOUS SPIRITS

KIERKEGAARD'S WRITINGS, XV

UPBUILDING DISCOURSES
IN VARIOUS SPIRITS

by Søren Kierkegaard

Edited and Translated
with Introduction and Notes by

Howard V. Hong and

Edna H. Hong

PRINCETON UNIVERSITY PRESS
PRINCETON, NEW JERSEY

Copyright © 1993 by Howard V. Hong
Published by Princeton University Press,
41 William Street, Princeton, New Jersey 08540
In the United Kingdom: Princeton University Press, Chichester, West Sussex

All Rights Reserved

Library of Congress Cataloging-in-Publication Data

Kierkegaard, Søren, 1813–1855.
[Opbyggelige taler i forskjellig aand. English]
Upbuilding discourses in various spirits / by Søren Kierkegaard;
edited and translated with introduction and notes by Howard V. Hong
and Edna H. Hong.
p. cm. — (Kierkegaard's writings; 15)
Translation of: Opbyggelige taler i forskjellig aand.
Includes bibliographical references and index.
ISBN 0-691-03274-2
1. Christian life—Lutheran authors.   I. Hong, Howard Vincent,
1912– .   II. Hong, Edna Hatlestad, 1913– .   III. Title.
IV. Series: Kierkegaard, Søren, 1813–1855. Works. English. 1978 ;
15.
BV4505.K46   1993   92-33248

Preparation of this volume has been made possible in part by a grant from
the Division of Research Programs of the National Endowment
for the Humanities, an independent federal agency

Princeton University Press books are printed
on acid-free paper and meet the guidelines for permanence and durability
of the Committee on Production Guidelines for Book Longevity
of the Council on Library Resources

Designed by Frank Mahood

Printed in the United States of America

1 3 5 7 9 10 8 6 4 2

CONTENTS

Part Three
THE GOSPEL OF SUFFERINGS
CHRISTIAN DISCOURSES
213

HISTORICAL INTRODUCTION

The months between the publication of *Concluding Unscientific Postscript to* Philosophical Fragments (February 27, 1846) and the publication of *Upbuilding Discourses in Various Spirits* (March 13, 1847) were for Kierkegaard a time of intensive writing in accord with a crucial change of plans.

The original plan was to "conclude" writing with the completion of *Postscript*[1] and to seek a position as a rural pastor.

> It is now my intention to qualify as a pastor. For several months I have been praying to God to keep on helping me, for it has been clear to me for some time now that I ought not to be a writer any longer, something I can be only totally or not at all. This is the reason I have not started anything new along with proof-correcting except for the little review of *Two Ages*, which again is concluding.[2]

> Up until now I have made myself useful by helping the pseudonyms become authors. What if I decided from now on to do the little writing I can excuse in the form of criticism. Then I would put down what I had to say in reviews, developing my ideas from some book or other and in such a way that they could be included in the work itself. In this way I would still avoid becoming an author.[3]

In keeping with this plan, Kierkegaard altered his pattern of writing and wrote only "reviews": *Two Ages: The Age of Revolution and the Present Age, A Literary Review* (March 30, 1846) and *The Book on Adler*[4] (published posthumously). But the continuation of *The Corsair*'s attacks upon him[5] and the public

---

[1] See Historical Introduction, *Concluding Unscientific Postscript to* Philosophical Fragments, pp. xi–xiii, *KW* XII.2.

[2] See Supplement, p. 356 and notes 1 and 2 (*Pap.* VII[1] A 4).

[3] *JP* V 5877 (*Pap.* VII[1] A 9). See Supplement, p. 356 and note 2.

[4] *KW* XXIV (*Pap.* VII[2] B 235). See Supplement, p. 363 (*Pap.* VII[2] B 242).

[5] See Historical Introduction, *The* Corsair *Affair*, pp. vii–xxxviii, *KW* XIII.

consequences of those attacks meant also an altered pattern of life for Kierkegaard. The most obvious change was that Copenhagen's preeminent peripatetic[6] could no longer walk the streets and converse with acquaintances and strangers.[7] Copenhagen was no longer the congenial walking place it had been for him.[8] Instead of walking, he took numerous drives for

---

[6] Kierkegaard was Copenhagen's "greatest peripatetic," as Villads Christensen has called him in *Peripatetikeren Søren Kierkegaard* (Copenhagen: 1965), p. 5. Andrew Hamilton, in the earliest English account of Kierkegaard, *Sixteen Months in the Danish Isles*, I–II (London: 1852), II, pp. 268–70, wrote:

> There is a man whom it is impossible to omit in any account of Denmark, but whose place it might be more difficult to fix; I mean Sören Kierkegaard. But as his works have, at all events for the most part, a religious tendency, he may find a place among the theologians. He is a philosophical Christian writer, evermore dwelling, one might almost say harping, on the theme of the human heart. There is no Danish writer more in earnest than he, yet there is no one in whose way stand more things to prevent his becoming popular. He writes at times with an unearthly beauty, but too often with an exaggerated display of logic that disgusts the public. All very well, if he were not a popular author, but it is for this he intends himself.
>
> I have received the highest delight from some of his books. But no one of them could I read *with pleasure* all through. His "Works of Love" has, I suppose, been the most popular, or, perhaps, his "Either—Or," a very singular book. A little thing published during my stay, gave me much pleasure, "Sickness unto Death."
>
> Kierkegaard's habits of life are singular enough to lend a (perhaps false) interest to his proceedings. He goes into no company, and sees nobody in his own house, which answers all the ends of an invisible dwelling; I could never learn that any one had been inside of it. Yet his one great study is human nature; no one knows more people than he. The fact is *he walks about town all day*, and generally in some person's company; only in the evening does he write and read. When walking, he is very communicative, and at the same time manages to draw everything out of his companion that is likely to be profitable to himself.
>
> I do not know him. I saw him almost daily in the streets, and when he was alone I often felt much inclined to accost him, but never put it into execution. I was told his "talk" was very fine. Could I have enjoyed it, without the feeling that I was myself being mercilessly pumped and sifted, I should have liked [it] very much.

[7] See Supplement, p. 356–57 (*Pap.* VII[1] A 107).
[8] See Historical Introduction, Corsair *Affair*, pp. xxix–xxxi, *KW* XIII.

solitude in wooded areas near Copenhagen,[9] and in May 1846 he spent a fortnight in Berlin.[10]

"And now that I have remodeled my external life, am more withdrawn, keep to myself more, have a more momentous look about me, then in certain quarters it will be said that I have changed for the better."[11] And in quite another sense there was a change, and for the better in quite another sense. The major consequence of the *Corsair* affair (apart from Kierkegaard's success in separating editor Meïr Goldschmidt from the paper[12] and ending its reign of terror[13]) was that Kierkegaard's plan was remodeled. The *Corsair* affair was a kind of *felix culpa*, a happy fault that, as an essential element in his own education, was the occasion for his giving up the rural pastorate idea and the plan to lay down his pen: "Now I stand resolved and rooted to the spot in a way I have never been."[14]

Out of Kierkegaard's greater self-knowledge, sharpened insight into human life, and deepened awareness of the implications of the Christian faith came what may be called his "second authorship." *Concluding Unscientific Postscript* may be called the "turning point," but the experience of 1846, the *Corsair* experience, was the impelling point,[15] and *Upbuilding Discourses in Various Spirits* was the first yield in the second authorship. A clue to the distinctive nature of the second authorship is the subtitle "Christian Discourses," which was used for the first time in that work.[16]

Kierkegaard was very prolific during the fourteen months

---

[9] See *JP* V 6013 and note 1606.

[10] *JP* V 6013 (*Pap.* VIII¹ A 163): "I know very well that Heiberg [Johan Ludvig] and the like Christianly explain my walking the street as so much vanity—that I do it to be seen. I wonder if it is also to be seen that I walk about even more, if possible, in Berlin, where not a soul knows me?"

[11] See Supplement, p. 356–57 (*Pap.* VII¹ A 107).

[12] See Historical Introduction, Corsair *Affair*, pp. xv–xvi, xxiv, *KW* XIII.

[13] Ibid., pp. ix–x

[14] See Supplement, p. 361 (*Pap.* VII¹ A 229) and pp. 357–61 (*Pap.* VII¹ A 221, 222).

[15] See Historical Introduction, *Postscript*, pp. xi–xiii, *KW* XII.2.

[16] See pp. 213, 215; Supplement, p. 386 (*Pap.* VIII¹ A 20).

before the publication of *Discourses in Various Spirits*. In addition to writing that work, he completed the "reviews" of *Two
Ages* and of Adler's works and also developed to a considerable
extent a series of lectures on communication.[17] After the publication of *Two Ages*, he considered the possibility of a series of
short pieces of varied contents,[18] including one on the lilies and
the birds. Early in the autumn of 1846, he pondered a collection
of sermons under the title "The Gospel of Sufferings," to be
followed by "three short but delightful discourses: What We
Learn from the Lilies in the Field and from the Birds of the
Air."[19] The idea of publishing small parts at a low price[20]
persisted but gave way to the decision to publish four works,[21]
including "The Book on Adler," in one volume under the title
"Minor Works." Finally "The Book on Adler" was omitted,
and the three remaining works became the three parts of *Discourses in Various Spirits*.[22] Three separate title pages of the three
parts are mementos of the earlier plan. In the original edition,
the three parts also have separate pagination. In two journal
entries,[23] Kierkegaard discusses at some length the relations of
the three parts, and in the context of the internal coherence of
the three-part work it is readily apparent that "The Book on
Adler" was planned as an appendage.

Presumably the customary edition of five hundred copies was
printed, but no record of sales is included in Brandt and Rammel's work on Kierkegaard's publications and finances.[24] The
discourses were not reprinted during Kierkegaard's lifetime.
Kierkegaard had hitherto been his own publisher, and the edition of the discourses was the first in a series of works pub-

---

[17] See *JP* I 648 (*Pap.* VIII[2] B 79).
[18] See Supplement, pp. 361–62 (*Pap.* VII[1] B 212, 213).
[19] See Supplement, pp. 362–63 (*Pap.* VII[1] A 160).
[20] See Supplement, pp. 365 (*Pap.* VII[1] B 219, 220).
[21] See Supplement, p. 363 (*Pap.* VII[1] B 214).
[22] See Supplement, pp. 364, 366 (*Pap.* VII[1] B 218, 192:1–2).
[23] See Supplement, pp. 388–91 (*Pap.* VIII[1] A 15, 16).
[24] See Frithiof Brandt and Else Rammel, *Søren Kierkegaard og Pengene*
(Copenhagen: Munksgaard, 1935).

lished on an honorarium basis with the Reitzel Forlag.[25] For
the volume of discourses, Kierkegaard received 225 rix–dollars
(approximately $1125 in 1973 money).

There were two brief reviews and one long review of the
work. In the *Berlingske Tidende*,[26] the anonymous announce-
ment is extended by a few lines in praise of the work as surpass-
ing Kierkegaard's previous works of a similar nature because of
the artistry of the writing, the consistency of development, the
deep earnestness, and the clear view of what Christianity is and
what it requires. An anonymous review in *Nyt Aftenblad*[27]
essentially consists of a letter of thanks for the opportunity of
setting forth the best and highest thoughts of a solitary who,
against the stream of preoccupation with social salvation and
vain temporal striving, is concerned with the holy, the eternal,
and individual life. The long review by Ludvig Nicolaus
Helveg,[28] a Grundtvigian pastor and church historian, begins
by noting the author's intention to be a vanishing occasion, at
most a prompter in relation to the reader. The reviewer then
briefly discusses Part One as illustrative of the author's characteristic style and as analogous to Kant's principle of univer-
sality. Part Two, Helveg continues, exhibits the characteristic
mark of the author's conception: "The quiet rest in the mater-
nal lap of loving providence that nature proclaims"[29] is interpreted psychologically as a movement of thought, the abstract
thought of man as man. In Part Three, the author's intention is
said to be to present the essence of Christianity, which again is
defined altogether psychologically and which in its purely log-
ical form leads more to a Kantian stoicism than to a Christian
confession of sin. The reviewer concludes with the judgment
that the discourses are not upbuilding in the usual sense, be-

---

[25] Ibid., pp. 22–23. With regard to the publishing of Kierkegaard's works,
see also Corsair *Affair*, p. 302, note 406, *KW* XIII; *Kierkegaard: Letters and
Documents*, Letters 152–157, *KW* XXV.

[26] See *Berlingske Tidende*, 85, April 14, 1847, col. 1.

[27] See *Nyt Aftenblad*, March 18 and 19, 1847. col. 5, 5.

[28] Anon. (Ludvig Helveg), *For Literatur og Kritik*, V, 1847, pp. 299–306.

[29] Ibid., p. 302.

cause they betray, even where they are simplest and most intimate, that they are a dialectical work of art that puts thought
into motion instead of comforting and addressing the heart.

On the whole, many readers are more likely to agree with
the observation of the Danish scholar Eduard Geismar on Part
One of *Upbuilding Discourses in Various Spirits*: "I am of the
opinion that nothing of what he has written is to such a degree
before the face of God. Anyone who really wants to understand Kierkegaard does well to begin with it."[30]

[30] Eduard Geismar, *Søren Kierkegaard, hans Livsudvikling og Forfatter-
virksomhed*, I–VI (Copenhagen: 1927), V, p. 11.

UPBUILDING DISCOURSES
IN VARIOUS SPIRITS

by Søren Kierkegaard

Part One[1]

AN OCCASIONAL DISCOURSE

TO

"THAT SINGLE INDIVIDUAL"[2]

THIS LITTLE BOOK

IS DEDICATED

Although this little book (it can be called an occasional discourse, yet without having the occasion that makes the speaker and makes him an *authority* or the occasion that makes the reader and makes him a *learner*) in the situation of *actuality* is like a fancy, a dream in the daytime, yet it is not without confidence and not without hope of fulfillment. It seeks that single individual, to whom it gives itself wholly, by whom it wishes to be received as if it had arisen in his own heart, that single individual whom I with joy and gratitude call *my* reader, that single individual, who willingly reads slowly, reads repeatedly, and who reads aloud—for his own sake. If it finds him, then in the remoteness of separation the understanding is complete when he keeps the book and the understanding to himself in the inwardness of appropriation.

[4]When a woman works on a cloth for sacred use, she makes every flower as beautiful, if possible, as the lovely flowers of the field, every star as sparkling, if possible, as the twinkling stars of the night; she spares nothing but uses the most precious things in her possession; then she disposes of every other claim on her life in order to purchase the uninterrupted and opportune time of day and night for her sole, her beloved, work. But when the cloth is finished and placed in accordance with its sacred purpose—then she is deeply distressed if anyone were to make the mistake of seeing her artistry instead of the meaning of the cloth or were to make the mistake of seeing a defect instead of seeing the meaning of the cloth. She could not work the sacred meaning into the cloth; she could not embroider it on the cloth as an additional ornament. The meaning is in the beholder and in the beholder's understanding when, faced with himself and his own self, he has in the infinite remoteness of separation infinitely forgotten the needlewoman and her part. It was permissible, it was fitting, it was a duty, it was a cherished duty, it was a supreme joy for the needle-

woman to do everything in order to do her part, but it would be an offense against God, an insulting misunderstanding to the poor needlewoman, if someone were to make the mistake of seeing what is there but is to be disregarded, what is there—not to draw attention to itself but, on the contrary, only so that its absence would not disturbingly draw attention to itself.

                                                              S. K.

On the Occasion of a Confession

[5]Father in heaven! What is a human being without you! What is everything he knows, even though it were enormously vast and varied, but a disjointed snippet if he does not know you; what is all his striving, even though it embraced a world, but a job half done if he does not know you, you the one who is one and who is all! Then may you give the understanding wisdom to comprehend the one thing; may you give the heart sincerity to receive the understanding; may you give the will purity through willing only one thing. Then, when everything is going well, give the perseverance to will one thing, in distractions the concentration to will one thing, in sufferings the patience to will one thing. O you who give both the beginning and the completing,[6] may you give to the young person early, when the day is dawning, the resolution to will one thing; when the day is waning, may you give to the old person a renewed remembrance of his first resolution so that the last may be like the first, the first like the last, may be the life of a person who has willed only one thing. But, alas, this is not the way it is. Something came in between them; the separation of sin lies in between them; daily, day after day, something intervenes between them: delay, halting, interruption, error, perdition. Then may you give in repentance the bold confidence to will again one thing. Admittedly it is an interruption of the usual task; admittedly it is a halting of work as if it were a day of rest when the penitent (and only in repentance is the burdened laborer quiet) in the confession of sin is alone before you in self-accusation. Oh, but it is indeed an interruption that seeks to return to its beginning so that it might rebind what is separated, so that in sorrow it might make up for failure, so that in its solicitude it might complete what lies ahead. O you who give both the beginning and the completing, may you give victory on the day of distress so that the one distressed in

repentance may succeed in doing what the one burning in desire and the one determined in resolution failed to do: to will only one thing.

Everything has its time,[7] says Solomon, and this is how experience speaks of the past and the traversed when the old person reliving his life lives it only in reflective recollection, when wisdom in the old person has outgrown the impressions of life, which as immediately present, in the hustle and bustle of life, are something different from what they are as the past for calm recollection. The time of work and exhaustive effort is over, the time of desire and dance; life makes no more demands upon the old person, and he makes no more demands upon it; by being present, one thing is no closer to him than another, does not change his judgment in the expectation, does not change it in the decision, does not change it in regret. It has all been equalized by the pastness that as something completely past has nothing present to relate to. Oh, what bleakness of old age if this were what it means to be old, if it were true that life at any moment can ever be regarded by a living person as if he himself did not exist, as if life were merely a past event but had no present task whatever for the living person, as if the living person and life were separated in life in such a way that life was over and done with and he had become an absentee. Oh, what lamentable wisdom if everything human were as Solomon said and if the discourse on it had to end in the same way as the one about there being a time for everything—with the familiar words "What benefit from all his striving does he have who exerts himself" (Ecclesiastes 3:9)!

Perhaps the meaning would have been clearer if Solomon had said: There *was* a time for everything, everything *had* its time—in order to show that as an old man he is speaking about the past, and that he is actually not speaking to anyone but is speaking to himself. The person who speaks about that human life which changes over the years must indeed be careful to tell his listener in which period of life he is himself; and the wisdom that pertains to the changeable and temporal in a person must, as must everything fragile, be dealt with carefully, lest it do harm. Only the eternal applies at all times and is always, is always true, pertains to every human being of whatever age; the changeable is and is changed when it has been, and therefore the discourse about it is subject to changeableness. What is said by the old person about the past may be wisdom, but it surely would be foolishness in the mouth of a youth or adult if said about the present: The youth would be unable to understand it, and the adult would be unwilling to understand it. A somewhat older person can already agree totally with Solomon in saying: There is a time to dance for joy—and why can he agree with him? Because for him the time for dancing is over, and consequently he speaks of it as one who speaks of something bygone. And whether in those days when there were youthfulness and the pleasure of dancing he grieved that it was denied him or he gladly accepted the invitation to the dance, the somewhat older person will nevertheless calmly say: There is a time for dancing. But daring to hurry off to the dance and having to sit imprisoned at home are for youth two such different things that it does not occur to youth to link them equally and say: There is a time for the one and a time for the other. A person changes with the years, and every time some phase is accomplished he speaks impartially of its varied content, but this does not mean that he has become wiser, for he is only saying thereby that he has changed. There may be something now that stirs him in the same way as dancing stirred the youth, something that occupies him in the same way as a toy occupies the child. This is how a person changes with the years; the old person is the last change, and he speaks impartially of it all, all the changeable that now is past.

But is the story finished here? Has everything been heard that can be said about what it means to be a human being and about human life in time? Surely the most important and the most crucial thing has been left out, because discourse about the natural changes of human life over the years as well as about what happens externally is not essentially different from discourse about plant or animal life.

The animal, too, is changed over the years, in its old age has cravings different from those in its earlier years, also has at certain times its joy in life and must in turn endure hardships. Indeed, late in autumn the flower can utter the wisdom of years and truthfully say: For everything there is a time; "there is a time to be born and a time to die";[8] there is a time to play lightheartedly with the spring breezes and a time to be snapped off by the autumn storms; beloved by the spring, there is a time to blossom exuberantly by the running water and a time to wither and be forgotten; a time to be sought out for its loveliness and a time to be unrecognizable in its wretchedness; there is a time to be nursed with care and a time to be cast out in contempt; there is a time to delight in the warmth of the morning sun and a time to perish in the cold of the night—everything has its time; what gain does he who exerts himself have from all his striving? Indeed, when it is decrepit, the animal can speak with the wisdom of years and truthfully say: Everything has its time; there is a time to leap for joy and a time to crawl along the ground; there is a time to awaken early and a time to sleep late; there is a time to run with the herd and a time to go apart to die; there is a time to build a nest with its beloved and a time to sit alone on the roof; there is a time to fly free upward toward the clouds and a time to sink oppressed to the earth—everything has its time; what gain does he who exerts himself have from all his striving?

VIII
122

And if you were to say to the flower, "Is there nothing more to tell?" it would answer, "No, when the flower is dead, the story is finished"—otherwise, of course, the story would have had to be a different story from the beginning and in the development and would not have become different only at the end. Suppose that the flower ended its reply in another way and added, "The story is not finished, because when I am dead I become immortal"—would this not be strange talk? In other words, if the flower were immortal, the immortality would certainly have to be precisely what would prevent it from dying, and then the immortality would have to have been present every moment of its life. And the talk about its life would in turn have to have been entirely different in order to express the difference of immortality from everything changeable and from the diversity of the corruptible. Immortality could not be a final change that intervened, if one wants to put it that way, in death as the concluding age; on the contrary, it is a changelessness that is not changed with the change of the years. This is why the wise Solomon added to what the old person said about there being a time for everything, "God has made everything beautiful in its time; he has also put eternity into the heart of human beings" (Ecclesiastes 3:11). The sage speaks this way because the discourse about the change and the changed discourse about the change is, after all, confusing, even the old person's—only the eternal is upbuilding; the wisdom of the years is confusing—only the wisdom of eternity is upbuilding.

If, then, there is something eternal in a human being, this must be able to be and able to be claimed throughout every change. Thus neither can it be wisdom to talk impartially about it and say that it has its time just as the corruptible has, that it has its cycles just as the wind does, which really never makes any headway, that it has its course just as the river, which still never fills the ocean. Nor can it be wisdom to speak impartially about the eternal as one speaks of the past when it is gone, and gone in such a way that it cannot be related at all to a person present, not even in regret, but only to an absentee, because regret is indeed the relation between a past and someone who is living in the present time. It would be unwise of the youth to want to speak impartially of the delight of dancing and of its opposite, because this wise foolishness would betray that the youth in his youth would have outgrown youth. But with respect to the eternal, no time ever comes when a person has outgrown it or has grown older—than the eternal! If there is something eternal in a human being, then the discourse about it must be different; it must say that there is something that should always have its time, something that a person should always do, just as an apostle declares that we should always thank God.[9] Something that has its time must duly be regarded as an associate and equal of something temporal that likewise must have its time in turn, but the eternal is the dominant, which does not want to have its time but wants to make time *its own* and then permits the temporal also to have its time. Thus Scripture declares: The one should be done; the other

VIII
123

should not be neglected.[10] But that which must not be neglected is, of course, that which can come under consideration only when that which should be done is done. So also with the eternal. If, then, any worldly wisdom wants to change what should pertain to the eternal in a human being into something also temporal, this would be foolishness, whether it is an old person or a youth who is speaking, because with regard to the eternal the years constitute no justification for talking foolishly, and youth constitutes no exclusion from being able to comprehend what is right. If someone were to expound that godliness is to belong to childhood in the temporal sense and thus dwindle and die with the years as childhood does, is to be a happy frame of mind that cannot be preserved but only recollected; if someone were to expound that repentance as a weakness of old age accompanies the decline of one's powers, when the senses are dulled, when sleep no longer strengthens but increases lethargy—this would be ungodliness and foolishness. It is of course true that there was the one who over the years forgot the godliness of childhood, was cheated of the best and deceived by the most presumptuous; it is of course true that there

was the one whom repentance did not catch up with before the painfulness of old age, when he did not have even the strength to sin, so that repentance was not only late but the despair of late repentance became the final stage—but this is no story about an event that is to be cleverly explained or is itself presumably even to explain life: it is a nightmare. And even if a person became a thousand years old, he still would not be old enough to dare to speak of it in any other way than the young speak of it—with fear and trembling.[11] In relation to the eternal, a person does not in a temporal sense grow older than the eternal, therefore not in the sense of pastness either. No, human language calls it maturity and an advantage to have outgrown, as an adult, the childish and the youthful, but to want at any time to have outgrown the eternal it calls falling away from God and perdition, and only the life of the ungodly "will be like the snail, which dissolves into slime as it goes along" (Psalm 58:8).

So, then, there is something that must always be done,

something that is not to have its time in the temporal sense—and if, alas, it is not done, if it is neglected, or if even the opposite is done—then there is again something (or rather it is the same thing that comes back again, presumably changed but not changed in essence) that always must be done, something that is not to have its time in the temporal sense—*that must be repented and regretted.* We dare not say of repentance and regret that it has its time, that there is a time to be carefree and a time to be crushed in repentance. Such talk would be unpardonably slow compared with the concerned haste of repentance; it would be ungodly compared with godly grief,[12] pointlessly procrastinating about what should be done this very day, in this moment, in the moment of danger. There is indeed a danger; there is a danger that is called going astray; it does not stop by itself but still continues and then is called perdition. But there is a solicitous guide, an expert, who makes one aware, who shouts to the wanderer so that he is on his guard. This guide is regret; he is not as nimble as the suppleness of the imagination, which serves the wish; he is not as strongly built as the victorious intention—he comes slowly afterward, aggrieved, but he is a trustworthy and sincere friend. If the voice of this guide is never heard, then it is precisely because the way of perdition is being followed, for when the invalid, wasting away in consumption, feels most healthy, the sickness is at its worst. If there was someone who early hardened his heart to regret nothing and who regretted nothing—ah, it will surely come back again, provided that this can be regretted at all. So strange a power is regret, so sincere is its friendship, that there is in fact nothing more terrible than to have escaped it entirely. A person may wish to sneak away from much in this life and he may succeed, so that the indulged one can say in the last moment: I escaped all the toil and moil in which other people drudge. But if anyone wants to run away from, to be defiant toward, or to sneak away from regret—alas, which is worse, to say that he failed or—that he succeeded!

Over every human being's journey through life there watches a providence who provides everyone with two guides: the one calls forward, the other calls back. Yet they do not contradict

VIII
125

each other, the two guides, nor do they let the traveler stand there irresolute, confused by the double call; on the contrary, the two have an eternal understanding with each other, for the one calls forward to the good, the other calls back from the evil. Nor are they blind guides—this is precisely why they are two, because in order to safeguard the journey there must be a looking ahead and a looking back. Alas, perhaps there was many a one who went astray by mistakenly continuing a good beginning, since the continuation was on a wrong road, by unremittingly pressing forward—so regret could not lead him back to the old road. Perhaps there was someone who went astray in the prostration of the repentance that does not move from the spot—so the guide could not help him to find the road forward. When a long procession is to start, there is first a call from the person who is in the lead, but everyone waits until the last one has answered. The two guides call to a person early and late, and if he pays attention to their calls, he finds the road and can know where he is on the road, because these two calls determine the place and indicate the road, the call of regret perhaps the better, since the casual traveler who goes down the road quickly does not get to know it as does the traveler with his burden. The one who is only striving does not get to know the road as well as does the one who regrets; the former hurries ahead to something new, to something new—perhaps also away from the experience; but the one who regrets comes along afterward, laboriously gathers up the experience.

The two guides call to a person early and late—and yet not so, for when regret calls to a person it is always late. The call to find the road again by seeking God in the confession of sins is always at the eleventh hour. Whether you are young or old, whether you have offended much or little, whether you are guilty of much or have left much undone, the guilt makes this an eleventh-hour call; the concern of inwardness, which regret sharpens, grasps that this is at the eleventh hour. In the temporal sense, old age is the eleventh hour, and the moment of death is the last moment of the eleventh hour; the indolent youth talks of a long life that is supposed to lie ahead of him; the indolent old man hopes that he will not die for a long time

VIII
126

yet—but repentance and regret belong to the eternal in a human being, and thus every time repentance comprehends the guilt it comprehends that it is in the eleventh hour, that hour which human indolence knows very well exists and will come when it is spoken of in generalities, but not when it applies personally to the indolent person himself, for even the old man believes that there is still time left, and the indolent youth fools himself if he thinks that age difference is the main factor with regard to the closeness of the eleventh hour. This is why it is so good and so necessary to have two guides, because whether it is the wish of lightly armed youth, which presumably wants to press forward victoriously, or it is the manly resolution, which wants to fight its way through life—they both have an idea of a long time at their disposal; they count on a lifetime or at least a few years in the plan for their striving—and this is why so much time is wasted and why the whole thing so easily ends in error. But repentance and regret know how to associate with time in fear and trembling. When regret wakes up troubled, be it in the youth or in the old man, it always wakes up at the eleventh hour. It does not have much time at its disposal, because it is indeed the eleventh hour; it does not deceive with a false notion of a long life, because it is indeed the eleventh hour. And in the eleventh hour one understands life quite differently than in the days of youth or in adulthood's busy time or in the final moment of old age. The person who repents at any other hour of the day repents temporally; he fortifies himself with a false and superficial notion of the insignificance of guilt; he fortifies himself with a deceptive and busy notion of the length of life—that person's regret is not in true inwardness. O eleventh hour, how changed everything is when you are present; how still everything is, as if it were the midnight hour; how earnest everything is, as if it were the hour of death; how solitary, as if it were among the tombstones; how solemn, as if it were in eternity! O strenuous hour of work (although the task is at rest) when the accounting is made and yet there is no accuser, when everything is mentioned by its proper name and yet there is no one who speaks, when every idle word[13] must be repeated in the transformation of eternity! What an expensive

purchase when regret must pay dearly for what seemed so
negligible to irresponsibility and busyness and proud striving
and impatient passion and public opinion! O eleventh hour,
how terrible if you should linger on, more terrible than if death
were to go on for a whole life.

Repentance, then, must have its time if everything is not to
be confused, for there are indeed two guides, the one beckoning a person forward, the other back. But it must not have its
time in the temporal sense, not belong to a certain period of
life, as fun and games belong to childhood, as the excitement of
erotic love belongs to youth; it must not come and disappear as
a whim and as a surprise. No, regret must be an action with a
collected mind, so it can be spoken about for upbuilding, so it
may of itself give birth to new life, so that it does not become an
event whose mournful legacy is a sorrowful mood; repentance
in the sense of freedom with the stamp of eternity must have its
time, yes, even its time for preparation. In connection with
what must be done, the time of concentration and preparation
is no protraction; on the contrary, it is a respect, a holy fear, a
humility, lest what must be done in true sincerity become futile
and rash. That one wants to prepare oneself is no indolent
postponement; on the contrary, it is a concern of inwardness
that is already in harmony with what must be done. In the
eternal sense, there must be repenting at once; indeed, there is
not even time to say it. But a human being, of course, lives in
temporality, which goes on in time—so, then, the eternal and
the temporal seek to make themselves understandable to each
other, inasmuch as temporality does not plead for postponement in order to shirk but, conscious of its own weakness, asks
for time to prepare itself, inasmuch as eternity yields, not so as
to abandon its requirement but by gentle treatment to give
frailty a little time. The eternal with its "at once" must not
become the sudden, which merely confuses temporality; on
the contrary, it must be of assistance to temporality throughout
life. Just as the superior in relation to the limited, just as the
adult in relation to the child can force the requirement to such
an extreme that the result is that the limited and the child are
almost weakened in mind, so also the eternal in the imagina-

tion of an excited person may try to make temporality mad. But the godly grief of repentance and the concern of inwardness must above all not be confused with impatience. Experience teaches that to repent at once is not always even the right time to repent, because in this moment of haste, when the engaged thoughts and various passions are still busily in motion or at least tensed in the relaxation, repentance can so easily be mistaken about what really should be repented, can so easily confuse itself with the opposite: with momentary remorse, that is, with impatience; with a painful, tormenting worldly grief,[14] that is, with impatience; with a desperate pulling apart within itself, that is, with impatience. But impatience, however long it continues to rage, however darkened the mind becomes, never becomes repentance; its weeping, however convulsed with sobs, never becomes the weeping of repentance; its tears are as devoid of beneficent fruitfulness as clouds without rain, as a spasmodic shower. But if a person incurred some greater guilt but also improved and year by year steadily made progress in the good, it is certain that year after year, with greater inwardness—all in proportion to his progress in the good—he will repent of that guilt from which he year after year distances himself in the temporal sense. It is indeed true that guilt must stand vividly before a person if he is truly to repent, but momentary repentance is very dubious and is not to be hoped for at all simply because it perhaps is not the deep inwardness of concern that sets forth the guilt so vividly, but only a momentary feeling. Then regret is selfish, sensuous, sensuously powerful in the moment, inflamed in expression, impatient in the most contradictory overstatements—and for this very reason is not repentance. Sudden repentance wants to collect all the bitterness of sorrow in one draft—and then be off. It wants to get away from guilt, away from every reminder of it, fortifying itself with the delusion that it is for the sake of not being delayed in the good; it wants the guilt to be completely forgotten with the passage of time—and this again is impatience. A late sudden repentance perhaps will make it obvious that the first sudden repentance did not have true inwardness. It is said to have happened that a man who by his

VIII
128

misdeeds became liable to punishment under the law returned to society a reformed man after having served his sentence. Then he went to a foreign country where he was unknown and where he became known for his upright conduct. All was forgotten; then came a fugitive who recognized the esteemed man as his peer back in those wretched days. To meet was an appalling recollection; to shudder at it in passing was a deadly anxiety. Even silent, it shouted with a loud voice, until it became vocal in that dastardly fugitive's voice. Then despair suddenly seized the man who seemed redeemed, and it seized him just because repentance was forgotten, because this civically reformed man was still not surrendered to God in such a way that in the humility of repentance he remembered his former condition. In the temporal and sensuous and civic sense, repentance is still also something that comes and goes over the years, but in the eternal sense it is a quiet daily concern. It is eternally false that guilt becomes something different even if a century passed by; to say anything like that is to confuse the eternal with what the eternal least resembles, with human forgetfulness. If on that basis someone brashly and presumptuously proclaims exemption from the good because, after all, everything is forfeited anyway, this is ungodliness that will pile new guilt upon guilt.

VIII
129

Let us really think this matter through. The guilt is certainly not increased by its appearing more and more sorrowful to the reformed person. Neither is it a gain that the guilt is totally forgotten; on the contrary, it is loss and perdition; but it is a gain to gain inwardness to regret the guilt more and more fervently. It is not a gain to note by one's forgetfulness that one is growing older, but it surely is a gain if by regret's change from inwardness to inwardness someone noted that he was becoming older. It is said that the age of a tree can be reckoned by looking at the bark—one can also truly know a person's age in the good by the inwardness of the repentance.

There is a battle of despair; it is contending with—the consequences. The enemy continually attacks from the rear, and yet the contender must go forward. If so, repentance is still young and weak. There is a suffering of repentance; it certainly does not bear the punishment impatiently, yet at every moment it is writhing under it. If so, repentance is still young and weak. There is a quiet, sleepless sorrow at the thought of what has been wasted; it does not despair, but in its daily grieving it never rests. If so, repentance is still young and weak. There is a toilsome progress in the good that is like the gait of one whose feet are blistered; it is willing enough, would so like to walk swiftly, but its bold confidence has been damaged and the pain makes its walking precarious and agonizing. If so, repentance is still young and weak. But if a surer step is made on the path, if the punishment itself becomes a blessing, if the consequences become even redemptive, if the progress in the good is visible, then there is a mitigated but deep sorrow that recollects the guilt. It has removed and overcome what could deceive and confuse the vision; this is why it is not mistaken but sees only that one sad thing: this is the adult, the strong, the powerful repentance. Of the sensuous it holds true that it depreciates with the years and diminishes with the years. It may be said of a dancer that her time is over with her youth, but not so with a penitent. Of repentance it must be said that, if it is forgotten, then its strength was nothing but immaturity, but the longer and more deeply it is preserved, the better it becomes. The more closely one views guilt, the more appalling it looks, but repentance is most pleasing to God the farther away on the path of good it catches a glimpse of the guilt.

VIII
130

Thus repentance must not only have its time, but even its time of preparation; if it is indeed to be a quiet daily concern, it will still be able, well prepared, to collect itself for the solemn occasion also. *Confession* is such an occasion, the holy act that ought to be preceded by preparation. Just as a man changes his clothes for a celebration, so a person preparing for the holy act of confession is inwardly changed. It is indeed like changing one's clothes to divest oneself of multiplicity in order to make up one's mind about one thing, to interrupt the pace of busy activity in order to put on the repose of contemplation in unity with oneself. And this unity with oneself is the celebration's simple festive dress that is the condition of admittance. One can see multiplicity with a distracted mind, see something of it, see it in passing, see it with half an eye, with a divided mind, see it and yet not see it; in busy activity one can be concerned about many things, begin many things, do many things at one time and do them all halfway—but one cannot *confess* without this unity with oneself. In the hour of confession, he who has not truly made up his mind is still only distracted if he remains silent, is not collected; he is still only talkative if he speaks—without confessing.

But the person who truly made up his mind, that person is *quiet.* And this is also like changing one's clothes, to take off everything that is noisy since it is empty, in order, hidden in quietness, to become disclosed. This quietness is the simple solemnity of the holy act. In a worldly sense it holds true that the more musicians there are at dances and banquets the better, but in the godly sense it holds true that the deeper the quietness the better. —When the traveler leaves the noisy main highway and comes to the quiet places, he feels as if he had to talk with himself (for the quietness is soul-stirring!), feels as if he had to say what lies hidden in the depth of his soul. He feels, according to the poet's explanation, as if something ineffable forced its way out of his innermost being, that inexpressible something for which language still has no expression, because even *longing,* after all, is not the inexpressible itself—it is only hastening after it. But what quietness means, what the surroundings are saying with this quietness: that is the inexpressible. [15]The trees' wonder, provided it is the trees that contemplate the traveler in wonder, explains nothing. And the echo of the forest indeed explains that the voice does not penetrate through to an expla-

VIII
131

nation by that road; no, just as an impregnable fortress throws back the enemy's attack, so the echo throws back the voice, however loudly the traveler shouts. And the clouds trail only after their own thoughts, dream only about themselves, whether they seem to be pensively resting or they are enjoying the voluptuous, soft motion; whether they, transparent, scurry away, driven by the wind, or, darkened, collect themselves for struggle against the wind—they do not concern themselves about the traveler. And the ocean, like the wise man, is self-sufficient, whether it lies just like a child and amuses itself by itself with gentle ripples, like a child playing on its lips, or at midday lies, like a half-sleeping indulgent thinker, surveying everything around it, or at night it deeply ponders its own nature; whether with profound subtlety it makes itself into nothing in order to observe or it rages in its own passion. The ocean runs deep, it indeed knows what it knows; the one who runs deep always knows that, but it has no co-knowledge. And the host of stars is certainly a puzzling compilation; it looks as if they arrange themselves this way by mutual agreement. But the stars are so far away that they cannot see the traveler; it is only the traveler who can see the stars—so after all there is no agreement between him and the stars. This is the sadness of poet-longing based on a profound misunderstanding, because the person alone in nature is everywhere surrounded by a totality that does not understand him, even though it continually seems that it might arrive at an understanding. So it is with the inexpressible. It is something like the murmuring of the brook. If you are walking deep in your own thoughts, if you are busy, you do not notice it at all in passing, you are not aware that it exists, this murmuring. But if you stop, you discover it; and when you have discovered it, you must stand still; and when you stand still, it persuades you; and when it has persuaded you, then you must bend down listening to it; and when bending down you listen to it, it captures you; and when it has captured you, you cannot tear yourself loose from it; and when you cannot tear yourself from it, you are overcome—infatuated, you drop down beside it; every moment it seems to you as if the explanation has to come in the very next moment, but the brook goes on murmuring, and the traveler at its side only grows older.

Not so with the one who is confessing. The quietness grips him also, yet not in misunderstanding's pensive mood but with the earnestness of eternity. Nor is he like the traveler, led to these quiet places without really knowing how. He is not like the poet who wishfully seeks solitude and its mood. No, to confess is a holy act, an act for which the mind is collected in preparation. Thus the surroundings, too, know very well what they mean by the quietness—that they command earnestness. They know that it is their will to be understood; they know that

VIII
132

it is a new guilt if they are misunderstood. And the one who is present is an omniscient one who knows everything, remembers everything, what this person ever confided to him and what this person ever kept from his confidence; an omniscient one who again in this person's final moment will remember this hour, what this person confided to him and what this person kept from his confidence; an omniscient one who knows every thought from afar,[16] knows clearly all its paths, even when it sneaked past the person's own consciousness; an omniscient one to whom a person is disclosed in secret,[17] with whom there is conversation in silence lest anyone dare to try to deceive him, by talking or by silence, in the way that one person can hide much from another by remaining silent, at times even more by speaking. The person confessing is himself not like a servant who makes an accounting to his master of the administration entrusted to him because his master could not manage everything or be everywhere at once; the Omniscient One was present at every moment, for which an accounting must be made in the accounting. The accounting with regard to what has been done is made not for the sake of the master, but for the sake of the servant, who in turn must account for the way he used the moment of the accounting. The person confessing is not like someone confiding to a friend, whom he initiates, in advance or afterward, into something he did not know before; the Omniscient One does not find out anything about the person confessing, but instead the person confessing finds out something about himself. Therefore, do not raise the objection against the confession that there is no benefit in confiding to an omniscient one what he already knows; first answer the question whether it does not benefit a person to find out something about himself that he did not know! A hasty explanation can suppose that to pray is a futile act because a person's prayer does not, of course, change the changeless;[18] but in the long run would this be desirable, could not the changing person easily come to repent that he had managed to get God changed! Thus the true explanation is also the one and only to be desired: the prayer does not change God, but it changes the one who prays.

It is the same with the theme of this discourse: God does not find out anything by your confessing, but you, the one confessing, do. Much of what you could try to keep in obscurity you first get to know by letting an omniscient one become aware of it. Even horrible crimes are committed, even blood is shed, and many times in such a way that it must truly be said of the guilty one: He did not know what he was doing—perhaps he died without, through repentance, ever really getting to know what it was he did. Indeed, does passion ever really know what it is doing; is not this its ingratiating temptation and its apparent excuse, this delusive ignorance of itself because at the moment it has forgotten the eternal, because continued in a person it changes his life into nothing but moments, because it perfidiously serves its blinded master while working its way up to making him serve like a blinded slave! Hate and anger and revenge and despondency and depression and despair and fear of the future and trust in the world and faith in oneself and pride that mixes in even with sympathy, and envy that mixes in even with friendship, and the changed but not improved inclination—when this was present in a person, when was it without the delusive excuse of ignorance? If a person continued being ignorant of it, was it not precisely because he also continued being ignorant of an omniscient one? Yes, there is an ignorance that should not trouble anyone if the opportunity or the capacity to learn was denied him, but there is an ignorance of oneself that is just as lamentable for the learned one and the simple one, both of whom are bound in the same responsibility: this ignorance is called self-deception. There is an ignorance that little by little, as more and more is learned piecemeal, is changed into knowledge; but there is only one thing that can remove that ignorance, that self-deception—and not knowing that it is one thing, only one thing, that only one thing is needful,[19] is still to be in self-deception. The ignorant person may have been ignorant about much, may come to know much, and yet there remains much he does not know; but the self-deceived person, if he talks about the much and the multifarious, is still in self-deception, is much ensnared and much fortified by the multifarious. The ignorant person can

VIII
133

gradually acquire wisdom and knowledge, but the self-deceived person, if he won the one thing needful, would have won purity of heart.

So let us on the occasion of a confession speak on this theme:[20]

Purity of Heart Is to Will One Thing[21]

as we base our meditation on the Apostle James' words in the fourth chapter of his Epistle, verse 8:

Keep near to God, then he will keep near to you. Cleanse your hands, you sinners, and purify your hearts, you double-minded,

VIII
134

because only the pure in heart are able to see God[22] and consequently keep near to him and preserve this purity through his keeping near to them; and the person who in truth wills only one thing *can will only the good*, and the person who wills only one thing when he wills the good *can will only the good in truth*.

Let us discuss this, but let us first forget the occasion in order to come to an understanding of this theme and what the apostolic admonishing words ("purify your hearts, you double-minded") are opposing: *double-mindedness*; then in conclusion we shall more specifically utilize the occasion.[23]

I

IF IT IS TO BE POSSIBLE FOR A PERSON TO BE ABLE TO WILL
ONE THING, HE MUST WILL THE GOOD.

To will only one thing—but is this not bound to become a lengthy discussion? If anyone is really to consider this matter, must he not first examine one by one every goal that a person can set for himself in life, designate one by one all the many things that a person can will? And if this were not enough, since considerations of this sort easily become run-of-the-mill, must he not try willing one thing after the other in order to find out which one thing it is that he can will if it is a matter of willing only one thing? Indeed, if anyone would begin in this manner, he certainly would never be finished; or rather, how would it be possible that he could finish when he expressly started out on the wrong road and still continued to proceed further and further on the road of error that *leads* to the good only in a lamentable way—namely, if the traveler turns around and goes back, for just as the good is only one thing, so all roads *lead* to the good, even the road of error—if the one who turned around goes back on the same road.

O you unfathomable trustworthiness of the good; wherever a person is in the world, on whatever road he is traveling, if he wills only one thing, there is a road that leads him to you! Hence prolixity here would be a bad thing; instead of wasting many moments of the discourse on mentioning the multiplicity or even life's precious years on trying one's hand in the multiplicity, the discourse can, as life should, with desirable brevity stick to its subject. Indeed, in a certain sense nothing else can be discussed as briefly, that is, if it is really discussed well, as the good can, because without conditions and without circumlocutions, without introductory remarks and without compromises, the good is unconditionally the one and only thing that a person may will and shall will, and is only one thing. O blessed brevity, blessed the simplicity that swiftly grasps what sagacity, weary in the service of vanity, slowly comprehends! The sagacious person needs to take a lot of time and trouble to understand what the simple person at the joyous prompting of a pious heart feels no need to understand in lengthy detail, because he at once simply understands only the good. In other words, to will the good is not of such a nature that one person wills one thing but what he wills is not the good, another person wills one thing but what he wills is not the good either, and a third person wills one thing and what he wills is the good. No, it is not like that. The person who wills one thing that is not the good is actually not willing one thing; it is an illusion, a semblance, a deception, a self-deception that he wills only one thing—because in his innermost being he is, he must be, double-minded. This is why the apostle says, "Purify your hearts, you double-minded"; that is, cleanse your hearts of double-mindedness, that is, let your heart in truth will only one thing, for in this is purity of heart. It is of this same

VIII
135

purity of heart that the apostle is speaking when he says, "If any of you lacks wisdom, let him ask God . . . . . but in faith, not as a double-minded person" (James 1:5,6,8), because purity of heart is precisely the wisdom that is gained by praying; a man of prayer does not pore over scholarly books but is the wise man "whose eyes are opened—when he kneels down" (Numbers 24:16).

To the person, then, whose mind devoutly remains ignorant of the multiplicity, the discourse concisely says: The good is one thing. The more difficult discourse is addressed to the person whose mind *in double-mindedness* has formed dubious acquaintance with the multiplicity and with knowledge. If it is certain that a person in truth wills one thing, then he wills the good, because only the good can be willed in this way. But both these statements say one and the same thing—otherwise, of course, they would be speaking of different things. The one statement mentions the name of the good *directly*, defines it as being one. The other cunningly conceals this name; it almost seems as if it were speaking of something entirely different, but for this very reason it insinuates itself searchingly into a person's inner being, and however much he gives assurances, asserts, and brags that he wills only one thing, it penetratingly examines him and exposes the double-mindedness in him if the one thing he wills is not the good.

Surely there was in the world that person who seemed to will only one thing. Even if he had concealed it, he would not have needed to give assurances of it; there was plenty of eloquent testimony against him—how he inhumanly inured his mind, how nothing moved him, not tenderness, not innocence, not wretchedness, how his blinded soul had no eye for anything and his senses had an eye only for the one thing he wanted. Yet it was a delusion, a dreadful delusion, that he willed only one thing, because pleasure and honor and wealth and power and all that is of the world is only seemingly one thing. It is not one thing and does not remain one thing while everything is changed—and while he is changed; it is not the same amid all changes—on the contrary, it is the continually changed. Thus, even if he named only one thing, be it pleasure

VIII
136

or honor or wealth, he would not in truth be willing one thing. Or can he really be said to will one thing when the one thing he wills is in itself not one thing, is in itself multiplicity, a dispersion, a sport of changeableness and prey of corruptibility! In a time of pleasure, see how he craved one pleasure after the other; indeed, variation was his watchword. Is variation, then, willing one thing that remains the same? On the contrary, it is willing one thing that must never be the same; it means to will multiplicity, and someone who wills in this way is not only double-minded but is also divided in himself. So he wills one thing and in turn immediately wills the opposite, because the unity of pleasure is a delusion and a deception—what he wills is the variety of pleasures. When he had enjoyed to the point of nausea, when he had become weary and surfeited, what would he will if he were still to will one thing? He wanted new enjoyment; his enervated soul was furious that no resourcefulness was adequate to discover something new—something new! Change was what he called for when pleasure served him—change, change; and change was what he called for when he arrived at the limits of pleasure, when the servants were exhausted—change, change!

Now, obviously there are indeed changes in life that can allow a person to learn whether he wills one thing. There is the change of *perishableness* when the sensualist must take leave, when the dance and the hubbub of confusing sensations are over, when everything becomes quiet in earnest. There is the change of *death*. If at times perishableness might seem to forget itself so that it did not come, if it might seem as if the sensualist has managed to slip through—death does not forget itself, he does not slip past death; it has power over what belongs to this world and changes to nothing that one and only thing the sensualist wanted. Finally, there is the change of *eternity*; it changes everything—so only the good remains and becomes the blessed possession of the one who has willed only one thing. But that rich man whom no misery could touch, that rich man who, to his own curse, even in eternity must go on willing one thing,[24] ask him now whether he indeed actually wills one thing!

VIII
137

So also with honor and wealth and power, for in the prime of life, when he aspired to honor, did he really find some limit, or was it not the ambitious one's restless preoccupation to climb higher and higher; did he find some rest in his sleepless effort to capture honor and hold it fast; did he find some refreshment in the cold fire of his passion! And if he actually did win the highest of honors, is then earthly honor in itself one thing? Or in its multiplicity, when thousands and thousands are braiding garlands, is it really like the glorious carpet of the fields created by one hand? No, like the world's contempt, the world's honor is a vortex, a play of confused forces, a deceptive element in the divisiveness, an illusion, as when a swarm of insects in the distance seems to the eye like one body, an illusion, as when the noise of a crowd in the distance seems to the ear like one voice. Even if the honor were unanimous, it is still meaningless, indeed all the more meaningless the more thousands there are who constitute the unanimity, and the more swiftly it becomes manifest the more thousands there are who constituted the unanimity. And yet it was just the unanimity of these thousands that he wanted; it was not the approval of the good— they are quickly counted—no, of the thousands. Is this wanting to count, then, willing one thing—to count and count until there are enough [*slaae til*], to count and count until it goes wrong [*slaae feil*]—is this willing one thing? Therefore, whoever wants this honor or fears this contempt, even if he is said to will one thing, is nevertheless in his innermost being not merely double-minded but thousand-minded and divided. And so also is his life when he must grovel—in order to attain honor; when he must flatter his enemy—in order to attain honor; when he must court the favor of the one he despises—in order to attain honor; when he must betray the person he esteems—in order to attain honor, in order to attain honor, that is, in order to have contempt for himself at the pinnacle of honor—and yet to shudder before change. Change, yes, where does change rage as dissolutely as here; what changeover is more swift and sudden, like a blunder in a prank, like a chance move by a blind man, when the seeker of honor does not even have time to take off his robe of honor before insult and mockery seize him in it! The change, the *final* change, the most certain in the uncertain—however loudly the thunder of honor sounded over his grave, even if it could be heard over the whole world, there is still one person who cannot hear it, he the dead man, he who died with the honor, the only thing he had willed, but also from the honor, for it remains behind, it goes home again, it dies away like an echo. Change, the *true* change, when eternity *is*—I wonder if the crown of honor will be offered to him, the highly honored one, there! And yet eternity is more just than the earth and the world; in eternity a crown of honor is reserved for everyone who in truth has willed only one thing.

VIII
138

So also with wealth and power and everything that perishes when the world and its lust perish.[25] The person who has willed this, even if he willed only one thing, must to his own torment continue to will it when it has perished and by the torment of contradiction learn that it is not one thing. But the person who in truth willed one thing and therefore willed the good, even if he is sacrificed for it—why should he not in eternity will the same thing for which he would die; why should he not will the same thing when it has been victorious in eternity!

To will one thing, then, cannot mean to will something that only seemingly is one thing. In other words, the worldly in its essence is not one thing since it is the *nonessential*; its so-called unity is no essential unity but an emptiness that the multiplicity conceals. Thus in the brief moment of illusion what is worldly is multiplicity and therefore not one thing; then it changes into its opposite—that is how far it is from being and remaining one thing. Indeed, what else is desire in its boundless extreme but nausea? What else is earthly honor at its dizzy summit but contempt for existence? What else is the superabundance of wealth but poverty; does all the gold in the world hidden in avarice amount to as much as, or does it not amount to infinitely much less than, the poorest mite hidden in the contentment of the poor! What else is worldly power but dependence; what slave in chains was as unfree as a tyrant! No, the worldly is not one thing; multifarious as it is, in life it is changed into its opposite, in death into nothing, in eternity into a curse upon the person who has willed this one thing. Only the good is one thing in its essence and the same in every one of its expressions. Let love illustrate it. The person who truly loves does not love once for all; neither does he use a portion of his love now and then in turn another portion, because to exchange it is to make it a changeling. No, he loves with all his love; it is totally present in every expression; he continually spends all of it, and yet he continually keeps it all in his heart. What marvelous wealth! When the miser has amassed all the world's gold—in grubbiness—he has become poor; when the lover spends all his love, he keeps it whole—in purity of heart. —If a person is in truth to will one thing, the one thing he wills must indeed be of such a nature that it remains unchanged amid all changes; then by willing it he can win changelessness. If it is continually changed, he himself becomes changeable, double-minded, and unstable. But this continual changeableness is precisely impurity.[26]

VIII
139

But neither is willing one thing *that drastic error of presumptuous, ungodly enthusiasm: to will the great, no matter whether it is good or evil.* Be he ever so desperate, a person who wills in this way is nevertheless double-minded. Or is not despair [*Fortvivlelse*] actually double-mindedness [*Tvesindethed*[27]]; or what else is it to despair but to have two wills! Whether he, the weak one, despairs over not being able to tear himself loose from the evil or he, the presumptuous one, despairs over not being able to tear himself completely loose from the good—they are both double-minded, they both have two wills; neither of them in truth wills one thing, no matter how desperately they seem to be willing it. Whether it was a woman whom desire plunged into despair or it was a man who despaired in defiance; whether a person despaired because he got his will or despaired because he did not get his will, everyone in despair has two wills, one that he futilely wants to follow entirely, and one that he futilely wants to get rid of entirely. This is how God, better than any king, has safeguarded himself against every rebellion. It certainly has happened that a king has been dethroned by a rebellion, but the furthest any rebel against God carries it is to the point of despairing himself. Despair is the limit—to this point and no further! Despair is the limit; here the ill nature of cowardly, fearful self-love meets the presumptuousness of the proud, defiant mind; here they meet in equal powerlessness.

Only all too soon one's own experience and experience with others teach how far the lives of most people are from what a human life ought to be. All have their great moments, see themselves in the magic mirror of possibility that hope holds before them while desire flatters, but they speedily forget the vision in the everyday. Or perhaps they utter enthusiastic words, "for the tongue is a little member and boasts of great things"[28]—but by loudly proclaiming what ought to be practiced in silence the talk takes the enthusiasm in vain, and the inspired words are quickly forgotten in the trivialities of life; it is forgotten that such words were said about this person; it is forgotten that it was he himself who said them. Then perhaps one day recollection awakens with horror, and regret seems to give new strength; alas, this also would become only a big moment. They all have intentions, plans, and resolutions for life, indeed, for eternity. But the intention quickly loses its youthful vigor and becomes decrepit, and the resolution does not stand firm and does not resist; it vacillates and is changed with the circumstances, and memory fails—until by habit and association they learn to console each other, as one says, until they even find it upbuilding instead of traitorous if someone proclaims the feeble consolation of excuses that encourages and fortifies the lethargy. There are people who find it upbuilding that the requirement is affirmed in all its sublimity, in all its rigor, so that it penetrates the innermost soul with its requirement; others find it upbuilding that a wretched compromise is made with God and the requirement—and the language. There are people who find it upbuilding if someone will call to them, but there are also sleepy souls who not only call it pleasant but even upbuilding to be lulled to sleep.

This is indeed lamentable, but then there is a wisdom that is not from above;[29] it is earthly, corporeal, and diabolical. It has discovered this universally human weakness and lethargy; it wants to help. It sees that it is a matter of the will and now loudly proclaims, "Without willing one thing, a person's life

VIII
140

becomes wretched mediocrity and misery. He must will one thing, regardless of whether it is good or evil; he must will one thing—therein lies a person's greatness." But it is not difficult to see through this drastic error. Holy Scripture teaches for our salvation that sin is a human being's corruption[30] and therefore deliverance is only in purity through willing the good. That earthly and diabolical wisdom distorts this into tempting perdition: weakness is a person's misfortune; strength is the only deliverance. "When the unclean spirit goes out of a person, it wanders through dry and empty places but finds no rest; then it returns and has in company with itself"[31] that impure sagacity, the wisdom of the desert and the empty places, that impure sagacity that now drives out the spirit of lethargy and mediocrity—"so the last is worse than the first."[32] How is one to describe the nature of such a person?

It is said that a singer can rupture his voice by outvoicing himself; similarly the nature of a person like that is ruptured by outvoicing itself and the voice of conscience. It is said of someone dizzily standing on a high place that everything runs together before his eyes; similarly, a person like that has become dizzy out in the infinite, where everything that is eternally separate runs together so that only the great dimension remains— that is, the deserted and empty, which always gives birth to dizziness. But however desperately he seems to will one thing, such a person is nevertheless double-minded. If he, the self-willed person [*Selvraadig*], might have his will [*raade*], then there would be only one thing and he would be the only one who would not be double-minded, the only one who would have cast off every chain, he the only one free. But free—the slave of sin is indeed not, nor has he cast off the chain "because he mocks it";[33] he is under constraint and therefore double-minded, and certainly he must not rule. There is a power that constrains him; he cannot tear himself loose from it; indeed, he cannot even quite will it—this power, too, is denied him. If you, my listener, were to see such a person (although he certainly is rare, just as weakness and mediocrity are undeniably more common), if you were to meet him in what he himself

VIII
141

would call a weak moment (alas, what you might call a better moment), if you were to meet him when he had found no rest in the desert, when his dizziness had passed for a moment and he felt an anguished longing for the good,[34] when shaken in his innermost being and not without sorrow he was thinking of that simple one who despite his frailty nevertheless wills the good—you would then discover that he had two wills, and his anguished double-mindedness. Despairing as he was, he thought: What is lost is lost—yet he could not help but turn around once more in longing for the good, no matter how dreadfully embittered he had become against this longing, a longing that demonstrates that, just as a person, despite all his defiance, does not have the power to tear himself away completely from the good, because it is the stronger, he also does not even have the power to will it completely.

[35]You may even have heard that despairing one say, "Yet something good goes down with me." When someone finds his death in the waves, he sinks although not yet dead, comes up again, and finally a bubble comes out of his mouth—when this has happened, he sinks in death. That bubble was his last breath, the last reserve of air that could make him lighter than the ocean. So also with those words. In those words he breathed out his last hope of rescue; in those words he gave himself up. Suppressed, there was still in that thought a hope of rescue; in that thought there was still hidden in his soul a possible way of rescue. Once the words are spoken, confidentially to another person (oh, what a dreadful misuse of confidentiality, even though the despairing one uses them only against himself!), once these words are heard, then he goes down forever. Alas, it is terrible to see a person rushing headlong to his own downfall; it is terrible to see him dancing on the edge of the abyss without suspecting it; but this clarity about himself and his own downfall is even more terrible. It is terrible to see a person seek solace by plunging into the vortex of despair, but even more terrible is the composure that in the anguish of death a person does not call out in a scream for help, "I am going down, save me!" but calmly wants to be a witness

VIII
142

to his own perdition. What colossal vanity not to want to draw people's attention to oneself by one's beauty, by wealth, by talents, by power, by honor, but to want to beg their attention by one's perdition, to want to say of oneself what compassion at most would sadly dare to say of such a one at his grave: Yet something good went down with him! What dreadful double-mindedness to want in one's perdition to derive a kind of advantage from the fact that the good exists, the only thing one has not willed! Now, of course, it manifested itself, the other will, even though it was so weak that it became a pandering to perdition, an attempt to become noteworthy—by perdition.

To will one thing, then, cannot mean to will that which by nature is not one thing but only by means of a dreadful falsehood seems to be that, something that only by means of the lie is one thing, just as the person who wills only this alone is a liar, just as the one who conjures up this one thing is the Father of Lies. The deserted and empty is not truly one thing but is truly nothing and is the perdition in the person who wills only this one thing. But if a person is to will only one thing in truth, this one thing must be one thing in the truth of its innermost being; it must by an eternal separation differ from the heterogeneous so that in truth it can continue to be one thing and to be the same and thereby form in likeness to itself the one who wills only this one thing.[36]

In truth to will one thing can therefore mean only to will the good, because any other one thing is not a one thing and the person willing who wills only that must therefore be double-minded, because the one who craves becomes like that which he craves. Or would it be possible that a person by willing evil could will one thing even if it were possible that a person could harden himself to willing only evil? Is not evil, just like evil people, at odds with itself, divided in itself? Take someone like that, separate him from society, lock him up in solitary confinement—is he not divided against himself there, just as the bad alliance of such similar minds is a divided union. But even if the good man lived in an out-of-the-way place in the world and never saw anyone else, he is still at one with himself and at one with all, because he wills one thing and because the good is one thing.

Then everyone who in truth is to will one thing must be led to will the good, even though it may sometimes be that a person begins by willing one thing that yet in the deepest sense is not the good, but probably something innocent, and then little by little is transformed into willing one thing in truth by willing the good. For example, sometimes erotic love has probably helped a person along the right road. He faithfully willed only one thing, his love; for it he would live and die, for it he would sacrifice everything, in it alone he would have his happiness. In the deepest sense, however, falling in love is still not the good but possibly became for him a formative educator that finally led him, by winning the beloved or perhaps by losing her, in truth to will one thing and to will the good. Thus a person is brought up in many ways; an honest erotic love is also an upbringing to the good.

Perhaps there was someone whom enthusiasm gripped for a specific endeavor. Full of enthusiasm, he willed only one thing; he would live and die for this endeavor, he would sacrifice everything for it, in it alone would have his happiness— because erotic love and enthusiasm are not content with a divided heart. Yet his endeavor may still not have been in the deepest sense the good; thus the enthusiasm became for him the teacher he presumably outgrew but to whom he also owed very much. As stated, all roads lead to the good if a person in truth wills only one thing; and if there is indeed any truth in his willing one thing, this also assists him to the good. But the danger is that the person in love and the enthusiast take a wrong turn and swing off to the great instead of being led to the good. It is certain that the good is truly the great, but the great is not always the good. One can woo a woman's favor by willing something if only it is great; it can flatter the girl's pride and she can reward one with her worship. But God in heaven is not like the folly of a young girl; he does not reward the great with admiration, but the reward of the good person is to dare to worship in truth.

II

IF A PERSON IS REALLY TO WILL ONE THING IN TRUTH,
HE MUST WILL THE GOOD IN TRUTH

*A. If a person is to will the good in truth, he must make up his
mind to will to renounce all double-mindedness.*

Consequently, if it is to be *possible* for a person to be able to will
one thing, he must will the good, because only the good is this
unity; but if it is to become *actual* that he wills only one thing,
he must will the good in truth.

Who could rightly discuss this here, since here the discourse
is indeed about the lives of most people; they will the good, and
yet there is so much double-mindedness in the world. The
speaker also has his life here, surely has his flaws also, his share
of double-mindedness. Would that the discourse might not
seem to want to judge or accuse others, because that, too,
would certainly be double-mindedness—to want to judge
others instead of oneself! Would that the discourse might not
seem to make the requirement valid, binding for others but
exemptible for the speaker, as if he had only the task of speaking, because this, too, is indeed double-mindedness, just like
that of wanting to preach comfort to others but refusing to let
oneself be comforted, which is hidden pride. However artfully,
sympathizing in sadness and kindness, he knows how to comfort others, if he also thinks that for himself there is no comfort,
this is hidden pride and thus double-mindedness. Oh, would
that the discourse might not wound anyone except for his healing; would that the discourse might exasperate no one and yet
be the truth; would that it might penetrate with the truth to
disclose what is hidden; would that it might annihilate double-
mindedness and win hearts for the good—not by persuasion,
since this also is very easily double-minded: to want to enjoy
the pleasure of persuasion, to long for it, to want to calm
oneself with it—and because of that forget the task. No, would
that the discourse might repel all and make only the good
appealing to them!

1. *First* it must be said, something that is easy to see, *that the person who wills the good for the sake of reward does not will one thing but is double-minded.*

The good is one thing; the reward is something else. It may indeed come, and it may fail to come until later, until the very end. If, then, he wills the good for the sake of reward, he is not willing one thing but something double. It is now apparent that in this way he will not go very far on the path of the good, because it is really the same as if a person, instead of doing what is natural, using both eyes to look at one thing, were to use one eye to look to the one side and the other to look to the other side—it will not work, it only confuses the vision. We are not, however, speaking about that now but only about its being double-mindedness.

This matter often was the topic of discussion in ancient times also. There were brazen teachers of brazenness who thought that justice was to do wrong on a large scale[37] and then to be able to make it appear that one nevertheless willed the good. Thus they had, so they thought, double advantage, the wretched advantage of being able to do wrong, of being able to have their will, of letting their passions rage, and the hypocritical advantage of seeming to be good. But in ancient times there was also a simple wise man whose simplicity became a trap for the quibbling of the brazen;[38] he taught that in order to be really sure that it was the good that one willed, one should avoid even appearing to be good—presumably lest the reward should become tempting. The good and the reward are so different that, if the reward is coveted separately, the good is the ennobling and sanctifying element, and the reward is the tempting element, but the tempting is never a good thing. The reward we are speaking of here is the world's reward, because the reward that God has eternally joined together with the good has nothing dubious about it and is also adequately sure. Neither things present nor things to come, neither heights nor depths, neither angels nor devils will be able to separate it from the good.[39] But if the world itself is not good in its innermost being, if, as Scripture says, it is even in the power of evil,[40] or

VIII
145

if, on the other hand, the one who does not will the good is far from being the rare exception, then the reward of the world is indeed dubious, then it more likely will reward what it regards as the good, what to a certain degree looks like the good, what, as those brazen ones taught, has the semblance of the good— and those brazen ones did not lack acquaintance with the world. But then the reward is indeed the tempting element.

The matter is not difficult. If a man loves a girl for the sake of her money, who would call him a lover? After all, he does not love the girl but the money; he is a fortune hunter, not a lover. But if someone said, "It is the girl I love, and she has money," and would ask us for our opinion, since it is not our business to judge, the answer would presumably be, "This money poses a problem. Money is said to have great influence; one can easily be mistaken, and it is very difficult to know oneself." If this matter concerned him very deeply, he might very well wish the money to vanish if only to test his love. A proper lover presumably would say, "The girl has only one defect, that she has money." And what, now, may the girl say? If she said, "The advantage I want to have is that it is I who have made him rich," then I wonder if she could be called a proper lover—after all, she did not love him but the money. If, however, the two in love are in agreement about doing a good work with this money that was an obstacle to them, then it would be made possible for them to will love alone. Would that no one at this point might get busy to disturb the innocent imagery of this beautiful thought by telling us about "what life will surely teach those two." Alas, there is a miserable knowledge, a scurvy acquaintance with actuality, that is not merely miserable and scurvy but also on all occasions assumes an air of importance, as if this knowledge were anything but a disgrace to everyone who cravenly and traitorously and enviously and pompously dares to express it, as if this acquaintance were anything but contemptible double-mindedness that wills and does not will and therefore only lies, lies about the good and the good person. Yes, what someone once said of memory applies to this knowledge, namely, that one should rather wish to learn the art of forgetting.[41] It holds true that one can learn

VIII
146

that knowledge easily enough and learn easily enough from all
the contemptible wretches that we should rather wish and pray
that there was an art that could teach one to want to be ignorant
of it.

So, then, to want the girl without wanting the money. Let us
reflect on the good where everything is perfect, where the
innocent fantasy of beautiful thought is earnestness and truth.
To will the good for the sake of reward is double-mindedness;
therefore to will one thing is to will the good without regard
for reward; in truth to will one thing is to will the good but not
to want the reward for it in the world. Quite true, the reward
may indeed come without a person's willing it; it can come
from God also in the external realm, but if he bears in mind
that all rewards in the external realm can become what the
world's reward always is, a temptation for him, then he must,
in order really to be able to will the good, defend himself
against the reward, although he nevertheless must not forget
that to defend himself in this way can in turn be a temptation to
pride. But, now, if this is the case with the reward for the good
in the world, that the world's reward is so hazardous, then the
good has in this world almost an upbuilding quality (even
though this upbuilding is, as it were, mitigated in eternity's
beatific smile), that the person who in truth wills it by willing
one thing is rarely led into the difficulty of being tempted by
the reward. That the good is its own reward, yes, that is eternally certain. There is nothing so certain; it is not more certain
that there is a God, because this is one and the same. But here in
the world the good is often rewarded temporarily with ingratitude, with lack of appreciation, with poverty, with contempt,
with many sufferings, at times with death. This is not the
reward we speak of when we say that the good has its reward,
but it is the reward that comes in the external realm and comes
first. It is precisely this that is feared by the person who wills
the good for the sake of reward, because he has no time to wait,
has no time, no year, no life to give away—for an eternity.
Thus it is so far from being desirable that the reward come in
the external realm that on the contrary it is both beneficial and
encouraging that the reward does not come in the external

VIII
147

realm, so the double-mindedness in the internal being might perish and the reward in heaven might become all the greater.

To will the good for the sake of reward is a kind of symbol of double-mindedness, and a double-minded man, according to the Apostle James, is unstable in all his ways.[42] Neither will he achieve anything, because a double-minded man, says the same apostle, must not expect to obtain what he prays for.[43] Therefore, even if such a double-minded person, who wills the good for the sake of reward, brags and boasts—and fools himself into thinking that he gained what he was after, even if many an infatuated person foolishly thinks the same—let us not deceive each other, my listener, or let an illusion do it! In other words, it is certainly possible that he gains the good things that are called reward, but he does not obtain them as reward, at least not in truth, that is, if willing the good in truth is distinguishable by willing it without reward. O you marvelous accord of the good with yourself, that you do not let yourself be deceived! If for the sake of reward a double-minded person pretends to will the good, and if he seems to obtain the reward, he still does not obtain it, because what he obtains he does not obtain as reward—for the good. Indeed, it is so far from the case that he in truth *obtains it as reward* that, precisely when he obtains it, he in truth *loses the reward!* A deceitful lover may be able to deceive the girl who has money so that it seems that he loves her although he actually loves her money, and she, happy, perhaps even grateful, lives on in the delusion that she is loved—but no one can deceive the good, no, not in all eternity! Not in all eternity—yes, it is there that one can deceive it least of all. Here in the world it can perhaps be done—not a deceiving of the good but a deceiving of people by the semblance of the good. This kind of thing does not escape the attention of the good; at times it concentrates its wrath on such a person and exposes his deception. But frequently the good allows the deceiver to go on, because it is well aware that it is the stronger. Only a weak and soft person wants to have his rights at once, wants to be victorious in the external realm at once, simply because he is weak and therefore must have an external proof—that he is the stronger. The person who in truth has power and in truth is the stronger calmly grants the weak one a free hand; he seems to allow him to make a show of being the stronger. So also with the good; when it puts up with such a deceiver, it is as if it secretly said to him, "Well, have a jolly time with your show of deception, but just remember, we two will discuss this again."

The double-minded person stands at the crossroads; two prospects appear there: the good and the reward. It is not in his power to reconcile them, because they are heterogeneous; only the reward that God internally and eternally adds to the good, only that reward is truly homogeneous with the good. So he stands there pondering and deliberating. If he totally abandons himself to this pondering, he remains standing there—a symbol of double-mindedness. But then he presumably tears himself loose from deliberation and now goes ahead. Along which of the roads? Well, do not ask him about that; perhaps he was able to answer learned questions and display extensive knowledge, but there is one thing he cannot do, indeed, the only thing he cannot do—he cannot answer the question about which of the two roads he is taking. Pondering in deliberation, he has somewhat disturbed his vision by repeatedly seeing the heterogeneous together; he believes that he has discovered that there is a third road—and it is along this road he is walking.

This third road has no name since it does not exist at all, and thus it is explainable that he, especially if he is to be honest, cannot say which road he is taking. If he is to be honest, since otherwise he certainly would declare that he is taking the road of the good, he would of course attach great importance to convincing people of it—so that they could honor him, which is part of the reward to which he aspires. The third road is the secret he keeps to himself.

And how, then, does he proceed along this third road, which is narrower than an acrobat's tightrope, since it does not exist at all? Does he go along smoothly and steadily like someone who has a definite goal before his eyes, like someone who therefore does not look around very much lest he be disturbed, like someone who keeps his eyes on that one thing, the goal? No, he walks that way only on the road of the good—with only the good before his eyes. Or does he walk along like someone who pursues every pleasure on the broad highway of desire? No, he is not walking that way either. Is he walking like a carefree youth who intrepidly looks around at everything? Alas, no, he is too old for that.

How, then, does he walk? He walks very slowly, according to the circumstances due to the difficulty of the road. He feels his way with his foot, and when he finally puts his foot down and takes a step, he promptly looks at the clouds to see from which direction the wind is coming and whether the smoke is rising straight up from the chimney. He is looking, namely, for the reward, the world's reward, which is like the clouds, the wind, and the smoke from the chimney. So he is continually making inquiries, scanning the faces of passersby in order to find out the status of the reward, what the prices are, what the demand of the times and of people is concerning the good if they are to reward it.

What, then, does he actually will? Well, do not ask him about that; he perhaps would be able to answer every other question, with the exception, however, of the one about the road. But this one, if he is to be honest, he cannot answer definitely. Otherwise, of course, the answer is promptly at hand: that he wants the good and abhors vice—when it *seems* to be abhorrent; that he wants the approval of good people—when they are in the majority and have the power; that he wants to be useful to the good cause—when it is so good as to be useful to him. But in honesty he does not dare to say definitely what he wills. He does not even dare to say loudly and decisively with the full voice of conviction that he wants the good; he says it with the toneless caution of double-mindedness. After all, he knows well enough that the good and the reward are heterogeneous. Suppose, now, that these two came into conflict because of some uncircumspect comment; suppose he became regarded as willing the good to such a degree—that the reward failed to materialize, which is said to have happened before in the world. What, then, does he will? Does he will the good and even avoid the appearance of doing so? No, definitely not. Does he, then, will the reward? Yes, but he is unwilling to say that directly. Does he, then, will the good? Well, now and then, perhaps in common decency, as one says. Thus he makes a show of willing the good—for the sake of honor and reward; once in a while he sincerely wills the good—in common decency.

So much for the coveter of reward; so double-minded is he that one does not really know whether to laugh or cry over him, unless one knows that all double-mindedness is indeed perdition, for then one certainly knows what to do, especially if one has a share of it. This matter of willing the good for the sake of reward can also have a somewhat different aspect. Perhaps there was someone who truly and sincerely willed the good. Humble before God, quickened in his enthusiasm, in good spirits when the world and the public were working against him, he understood that this was the reward and that there was nothing more to be said about it. Strong through God, strengthening himself only through his confidence, he almost never wished to be rewarded by the world in any other way. But then he became weary, grasped for the reward as the nearest at hand and for the easier understanding of the reward, because the closer understanding is to misunderstanding the easier it ordinarily becomes. He could not see it through [*holde ud*] with the eternal, he could not endure [*udholde*] the opposition of the world and of the people. So at first he claimed the reward with the understanding that after all there should be a compromise between the good and the world; finally he claimed the reward alone—that is how he regressed. What a sad end to a good beginning! O you the good's keen jealousy for yourself, that you perhaps allowed him to obtain the reward in the world just when you rejected him, allow him to obtain the world's recompense when he ungratefully forgot what a blessing it is to have your reward while the world denies its reward!

Or he did not begin so loftily but yet began with willing the good in truth. Without knowledge of the world, without being formed in inwardness by the conception of the possibility of what can happen to a human being, he piously hoped that the good would not lack its reward—which understood eternally

VIII
150

is eternally true and sacred truth, but in the sense of the temporal is uncertainty and futile sagacity. So he went out into the school of experience, because we indeed all go to school as long as we live. Life's school is for adults and thus is somewhat more rigorous than the school the children attend, where the alert and diligent rise above their peers. So life schooled him rigorously, but he resisted; he reduced the requirements, did not wish to betray the good. Alas, it seemed as if this, too, would be of no help. He believed that in the good he had a claim upon life; now it seemed to him as if it were the good that only had claims upon him. So his bold confidence dwindled away. He looked around and saw how many others grabbed rewards; the tempter began to make him faintheartedly uneasy about why he did not want to be like others, why he wanted to pursue the uncertainties of the imagination instead of grasping the certainties. Then his mind changed. The same thing happened to him in life as would no doubt happen to the better pupil in school if there was no teacher—the mediocre would gain the upper hand and gain the power to corrupt the better pupils, because the good pupil had no recourse to a teacher. In life there is no visible teacher who encourages the good pupil, because we are indeed all pupils. If the good pupil is going to see it through, he must find encouragement in himself. This he did not find. His courage was broken; perhaps he did not find what he was seeking in the world either. And so he succumbed— he, the deceived one, whom the world defrauded of the reward when he willed the good, and whom the world nevertheless deceived most terribly when it got him to give up the good.

VIII
151

2. *Next* it must be said *that the person who wills the good only out of fear of punishment does not will one thing but is double-minded.* To will the good only out of fear of punishment is the other side of coveting reward, in essence therefore the same as willing the good for the sake of reward inasmuch as avoiding an evil is a gain of the same kind as acquiring an advantage. The good is one thing, punishment something else. Therefore the double-minded person does not will one thing when he wills the good on the condition of thereby avoiding punishment. The condi-

tion indicates precisely the double-mindedness; if this were not there, neither would he *fear* merely the punishment, because the punishment is certainly not what a person should fear. He should fear doing wrong; but if he has done wrong, then, if he actually wills one thing and wills the good in truth, he must even desire to be punished so that the punishment can heal him just as the medicine heals the sick. If the sick person fears the bitterness of the medicine, if he fears "to let himself be cut and cauterized by the physician," then he actually fears getting well, even if in his delirium he loudly and solemnly protests that this is not at all the case, that on the contrary he very much wants his health. The protesting exposes, only more clearly the more fervent it is, his double-mindedness: that he *desires* his health and yet does not *will* it, although *he has that in his power*. To desire what one is incapable of doing is not double-mindedness, because what hinders is not in the power of the person who desires. But when the person who desires is himself the one who hinders, who prevents himself from obtaining his desire, not by giving it up, because then he is at one with himself, but by not willing and yet willing to continue to desire—then the double-mindedness is as clear as it can be, or it is then clear that it is double-mindedness. If a person fears the shame of being caught in an error, not the error itself, then he is so far from being helped out of the error by this fear that he is led into something more corrupting—even if in other respects he was not in error.

VIII
152

So, also, when someone wills to do the good out of fear of punishment—that is, it can be done in this manner, if it does not come to be like the fearful person's reducing his life to sheer sickliness out of fear of becoming sick—fear is so far from helping him to do the good in truth that it ruins him precisely because the punishment is the medicine. But then everyone, even a child, knows that nothing is so dangerous as a medicine when it is used—but in the wrong way. Even if it does not end in death, driving the sickness inward is perilous. Spiritually understood, it is a pernicious sickness, the sickness *of not fearing what a person should fear*, the sanctity of shame, God in heaven, the command of duty, the voice of conscience, eternity's responsibility. In order to be protected against or rescued from this sickness, it is beneficial for a person to punish himself, "to beat his breast and scourge his heart."[44] It is even more beneficial that he be punished, so that the punishment will keep him awake and sober and, however more specifically this is understood, will become his lot in life and for his good, indeed, truly for his good if he allows himself to be punished.

But then, spiritually understood, there is another sickness, the even more pernicious sickness of *fearing what a person should not fear and ought not to fear.* The first sickness is defiance and obstinacy and self-willfulness; the second is cravenness and servility and hypocrisy, and the latter is appalling just as the sickness is when the physician to his horror sees that the patient has used the medicine—in the wrong way. It may very well seem that the person who wills the good out of fear of punishment cannot yet be called sick, because he does indeed will the good. But surely the punishment is not the sickness? So he is nevertheless sick, and his sickness is just this: confusing the sickness and the medicine. [45]It might seem that the one who wills the good out of fear of punishment cannot be said to have used the medicine and thus not to have used it wrongly either, because he does will the good, does will to be healthy, out of fear of having to use the medicine. Spiritually understood, however, where the sickness is not physical, like fever in the blood, and the medicine is not something external, like drops in a bottle, there fear amounts to using and having used, having taken the medicine—in the wrong way. This shows up clearly in the most pernicious and morbid symptoms of that other sickness. Fear of poverty has been seen to make the prodigal suddenly stingy but has never been seen to make him thrifty— and why not? Because the fear of the medicine was: taking it in the wrong way. Fear of physical debility has certainly taught the profligate to observe moderation in his debauchery (because his fear was taking the medicine in the wrong way), but it has never made him chaste. Consequently, instead of forgetting God in the vortex of vice (lamentable dissipation!), it taught him to mock God daily by moderation—in debauchery (abominable composure!). And certainly fear of punishment has made the sinner into a hypocrite who in the loathsome double-mindedness of hypocrisy made a show of loving God (since the fear was taking the medicine in the wrong way), but it has never made him pure of heart. This is certain: the punishment is not the sickness but the medicine. For example, for the thoughtless person, being confined to the sickbed can be a punishment, but if he truly understands it as punishment, then the sickness, the fever, or whatever the sickness may be, is the medicine. On the contrary, all double-mindedness that wills the good only out of fear of punishment is ultimately recognizable by this: that it regards the punishment as a sickness. Even if the double-mindedness is an exaggerated worry, something with which one can sincerely sympathize, as when the sick one's frightened imagination alters the effect of the medicine, the evidence is there that the punishment is confused with the sickness, that the sufferer nevertheless does not in truth will to be free *from* the sickness but in untruth to be free *of* the medicine.

But which is the punishment that is feared; how is it to be more definitely understood? When we deliberate on this, the double-mindedness becomes more definitely obvious, because the differences in the nature and the various dangers of one and the same sickness are proportionate to the various wrong conceptions of the punishment. *By punishment someone perhaps thinks of* what is seldom mentioned these days, *the punishment of eternity,* and it might seem that the person who wills the good out of fear of this punishment is not double-minded, since he assigns the punishment to eternity, thus to the same place where the good has its home. And yet he does not will the good; he wills it only out of fear of punishment. So—if there were no punishment! In this "if" lurks the double-mindedness. If there were no punishment!! In this "if" hisses the double-mindedness. If there were no punishment, or if at least there were someone who could convince him that the punishment of eternity is a figment of the imagination, or if it became customary to think this way, or if he could journey to a foreign country where it was customary, or if cowardly and hysterical superstition could invent a cheap means of expiation!!! Look at the double-mindedness! Look, it can just as well seek its consolation in unbelief [*Vantro*] as in superstition [*Overtro*]; and even if it is not double-mindedness that seeks them out, it is they who strain after double-mindedness until it becomes evident.

If double-mindedness were to be designated briefly with one single appropriate term, what would be more descriptive than this "if" or "in case"! When the will gains command in a person through his willing the good and willing only one thing in truth, then there is no "if"; but double-mindedness continually stops itself in its "if." It does not have the momentum of eternity within it and the passability of the infinite before it; it gets ahead of itself and meets itself so that it stops itself. [46]It is said that by the holy sign of the cross one can stop the evil spirit so that it cannot move from the spot; double-mindedness likewise brings itself to a standstill at its sad sign by its "if." For a moment it perhaps seems as if the double-mindedness did not exist; the double-minded person is perhaps able to talk in such a way that it is deceiving. But when a person is going to act and there is double-mindedness in him, it is immediately present in his immobilizing "if." It is quite true that a person can fill up time with his talking, but eternity discloses the nature of his act. Only for the one who wills the good in truth, only for that person can what is taught about the punishments of eternity be eternally true; for the one who merely fears them, for him it cannot be eternally certain because there is nothing eternal in him, since the eternal can be in him only if he wills the good in truth. There is only one evidence that there is the eternal—faith in it; fear is a vacillating evidence that demonstrates that the fearful one does not believe, just as when the devil believes but trembles[47]—because he does not believe. Only one thing can help a person to will the good in truth: the good. Fear is a deceitful aid; it can sour one's delight, make life arduous and miserable, make a person old and decrepit, but it cannot help one to the good, since fear itself has an erroneous conception of the good—and the good does not let itself be deceived.

But is not part of the true nature of the good also this jealousy for itself, that it will not tolerate any other, any alien helper, the intervention of any divisiveness that would cause confusion, so that when the good took its place at the goal, where the reward beckons or where the good itself beckons to a person, it would then unwillingly be obliged to see and tolerate that there were two roads, two strivers, the one because he willed the good in truth and, humble but joyful, heeded the beckoning, the other because fear drove him there! From the spiritual point of view, should two such different people be able to arrive at the *same place*! Spiritually understood, the place is not something external to which *also* the slave comes *against his will* when the overseer uses the whip, and the road is not such that it makes no difference whether one journeys forward or backward; but the place and the road are within a person, since the place is the blessed state of the striving spirit, the road the continual transformation of the striving spirit. No, just as the good is only one thing, so it also wants to be alone in helping a person. [48]The good nurses and takes care of the infant, brings up and feeds the youth, strengthens the adult, watches over the old; the good teaches the one who is striving, helps him, yet only in the way the loving mother teaches the child to walk alone. The mother is far enough in front of the child so that she cannot actually hold onto the child, but she stretches out her arms; she imitates the child's movements. If it merely totters, she quickly bends as if to grasp it—thus the child believes that it is not walking alone. The most loving mother can do no more if there is to be any truth in this matter of the child's walking alone. And yet she does do more, inasmuch as her face, her countenance—indeed, it is beckoning like the reward of the good and the encouragement of eternal happiness. So the child is walking alone, with its eyes fixed on its mother's face, not on the difficulty of the way, supporting itself by the arms that do not hold onto it, striving to reach the refuge in its mother's arms, scarcely suspecting that just then it is showing that it can do without them—for now the child is walking alone.

Fear, on the other hand, is a dry nurse for the child—it has no milk. It is an anemic disciplinarian for the youth—it has no beckoning encouragement. It is an envious sickness for the adult—it has no blessing. It is a horror for the old—when it

VIII
155

turns out that the painfully long *school time* did not lead to eternal happiness. Fear also will help a person, will teach him to walk alone, but not as the loving mother does, because it is fear itself that continually pushes the child over. It will help him forward, but not as the loving mother's beckoning does, because it is fear itself that weighs upon him so he cannot move from the spot. It will lead him to the goal, and yet it is fear itself that makes the goal fearful to him. It will help him to the good, and yet such a learner never wins the favor of the good.

Neither does he ever become God's friend, because, as Scripture teaches, not only thieves and robbers but also the timorous cannot enter into the kingdom of heaven[49]—after all, he does not will it itself; he wills it only out of fear of punishment. Is he not, then, double-minded even if he were not the kind of person who would reveal himself as an entirely different person if you saw him in his dreams, when in sleep he has thrown off the constraint of fear, when everything is as he actually wanted it to be, and he is as he actually is and as he would be when awake if fear were not there, for from olden days it is said that one learns to know a person's soul through his dreams.[50]

When the punishment is thought of as eternity's punishment, it looks deceptively as if it were not double-mindedness to will the good only out of fear of punishment. But it nevertheless is double-mindedness; even if it were a better person who in the painfulness of fear maintained a kind of toilsome unpunishability out of fear of punishment, he nevertheless is double-minded. *He is continually doing what he does not really will*, or what he still has no pleasure in doing, because the pleasure is only shallow, sensate pleasure, and of the sensate pleasures the shallowest is the pleasure whose miserable glory consists solely in avoiding something, so that the pleasure is not in itself but only by way of a contrast. *Neither does he relate the punishment to God and to the good*; on the contrary, in his conception the good is one thing, the punishment something entirely different. But then, of course, the good is not one thing; therefore by his double-mindedness he produces a strained relation between the good and the punishment. He wishes that the punishment did not exist, and thereby he also actually wishes that the good did not exist, since he otherwise must of course have another relation to the good than the one through punishment. Now, punishment does exist; so he does the good out of fear of punishment. But someone who wills the good in truth understands that the punishment exists only on account of the transgressions; he devoutly understands that the punishment is like everything else that befalls one who loves God—a helping hand. The double-minded person shuns the punishment as a suffering, a misfortune, an evil, and thereby completely severs himself and his understanding of the punishment and the punishment from the good. This self-willfulness is like the infantile notion of the child, who, in its lack of understanding, even divides its father's nature, for the child supposes that its father is the loving one, that on the other hand the punishment is something a bad man has invented; but that the loving father himself would have invented the punishment out of love for the child will not become clear to it.

So it is also with the relation between the good and the punishment: it is the good that out of love for the learner has invented the punishment. And indeed we all go to school, except that life's school is for adults and therefore the punishment is of a more serious nature than it is where children go to school. It is less tangible and therefore all the more serious, less instantaneous and therefore all the more serious, less external and therefore all the more serious. It does not follow the offense in quick succession and is therefore all the more serious. 51One is not let off because it seems as if the punishment has been forgotten, and for that very reason it is all the more serious, but by its very seriousness it is truly for the good, if a person wills it. Double-mindedness does not will it but goes on having a soft, sensuous conception of punishment and a powerless will for the good. Therefore it often happens with such a double-minded person that his life deteriorates further the older he becomes, when youth, in which there was still something better than fear, is lost, and when fearfulness conspires with sagacity to make him into a slave, so to speak, of the good. So different is it—the person who wills the good in truth, he is the only free person, free through the good. But

VIII
157

then someone who wills the good only out of fear of punishment does not will the good in truth, and therefore the good
only makes him a slave.

*Yet perhaps double-mindedness very rarely thinks of eternity's pun-
ishment; the dreaded punishment is more often understood in an
earthly and temporal sense.* Of the person who wills the good
only out of fear of this punishment, it must be said with special
emphasis that he fears what one should not fear and ought not
to fear: financial loss, loss of reputation, lack of appreciation,
disregard, the opinion of the world, the mockery of fools, the
laughter of light-mindedness, the cowardly whining of deference, the inflated insignificance of the moment, the delusive,
misty apparitions of miasma. Indeed, just as that double-
minded person who willed the good for the sake of reward was
unstable in all his ways, so also this double-minded person
becomes unstable because he is always on the lookout for the
inconstant, the continuously changed, and always fears what a
person should not fear, fears what has the power to wound,
mistreat, corrupt, and kill the body but over the soul has no
power, if it does not get that through fear.[52] If a person is not to
love the world, the lust of the eyes, the lust of the flesh, the
pride of life,[53] if he is not to crave what is the world's—money
in his hands and the esteem of people—then neither should he
fear what is the world's, neither the world nor people, neither
the exclusion of poverty nor of persecution. If he does that,
then he is the prey of double-mindedness, just as in double-
mindedness he is the people's slave.

Yes, there is a sense of shame that is to the good—woe to the
person who discards it. It is a rescuing attendant through life—
woe to the person who breaks with it. It is in the service of
sanctification and of true freedom—woe to the person who is
offended by it as if it were a constraint! If a person went
through life alone, which according to Scripture is not supposed to be good,[54] but went through it attended by this sense
of shame, ah, it will surely become good and become one
thing! If the solitary one stumbled, if that sense of shame still
attended him, we would not cry out as did the Preacher, "Woe
to the solitary one," nor say with the Preacher, "Woe to the

solitary one; if he falls, who will raise him up?"[55] because this sense of shame is more concerned for him than his best friend, will help him better than all human sympathy, which easily leads to double-mindedness—not to will one thing.

It is certain that ordinarily a person acts more sensibly, shows more energy, apparently more self-control, when others are watching him than when he believes himself unobserved. But the question is whether this sensibleness, this energy, this self-control are in truth, or whether through the persistence of his attention in the untruth of appearance they do not easily light the inconstant flame of double-mindedness in his soul. Everyone who when before himself is not more ashamed than he is before all others will, if he is placed in a difficult position and is sorely tried in life, end up becoming a slave of people in one way or another. What is it to be more ashamed before others than before oneself but to be more ashamed of seeming than of being? Indeed, conversely, a person ought to be more ashamed of being than of seeming; otherwise he cannot will one thing in truth, since in his wooing deference to appearance he only covets the changing semblance and its reflection in public favor. The sagacious person who fears the opinion of others and is ashamed before others—if he is not more ashamed before himself, alas, his slyness might succeed in becoming impenetrable or succeed in fooling him into thinking that it is—and then, what then? The person who does not misuse his power because he fears people's opinion and is ashamed before people—if he is not more ashamed before himself, alas, perhaps he would succeed, or a lip-serving attendant may fool him into thinking that it could be done so cunningly that not even God could see through it—and then, what then? But the discourse does not need to wait for what will happen, that is, for the expression of his double-mindedness, because the discourse is only about his double-mindedness, and that is already obvious. Whether it becomes obvious to people or not, the double-mindedness is there nevertheless, and the double-minded one is miserable. Therefore let us not forget that what is true has the right to call anyone miserable who is in untruth, even when he himself and everyone else consider him happy, because from the standpoint of truth it does not help a person not to know that he is miserable, since that is only one misery more.[56] But the person who is more ashamed before himself is strengthened thereby in willing one thing. However cunning the slyness was, the inventor himself can of course see through it; even if it could be concealed from all people, how could the concealing of it tempt him, since he cannot really conceal it from the one who is privy to the secret, before whom he is most ashamed!

In saying this, we do not mean to imply that anyone has ever lived, even in the most corrupt of times, in such a way that there was no one whose judgment he, for his own good, could and would fear with a beneficial sense of shame, whose judgment could be instructive to him in willing the good in truth. But if this sense of shame before the respected one is to become truly beneficial to the modest person, it is still an unavoidable condition that he be most ashamed before himself. Therefore it is legitimate to say that it is truly most beneficial for a person to have a sense of shame before one who is dead, and if he has it before a living person, then to have it before him as before one who is dead and—or if it seems more appealing to you, my listener, I shall use another expression that still says the same thing although it also couches the explanation beautifully, that is—to have a sense of shame before him as before one who is *transfigured*. One who is dead is indeed a transfigured person. The living person can still make mistakes, can still be changed, can still be carried away in a moment and by a moment. If he is truly worthy of respect, he himself in admonition will call it to your attention, lest through your relation to him you be led into the double-mindedness of being another person's adherent. The living person can perhaps be too favorable toward you, perhaps also too unfavorable. If you associate with him every day, your sense of shame will perhaps lose some of its solemnity or perhaps bring on such a violent sickness that you might wish for some magic charm in order to infatuate the person you respect, might want to insinuate yourself into his favor or at least work yourself up in his favor in every way, because his estimate of you had become the most important thing to you. What a great risk and what a great temptation to be double-minded! It does not disappear until you associate with him as with one who is dead—distance yourself from him, but never forget him. It does not disappear until you are separated from him as by death, when you do not come too close to him in the earthly and temporal sense but only eternally recollect what he himself would call the best in his nature! One who is trans-figured cannot be persuaded; favor and persuasion and rashness belong to the moments of earthly life. One who is dead does not perceive these promptings; the transfigured one cannot and does not want to understand them. If you refuse to give them up, then you must give him up, then you must, if you dare to, insult the transfigured one, break with him, yes, annihilate him, for if he is not the transfigured one he does not exist at all. One can speak with a living person in another way because he also exists in the earthly sense, and if you managed to get him changed a little (alas, to your own deprivation and to his dispar-agement!) you would still have him to cling to, so to speak, you would still have his words, his audible approval, and in your alliance it perhaps would escape both of you that a change had taken place. But the transfigured one, not visible to the mortal eye, not audible to the mortal ear, exists only as transfigured, only in the blessedly still silence of a sense of shame. He cannot be changed, not in the least, without its being noticed at once and without the loss of everything and his disappearance. The transfigured one exists only as transfigured; he cannot be changed into something better—he is indeed the transfigured one; he cannot be changed—he is indeed one who is dead—he remains true to himself, the one and the same, the transfigured one! How, then, could one become double-minded who, by a sense of shame before him, is strengthened in willing the good! Even the honest man, to be sure, is surprised by many a frailty, even at times takes a wrong road; but then he has one hope, that there is a God, a righteous Governance, who by punishment will surely arouse him and lead him back. So different is it—the person who wills the good in truth *even hopes for punishment*, but

VIII
160

accordingly the person who in his double-mindedness *wills the good only out of fear of punishment* is far from willing the good in truth.

The double-minded person stands at the crossroads; then two visions appear, the good and the dreaded shape of punishment. To him the two are not homogeneous, for it is undeniable that the punishment God in his wisdom has attached to every transgression is a good, but it is that only when it is received with gratitude, not when it is only feared as an evil. The double-minded person pays less attention to this punishment; he is more concerned about the world's punishment, but the good and the world's punishment are not homogeneous. Or has the world actually become so perfect and so holy that it is like God, that what it rewards is the good, what it punishes the bad? Could such deification of the world ever occur to anyone who before God trusts that he has a view of life according to which he wants to shape his life? We do indeed hear, especially in places where people gather in a festive mood to deceive each other with many speeches, we do indeed hear glorious words about how the world is progressing and about our age and our century.

But, my listener, did you dare as a father (and I am sure that you have a lofty conception of the meaning of this name and a solicitous conception of the responsibility attached to it!), did you dare as a father to say when you sent your child out into the world, "Just go in confidence, my child; pay attention to what the majority approve and the world rewards; it is the good, but what it punishes is the bad. Nowadays it is not as it was in the days of old, when the opinion of the many was like foam on water, meaningless yet clamorous, blind yet crucial, impossible to follow because it changes faster than a woman changes color. Nowadays the outcome is no longer doubtful; the good is immediately victorious. Nowadays no sacrifice is demanded, no self-denial, because the world wills the good. Nowadays the opinion of the many is the opinion of the wise; the single individuals are the fools. Nowadays the earth is the kingdom of God; the kingdom in heaven is only a reflection. Nowadays the world is the most trustworthy thing we have, the only thing one can build upon, the only thing one can swear by."

But the discourse does not need to ask you, my listener, for it is sure of your answer in advance. But I would like to ask the most fervent speaker at those festive occasions: Would you dare, if you as a *father* were to speak to *your* own *child*, would you dare to say anything like that? Or would you dare to say anything like that if it was a youth who with all the devotedness of his honest soul fastened his trusting gaze upon you, convinced that since you said it it must be true, and in gratitude committed himself by a sacred vow to follow the guidance of your learning throughout life? Or if you saw with your own eyes an engaging youth's beautiful enthusiasm when he read and heard about the great men who struggled against harsh fates and suffered hardships in the world, the glorious ones whom the world repudiated because it was not worthy of them—would you dare, if no clamor incited you to speak in delirium but only in the stillness of confidence, if the trust of the engaging youth and his inexperience obliged you to speak the truth—would you dare to lay your hand upon your heart and say, "Such things do not happen anymore; nowadays the world has become enlightened and perfected; nowadays to seek first this world and its practices is the same as it was in the old days to seek first the kingdom of God and his righteousness."[57]

Alas, as one grows older, one gradually becomes habituated to a great deal in life. Among other things, one also becomes accustomed to saying a great deal that one does not really mean; among contemporaries one becomes accustomed to talking within so many presuppositions that the simple and the lofty things almost sink into oblivion. Now and then one drops a remark that expresses a continuous, incessant, long-standing indignation, "Of course one knows what the world is like"; and at other times the world is praised to the point of deification. But neither comment makes any deeper impression upon the speaker, because the first does not awaken him, does not in fear and trembling at least shock him into wanting to save himself since the world is so bad; and the second does not

VIII
162

strengthen the speaker to will the good enthusiastically, out of confidence in the perfection of the world.

Alas, one so easily becomes habituated in life, in habit's dull round of association with others, to the point of almost abandoning oneself while one plays with platitudes. But even one as pitiably spoiled as that, when speaking responsibly and admonishingly to a child, a youth, a young girl, speaks with a sense of shame. There is a beautiful like for like here: the youth approaches an older person with a sense of shame, and when the older person is speaking admonishingly to a youth he always speaks with a sense of shame. Would to God that everyone who has the opportunity to speak admonishingly to the youth would himself also have some benefit from the shame of the admonition!

In his *admonishing*—because on this the accent lies—the older person will not present a horror picture of the world to the youth, certainly not; such a thing is not earnestness anyway but only morbid imagination. But in his *admonishing* he will shudder at the thought of leading the youth directly into the danger of double-mindedness by deceptively fastening his attention upon the world's punishment, by defiling the pure one instead of impressing upon him a holy fear and a sense of shame before the good—defiling him by teaching him to fear financial loss, loss of reputation, lack of appreciation, disregard, the judgment of the world, the mockery of fools, the laughter of light-mindedness, the cowardly whining of obeisance, the inflated insignificance of the moment, the delusive, misty apparitions of miasma. Indeed, for many people these high-minded thoughts are only all too much like gold-plating, which comes off in the double-mindedness of life, which gnaws and gnaws. But even the most eroded of such persons, when he speaks admonishingly to a youth, remembers that he dare not say anything else—out of a sense of shame. In his *admonishing*, even he will say (for it is no exceptional speaker who is being introduced here, and therefore praise of the good is all the more glorious because it does not need the aid of eloquence, because it is the most lamentably pampered in this life who speaks, please note, admonishingly to a youth)—even he will say,

"Fear not; be slow to judge others, but keep an eye on yourself; stand firm in willing one thing, in willing the good in truth, and then let this lead you wherever for the time being it will lead you—because eternally it leads you to victory. Temporally, let it lead you to prosperity or to deprivation, to honor or derision, to life or to death; just do not let go of this one thing. Holding its hand, you walk safely even in danger; even in mortal danger you walk as safely as the child holding its mother's hand, indeed, more safely, because the child does not even know the danger." Thus in his admonishing he would warn against fear of the world's punishment, which is double-mindedness. VIII
163

At times mention is made of "suffering punishment when one does good"—how is this possible, from whom is this punishment to come? Certainly not from God! Consequently from the world—when this in its wisdom makes a mistake, rewards evil and punishes the good. But, no, the words are spoken figuratively, are not what they say, do not mean what they say. The word "world" does indeed have a mighty and terrible sound, and yet it has to obey the same law as the lowliest and most wretched human being. But even if the world were to concentrate all its power, there is one thing it is unable to do—it cannot *punish* an *innocent person*, no more than it can kill a dead person. Admittedly the world has power, can cause a person a lot of trouble while he is alive, can make his life sour and arduous, can rob him of his life, but it cannot punish an innocent person. Here, amazingly, is a boundary, a boundary that is invisible as a line; it can easily be overlooked with the eye, but it has the powers of eternity with which to restrain! It perhaps escapes the world, whose attention is turned to the great—and the boundary is an insignificant one, for the time being is an unobtrusive, negligible factor, but nevertheless it is there. Perhaps it is completely hidden from the eyes of the world, because this, too, can be a part of the innocent person's suffering—that the world's injustice acquires the appearance of punishment—in the eyes of the world. But the boundary is there nevertheless, is nevertheless the strongest. And even if all the world raged in rebellion and everything was in tumult, the boundary is there nevertheless, and on the one side with the innocent: justice, and on the other side for the world: the eternal impossibility of punishing an innocent person. Even when the world wants to wipe him out and get rid of him, it cannot get rid of the boundary, although it is invisible—perhaps that is why. Even in the moment of his sacrificial death, the boundary is there. Then it tightens with the strength of eternity; then it makes a cleft with the chasmic abyss of eternity! The boundary is there, and on the one side with the innocent: justice, and on the other side for the world: the eternal impossibility of punishing an innocent person.

[58]The good person is strong, stronger than the whole world when he in truth stands on the other side of the boundary within the bastion of eternity; he is strongest when he seems to be getting the worst of it. But the powerless double-minded person has moved the boundary line because he wills the good only out of fear of the world's punishment. If the world actually is not the land of perfection, then in his double-mindedness he has surrendered to the force of mediocrity or pledged himself to evil.

VIII
164

3. [59] *Further, it must be said that the person who self-willfully wills the good, wills its victory, does not will one thing but is double-minded.* If a person wills the good only in order that *he* can be victorious, he wills the good for the sake of reward, and his double-mindedness is obvious, as the discourse tried to show earlier. He does not want to serve the good but to make use of it, regards it as a benefit. But if a person wills that the good shall be victorious, if he does not call the outcome of the struggle victory if he is victorious, but only if the good is victorious— how can he then be called and be double-minded? Well, if he is double-minded (the boundary determination between the pure and the double-minded here is a special difficulty), then his double-mindedness is more cunning and concealed, is even more presumptuous than that obvious and obviously worldly double-mindedness. It is a powerful delusion that seems to come closest to the purity of heart that wills the good in truth, although it is furthest removed, like the heights from the

depths, like heaven-storming pride from the lowly dwelling of humility, like the arrogant equality of presumption when it is achieved by falsifying an eternal, essential distinction. He does not will the good for the sake of reward; he wills that the good shall be victorious; but he wills that it shall be victorious *through him*, that he shall be the *instrument*, he the *chosen one*. He does not want to be rewarded by the world, which he scorns, or by people, whom he looks down upon, and yet he does not want to be an unworthy servant.[60] A proud consciousness is the reward he demands, and in this demand is his violent double-mindedness, yes, violent, for what else does he want but to take the good by violence[61] and by violence to obtrude himself and his services upon the good! And even if he is not guilty of this last presumption, if he still in any way does not will as the good wills, does not will the victory of the good as the good wills it, then he is double-minded, even if he knows how to hide this from people, even if he wants to hide it from himself, even if language's true expression momentarily seems to hide it by calling his frame of mind obstinacy, self-willfulness, for does this seem, especially when it is strong enough to venture the utmost, does this really seem to be double-mindedness? No, it does not seem to be double-mindedness, but it is.

For this double-minded person, then, the good is one thing, its victory something else, or at least its victory through him is something else. Now it is definitely so that eternally the good has always been victorious, but in time it is different. In time it takes a long time, the victory is slow, its uncertainty a slow linear measuring; the faithful servant's life went on over and over, and at the end it seemed as if he had accomplished nothing for the good. And yet he was the faithful servant who willed the good in truth, and he was also loved by the good, which values obedience more than the fat of rams.[62] "Alas, why did time come into existence! If the good has always been victorious eternally, why must it drag itself slowly forward through the duration of time or almost perish in the slowness of time, why must it struggle laboriously through what makes time so long, through uncertainty! Why should the single individuals who will the good in truth be so split up, so separated

VIII
165

that they are scarcely able to shout to one another, scarcely catch sight of one another? Why should time rest like a weight on them, why should the separation delay them when it is so swiftly accomplished in eternity? Why was an immortal spirit placed in the world and in time, just as a fish is pulled out of the water and cast onto the beach?"

Whoever asks questions like these (and even if he sighs as he asks, the utterance remains the same) had better be on his guard, because he scarcely knows of which spirit he is speaking. Alas, often enough people confuse impatience with humble, obedient enthusiasm; the impatient person himself is all too inclined to this confusion. If early and late a person is on the go "for the sake of the good," makes a big noise, is sheer unrest, hurls himself into time as a sick person throws himself on his bed, throws off all consideration for himself as a sick person his clothes, scorns the rewards of this world, keeps people at a distance—then many think, as he himself imagines, that he is enthusiastic. And yet he is anything but that, because he is double-minded, and double-mindedness no more resembles enthusiasm than a tornado resembles a steady prevailing wind. Indeed, all impatience is like this—it is a kind of ill-nature. Already with the child this is the cause, that the child will not take time; it emerges in that double-minded person because temporality and eternity cannot be reconciled in the same person. He cannot and he will not understand the slowness of the good, that in its compassion it is long-suffering, that in its love for the free it will not use power, that in its wise understanding of the weak it shuns every deception; he cannot and he will not humbly understand that the good can do without him. Double-minded is he, this person who with his enthusiasm seems able to become an apostle but can also become a Judas who traitorously wants to expedite the victory of the good. Offended is he, this person who with his enthusiasm seems to love the good so dearly—he is offended by its lowliness when it is clad in the slowness of time. He is not devoted to the good in unprofitable service; he only effervesces, and the person who effervesces loves the moment, and the person who loves the moment fears time—he fears that the duration of time

will make his double-mindedness manifest. And he counter-
feits eternity, because otherwise eternity might make it even
more manifest. A counterfeiter is he; for him eternity is the
deceptive illusion of the horizon, for him eternity is the bluish
boundary of time, for him eternity is the dazzling jugglery of
the moment.

Such a double-minded person is perhaps more difficult to
recognize in this world, because his double-mindedness is not
obvious within the world and has no informer and no confi-
dant in the world's rewards and punishments, since he has
overcome the world, although by a higher deception, since his
double-mindedness is first recognizable at the boundary where
time and eternity touch each other, is recognizable there and at
all times recognizable by the Omniscient One. He will not be
satisfied with the blessed assurance that comforts beyond all
measure—that eternally the good has always won the victory,
the blessed assurance that is a property guarantee beyond all
understanding, the blessed assurance that the unprofitable servant can have within himself at every moment, even when time
is the longest and he seems to accomplish the least, the blessed
assurance that gives the unworthy servant the bold confidence
to speak more proudly than that kingly saying "All is lost
except honor"[63] when he also lost honor but says, "Nothing is
lost but everything is gained." But this double-minded person
is not so easily recognizable in the world, because it is not for
the sake of reward that he wills the good, in which case he
would be disclosed in his ambition or in his despair, and it is not
out of fear of punishment that he wills the good, in which case
he would be disclosed in his cowardly avoidance of punishment or in his despair when he still did not avoid it. No, he is
willing to sacrifice everything, he fears nothing, but he is not
willing to sacrifice himself in daily self-denial—this he fears.

The double-minded person stands at the crossroads; then
two visions appear, the good and the good in its victory or even
in its victory through him. The latter is presumptuousness, but
even the two first visions are not exactly the same. In eternity
they are, but not in time. And they must be separated; the good
wills it so. The good puts on the slowness of time like a shabby

suit of clothes, and in accord with this change of clothes, the double-minded person must be dressed in the humble character of the unprofitable servant. But with his sensate eyes he is not permitted to see the good in its victory; only with the eyes of faith can he aspire to its eternal victory. Therein lies his double-mindedness, because just as there is a double-mindedness that divides in the nature of the good what the good itself has united eternally, so his double-mindedness is that which unites what the good has divided in time. The one double-minded person forgets the eternal and thereby makes time empty—the other makes eternity empty.

4. *Finally*, before it leaves double-mindedness in order, as it were, to show the pure side, the discourse should *call to mind the multifarious double-mindedness, the double-mindedness of weakness* as seen in actual everyday life, *or that the person who wills the good only to a certain degree is double-minded.* To say that double-mindedness wills the good only to a certain degree is basically the expression for all double-mindedness in its relation to the good. But what was developed earlier (which perhaps could be called double-mindedness's false transactions in great matters) did at least have a certain semblance of oneness and unity with itself insofar as it was a single thing that was pursued with a one-sidedness, while the one-sidedness, however amazing this may seem, was precisely double-mindedness in the one-sided person. The transactions of daily life, however, are not in great matters. In daily life it is even more rare to see just one person who wills something wrong with a certain consistency and effort [*Anstrængelse*[64]]. In daily life, the transactions are made in smaller matters, whereby the double-mindedness becomes *more multifariously compounded* in the single individual. Just as a merchant who handles only one ware is a rarity, so also the double-mindedness that has a certain spurious unity; but just as a merchant ordinarily handles different wares, so also double-mindedness ordinarily is multifarious. Thus the wrong road becomes less recognizable as this particular wrong road. No, the wrong roads cross one another—and the right road—in the most diverse ways, and the single individual is in this crossing

in the most diverse ways. His life is surely definable as double-mindedness, but it is not easy to define it more specifically, because not even within his double-mindedness is he of one mind about anything specific, but in his indefiniteness is tossed about by every breeze,[65] because he learns and learns and yet never comes to a knowledge of the truth[66] or approaches it, since he rather gets further and further away the more he learns from this confused and confusing instruction. This double-mindedness has an advantage over the previous double-mindedness in that its good side is that it nevertheless weakly wills the good and it does not have the stubbornness of that earlier double-mindedness, but the weakness is perhaps sometimes just as incurable.

VIII
168

This double-mindedness is difficult to discuss, because it resembles everything and because it continually varies with the ups and downs of life—so swiftly that it can have changed several times while the discourse is scarcely ready to describe one manifestation. Motley-colored, it plays not only in all possible colors, but there is not even any law for this play of colors that blends the colors and shades of colors in ever-new confusion—so there is continually something new under the sun,[67] and yet it is continually the old double-mindedness. Yes, what makes it even more difficult to discuss is that in daily life, where it properly belongs, it deals with itself within the definition of double-mindedness by way of comparison. Thus, by being a little less double-minded than the other, the one double-minded person claims distinction, although his degree of distinction is within the essential likeness. In this way it finally seems as if that genuine eternal claim, which requires purity of heart by willing one thing, has been abolished, removed from the government, placed in the desuetude of dismissal so removed from daily life that it cannot come up at all. In the motley, teeming crowd, in the noise of the world, little attention is paid from day to day and year to year to whether a person completely wills the good if only he has influence and power, is in a big enterprise, is somebody to himself and to others. "What timid and miserable pettymindedness," one thinks, "to be so particular!" One does not even think that there is anything presumptuous in what one says. No, one drops the clever remark in passing and hurries on, while the remark also hurries on from mouth to mouth in the motley and teeming crowd. And in the busy life, in all the dealings from morning to night, it is not such a scrupulous matter whether a person completely wills the good—as long as he is enterprising, not to mention a thief,[68] in his job, as long as he saves and accumulates, as long as he has a good reputation and, incidentally, avoids scandal (for whether he is actually guilty or not is of minor importance, something neither he nor the world has time to investigate—the only danger of scandal is the halting of his enterprise): "What is the point of such a delay in the midst of the rush of busyness!" And in the world there is always hustle and bustle. Yes, it is quite true, this is how it looks in the world.

VIII
169

This is how it seems in the world, this is how it must seem within the illusory horizon of temporality; but in eternity it will make a tremendous difference whether or not one was scrupulous. Yet eternity is certainly not like a new world, so that the person who had lived in time according to the ways of time and busyness, when happy and well he had arrived in eternity, now could try his hand at adopting the customs and practices of eternity. Alas, time and busyness think that eternity is very far away, and yet in drama the producer has never at any time had everything in readiness for the stage and the transformation of the performers in the way eternity has everything ready with regard to time—everything, down to the least detail, down to the needless words that are spoken,[69] has everything ready at every moment—although it holds back.

Would that the discourse, far from delaying anyone who wills the good in truth or calling anyone away from useful activity, might nevertheless halt a busy person, because this busyness is indeed like a spell. And how sad to note how its power grows with the increasing buzzing, how the spell spreads, seeks to trap the earlier prey so that childhood or youth are scarcely granted the stillness, the remoteness, in which the eternal attains a divine growth. And even if this busyness hurriedly makes an admission, in its superficial wisdom itself perceives the advantage of also having a busy man along who occasionally proclaims in haste that higher view of life about willing the good in truth—alas, is it really right that almost everyone is more or less exempted from doing what everyone, each one individually, should do, but then that someone, for the sake of completeness, in the hustle and bustle is given the task of proclaiming that higher requirement—that higher requirement, which if it were to be met in any way whatever, even in frailty and imperfection, would take the collected mind of every human being, his steadfast diligence, his best powers!

So, then, *in busyness there is double-mindedness.* Just as the echo lives in the forest, just as stillness lives in the desert, so double-mindedness lives in busyness. Therefore, that someone who wills the good only to a certain degree is double-minded, has a distracted mind, a divided heart, scarcely needs to be explained. But the basis may well need to be explained and developed—that in busyness there *is neither the time nor the tranquillity to acquire the transparency* that is necessary for understanding oneself in willing one thing or for just temporarily understanding oneself in one's unclarity. No, busyness—in which one continually goes further and further, and noise, in which the true is continually forgotten more and more, and the multitude of circumstances, incentives, and hindrances— VIII continually makes it more impossible for one to gain any 170 deeper knowledge of oneself.

A mirror, it is true, has the feature that a person can see his image in it, but then one must stand still. If one hastily hurries by, one gets to see nothing. If a person perhaps carries with him a mirror that he does not take out, how would he get to see himself? Likewise, the busy person hurries ahead carrying *with him* the possibility of understanding himself, but the busy one keeps on running and never comes to the understanding— indeed, for him it recedes more and more into oblivion—that he is carrying the possibility *with him.* And yet one hardly dares to say this to the busy person, because however short of time he usually is, he on occasion still has plenty of time for a multitude of excuses, through the use of which the last is worse than the first, excuses that have just about as much wisdom as the ship passenger's belief that the ocean is moving, not the ship. One hardly dares to say it to him, for however short of time he is, he on occasion still has plenty of time, along with the like-minded, "to pick from their wisdom the unripe fruit of ridi-cule"[70] in order to deride the speaker as an incompetent in life, as someone the busy person in his sagacity looks down upon—from the exalted viewpoint of his excuses. Everywhere the busy person also has common agreement against the speaker, everywhere in the increasing buzzing of multifarious busyness and in the swarming multitude of excuses. Just like poisonous fumes over the fields, like the hosts of grasshoppers over Egypt,[71] so excuses and the hosts of them become a general plague that nibbles off the sprout of the eternal, become a corrupting infection among the people—with everyone who catches it there is always one more excuse available for the next person. Whereas ordinarily it cannot escape anyone that a sick-ness becomes more and more dangerous, more and more viru-lent the more it spreads, it is just the opposite with excuses—the sickness seems to become milder and milder, the condition more and more pleasant, the more there are who catch it. And then when we all agree that this miserable and stunted health of these excuses is the very best there is, of course there is no one to say anything else. If, then, there were a single individual who could not persuade himself to yield, if he should even strongly object to all this excusing—ah, the end is not yet, there is continually one excuse left. It stands outside his door and solicits him: "Of what use is it for a single human being to want to resist?" Thus again excuses are even worse than a virulent sickness, since no one dies of it because the others died of it.

VIII   So, then, perhaps the double-minded person has *a feeling for*
171 *the good*, a vivid feeling. If someone speaks about the good, especially in a poetic way, he is quickly moved, easily prompted to dissolve in emotion. If the world goes against him a little and then someone tells him that God is love, that his love passes all understanding,[72] that God in his providence embraces even the sparrow, which does not fall to the ground without his will[73]—if someone would speak about this, especially in a poetic way,

he is gripped by it, grasps for faith as one grasps for a wish, and with faith he grasps for the help wished for. Thus in the faith belonging to the wish he has a feeling for the good. But perhaps the help is slow in coming; instead someone who is suffering comes to him, someone he is able to help. But this sufferer finds him impatient and forbidding; this sufferer must be satisfied with the excuse "that at present he is not disposed or in the mood to concern himself with other people's sufferings since he himself has adversities." Yet he thinks that he has faith, faith that there is a loving providence who helps the sufferer, a providence who also uses human beings for his instruments.

Perhaps now the desired help comes; once again he is quickly blazing with gratitude and languishing in a sentimental notion of the goodness of a loving providence. Now, so he thinks, he has really grasped faith; now it has been victorious in him over every doubt and every objection—alas, and that other person who is suffering is completely forgotten. What else is this condition but double-mindedness! If there is going to be any mention whatever of objections to faith, of events and occurrences that seem to make an objection to it and to the solicitous care of a loving providence, then that other sufferer, who was not helped, who even by the one who could help was rebuffed and dismissed with the excuse that he did not happen to be so disposed, that other sufferer is indeed the stronger objection. But it totally escapes the double-minded person that in the very moment when he thinks that faith is victorious in him he contradicts this conviction in action. Or is it not double-mindedness to think one has a conviction that one oneself contradicts in action? Or is it not truly the only demonstration of someone's having a conviction that his own life expresses it in action? Is not this the only guarantee that a person's so-called conviction is not changed every moment according to various things that happen to him and immediately change him and change everything for him, so that today he has faith and tomorrow has lost it and gains it again the day after tomorrow, until something very unusual happens so that he loses it almost entirely, assuming that he had it in the first place!

Suppose there were two people: one double-minded person

who thought that he had acquired faith in the loving providence because he himself had experienced being helped, even
though he, unmoved, had dismissed a sufferer whom he could
help, and another person whose life of self-sacrificing love was
an instrument in the hand of providence, so he helped many a
sufferer while the help he himself had wanted was denied him
year after year—which of these two was truly convinced that
there is a loving providence who takes care of those who suffer?
Is it not a beautiful and a convincing conclusion: Should not he
who planted the ear hear?[74] But is not the opposite conclusion
just as beautiful and convincing: Should not he whose life is
sacrificing love believe that God is love? Yet in the midst of
busyness there is neither time nor tranquillity for the quiet
transparency that teaches equality, that teaches one to be willing to pull in the same yoke with others, the noble simplicity
that is in inner harmony with every human being; there is
neither the time nor the tranquillity to acquire a conviction.
That is why in life's busyness even faith, hope, and love and
willing the good become nothing but flabby words and
double-mindedness. Or is it not double-mindedness to live
without a conviction or, more correctly, to live in the continual
and continually changing delusion that one has and one does
not have a conviction!

This is the way feeling tricks the busy person in double-
mindedness. After the remorse of a flash of repentance died
down in exhaustion, he perhaps had a conviction, so he
thought, that there is a mercy that forgives sin; but he himself
harshly denied forgiveness to the person who was guilty of
something against him. Thus he trustingly believed that he
had, so he thought, a conviction that there is such mercy, and in
action he denied that it exists; in his action he did his part to
demonstrate that it does not exist. Suppose there were two
people—that double-minded one and then another person
who would willingly forgive his debtor if only he himself
might find mercy—which of these two was truly convinced
that such mercy does exist? The latter did at least have the
evidence that it exists in that he himself practices it; the former

has no evidence at all for himself and only the counterevidence he himself provides.

Or the double-minded person perhaps had a sense of right and wrong; it flamed up powerfully in him, especially if someone would poetically describe the zealous men who in the service of the truth self-sacrificially upheld right and justice. Then if some wrong was done to him personally, it seemed to him as if a sign would have to appear in heaven and on earth, as if the world order could no more sleep than he until this was rectified; and it was not selfishness that inflamed him but his sense of justice—so he thought. And when he did get his rights, however much wrong it cost against this one and that one, he once again praised the perfection of the world. The feeling had indeed transported him, but it had also carried him away so that he had forgotten the most important thing: in the service of the truth to uphold right and justice with self-sacrifice. Which of these two is really convinced that there is justice in the world: the one who suffers wrong in order to do the right, or the one who does wrong in order to get his rights?

VIII
173

Immediate feeling is certainly the first, is the vital force; in it is life, just as it is indeed said that from the heart flows life.[75] But then this feeling must "be kept," understood in the same way as when it is said, "Keep your heart, for from it flows life." It must be cleansed of selfishness, kept from selfishness; it must not be left to its own devices, but, on the contrary, that which is to be kept must be entrusted to the power of something higher that keeps it—just as the loving mother prays to God to keep her child. In immediate feeling, one human being never understands the other. As soon as something happens to him personally, he understands everything differently. When he himself is suffering, he does not understand another's suffering, and when he himself is happy he still does not understand it. Immediate feeling selfishly understands everything in relation to itself and therefore is in the disunion of double-mindedness with all others, because there can be unity only in the soundly understood equality of sincerity, and in selfish shortsightedness his conviction is continually being changed, or it is chance that it is not changed, since the reason for this is that by chance his life is not touched by any change. But such firmness of conviction is a delusion on the part of the pampered, because a conviction is not firm when everything forces it upon one, as it were, and makes it firm, but its firmness manifests itself in the ups and downs of everything. Rarely, indeed, does a person's life avoid all changes, and in the changes the conviction of immediate feeling is a delusion, the momentary impression blown up into a view of life as a whole.

VIII
174

Perhaps the double-minded person did have a *knowledge of the good*; in the moment of contemplation it appeared so distinctly before him, so clearly, that the good truly did have all the advantages on its side, that it truly was a gain both for this life and the life to come. Yes, he felt in his heart as if he must be able to convince the whole world of it. Perhaps, however, it was not required of him that he should go out with his acquired conviction to convince others, but the ordeal did not fail to come that would test—his acquired conviction.

Alas, contemplation and the moment of contemplation, despite all its clarity, easily conceal an illusion, because its moment has something in common with the counterfeited eternity. There is a foreshortening that is necessary in order for the contemplation to come about; it must shorten time considerably—indeed, it actually has to call the mind and thought away from time in order to complete itself in a counterfeit eternal rounding off. In this it is something like the work of an artist in drawing a map of a country. The drawing, of course, cannot be as large as the country; it becomes infinitely smaller, but it also becomes all the easier for the viewer to survey the outlines of that country. And yet if that viewer were suddenly set down in the actuality of that country, where the many, many miles have all their force, he very likely would not be able to recognize the country or gain any notion of it or as a traveler get his bearings in it. The same thing will also happen to the double-minded person. His knowledge has certainly been an illusion. What was compacted airtight, as it were, in the completeness of the contemplation must now be stretched out to its full length; it is no longer a rounding off but is in motion. Life is like a poet and thus different from the contemplator, who always comes to a finish; the poet wrenches us out into the middle of life. Now the double-minded one stands there with contemplation's drawing; time, which was omitted in the contemplation, begins to assert its rights. Of course, time has no right in all eternity to deny that the good indeed has all the advantages on its side, but it has permission to stretch out time and thereby to make the understanding, apparently so straightforward in contemplation, somewhat more difficult. Thus the understanding does not become less straightforward simply by becoming warped and crooked but by becoming less straightforward—in pressing on. Now instead of keeping the contemplation with him and keeping to the contemplation in order straightforwardly, but step by step, to penetrate time with it, the double-minded person lets time separate him from the contemplation. Is this not double-mindedness: to be in time without any contemplation, without any definite thought, or more accurately, to be continually in time and to be continually deceived by contemplating or having contemplated! He had thoughtlessly mistaken the moment of contemplation for earnestness, and then when earnestness did come, he threw away his contemplation and mistook the moment of contemplation for a deception—until he once again became earnest in a moment of contemplation.

VIII
175

Or perhaps the double-minded person admitted to himself that he had done wrong, had acted badly, had taken a wrong road. But when in deliberation it became so obvious, so attractive that it is like this, that the punishment is like a medicine, well, it seemed to him that no physician ever made the medicine as agreeable as this deliberation seemed to make the punishment appealing. But when the punishment came and, as the physician also knows, momentarily made the condition worse in order properly to intervene curatively—then he became impatient. In his deliberation he had thought himself cured, had thought how good it would be when it was over—that is, when it was over. For example, the lazy person always has an inordinate imagination; he promptly thinks of how he is going to arrange things for himself and how comfortable he will be as soon as this and that are done; he thinks less about the fact that it is this and that which he is to do. In deliberation this does seem very inviting, but when he is to start out on the road, everything is changed (since deliberation is far beyond the road [*Overveien er ude over Veien*]). Instead of keeping the deliberation and the calculation with him and keeping himself to it to the letter, he discards the deliberation. He has thoughtlessly taken the deliberation in vain, as if it were the healing by the medicine, and when the healing is to begin, he thoughtlessly mistakes the deliberation for a deception. Is this not double-mindedness: to be sick, to put oneself in the care of the physician, and then to refuse to trust the physician but self-willfully stop! Is this not double-mindedness: when the sick person perhaps has gone into the sauna, where the temperature is rising, but now suddenly finds it too hot and runs out, exposed to every danger! Is it not double-mindedness if he still has a remnant of deliberation left, and thereby an idea that he actually is sick, and therefore soon begins his cure again in the same manner!

In the knowledge, as contemplation and deliberation, that is the distance of eternity from time and actuality, there presumably is truth, and the knower can understand the truth in it, but he cannot understand himself. It is true that without this knowledge a person's life is more or less devoid of thought, but it is also true that this knowledge, because it is in a counterfeit eternity for the imagination, develops double-mindedness if it is not honestly gained slowly through purity of the will.

Thus the double-minded person perhaps had *a will for the good*, because surely the person who is deceived into double-mindedness by feeling or by that remote knowledge also has a will, but this gained no power, and the seed of double-mindedness lay in the inner psychical misrelation. Consequently, he has a will for the good; he is not without purpose and intentions and resolves and plans for himself and is not without sympathy's plans for others. But something has escaped him—namely, he does not think that the will in itself is or ought to be the firmest of all, that it should be as hard as a sword that could cut stone and yet would be so soft that it could

VIII
176

be wound about the waist. He does not think that it is the will a person should lean on, yes, that when everything goes to pieces it is the will a person must cling to. He does not think that the will is the mover but that it itself is to be moved, that in itself it is vacillating and therefore must be propped up, that it must be moved and supported by reasons, considerations, the advice of others, experiences, and rules of conduct. If we want to compare the will to the momentum of a ship, which is indeed fitting, the will in a human being with the momentum of a ship, in which it (the human being) is brought forward, then he, on the other hand, thinks that the will, instead of actuating everything, is itself something that must be dragged forward, that it is reasons, considerations, the advice of others, experiences, rules of conduct that trot alongside, as it were, and pull or drag the will forward, so that the will is compared to a ship, indeed, to a freighter. But at the same moment the will is made powerless, reduced "to a certain degree," accordingly as there are reasons and considerations and advice and accordingly as these mutually relate to each other. He has turned everything upside down. What in life has a delaying effect—for everyone who with the momentum of eternity is steering toward a better world—he thinks is the moving force; and what is supposed to be the moving force he makes into something that delays or at least into something intrinsically immovable. Such a person, of course, is bound to remain in double-mindedness, busy with small errands on the inland waters of double-mindedness, when, instead of gaining momentum out of all the delaying factors through the will for the good, he sails only with the speed of the delaying factors.

A person enters upon his life; hoping everything good for himself and wishing others the same, he steps out into the multifariousness of the world like someone who comes from the country into the big, noisy city, into the multifariousness where people busily and hurriedly rush past each other, where everyone tends to his own business in the vast crisscrossing where everything is in the process of passing, where at each moment what one has learned seems confirmed and at the very same moment refuted, yet without any halt in the unrest of the works. He steps out into the multifariousness, the all-too-large school of experience, for here one can experience everything possible, or that everything is possible, even what the inexperienced would least believe—that the good sits at the head of the table and crime next highest, or crime at the head and the good next highest—very congenially. So there he stands. He has a latent susceptibility to the sickness of double-mindedness; his feelings are entirely immediate, his knowledge is fortified only by observation, his will is not mature—swiftly, alas, so swiftly, he is infected, one more victim. This is not anything new, but an old story. What happened to him happened to thousands before him—in passing, he himself says this as his own excuse, because he has received the initiation of excuses.

At this point a speaker, who is just as double-minded as that double-minded one and therefore actually only wants to deceive us, might picture for us willing the good as alluring, alluring with the prospect of becoming something in the world; he might end his description by saying that the double-minded person would become nothing in the world—in order to terrify us. But we do not wish to deceive; even less do we wish to do the terrible thing of terrifying by means of a deception, which is akin to recommending a lie. We only wish to say that from the point of view of the eternal that double-minded person amounted to nothing. In temporality, however, he probably became, in proportion to his capacities and his indefatigable busyness, a prosperous man, or to a certain degree a prosperous man, an esteemed man, or to a certain degree an esteemed man, or whatever he could become within the range of "to a certain degree," which is not at all to deny that he could indeed become the richest man in the world, because even being the richest is only something to a certain degree, whereas only the categories of eternity are above a certain degree. Just like its truths, temporality and everything pertaining to it are to a certain degree; only eternity and its truths are eternal.

Therefore let us not deceive ourselves and say that, in an earthly sense, one goes furthest in temporality by willing the good in truth; do not let the discourse be just as double-minded

VIII
177

as the world is. No, in an earthly sense, one goes furthest in temporality with double-mindedness and mainly, it must be admitted, with the double-mindedness that has an artificial gloss of integrity and unity with itself. See, honesty lasts the longest; it lasts also when the rich man becomes poor through his honesty; it lasts also when the once rich and later poor man is dead and gone. And when the world has perished and is forgotten, when there is no longer poverty or wealth or money, when the once rich and later poor man has long forgotten the sufferings of poverty—then his honesty still survives. And yet one is to think that honesty is involved only with money and the value of money, that, just like dishonesty, it ends with the end of the money world. Of course, honesty is involved with wealth and poverty and money, but it is also involved with the eternal, and not, in a double-minded way, with money and with the eternal; in money matters it is involved—with the eternal. Therefore it lasts; it does not last longest to a certain degree—it lasts.

VIII
178

Therefore that statement is no proverb; it is an eternal truth, it is eternity's invention. There is, however, a proverb that says that it takes a little more than honesty to get through the world. But the questions to which these two statements reply are also extremely different—that which asks about what lasts, and that which asks: How do I get through? The person who merely asks how to get through does not really want to go further. But the one who asks about what lasts has already come through; he has already passed over from temporality into eternity, although he is still living. The one makes inquiries only *to a certain degree*; the other asks *eternally*, and if, in an hour of temptation when his honesty was being tested, he asked correctly, he again receives immediately and hereafter eternity's answer: Yes, it does last! —Oh, it is indeed better to go to the house of mourning than to go to the banquet house,[76] and even there one can learn that "in a hundred years everything will be forgotten."[77] Yes, the banquet and the doughty companions will be forgotten long before that, but truly the eternal will not be forgotten, not in a thousand years.

B. If a person is to will the good in truth, he must will to do everything for the good or will to suffer everything for the good.

My listener, if it seems suitable to you, before going any further, we shall recall the progress of the discourse up to this point, since the discourse also has its developing task and not until this is completed with the requisite slowness, so that we agree with one another about what the discourse presupposes, not until then can the discourse with assurance use the attractive dispatch that is so vital to discourse.

Accordingly, purity of heart is to will one thing, but *to will one thing* could *not mean to will the pleasures of the world and what pertains to them,* even if a person named only one as his choice, since this one thing would still be one thing only by a deception. *Neither could willing one thing mean to will the great as vanity understands it,* which only in dizziness seems to be one thing. In order **to will one thing in truth one must will the good**. This was the first presupposition, *the possibility of being able* to will one thing, but in order **really to will one thing in truth, one must will the good in truth**. Every willing of the good, however, that does not will it in truth must be called *doublemindedness*. So there was a *double-mindedness* that *more forcefully* and acting in a kind of consistency with itself seemed to will the good but yet deceptively wanted something else—it willed the good *for the sake of reward, out of fear of punishment,* or *in self-willfulness*. But there was another double-mindedness, *the double-mindedness of weakness,* the one that is most common among people, the multifarious *double-mindedness* that wills the good with a kind of sincerity, *but only to a certain degree.*

Now the discourse goes further. If a person is to will the good in truth, **he must will to do everything for it**, or **he must will to suffer everything for it**. This in turn we interpret as a classification that divides people, or draws attention to the division that actually exists, into those who act and those who suffer, so that when the discourse is about willing to do everything we are also thinking about the suffering that can be linked to it, without, however, calling such a person a sufferer, since he essentially is one who is acting. But by those who

VIII
179

suffer we are thinking of those whom life itself seems to have assigned to quiet and, if you will, useless sufferings, useless because the sufferings do not benefit others, do not benefit any cause, but instead are a burden to others and to the sufferers themselves.[78]

1. *If a person is to will the good in truth, he must will to do everything for the good.* First we shall discuss: to will to do everything for the good. Everything—but if everything is to be mentioned, will not this discourse easily become limitless in range, will it not become impossible to obtain a good grasp of all the diversities? And will not the discourse thereby become indefinite since the good can indeed require the most diverse things of different people, can sometimes require that a person shall leave his prestigious position and attire himself in lowliness, shall give away his possessions to the poor,[79] shall not even dare to bury his father.[80] And then in turn it can require of others that they should take over the power and rank that are offered, that they should take over the productive power of wealth, that they should bury the father and perhaps a great portion of their lives should be devoted to the faithfulness that is faithful in little,[81] inasmuch as one's own life has no demands of its own but is faithful only to the memory of one who is dead! Therefore, instead of proliferating the details to the point of confusion and distraction, whereby also the status-competition of pettymindedness is so easily brought to mind when one person thinks that by doing one thing he is doing more for the good than another who does something else, even though both of them, if according to the requirement they are doing everything, are doing equally much, and if neither of them is doing everything, both are doing equally little— instead of proliferating the details, let us instead simplify all this in its essential unity and equality by saying that to will to do everything is: *to will, in the decision, to be and to remain with the good,* because the decision is precisely the decisive everything, just as it is the essential one thing. Then there is no tempting occasion for the misguided status-competition of pettymindedness. Then the discourse can be briefer; it need not mention

VIII
180

the many names of the multiplicity and yet is precisely in the truth since this essential brevity corresponds to the full-bodied brevity, as it is in life, of willing in the decision to be and to remain with the good. In other words, let no one think that this is a prolix affair. On the contrary, this is what in the sense of eternity reduces, if I may put it this way, all life's fractions (for eternity's length is the true foreshortening), resolves all its difficulties. In the decision, it is by this willing to be and to remain with the good that so much time is gained, because what takes people's time when they complain of the lack of time is irresolution, distraction, half thoughts, half decisions, indecisiveness, great moments—great moments, this is why we said "to be and *to remain*," lest the decision be confused with the quixotism of a high-minded moment. The person who in the decision wills to be and to remain with the good can find time—for all kinds of things—no, that he cannot do, but neither does he need to, because he wills only one thing, and for that very reason he will not be dealing with all kinds of things, and for that very reason he has plenty of time for the good.

To will, in the decision, to be and to remain with the good is truth's brief expression for willing to do everything, and in this expression the equality is maintained that recognizes no distinction with regard to that more essential diversity of life or of the human condition: to be acting or to be suffering, since the one who is suffering can, in the decision, also be with the good. It is of importance to the idea and to the discourse that there be no divisiveness or occasion for divisiveness, that the discourse not occasion the one who is acting, who can do so much in the external world, to compare himself conceitedly with the sufferer, or occasion the sufferer, who seems to be wasting his time burdensomely in useless sufferings, to compare his uselessness, his wretchedness, his not merely superfluous but *for others burdensome* existence despairingly with the great exploits of those who act. Alas, in addition to his grievous innocent suffering, such an unhappy person often must bear the severe judgment of arrogance and busyness and obtuseness, which no doubt can chide him, no doubt can affront him, but cannot understand him.

VIII
181

But now we are discussing *doing* everything, discussing the people to whom in one way or another the external world is assigned as a stage. With respect to the highest, with respect to willing to do everything, it makes no difference at all, God be praised, how big or how little the task. Oh, how merciful the eternal is to us human beings! The eternal does not recognize all the corruptive strife and comparison that condescends and insults, that sighs and envies. Its requirement is equal for everyone, the greatest who has lived and the lowliest. Yes, the sun does not shine more equally upon the peasant's hut and the ruler's palace than the eternal looks equally upon the highest and the lowliest—equally? No, not equally, for if the highest one does not will to do everything, then eternity looks upon him with wrath. And if through human ingenuity the rich man should ever finally manage to trick the sun into shining over his palace more invitingly than over the hut of poverty, the good and eternity can never be tricked in this way. The requirement is equally the same for everyone: to will to do everything; if it is fulfilled, the good shines its blessing equally over everyone who makes the decision and continues in it.

Should we now recommend the *decision* in an earthly and temporal way; should we say, "You might just as well jump into it as creep into it, just as well risk it first as last, because although life may be a bed of roses for you for a time, the difficult time of troubles will surely come, and then it is always best to be prepared"? Ah, let us never want to sell what is sacred, or rather, let us never forget that in that sense eternity is not for sale, that it values itself too highly to be sold if it is going to be purchased by a bargain hunter, an adventurer. Yes, if a temple robber is one of the most contemptible among criminals, then this varnished sagacity, which shrewdly wills the highest without willing it in truth, is the same. But even if the temple robber succeeds in stealing the sacred treasures, in *actually* taking possession of them because they are something external, that sagacious fellow never succeeds in stealing the decision or in stealing his way into the decision. The executive justice that eternally carries out justice is so vigilant that every crime not only does not become dangerous for the eternal, but

VIII
182

does not even, in the sense of imperfection, actually come into existence, since the crime becomes a self-accusation. In relation to the eternal, the worst crime is similar to that of the temple robber if, instead of stealing the sacred vessels, he went to the authorities and said: I intended to steal the sacred vessels. The stealing of the decision likewise failed, but the guilty one simply reports to the eternal and says: I intended to steal the decision. Eternally there is no illusion, and likewise, just as it is morally, there is no *actual* possession—of stolen property. Therefore let us not deceptively and foolishly recommend the decision. If someone wishes to sneak through life, let him do so, or would that the truth still might seize him so that he wills the decision for the sake of the good, but let us not delude him into thinking that by means of a trick he could slyly take the decision along with him on his sneaking way through life.

The decision is to will to do everything for the good—it is not sagaciously to will to have advantage from the good. Alas, but in every human being there is a power, a dangerous and also a great power. This power is *sagacity*. Sagacity is continually averse to the decision; it fights for its life and honor, because if the decision wins, then sagacity is the same as having been put to death, reduced to being a disdained servant, to whose words one pays great attention but whose advice one disdains to follow.

Inwardly a person uses *sagacity in a pernicious way* to prevent himself from stepping out into the decision. It can be misused in countless ways, but in order again not to proliferate the unimportant and thereby draw attention away from what is important, we shall again describe this misuse with one definite phrase: *to seek evasion.*

To desert one's post, to flee in battle, is always dishonorable, but then sagacity has come up with an ingenious turn that obligingly forestalls flight—it is evasion. Therefore, through evasion one never gets into danger and as a result does not lose one's honor by fleeing in danger. On the contrary, one does not get into danger—that is one advantage; and one wins great honor for being so very sagacious—that makes two advantages. Only eternity, the good, and thus also Holy Scripture have another opinion about evasions and the much-honored sagacious ones, for the reference is indeed to them when it is said, "Some shrink back to their own destruction" (Hebrews 10:39). Amazing! So a person can shrink from a danger, and just when he thinks he is safe and secure (which, of course, he would think, since he avoided the danger), he has sunk into destruction. VIII 183

So a sagacious person says, "Afterward is too late; who is going to help me after I have ventured too far out and am crushed; then I will be a cripple for the rest of my life, an object of scorn, a byword to the public; who will help me then?" Who will help him? Who else but the power in which he trusted when he ventured so far out—yet certainly not as one who is stronger and helps a weak person, but as one who helps when the unworthy servant does everything to do his master's will. [82] But now, with the help of evasions, the sagacious person talks as if the good were itself no power, or as if its power were negligible, so that consequently it was the sagacious one who (if he were to venture this) would help the good by doing everything. If that is the case, then it is indeed really true that there is no one to help him—if he actually ventured in this way, and if, then, there is actually the supervention of what a sagaciously resourceful imagination devises in order that evasion's wretched background can be forgotten because of a foreground that strikes terror into the heart. That is how groundless evasion is.

And now, even though the appalling thing did happen that the trustful venturer came to grief, since an earthly government ordinarily takes care of its faithful servants who in loyalty to their country walk the dangerous road, should not God and the good also take care of their faithful servants if only they are honest! And even if the appalling thing happened that when the honest, sincere person had risked everything, Governance then seemed to say to him, "My friend, I cannot use you"—ah, it is still true that the slightest bread of charity in the service of the good is infinitely more blessed than to be the most powerful one outside it. Truly, truly, it is indeed true, with trembling it is true for the ungodly that God is not fooled by a human being, but in grace it is also joyfully true for the honest and sincere person! Even if the honest person came to grief, perhaps it was precisely this that Governance had to use! Is it not often the case that the well is not filled in until the child has fallen in, whereas the most sensible talk and warning were of no avail. Now then, if the honest person is willing to be the child who falls into the well, has his venturing been futile?

Then another person says, "I do not have the strength to risk everything this way." Once again an evasion, an evasion by means of the word "everything"; the good can indeed also calculate and figure out the requirement in proportion to the strength he has. And then if he in honesty will venture, in the decision he will surely acquire the strength. But with the help of evasions the sagacious one wants to have the strength in advance, wants to take it in vain, just as when the warrior demands honors in advance in order to be sure of becoming singled out for distinction in the battle, and yet this simile is false, because the extent to which the battle gives strength is doubtful, but it is certain that the trust with which one ventures gives suprahuman strength, but it is also certain (what amazing accuracy!) that the person who does not have the trust does not comprehend it either. [83]See, the great warship does not learn its destination until it is out on the deep, whereas the sloop knows everything in advance. Spiritually understood, only the person who wills to do everything is out on the deep, regardless of whether he is the most eminent or the most lowly. The sloop is the sagacious person, regardless of whether he is the most eminent or the most lowly.

Then someone says, "The little bit I can do amounts to nothing." The sagacious one is polite; he underplays and says, "Please do excuse me——." He pretends as if the good were an aristocratic person and to will the good an aristocratic affair. But this is a misunderstanding—yet no, here it is an evasion. The good is not aristocratic; it asks for neither more nor less than everything, whether this is a little bit or not makes no difference. Before God the widow's mite—but it was all she owned—was just as great a sum as all the gold of the world heaped up in a pile, and if someone who owned all the world's

VIII
184

gold gave it all, he would give no more.[84] Indeed, if it had been a public fund drive, it would have been possible that the solicitor had both benevolently and superiorly said to the widow, "No, mother, please keep the mite." But the good—how should we express it—its goodness is so great that it knows no distinctions.

Someone else says, "I cannot justify it on account of my wife and children." Alas, even the civil government ordinarily . . . . . but this does not fit. Yet I wonder if he, the husband and father, could do anything better for his wife and children than to imprint upon them this faith in providence. Here it is not as in civil life, where the person who takes a risk hopes that the state will take care of his wife and children. No, in a spiritual sense he has taken the best care of them precisely by his venturing, because he has thereby demonstrated to them that he at least has faith in providence. Here it is not as in civil life, that the person who refrains from venturing can do so out of solicitude for his wife and children, because in a spiritual sense the fearful one shows that he is not solicitous about his wife and children's true welfare.

Then someone says, "Experience teaches that the best thing to do is to divide your strength so that you can win in one thing if you lose in something else; I owe it to myself and regard for my future not to put all my eggs in one basket." Yes, God grant that he will not have regard only for his future, because that is too little, but will set his sights on one thing only and remember that his future is—an eternity.

VIII
185

But who could ever say all that there is to say about evasions, who would ever engage in this futile labor, this shadow-boxing.[85] Even if someone were to do so, even if he succeeded in enumerating them all and in holding them together for a moment so that they did not slip away like real deserters and assume another character but remained in essence the same, there is always one evasion left, whether there would not still be one, whether a commendable sagacity would not let one discover by repeated examination that one reason had been overlooked and consequently one more evasion was still possible.

So, then, the double-minded person, inveigled by sagacity, gave in to evasions. "But then he did not amount to anything." Oh, let us not deceive young people, let us not sit and haggle and bargain in the antechamber of the holy, let us not create a profane introduction to the holy, as if one were to will the good in truth in order to amount to something in the world. Certainly the sagacious one did amount to something, even something great in the world. But there is a power called recollection; it is said to be as precious to all good people as it is to all lovers. Yes, it is even said to be so precious to lovers that they almost prefer the whispering of recollection to the sight of each other and say: Do you remember that time, and do you remember that time! See, [86]recollection visits the double-minded person also. Then it says to him: Do you remember that time . . . . . You knew very well in your heart, *and so did I,* what was required of you, but you shirked (to your own destruction)—do you recollect that? That was how you gained a great portion of your fortune (to your own destruction)—do you recollect that! Do you remember that time? . . . . . You knew very well in your heart, and *so did I,* what you ought to venture, and you knew what danger was involved; do you recollect that you shirked (to your own destruction)? Do you recollect . . . . . yet you are doing it very well, inasmuch as you wear the medal on your breast in recollection that you evaded to your own destruction! Do you remember that time . . . . . You knew very well in your heart and agreed with my solitary voice in your inner being what you should choose, but you shirked (to your own destruction)—do you remember that? It was the time when public favor and crowd applause hailed you as the righteous one—do you remember that! Indeed, it is your business to remember applause and public favor, because such things are unknown in eternity; but in eternity it is not forgotten that you shirked! Oh, what would it profit a person if he won the whole world but lost himself;[87] what would it profit him if he won time and what belongs to time if he broke with the eternal; what would it profit him if he *swept through* the world at full sail with the fair winds of applause and admiration when he runs aground on eternity; what does it profit the sick person to imagine, what everyone thinks, that he is healthy when the physician declares: He is sick!

Externally sagacity is also used in a pernicious way in connection with the decision; it is misused *outwardly*. And we are indeed speaking about those who act and about willing to do everything for the good. Sagacity can be misused here in many different ways, but once again let us not proliferate distractions but simplify the typical and name all these kinds of misuse with one name: *deception*. Thus the sagacious person knows how the good must be changed a little in order to win favor in the eyes of the world; he knows how much should be added and how much should be subtracted. He knows what ingratiating words should be whispered in people's ears, what should be entrusted to them in confidence and how the hand should be pressed. He knows where to veer away from truth's decision, how the turn should be made and how he himself should adroitly twist and turn—"so that he can be all the more effective for the good." But the secret of the deception to which all manifestations of it can be traced in one way or another is this: that it is not human beings, after all, who stand in need of the good, but the good that stands in need of human beings. Therefore they must be won, because the good is a poor beggar who is in need, rather than human beings who stand in need of the good and need it in such a way that it is the one thing necessary, that it must be purchased at any price, that unconditionally everything must be given up and sold in order to buy it, but also that the one who owns it owns everything. As is natural, however, everyone is fooled by the deception. An attempt is made to fool the good, which will never succeed in all eternity, since its seeming to succeed for two weeks or a generation is only a jest. The sagacious person, however, wins great esteem in the world— and is fooled; the majority divert themselves with the flattering sweets of the imagination—and are fooled! This was the secret of the deception—that it is the good that stands in need of people; the sagacious person's secret is that he cannot be totally satisfied with the good's meager reward but must earn a little on the side—by going around a little on the side. VIII 187

Inveigled by sagacity, the double-minded person gave in.

"But then he didn't accomplish anything in the world." No, let us not deceive; he accomplished a great deal. A great crowd of friends of the good, or of good friends, admiringly assembled around him; yes, it is true that in so doing they certainly thought they were in turn assembling around the good; but it inevitably must be a delusion, since the sagacious person himself went *around on the side*. There were many joined together, because they had the idea that the good is something extraordinary, and honor be to them and honor be to this true idea. But they also had the idea that the good is so extraordinarily great that there must be many joined together in order to purchase it. But this idea is not worthy of honor, even though it is deceitfully called modesty. It is an insult to the good, which in its infinite goodness does not disdain the poorest person but allows him, too, to bid and to buy—if he wills to do everything and thus honors the good in truth. But the good disdains all foolish honor and esteem when its greatness is to be compared to a piece of property that one individual does not have enough money to buy, and therefore a campaign for funds becomes necessary. With the support of the crowd, the sagacious person now erected a huge building—indeed, a tie-beam structure [*Bindingsværk*] (of course it took many to do it), but it looked good as long as it stood.

But recollection, recollection, which in the highest and most earnest sense, ennobling even the coarser expression, is what one in vulgar daily language calls a dun, recollection sometimes also visits the admired one. It softly says to him, "Can you remember the deceptive turn you gave the affair; that was how you won the blinded crowd and how you were able to erect the tower so high?" But the public favorite says, "Just be quiet; don't let anyone ever find out." "Well, all right," replies recollection, "you know that I am no petty trifler financially embarrassed because of unpaid accounts. It may be that no one will find out as long as you live, perhaps not even when you are dead and forgotten, but eternally, eternally it will be recollected."

Of what use would it have been to the unfaithful servant whose master went on a journey if the master journeyed so far

that he never managed to see him again in time, of what use
would it have been to him if the master who went on a journey
was recollection, which he is to meet in eternity! Of what use is
it to the condemned person that the day of punishment is postponed throughout his whole life, of what use is it to him if the
sentence passed upon him is still eternity's judgment and will
be carried out in eternity!

Thus the sagacious one *did accomplish* much. Well, let us
examine this thought: to accomplish something in the world;
there is so much impatient and misleading talk about this. It is
indeed good that everyone wants to accomplish something. It
is indeed earnestness to will this, but would it not also be
earnestness precisely to understand oneself and life with regard
to what it means to accomplish so extraordinarily much or
seemingly to accomplish nothing at all. If *temporality*, not understood as it can be imagined but as it is a fact recognizable in
actuality—if temporality were the *uniform transparency* of the
eternal, then every eternal willing in a person and every willing
of the eternal would be directly recognizable, according to the
assumption, in temporality's uniform sense that the person
who wills would himself become something in temporality
and to many would prove to be somebody. Then the eternal
willing in a person would be just as directly recognizable as the
volume of a scream is recognizable by the volume of sound in
space, as the size of the stone when thrown into the water is
recognizable by the size of the circle that is formed. If the nature
of temporality and of the eternal were such that they correspond to each other as echo to sound, then accomplishing
would be the reliable rendition of the eternal will in the human
being; one would be able to see immediately, by what a person
accomplished, how much willing of the eternal was in him.
But in that case it could never have occurred in temporality (to
mention the supreme and the most terrible example but also
the example explaining everything) that God's son, when he
was revealed in human form, was crucified, rejected by temporality; in the eternal sense he certainly willed the eternal, and
yet he became recognizable in temporality by being rejected
and thus he accomplished but little. The experience of the

VIII
188

apostles was the same as his, just as they expected, and it was the same for so many of the witnesses to the good and to the truth, in whom the eternal will flamed intensely.

Temporality, as it is knowable, cannot be the transparency of the eternal; in its given actuality, it is the *refraction* of the eternal. This makes the category "to accomplish" less direct. The more the eternal is in motion in the witness, the greater the refraction; the more the striving person is allied to temporality instead of willing the eternal, the more he accomplishes in the temporal sense. In many ways, or in all ways, this is how it is in temporality.

When a singular thinker, who through his singularity is more related to the eternal and less to the moment of temporality, addresses his discourse to people, he is rarely understood or listened to. If, however, a garrulous adherent comes to his aid so that the singular thinker can be—misunderstood—then it never fails, then there are many who promptly understand it. The thinker becomes a kind of superfluity in life, the adherent an energetic man who accomplishes so very much in temporality.

Only rarely can it hold true approximately that what the eternal accomplishes and what temporality accomplishes approximately correspond *accidentally*, for let us not insult God and the God-man by assuming that what happened to him was accidental, that his life expressed something accidental, perhaps something that would not happen to him in other times in another nation. If there is to be any meaning in the talk about accomplishing, then a distinction must be made between the moment's view of a matter and eternity's view of the matter. These are two opposite views, between which every human being must choose in regard to his own striving and in regard to every contemporary striving, because to judge—by the result (whereby an attempt is made to unite the judgment of temporality and the judgment of eternity at a later time)—cannot be done in the moment a person himself is to act, and neither can it be done in the moment someone else acts. Thus by means of an illusion a living generation often feels that it dares to pass judgment on a past generation because it failed to

VIII
189

understand the good person—and itself becomes guilty of the same thing with regard to a contemporary. And yet it is in relation to the contemporary that a person must demonstrate whether he has the view of the moment or of the eternal. Afterward it is easy to decorate the graves of the noble ones and say, "If they had only lived now!"—now, just when we are in the process of doing the same thing to a contemporary. The difficulty and the test as to what resides in the person passing judgment are precisely the contemporaneity. The view of the moment is the estimate that according to an earthly and busy understanding decides whether a person is accomplishing something or not.

And in this sense no cause has ever been lost in the way the cause of Christianity was lost when Christ was crucified; and no one has ever, in the sense of the moment, accomplished as little by a life solely committed to sacrifice as did Jesus Christ. Yet, in the eternal sense, at that same moment he had accomplished everything, because he did not foolishly judge by the result, which was not yet there either, or rather (for here is the conflict and the battlefield for the two views on what it means to accomplish something) the result was indeed there. Ask his contemporaries if you ever meet them—did they not say of the crucified one, "The fool, he wanted to help others and he cannot help himself,[88] but now the result, as everyone can see, shows what he was!" Did not his contemporaries say, especially there where the sagacious held forth, "The fool, he had it in his power to become king if he had only used his opportunity; if he had had just half of my sagacity, he would have been king. In the beginning I actually believed that it was craftiness on his part to allow such expressions of the people without giving in to them. I thought it was a ploy to incite them even more, but now the outcome really bears out the conclusion I have already reached lately, that he is a narrow-minded, infatuated fanatic!" Did not many a reasonable man and woman say: "The result shows that he was chasing after illusions. He should have married; then he would have been an esteemed teacher in Israel by now!"

At the same moment, however, in the eternal sense, the

VIII
190

crucified one had accomplished everything! But the views of the moment and of eternity on the same matter never have been so glaringly contradictory, nor can it ever be repeated; this could happen only to him. *At the same moment,* however, eternally understood, he had accomplished everything and therefore said with the certainty of eternity: It is finished.[89] He does not now make his appearance again after the passage of eighteen hundred years and, referring to the outcome, say: It is finished. On the contrary, he presumably would not even say it in that way; perhaps many centuries are needed before he can say it in the temporal sense. Therefore, what he cannot say even after eighteen hundred triumphant years he said eighteen hundred years ago at the very moment when everything was lost— he said, in the eternal sense: It is finished. It is finished—he said that just when the mob and the priests and the Roman soldiers, and Herod and Pilate, and the loafers on the streets and the crowd at the gate and the journalists, if there were such people then, in short, when all the forces of the moment, however different the mentalities might be, were united in this view of the matter—that all was lost, dreadfully lost. It is finished, he said—himself nailed to the cross; when his mother stood near—as if nailed to the cross; when the disciples' eyes seemed to be nailed to the cross in horror at this sight—that is, when motherliness and loyalty submitted to the moment's view of the matter that all was lost. Oh, let us still learn wisdom in minor situations from this most terrible event that occurred once (and it is not to the world's credit that it happened only once, since the reason is indeed this, that the crucified one is eternally essentially different from every human being); let us never deceive young people with foolish talk about accomplishing; let us never make them busy in the service of the moment instead of patiently willing something eternal; let us never make them quick to pass judgment on what they perhaps do not understand rather than content to will something eternal themselves! Let us really consider that one generation is not better because it understands that a previous generation did wrong, if at the moment it does not itself understand how to distinguish between the views of the moment and of the eternal on the matter!

But the person who wills the good in truth uses sagacity *inwardly: in order to prevent all evasions and thereby to help himself out and to keep himself out in the decision.*

Sagacity certainly is a great power, but he treats it as an inferior servant, as a sly object of contempt—to be sure, he listens to what it says but does not act accordingly. He uses it against himself as a spy and informant who promptly reports every evasion, yes, reports even the suspicion of an evasion. In the same way the thief knows the secret paths—and takes them; the authorities also know them and take them—in order to discover the thief; but as knowledge the knowledge of both is the same.

This is how he uses sagacity. Whether or not it is true that at every person's birth two angels are born—his good and his bad angel—I do not know. But this I do believe (and I am willing to listen to any objection, but I *will* not believe it), that at every person's birth there comes into existence an eternal purpose for that person, for that person in particular. Faithfulness to oneself with respect to this is the highest thing a person can do, and as that most profound poet has said, "Worse than self-love is self-contempt."[90] But in that case there is one guilt, one offense: unfaithfulness to oneself or *a disowning of one's own better nature.* Someone guilty in this way is not like the thief or the robber. The civic authorities do not pursue him; his guilt can pass off so quietly that no one suspects it; is it therefore perhaps nothing? Many do indeed think that a person in investigating can equally well apprehend the truth, in cultivating the beautiful can equally well produce it, and in living can equally well accomplish the good even if he is also secretly a little unfaithful to himself, moves the boundary line of inwardness a little by being a little less scrupulous in order to win earthly advantages, so that when he by unfair means has gained them he "can really work for the good, the beautiful, and the true." Accordingly, one has so low an opinion of the good and beautiful and true as to believe them capable of employing everyone as a useful instrument to coax his sweet-sounding agreement—everyone, even the person who has made a mess of himself. Yes, one can deceive oneself and other people, but when eternity is listening, listening to discover whether the string playing is pure and harmoniously synchronized, ah, it promptly discovers discord and unsureness. It rejects such a person, just as the expert rejects a stringed instrument if it is damaged. Alas, it is indeed a shallow sagacity (however much it boasts of the earthly advantages it won as proof—of its shallowness; however much it points to the emblems of distinction and thereby in turn to—the concealed lostness inside) that sagaciously swindles itself out of the highest. Only that sagacity is true that helps a person to make every sacrifice in order to will the good in truth.

Therefore the person who wills the good in truth uses sagacity *against evasions*. But then does he not fail to become something great in the world? Perhaps, perhaps not; but one thing he does become, definitely, he becomes a friend, a lover of recollection. [91]And when in some quiet hour recollection pays him a visit (and already here, what a difference there is from that visit when recollection menacingly knocks on the double-minded person's door!) and says to him, "Do you recollect that time, that time when the good resolution won the victory in you?" And he answers, "Yes, my dear fellow!" But then recollection goes on to say (and recollection is said to be so dear to lovers that they almost prefer, even to the sight of one another, the whispering of recollection when they say, "Do you remember that time?" and "Do you remember that time?")—recollection goes on to say, "Do you remember all the troubles and sufferings you had for the sake of your resolution?" He answers, "No, my dear fellow, I have forgotten that—let it be forgotten! But if sometimes in the stresses of life and struggle, when everything is confused for my troubled thoughts, I ever seem to have forgotten also what I know I have willed in honesty—O you messenger from eternity, recollection, you who have your name from the act of recollecting—if that happens, then visit me and bring with you the desired, the strengthening reunion!" And recollection answers in parting, "That I do promise you—I swear it by eternity!" So they are separated again, and so it must be here in temporality; deeply moved, he once again watches it disappear as one watches the transfigured one; now it has vanished, and also the quiet hour. It was only a quiet hour, not any great moment—therefore he hopes that recollection will keep its promise. He preserves in his inner being that stillness in which he meets recollection when it deigns to visit him. This is his reward, and for him this reward is beyond measure. Just as a mother carrying her beloved child asleep in her arms along a difficult road is not worried about what may happen to her but fears only that the child may be disturbed and disquieted, so he does not fear the world's troubles for his own sake but is only worried that they might disturb and disquiet that possibility of the visit slumbering in his inner being.

VIII
193

The person who in truth wills the good also uses sagacity *outwardly*. It is no disgrace to be sagacious—it is a good thing; it is no disgrace that the authorities are sagacious, that they sagaciously know how to track down the criminal's secret path in order to arrest him and disarm him. Being sagacious, the good person is informed about the way the world wants to have the good falsely made attractive, how the crowd wants to be won over, the dreaded crowd that "wants the teacher to tremble before his audience and flatter them." [92]He knows all this—in order not to act accordingly, but in order by his opposite behavior to preclude, if possible, the illusions, lest he himself illegitimately come to gain advantage from the good (gain money, distinction, and admiration) or deceive anyone by a delusive appearance. Instead he wants, if possible, to keep the good away from contact with the crowd, to try to split it up in order to get hold of the single individual or each one separately. He will be reminded of what that simple wise man of old says, "There where the people come together in a great crowd, in the assemblies, in the theaters, in the camps or wherever else there is a gathering of the crowd, and there where with loud uproar they censure some of the things that are said and done and praise others, but in both cases with excessive cries and clamor and clapping of hands, there where even the rocks and the place where they are assembled echo the noise and repeat twofold the tumult of the praise and the censure—how would it be possible that there a young man's heart, as the saying is, would begin to throb?"[93] Yet this is just what is needed to will the good in truth, that the heart throb in the man, but with the fresh vitality of youth. Therefore the good person, if he is also sagacious, will realize that if anything can be done for the good, he must get people separated as individuals. The same people, who as individuals are able to will the good in truth, are immediately corrupted as soon as they unite and become many, and therefore the good person will neither try to have a *crowd* for help in splitting up the *crowd* nor try to have a *crowd behind him* while he is splitting up the *crowd in front of him*.

But how the good person will use sagacity outwardly cannot ordinarily be stipulated in detail, because in relation to each time and the conditions of each time the need may be quite different. The rigorous judge who went out into the desert and lived on grasshoppers[94] knew how he should decisively communicate to his contemporaries that it is not the truth that needs people but people who need the truth—therefore they had to come to him, come to him out in the desert, and there was no opportunity out there for them to be able to embellish the truth, to be able graciously to do something for it, out there where the axe did not lie in the forest but at the foot of the solitary tree, and every tree that did not bear good fruit would be chopped down.[95] Yes, there certainly have been self-appointed judges since that time who erred and slashed at a whole forest—and the crowd found it almost flattering.

At another time there was that simple wise man who by way of jest worked for the good. In his sagacity he knew what his light-minded people needed lest they directly take in vain the earnestness of the good and thereby be led to pay the wise man much money, a remuneration for their being deceived.[96] The character of the jest prevented them from directly taking the earnestness in vain; the adverseness of the jest, on the other hand, made their light-mindedness apparent—this was the judgment. Without this sagacity, the light-minded public probably would have aped him—in being earnest. Now, however, he presented them with the choice, and lo, they chose the jest; they utterly failed to see that there was any earnestness in it—because there was no earnestness in them. This was the judgment, and the judge's conduct, his art, was paganism's supreme ingenuity; Christianity again has another view.

Yet this, too, cannot be universally developed more explicitly; it pertains only to those initiates whose secret it is. Thus one can learn to know a whole generation by observing such an individual, deducing from him to the generation, from the character he found it necessary to assume to how the age must have been. But this is acknowledged by all and is certain: that anyone who wills the good in truth is not in the world to conjure up a semblance of the good, so that this gains attractiveness in the eyes of the world and he himself becomes a most beloved man; he does not have the task of transforming the good into the cause of the moment, into something to be voted on in a clamoring assembly, or something that in haste must have some adherents who also will the good after a fashion to a certain degree. No, he always has the task, not by words nor by intention but by the inwardness of honesty in his own life, to effect the maximum disclosure of an opposite environment, not by judging in words but by his life unconditionally serving the good in action. The task is his own commitment in the service of the good; passing judgment is not his occupation, not his work, but is a concomitant because a surrounding world relates to him.[97] Passing judgment is not his action, because his action is to will the good in truth; passing judgment is his suffering, in that the surrounding world is disclosed by the way it makes him suffer, while by these very sufferings it helps him to test himself to see whether what he wills is indeed the good or whether he is trapped in a deception himself. The person who wills the good in truth must above all not be busy but must in quiet patience leave everything up to the good itself, what reward he is to have, what he is to accomplish. He does not dare to permit himself one mediating word, not one hint; he does not dare to ask for the slightest relief from the world. He only has to give himself over to the good and the

VIII
195

cause and anyone who possibly could be helped by him. He is no judge; on the contrary, he is the very opposite—he is the one who is judged. His only effect is that the surrounding world is disclosed by the way it judges him.

But in that case he does not accomplish anything;[98] he gets the opposition of people to put up with, and then he succumbs. Well, probably not at first, and eternally never. Presumably not at first, because the person who through trust in God is truly enthusiastic is not like a candle stub whose little flame blows out in a breeze. No, he is like a conflagration—the storm cannot stop it; and the fire in his conflagration is like that Greek fire—water cannot put it out! And even if he finally does succumb to the world, that does not mean that either he or the good has lost—but to be on top in the world, like that ordeal called ordeal by water, is usually a sign of guilt. Quite true, because the world is more allied with the mediocre than with the truly good, precisely for that very reason he will accomplish, in the sense of the moment, much less by not yielding, by not bargaining, by not making himself cozy and comfortable, by not wanting to have advantage for himself—but recollection, recollection! Let us never forget recollection; one would indeed think that this could be forgotten least of all. Recollection will be unable to remind him of the time when he sneaked along a devious path in order to avoid a decision, of the time when he gave the matter another turn in order to please people, of the time when he deserted his post in order to let the storm pass over, of the time when he yielded in order to find some relief in his awkward situation; of the time when he sought support and alliance with others—perhaps, as it is called, to work all the more for the victory of the good, that is, to make his situation a bit less difficult in comparison with standing alone somewhat apprehensively, as in a midnight hour "with musket loaded at his dangerous post."[99]

No, what he accomplishes and what he does not accomplish in the sense of the moment are not his affair; what he accomplishes is always that he remains the friend of recollection and its lover. Whether or not he will be recollected in the world—this recollecting, like the moment, is also a series of moments—

he is sure of eternity's recollection. When he leaves the world, he leaves nothing behind, he takes everything with him; he loses nothing, he wins everything—because "God is everything to him."

2. *If a person is to will the good in truth, he must will to suffer everything for the good.* This pertains to those who act, but of *the suffering one*, if he is to will the good in truth, it is required *that he must will to suffer everything for the good* or, since what is expressed is essentially the same as explained earlier (and therein lies the eternal's equal participation with the diversity of earthly life), *in the decision he must will to be and to remain with the good.* One can indeed also suffer and suffer and continue to suffer without ever coming to any decision in good understanding and agreement with the suffering. A person may have suffered a whole lifetime without its being possible in any way to say truthfully of him that he has willed to suffer all for the good. [100]But the suffering of the sufferer is different from the suffering of the one who acts, inasmuch as when the latter suffers, his suffering has significance for the victory of the good in the world; whereas when the sufferer takes upon himself the sufferings allotted to him, he wills to suffer everything for the good, that is, in order that the good may be victorious in him.

VIII
197

So, then, the sufferer must will to suffer everything. Everything, but how is the discourse to be composed at this point, since, alas, the sight and knowledge of sufferings can easily disrupt the composure; how can the discourse be composed with brevity, since sufferings can be very different—and so prolonged. Here again let us not proliferate the distractions but simplify the typical; let us call all discussion about suffering back to the *wish*. The wish is indeed the sufferer's relation to a happier temporality (faith and hope are the relation to the eternal through the will), and the wish is, as it were, the tender spot where the suffering hurts, the tender spot that the suffering continually touches. Where there is no longer any wish, the suffering, even if there could be any question of suffering, is an animal suffering, not a suffering that is distinctive for a human being. It is a kind of spiritual suicide to want to kill the wish, [101]because we are not speaking of wishes but of the wish with the essential accent of excellence, just as we are not speaking of transient sufferings either but of one who is suffering essentially. The wish is not the healing; that is only through the eternal. But the wish is the life in the suffering, the health in the suffering, is the maintenance of the suffering, for it is as a thinker has said: "Temporality's comfort is a dubious matter, because it lets the wound close although it is not healed, and yet the physician knows that recovery comes through keeping the wound open."[102] In the wish the wound is kept open so that the eternal can heal; if the wound grows over, if the wish disappears, then eternity cannot heal, then temporality has really bungled the illness.

So let us speak about the wish and thereby about sufferings; *let us properly dwell on these, convinced that one learns more profoundly and reliably what the highest is by reflecting on sufferings than by reflecting on achievements, in which there is so much that is distracting.* There are, of course, wishes that die at birth; there are wishes that are forgotten like yesterday; there are wishes that one outgrows and later scarcely recognizes; there are wishes that one learns to give up, and how good it was that one gave them up; there are wishes to which one dies, which one hides, just as a departed one is hidden in transfigured recollection— these are the wishes that could be the more or less dangerous sicknesses to which a person who acts is exposed, while the healing here can be that the particular wish disappears. But then there is also a wish that dies slowly, that remains with *the person who suffers essentially* in the loss and dies only when he dies, because wishes pertain to the particular and the multifarious, but the wish pertains essentially to the whole life.

But if the matter of the wish is so sad, how joyful is the matter of hope! There is a hope that is born and dies; a brief hope that is forgotten tomorrow; a childish hope that the adult does not recognize; a hope to which one dies; but then—in death, in the decision of death, there is born a hope that does not die at birth, because it is born in death; *through this hope,* underneath the pain of the wish, *in the decision the suffering one is with the good!*

So it is with the hope in which the suffering one aims from a distance, as it were, at the eternal. Even more joyful is the matter of faith, for there is a faith that disappoints and disappears; a faith that is lost and regretted. There is a faith that is like death when it swoons, but then—in death, in the decision of death, there is won a faith that does not disappoint; is not regretted, does not die. It *grasps* the eternal and *holds it fast*; through this faith, underneath the pain of the wish, in the decision the suffering one is with the good.

So it is with faith, in which the suffering one draws the eternal closer to himself, and with love it is most joyful of all. For there is a love that flares up and is forgotten; there is a love that unites and separates; there is a love until death, but then—in death, in the decision of death, there is born a love that does not flare up, does not equivocate [*tvetyde*], is not until death, but on the other side of death it abides—in this love, underneath the pain of the wish, in the decision the suffering one *abides* with the good.

O you suffering one, whoever you are, do you want, double-minded [*tvesindet*], to seek the palliative of temporality that makes you forget your suffering—so you think, but no, it makes you forget the eternal! Do you want, double-minded, to despair [*fortvivle*] because all is lost—so you think, but there is indeed everything to gain with the eternal! Do you want, double-minded, to despair? Have you reflected upon what it means to despair? It means to deny that God is love! Really think this through, that a person who despairs is giving up on himself—yes, that is what he thinks—no, he is giving up on God! Ah, do not weary your soul with makeshift, temporary palliatives; do not grieve the spirit with temporal consolations; do not suicidally kill the wish; through hope, through faith, through love you win the highest that the most powerful is capable of—*in the decision to be with the good!*

Let us speak further about the wish and thereby about sufferings. Discussion of sufferings can always be beneficial if it addresses not only the self-willfulness of the sorrow but, if possible, addresses the sorrowing person for his upbuilding. It is a legitimate and sympathetic act to dwell properly on the suffering, lest the suffering person become impatient over our superficial discussion in which he does not recognize his suffering, lest he for that reason impatiently thrust aside consolation and be strengthened in double-mindedness. It certainly is one thing to go out into life *with* the wish when what is wished becomes the deed and the task; it is something else to go out into life *away from* the wish. Abraham had to leave his ancestral home and emigrate to an alien nation,[103] where nothing reminded him of what he loved—indeed, sometimes it is no doubt a consolation that nothing calls to mind what one wishes to forget, but it is a bitter consolation for the person who is full of longing. Thus a person can also have a wish that for him contains everything, so that in the hour of the separation, when the pilgrimage begins, it is as if he were emigrating to a foreign country where nothing but the contrast reminds him, by the loss, of what he wished; it can seem to him as if he were emigrating to a foreign country even if he remains at home, perhaps in the same locality—by losing the wish just as among strangers, so that to take leave of the wish seems to him harder and more crucial than to take leave of his senses. Apart from this wish, even if he still does not move from the spot, his life's troublesome way is perhaps spent in useless sufferings, for we are speaking of those who suffer essentially, not of those who have the consolation that their sufferings are for the benefit of a good cause, for the benefit of others. It was bound to be thus— the journey to the foreign country was not long; in *one moment* he was there, there in that strange country where the suffering ones meet, but not those who have ceased to grieve, not those whose tears eternity cannot wipe away,[104] for as an old devotional book so simply and movingly says, "How can God dry your tears in the next world if you have not wept?"[105] Perhaps someone else comes in a different way, but to the same place. Silently the guiding necessity leads him on; duty, rigorous and earnest but not cruel, since it never is that, comes behind and brings up the rear of the procession. But the road is not the road

VIII
199

of the wish. Now he stops for a moment. Even the two stern attendants are moved by his suffering. Look, there a side-road branches off. "Good-bye, you wish of my youth, you friendly place where I had hoped to build and live with my wish!" The procession moves on—the guiding necessity silently in advance, duty behind, stern and earnest—not cruel, since duty never is that. Ah, see that road branching off to the side; it leads to the wish: "Good-bye to you, my desired sphere of activity, where I had hoped to forget youth's denied wish in the fulfilled joy of work." Then the procession moves on.

VIII
200

But the way it happens makes, of course, no difference— whether it is the place that changes and the sufferer remains on the spot, or whether the sufferer changes the place and goes there. If the place is still the same, it makes no difference if what gathered in one place is still what human language might be tempted to call "the hopelessness of useless sufferings." Sufferings themselves can have various names, but let us not proliferate the names but consider the essential, that the sufferer does not benefit others by his suffering, is a burden instead; and even if the latter is not the case, the former must still be the case if the suffering is to be counted as useless, if the sufferer is to be called a sufferer in the strictest sense. In the strictest sense—indeed, let us be rigorous only with ourselves so we do not promptly get permission to call ourselves sufferers when something goes against us; but let us be all the more gentle with the person who is suffering in the strictest sense. O you who are suffering in this way, whoever you are, if in his native land a person has come to the point where every way out is closed to him, he presumably will consider emigrating to a foreign land and there seek his fortune. But you may reply, "Why this talk, why should I emigrate and what use would a change of place be to me; after all, my lot is cast and will remain the same anywhere on this earth." "Well, yes, but let us understand each other. The journey of which we speak is not long, nor is your lot cast, unless you have already found the way out. It is only one step, one decisive step, and you have indeed emigrated, because the eternal is much nearer to you than any foreign country is to the emigrant, and yet the change, once you are there, is infinitely greater. So go with God to God. Continually take that one step more, that one step, which even the person who cannot move a limb can take, the one step that even the confined [*ikke paa fri Fod*] prisoner, even the chained prisoner whose foot is not free [*Fod ikke er fri*], can take—and in the decision you are with the good. No one, not even the greatest person who has ever lived, can do more than you.[106] But remember: your sufferings are indeed called useless, and we human beings could indeed be tempted to speak of the hopelessness of the useless sufferings, but this is merely human talk. In the language of eternity, the suffering that helped you to the highest certainly is not useless. Alas, it is useless and unused only if you do not allow yourself to be helped by it to the highest—so that you perhaps killed the wish and became spiritually, like dead flesh, without pain, because usually it is in the wish that the sufferer moans, while the eternal comforts."

VIII
201

Let us speak further about the wish and thereby about sufferings. It is indeed beneficial not to leave suffering too soon. *Let us dwell on it properly, convinced that there is no remedy more beneficial against the pernicious sickness of busyness than to consider properly the hard fate of those who suffer essentially*, and then very humanly to sympathize with them in the common concern of suffering. Alas, human sympathy often relates itself inversely to suffering, which becomes harder in the long run, and sympathy becomes weary in the long run; the suffering increases while the sympathy diminishes. In the first moment of suffering, human sympathy rushes up, but if the suffering drags on, human sympathy draws back; and in the busy person, when the busy sympathy is at an end, it sometimes is changed into a kind of bitterness against the sufferer. Yet wishes can be healed in time, can become past, but not the wish. There really is still a distinction, for there is a suffering of the wish that sympathy can become aware of, but there is also a suffering of the wish that evades every glance, that conceals itself and secretly accompanies the sufferer throughout his whole life. Yes, it accompanies—but in the lack. It accompanies the sufferer as an attendant throughout his life, but no sympathy attends it. But how should we speak about what possibly exists but withdraws in secrecy—and speak in such a way that the sufferer will acknowledge the description, that he will not turn away, hurt and impatient, from our busy discussion of sufferings, into which we either lack the capacity to think our way or do not have the time. In the delineation, let us then, if possible, tell the sufferer what he wants to hear and hope to heaven that whatever upbuilding there is in it might speak to his heart. [107]Suppose that dumb animals could have thoughts and could communicate their thoughts to each other but not to us—let us assume this. It almost seems to be so, because when the farmer's horse stands in the pasture in the summertime and tosses or shakes its head, well, no one can know definitely what it means. [108] When the two horses that have pulled side by side in the same yoke all their lives approach each other in the freedom of the evening as if in intimacy, when they seem to embrace each other, stroke each other, and pet each other by the movement of their heads; or when the wild horses call to each other so the forest echoes, when they are assembled in a great herd on the plains, as if for a meeting—suppose that they actually are able to make themselves mutually understood. But there was one horse that stayed by itself. When it heard the call, when it saw that the herd was assembled in the evening and it understood that they would now hold a meeting, it also came running, so that it might learn something about life and its conditions. It listened attentively to what the older horses expounded, how no horse may count itself happy before it is dead, [109] how no created life is subject to more lamentable ups and downs than the horse. And then the older one recited the many and various sufferings: to suffer hunger and cold, to work oneself almost to death, to be kicked by a cruel driver, to be mishandled by stupid masters who are impossible to please, who blame the horse and punish it for their own stupidity, and then finally in old age to be turned out during the winter into the barren forest.

With that the meeting broke up, and that horse, which had come at an eager gallop, went away saddened; "by sorrow of heart the spirit is broken" (Proverbs 15:13). It had understood very well what had been expounded, but nothing was hinted

VIII
202

about its sufferings. Yet every time it noticed that the other horses hurried to a meeting it came at an eager gallop, continually hoping that now something would be said about them. And every time it listened, it went away saddened; it understood better and better what the others were talking about but understood itself less and less, precisely because the others seemed to exclude it even though it was present.

O you suffering one, whoever you are, if your suffering is not concealed because you yourself want to conceal it, since in that case you are able to act and there must be a different kind of discussion, but if unintelligibility guarantees that it will not be disclosed; if you went about among people in this way, listened attentively to their explanations, sought their guidance, participated in their meetings, but every time the book was finished and every time the conversation was over and every time the Amen was said—then in sorrow of heart your breathing became difficult when you sighed: If only my suffering were like that! Ah, you nevertheless are not without an intimate relationship, unless it is your fault; it is offered to you, the highest and of the most high.

Nor are you without human sympathy. There is a common human concern that is called upbuilding. It is not common like the projects in which the crowd clamors and makes noise, because each participant is essentially alone with himself, but yet in the highest and most comprehensive sense it is a common human concern. The upbuilding view does not find rest before it has understood you. If one sinner who repents is more important to heaven than ninety-nine righteous persons who need no repentance,[110] then you, if you truly are the suffering one, are more important to the upbuilding view than ninety-nine busy people who have no need of upbuilding. Indeed, even if you did not exist, the upbuilding view does not find rest before it has understood this suffering also. Woe to the upbuilding discourse that only wants to chat with people about all sorts of inconveniences in life but does not dare to venture out into the more terrible sufferings. Such a discourse lacks bold confidence; it has a bad conscience if it calls itself upbuilding. The busy ones, who neither labor nor are burdened but are only busy, presumably think that they themselves have escaped if they themselves have avoided sufferings in life; therefore they do not wish to be disturbed by hearing about or thinking about terrible things. They have indeed escaped, they have also escaped having a view of life and have escaped into meaninglessness.

O you suffering one, you who seem to have been abandoned by the race you belong to, alone in the world—you still have not been abandoned by the God who created you. His intimacy surrounds you everywhere; it is offered to you at every moment: *in this intimacy in the decision you are with the good.* And the upbuilding view is always ready to remind you of it; that this exists will surely be a reassurance for the living. Just as it is a comfort for sailors to know that in difficult waters there are also pilots not far away, in the same way the upbuilding view lives near the breakers and reefs; daily accustomed to the sight of terrible things, it is quickly available with its humble help. It cannot help in the same way the pilot helps the ship: the sufferer must help himself; but then neither does he need to be indebted to the pilot and any other person as the sailor is indebted to the pilot. Yet if this sufferer, the same as anyone else, is to will the good in truth, he must will to suffer everything. Then he is in the decision—not the decision by which he becomes free from suffering but in the decision by which he becomes intimate with God when he wills only one thing, namely, to suffer everything, in the decision to be and to remain with the good—amidst the pain of the wish.

My listener, perhaps you are weary of all this talk about suffering—yet an upbuilding discourse never becomes weary; no, a mother will become weary of taking care of a sick child before the upbuilding discourse becomes weary of speaking about suffering. Perhaps you are, as we say, a fortunate fellow who finds this wearisome, but you would not be so fortunate as to desire unsympathetically to remain ignorant of sufferings. On the contrary, you crave this knowledge for your own sake so that you might be educated by its earnest perception! Or perhaps you are a sufferer who finds it wearisome that so much suffering is discussed when your particular suffering is not mentioned. Ah, just to think oneself vividly into another per-

VIII
204

son's suffering is a comfort, and to dwell all too specifically on one's own suffering easily leads to the double-mindedness that thinks that there is comfort for everyone else, only not for oneself. But this is not so. If it is true of sufferings that everyone has his own, great or small, it is surely true of comfort that there is comfort for all and essentially the same for all. But let us once again speak of the wish and thereby of sufferings, because the duration of time makes the suffering harder and harder, but the duration of time also depends upon when the suffering began. Indeed, a sagacious pagan has said that one can become accustomed to protracted sufferings,[111] but the question is whether the comfort is the right one. The point is not to find the handiest comfort but to will the good in truth, to will to suffer everything in order in the decision to be and to remain with the good.

Let us speak of a whole life of sufferings, or of those whom nature has wronged from the very beginning, as we humans are tempted to say, those to whom useless sufferings have been assigned from the very beginning—to be a burden to others and almost a burden to themselves—yes, worse yet, to be almost an innate objection to the goodness of Governance. Alas, accounts of the careers of many busy persons are written and occasion new busyness. Observation of those unhappy ones is an excellent antidote to busyness, *and yet by observing such people one profoundly learns what the highest is.*[112] But we shall not speak carelessly and incidentally, hurrying from the sight in hasty joy over being ourselves spared; neither shall we speak despondently.

Certainly it is glorious to be a child: to fall asleep on the mother's breast in order to awaken to see the mother, to be a child and know only the mother and the toy! We extol the happiness of childhood. The sight of it mitigates with its smile—so that over the years even the person who prospers does not forget his childhood. But thanks be to God that it is not true that this should be the highest. It can be omitted without losing the highest; it can be missed without having lost the highest. And certainly it is beautiful to be young: to be unable to sleep because of the tumult of joyful thoughts, to have fallen asleep and with the bird song to wake up early to continued gaiety! We extol the happiness of youth, we rejoice with the joyful,[113] we wish youth in its happiness to have gratitude, wish it to have gratitude in the future for the past; but thank God the truth of the matter is not that this should be the highest. It can be omitted without losing the highest; it can be missed without having lost the highest. And certainly it is blissful to be in love: to have only one wish, even if everything else is given or denied—one wish, the beloved—one longing, the beloved—one possession, the beloved! We extol the happiness of erotic love. Oh, that the happy one may be faithful in the daily appreciation of domestic life, so that one who was happy may be faithful in the unceasing appreciation of recollection; but thank God the truth of the matter is not that this should be the highest. It can be omitted without losing the highest; it can be missed without having lost the highest!

But now the sufferer! Alas, he had no happy childhood. Certainly mother love is faithful and tender, especially for a pitiful child, but a mother is also a human being. He lay on his mother's breast; she did not look at him with joy, but he saw her looking sad; when he awakened, he sometimes saw her crying. Even among adults it is true that when everyone is feeling sad and then the one fortunately endowed with a bright spirit and cheerful disposition comes through the door and says, "Here I am," and now the cheerfulness begins—then the clouds of sorrow retreat. One so endowed is rare, but even the most rarely endowed—what would he be able to do compared with the child when it opens the door, as it did once in the terrible pains of the hour of birth, and says: Here I am! Oh, the happiness of childhood to be so welcome!

Then he grew up to the days of youth. But he was not included in the play, and if someone asked: Why do you not wish to join in? Surely he would answer, "How can you have the heart to ask me that?" —So he went apart, but not to die, because he was indeed still in the days of his youth. —Then came the time of erotic love, but no one loved him. To be sure, there were a few who were attached to him, but it was compassion and sympathy. —Then he became a man, but he stood on the outside of life. —Then he died, but he was not missed. The little band who formed the company of mourners all said: It was a blessing that God took him away; and the pastor said the same. —So he was dead, and so he was forgotten—and all his useless sufferings. There was no joy and jubilation when he was born, only fearful dismay; there was no sorrow and pain when he died, only a quiet, sad joy.

Such was the course of his life, or rather, so it goes, for it is not an old story I am telling of something that happened to one individual in a bygone day. The same thing happens quite often; it is close enough to us, even if light-mindedness and sensuality, even if worldly wisdom and impiety wish to remain ignorant of it, wish to remove such unfortunates and to remove these somber reminders not merely from the carefreeness of art but also from the Church and from the upbuilding contemplation that is bound to know that Holy Scripture has almost a preference for the lame and the crippled, for the blind and the lepers. Yes, just as Christ, when the apostles began to be busy, set a child in their midst,[114] so an earnest person in those places where the crowd makes noise and clamor in the confused name of the century might indeed be tempted to place such an unfortunate in their midst. The sight of him really will not delay anyone who wills something eternal, but their busyness does not have anything to do with the eternal either.

He, the suffering one, participated in life—by living. But there was one thing with which his life was unfamiliar, something that is happiness in all the situations of life, as in the delight of love: like for like. Like for like, he never did have that, and he himself could not give it, because he was a suffering object of sympathy and compassion. No, like for like he never did have, not as a child, so that he could make his mother glad, so that if others had made her sad he merely needed to awaken smiling to make her glad. No, like for like he never did have, since he loved his playmate in a different way than his playmate loved him. No, like for like he never did have and therefore no mate either. In the many years of his life he could do nothing to reciprocate, and even in death he did not have like for like: being missed as he missed the dear ones. He died, but, whatever the mourners and the pastor said, God be praised, it is not true that he thereby was excluded from the highest.

O you suffering one, whoever you are, wherever you withdraw yourself from the sight of men lest you disturb them by reminding them of what is piteous—oh, do not forget that you, too, can do something; do not let your life go on in a useless counting of the days and years of useless sufferings; do not forget that you are able to do something. The idea is not, as it is sometimes said in the world to a supposed sufferer who because of a minor adversity promptly wants to sit on the sidelines—that he can still do something for others—because the upbuilding view does not regard the person who can do that as a sufferer in the strictest sense, but on the contrary, it deals with him rigorously. O you suffering one, even if you cannot in this way do something for others, and this is part of your suffering, you can still do—the highest; you can will to suffer everything and thereby in the decision be with the good. ^{VIII}

What blessed equality, that in the strictest sense the sufferer can unconditionally do the highest fully as well as the most gifted person in the most fortunate sense. Honor and praise be to the eternal: there is not a shade of difference, there is no wrongdoing and no preferential treatment, but equality. By willing to suffer everything, in the decision you are reappareled with the good—indeed, just as the dead person stands up and throws off his grave clothes, so you have thrown off the character of wretchedness. You are indistinguishable from anyone else among those whom you might wish to resemble, those who in the decision are with the good—they are all clothed alike, girded about the loins with truth, clad in the armor of righteousness, wearing the helmet of salvation![115] If it is true—and it is, after all, every good man's hope that there is a resurrection where there will be no differences, where the deaf will hear, the blind will see, the one who was miserably shaped will be as beautiful as everyone else—oh, there is indeed on this side of the grave something akin to a resurrection [*Opstandelse*] every time a person by willing to do everything or by willing to suffer everything stands up [*staa op*] by being in the decision and in the decision remains standing with the good. The only difference is the pain of the wish in the sufferer, but this can also be of help in coming out in the decision.

The sufferer must therefore will to suffer everything, and this means, just as with willing to do everything, to make the decision, means in the decision to be and to *remain* with the good. In other words, while the pain of the wish manifests that in a way the suffering continues, the healing also continues [*vedblive*] if the sufferer remains [*forblive*] in the decision. But there is a power that is strong in the moment, and that is *sagacity*. From it and from the moment, or through it and from the moment issues the corruption of human beings— inasmuch as a human being's salvation is in the eternal and through the eternal. *At this point, sagacity is misused inwardly*, since for the person who suffers essentially it is not easy to misuse it outwardly. Here again sagacity is rich in evasions, by which time is suspended and the decision is postponed. It wants to have only an earthly and temporal understanding of the decision; it has only the moment's understanding of a deci- sion, by which the suffering itself should cease. But the eternal really does not heal in this way. The paralytic does not become sound in body because he is healed by the eternal, the leper does not become clean, and the crippled well shaped. "But then talking of the eternal's help is a poor notion," thinks sagacity.

VIII
208 "Yes, what is even worse, the decision, if the sufferer conse- crates himself to the suffering, even makes his situation hopeless"—because the decision breaks with temporality's de- lusive hope.

When the eternal does not heal such a sufferer, the help of sagacity usually goes like this. At first the sufferer lives for a few years on an earthly hope, but when this hope is consumed and the suffering still continues, he becomes superstitious. His state of mind vacillates between drowsiness and a burning ten- sion, but then when the suffering continues, he finally falls into lethargic despair, only very rarely broken by an unnatural and terribly weakening overwrought state, just as when the gam- bler *just once more* hopes for a stroke of luck. Alas, in the long run we really come to see what sagacity and earthly hope are!

Yet to sagacity it seems very sagacious "not foolishly to give up an earthly hope for a possible fantastic healing"—in order to win the eternal. To sagacity it seems very sagacious "not to say farewell to the world decisively; after all, one still does not know what possibly could happen . . . . . and then one would regret"—having allowed oneself to be healed by the eternal. The earthly hope and the heavenly hope do indeed grow up and play together in childhood as peers, but in the decision the difference becomes manifest. But sagacity hinders this; it continually hinders the decision. It tenaciously procrastinates, has ever so many notions whose wisdom is this: that one must not take suffering and life too much to heart, that it still might be possible, who knows, etc. In other words, when the sufferer really takes the suffering to heart, he is helped by the eternal into the decision. To take one's suffering to heart is to die to temporality and sagacity and evasions, and to the sagacious men and women, and to anecdotes about this one and that one—in order to find rest in the blessed trustworthiness of the eternal. The sufferer can be compared to a sick person who turns from side to side and finally finds the position in which there is relief—even though the wish pains. Even if it were a trifle, one can never have taken something too much to heart if one took it to heart in such a way that one gained the eternal.

But the sufferer who does not want to be healed by the eternal is double-minded; the double-mindedness in him is the sickness that gnaws and gnaws and consumes the noblest powers, is the internal damage that is far more dangerous than to be crippled and paralytic. The double-minded person wills to be healed and yet does not will to be healed—that is, he does not will to be healed eternally. But the temporal healing is uncertain, and the distinct mark of his mounting uncertainty is the mounting restlessness in his double-mindedness. Even in the double-minded person's final moment, sagacity still is sitting beside his deathbed and explains that one cannot know what might happen suddenly and unexpectedly. By no means should the pastor be sent for, because sagacity is to such a degree afraid of the decision that it even regards the pastor's coming as a kind of decision—and one still cannot know what might happen suddenly and unexpectedly. Then the double-minded person dies, and now the survivors know with certainty that the deceased was not healed of his sufferings of many years in any sudden and unexpected way. Alas, for the person who loves the world in the sagacious sense of the moment, the eternal is a riddle. He is continually thinking: But if some temporal help suddenly turned up, I would indeed be deceived, I who in the decision of eternity was dead to temporality. This means that one still regards the temporal as the highest and the eternal as a kind of desperate standby. Therefore one postpones the decision as long as possible; and even if temporality's help is the most unreasonable of all expectations, goaded on in superstitious delusion one would rather hope for it than grasp the eternal. There is the continual fear that one would come to regret this, and yet the eternal, if one grasps it in truth, is the only, unconditionally the only thing of which one may unconditionally say: It is never regretted. But if a person feared that he would at some time regret the decision of the eternal, it serves him right that he at some time must regret bitterly that he let time go by. Ah, it is a foolish sagacity (however much it swaggers, however loquacious it is) that foolishly defrauds itself out of the highest comfort and by means of a mediocre comfort helps itself into an even more mediocre comfort, and ultimately into certain regret. If the sufferer uses his sagacity in such a way, it makes no difference that his double-mindedness looks a little better in the eyes of the world than that just described. If he uses it to hinder the decision of the eternal, he is still essentially double-minded, he is and remains essentially double-minded even if temporality's help did come—and he prided himself on his sagacity, that he sagaciously avoided the decision of the eternal—indeed, one would think it was a misfortune, that is, that he sagaciously avoided the decision of the eternal. The decision of the eternal is the only true salvation, and therefore it is double-mindedness also when the sufferer uses his strength to conceal the pain instead of allowing himself to be healed by the eternal. Such a sufferer does not will to be free from the suffering but only from the compassion,[116] inasmuch as this can also be a suffer-

ing. In this lies the contradiction in double-mindedness, for
only by the decision of the eternal does he become truly free
from the painfulness of the compassion, because he has essentially overcome the suffering through the decision—thus the
wish only pains, whereas the eternal heals.

[117]All double-mindedness with regard to sufferings has its
basis and its mark in the unwillingness of the double-minded
person to let go of temporality. Likewise the double-minded
talk that is sometimes addressed to those who suffer is identi-
fiable in that it consoles by means of temporality. Only all too
often the sufferer seems to shrink from accepting the highest
comfort, and the speaker seems to avoid offering the highest
comfort. On the other hand, the consoling talk consoles with
"No doubt things will get better"—perhaps. It urges a little
patience; it potters a little about the sufferer and says that by
Sunday everything will be all right. But why give an indigent
person, if for a moment we dare to compare the sufferer to such
a one, silver or even imitation metal if one has plenty of gold to
offer him, since eternity's comfort is pure gold. Let us keep in
mind a person who acts, although his suffering is always different from that of the one who suffers essentially. We read about
the apostles that when they were flogged they went away joyful
and thanked God.[118] Here there is no mention of a little patience, that no doubt things will get better by Sunday; but here
the victorious comfort of eternity and the scourged apostles
have been more than victorious. So, too, with the one who
suffers essentially; when eternity heals, the wish certainly continues to pain (and so it should, because the eternal does not,
after all, take the sufferer out of time), but there is no whimpering, no provisional distraction, no deceptive procrastination.
There is, of course, the opinion that when the person who
suffers essentially has whimpered his way through time and
then with all sorts of delusions has more or less managed to
make time pass or has killed time—that then eternity stands
open to him. Alas, no, the person who suffers essentially also
has a responsibility for how he has used time and has utilized
the earthly misery, whether he has utilized it to allow himself to
be healed eternally. But sagacity says, "Surely one must not kill

hope." "You hypocrite," replies the eternal, "why do you talk
so equivocally; of course there is a hope that should be killed,
just as there is a lust, a craving, and a longing that should be
killed—the earthly hope should be killed, because not until
then is one rescued by the true hope, and that is why the
sufferer should not even want to 'accept release' (Hebrews
11:35) on temporality's terms."

*But the sufferer who in truth wills the good expressly uses sagacity
against evasions, and in that way he uses it to help himself out in the
decision* and to escape the disappointments of the temporary.
He does not fear the pressure of the decision, which seems to
gather the suffering over him, because he knows that this pressure is the breakthrough of eternity, knows that in the decision
the nerve of temporality is severed, even though the pain remains in the wish. What undoubtedly often makes a sufferer
impatient is that he takes in advance, as it were, the suffering of
a whole lifetime and now shrinks from what is portioned out in
time; it would be easier to bear if he let each day have its
troubles.[119] In this sense the suffering will not be concentrated
in the decision, because the error is—that despite all his pre-
emption of suffering he still does not win anything eternal but
is only temporally terrified. But it is also certain that because of
temporality's uncertainty a sufferer over the many years can
talk himself out of the impact of the decision, and that is de-
moralizing. Therefore the sufferer who wills the good in truth
knows that sagacity is a faithless friend and only the decision is
trustworthy.

The person who acts wills to *do* everything for the good; the
person who suffers wills to *suffer* everything for the good—the
likeness is that in the decision both are able to be and to remain
with the good. Only the directions in which they work are
different—but a difference that must not be understood as if
the one excluded the other; the one who acts works outwardly
in order that the good may be victorious, and even his suffering
has its meaning in this; the one who suffers does everything (by
willing to suffer everything) for the good inwardly so that it
may be victorious in him. [120]But the good must indeed have
been victorious and must continue to be victorious in the inner

self of the person who acts if he is truly to work for the good
outwardly. And the one who suffers essentially can always
work for the good outwardly by the power of example and
work forcefully, since his life, just because much is denied him,
contains a challenge to the many to whom much is given; and
his life, if he in decision is and remains with the good, passes
rigorous judgment on the many who utilized irresponsibly the
much that was given them. Yes, even if it were denied the
sufferer to work by his example, even if he had been distanced
from all other human beings, he is participating in the great
common enterprise of humankind; at his solitary post he is, so
to speak, defending a difficult pass by rescuing his soul from
the ensnaring difficulties of all suffering—even if no human
being sees him, humankind feels with him, suffers with him,
is victorious with him! But wherever the good is truly victorious, the victory is essentially equally great whether the
good is victorious in many persons through one person or
whether it is victorious in the solitary, forsaken person through
him—the victory is essentially equally great. Praised be the
blessed equality of the eternal.

VIII
212

Yet one thing more before the discourse leaves sufferings.
Can a person be said *to will* suffering; is not suffering something he must be forced into against his will? If he can be
excused from it, can he then will it; and if he is bound in it, can
he then be said to will it? If we are to answer this question, let us
above all distinguish between what it is to will in the sense of
desire and what it is to will in the noble sense of freedom. Yes,
for many people it seems impossible to unite freedom and
suffering in the same thought. Therefore, when they see someone who with his possessions could live in clover, when they
see him exert himself as strenuously as any dutiful worker,
expose himself to many sufferings, choose the laborious path
of a higher calling—then they regard him either as stupid or as
crazy. They almost deplore that Governance has bestowed all
these favorable conditions on someone who does not know
how to use them at all. Even if they do not say it aloud, even if
they do not think about how lamentably they are betraying
their own interior being, they secretly think: We should be in

his place; we would really know how to enjoy life. Thus if someone can be excused from suffering, then it is either stupid or crazy to will it.

But what, then, is courage? Is it courage to go where pleasure beckons, to look and see where the pleasant is? Or does not showing courage [*Mod*] require instead that there be resistance [*Modstand*] (as the language itself seems to suggest), such as when the courageous one looks the danger in the face, since the danger is not something that delights the eye to see. Or, to illustrate this, is it not like the courageous rider's spurring his horse forward against some horror; one does not see in the eyes of the courageous one that the physical eyes shrink from the danger, because the courage penetrates the expression of the eyes themselves, but the rider and the horse illustrate how the courage is compounded. The rider is the courageous one, the horse is skittish, but the horse and its shying correspond to what is base in the man and his shying, which courage subdues. Thus courage freely wills the suffering. The courageous person has a traitorous internal resistance that is allied with the external resistance, but he is the courageous one, because despite all this he freely wills the suffering.

On the other hand (and this is what we must consider principally since we are speaking of the essential sufferer), the sufferer can freely take upon himself the suffering into which he in one way is forced, inasmuch as he does not have it in his power to liberate himself. Can only the free person say, "Chain me, I am not afraid"? Cannot the person in chains also say, "Of my own free will I take my imprisonment upon myself"—that is, the confinement in which he is? Indeed, here is the same situation. The opinion of most people is that this is an impossibility and accordingly the sufferer's state is one of a bewailing faintheartedness.

But what, then, is patience [*Taalmod*]? Is not patience the courage [*Mod*] that freely takes upon itself the suffering that cannot be avoided? The unavoidable is what will crush courage. Within the suffering person himself there is a traitorous resistance that is allied with the dreadfulness of unavoidability, and united they would crush him; but patience, despite this,

VIII
213

submits to the suffering and in just that way finds itself free in the unavoidable suffering. Thus patience performs an even greater miracle, if you will, than does courage, because courage goes freely into the suffering that could be avoided, but patience makes itself free in the unavoidable suffering. With his courage the free person freely allows himself to be imprisoned, but with his patience the prisoner makes himself free—yet not in the sense that the jailer would become alarmed and afraid. The external impossibility of being able to free oneself from the suffering does not prevent the internal possibility of actually being able to make oneself free in the suffering, of being able freely to take the suffering upon oneself since the patient one gives *his consent* by *willing* to submit to the suffering. One can be forced into the narrow prison, one can be forced into lifelong sufferings, and necessity is the coercer; but one cannot be forced into patience. If the coercion of necessity presses [*trykke*] down on a soul that does not have and does not want to have the resiliency of freedom, the soul does indeed become oppressed [*fortrykt*], but it does not become patient; patience is the counter-pressure of resiliency [*Gjentryk*] whereby the person who is constrained makes himself free in his constraint.

Can only the rich person be thrifty—because he has it in his power to be wasteful? Is it not possible also for the poor person to be thrifty, although he does not have it in his power to be wasteful, although he is forced to be—thrifty? No, that is exactly what he cannot be forced to be, even though he is forced to be poor. Alas, the wisdom of many people seems to be intent upon doing away with the good. When the person of independent means freely chooses a laborious life, people say he is eccentric, "He who could have such an easy life in idleness and in comfort could indulge his every wish"; and when one who is constrained is patient in his suffering, they say of him, "Shame on him—after all, he can't do anything else and is simply making a virtue of necessity." Unquestionably he is making a virtue of necessity; that is the secret, that is the most typical expression for what he is doing—he is making a virtue of necessity, he is deriving a category of freedom (virtue) from what is defined as necessity.

VIII
214 Precisely in this lies the healing through the decision of the eternal, that the sufferer freely takes upon himself the enforced suffering. Just as it is a relief to the sufferer to open himself in confidence to a friend, so also is it his salvation through the decision of the eternal that he *opens* himself to the eternal while the constraint of necessity compresses his heart, so to speak, and he complies eternally by *willing* to suffer everything. Is that person really imprisoned for whom the door stands open—the double door of eternity! Is that person really under constraint who is eternally free! When Paul said, "I am a Roman citizen," the governor did not dare put him in prison but placed him in open custody.[121] If a person dares to say: I am a free citizen of eternity, then necessity cannot imprison him—except in open custody.

My listener! If agreeable to you, we shall recall the development of the discourse. If a person is to will one thing, he must will the good; then it would be *possible* that he could will one thing. But if this is to become *actual*, he must will the good in truth. According to whether he was *one who acts* or *one who suffers, he must will to do everything for the good* or *he must will to suffer everything for the good.* He must will to do everything for the good or in the decision to be and remain with the good. But sagacity was inwardly misused to seek evasions, and it was outwardly misused in deception. The good person, however, used sagacity to prevent all evasions and thereby to help himself out and to keep himself out in the decision; he used sagacity to prevent every deceit outwardly. He must will to suffer everything for the good or in the decision to be and to remain with the good. The discourse paused to describe the state of the person who suffers essentially, because by contemplating sufferings we most trustworthily learn what the highest is. With regard to sufferings, sagacity is once again misused internally to seek evasions, but the good person uses sagacity specifically against evasions so that in the decision he might be and remain with the good by willing to suffer everything, by *willing* the imposed necessity of the suffering.

But *purity of heart is to will one thing.* It is this sentence that has been the theme of this discourse, which we linked to the apostolic words: Draw near to God, and he will draw near to you. Cleanse your hands, you sinners, and purify your hearts, you double-minded. The decision of the good is the decisive one, and a person cannot deceitfully and ingratiatingly keep close to God with the tongue while his heart is far away. No, since God is Spirit and is Truth,[122] one can in truth keep close to him only by willing to be holy as he is holy, by purity of heart. Purity of heart—this is a metaphorical expression that compares the heart to the ocean, and why specifically to that? [123]Because the ocean's depth is its purity, and its purity is its transparency, because the ocean is deep only when it is pure, and pure only when it is transparent. As soon as it is impure, it is not deep but shallow, and as soon as it is shallow it is not transparent either. When, however, it is deeply and transparently pure, then, however long one continues to look at it, it is one thing; then its purity is this constancy in one thing. That is why we compare the heart to the ocean, because its purity is this constancy in being deep and in being transparent. No storm may agitate it, no sudden gust of wind may move its surface; no drowsy fog may spread over it; there must be no dubious movement within it; no fleeting cloud may darken it; but it must lie still, deeply transparent. And if you see it this way today, you are uplifted by gazing at the ocean's purity, and if you see it this way every day, then you say it is constantly pure—like the heart of someone who wills only one thing. Just as the ocean, when it lies still this way, deeply transparent, aspires to heaven, so the pure heart, when it is still, deeply transparent, aspires solely to the good; or just as the ocean becomes pure when it aspires only to heaven, so the heart becomes pure when it aspires only to the good. Just as the ocean reflects the height of heaven in its pure depth, so the heart, when it is still and deeply transparent, reflects in its pure depth the heavenly sublimity of the good. If the least thing comes between them, between the sky and the ocean, between the heart and the good, indeed, even if it was impatience in desiring the reflection, then the ocean is not pure, then it does not purely reflect the sky.

VIII
215

III

My listener, it was on the occasion of a confession that this discourse was prompted. Even if use has not been made of the occasion after the reference to it at the beginning, it has never been forgotten in the discourse, which, like an invitation program for a festive occasion, has treated what was most pertinent to it. From its one starting point—to will one thing—the discourse has gone out along different paths and continually returned to its starting point. It has, so to speak, looked around in the world and observed human differences. At times it has described a specific error and the state of mind of the erring one on an enlarged scale so that one can better note and identify what seldom appears unmixed in the minor situations of daily life and therefore is more difficult to identify as this particular error. The discourse, as it consistently held fast to the requirement to will one thing, has become acquainted with many errors, delusions, deceptions, and self-deceptions; it has tried to track double-mindedness down its hidden path, to discover its hiddenness. The discourse, by making itself, if possible, understandable, has tried to come to an understanding with the listener. But the understandableness of this discourse and the listener's understanding are still not the true earnestness and by no means give the deliberation its proper emphasis. To achieve this, the discourse must *decisively* require something of the listener, and not merely require what has been required up to this point—that he as reader share the work with the one speaking. At this point it must unconditionally require his decisive self-activity, upon which everything depends.

So now, my listener, think about the occasion; and while the consciousness of sin sharpens the need for the one thing necessary, while the earnestness of this holy place strengthens the will in holy resolution, while the presence of the Omniscient One makes self-deception impossible, consider your own life. The discourse, which is without authority, will not presumptuously pass judgment on you. By thinking very vividly of this occasion, you are standing before a higher judge, where no human being dares to judge another, since he himself is a de-

VIII
216

fendant. The discourse does not address itself to you as a specific person, it does not even know who you are. But if you
think about the occasion very vividly, it will seem to you,
whoever you are, as if it were speaking directly to you. This is
not the merit of the discourse; it is the action of your self-
activity that you on your own behalf assist the discourse and on
your own initiative will to be the one intimately addressed as:
you. This is your self-activity; in this way it truly is that. Alas,
let us above all not draw any attention away from the decisive
issue to the speaker and the art of the discourse. If this happens,
then it is again the fault of busyness and double-mindedness
that the emphasis in a relation of interaction is put on the
wrong place, that the religious discourse is admired for its
artistry, its eloquence, and that because of this one totally forgets what every human being is capable of and what, please
note, is the highest. To be eloquent is nevertheless, in a godly
sense, a jest, a fortunate advantage like being beautiful, yet a
jest. The earnestness is to will to listen in order to will to do
accordingly; this is the highest, and every human being, God
be praised, is capable of it if he wills. But busyness places an
extremely earnest emphasis upon the jest and regards earnestness as nothing; it contentiously and frivolously thinks that to
be eloquent is the highest and that the listener's task is to judge
whether the speaker is that.

Lest there be any lurking irregularity or any unmentioned
double-mindedness, let me at this point, where the requirement is made for self-activity, briefly explain the relation between the speaker and the listener with regard to the religious
discourse. Allow me, again taking a stand against double-
mindedness, to illustrate it with a metaphor drawn from the
secular arts, and do not let this double-mindedly disturb you or
give you occasion to accuse the discourse of impropriety. If you
venture to attend performances of the secular arts, then you of
course have devoutly come to an understanding with yourself
about them and accordingly you yourself must have thought of
the religious together with secular art, even though in so doing
you have clearly perceived the difference. Otherwise there are a
cleft and a double-mindedness in your inner being, so that you

VIII
217

want to live secularly at times and once in a while consider the religious. As you well know, in the theater there is someone who sits and whispers. He is concealed; he is the insignificant one; he must be and wants to be overlooked. But then there is another person; he steps forth conspicuously, draws everybody's eyes to himself—hence his name, which is "actor" [*Skuespiller*, show player]. He portrays a specific person; in the beautiful sense of deceptive art, every single word now finds truth in him, truth through him—and yet he hears everything he has to say from that hidden one who sits and whispers. No one is so foolish as to regard the prompter as more important than the actor.

Now forget the jest of art. Alas, when it comes to the religious discourse, many people are so foolish that they regard the speaker from a secular point of view and see him as an actor and see the audience as spectators who judge the artist. But this is not the way it is, by no means. No, the speaker is the prompter; there are no spectators, because every listener should look inwardly into himself. The stage is eternity, and the listener, if he is the true listener (and if he is not, it is his own fault), is standing before God through the discourse. The prompter whispers to the actor what he has to say, but the actor's rendition is the main thing, is the earnest jest of the art; the speaker whispers the words to the listener, but the main thing, the earnestness, is that the listener, with the help of the discourse and before God, in silence speaks in himself, with himself, to himself. The discourse is not spoken for the sake of the speaker, so that he may be praised or criticized, but the objective is the listener's rendition. If the one speaking has a responsibility for what he whispers, then the listener has an equally great responsibility not to mistake his task. In the theater the performance is played before persons present who are called spectators, but at the religious address God himself is present; in the most earnest sense he is the critical spectator who is checking on how it is being spoken and on how it is being heard, and for that very reason there are no spectators. Thus the one speaking is the prompter, and the listener is present and open before God; he is, if I may put it this way, the actor, who in the true sense is acting before God.

Let us never forget this, let us not secularize the religious but eternally separate the religious and the secular precisely by earnestly thinking about them together. As soon as the religious address is viewed from the secular point of view (a view that is just as foolish as in the drama to regard the prompter as more important than the actor), the speaker becomes an actor and the listeners become critical spectators; in that case the *religious* address is performed *secularly* before some people who are present, but God is not present any more than he is in the theater. The presence of God is the decisive element that changes everything. As soon as God is present, everyone has the task before God of paying attention to himself—the speaker during his speech has the task of paying attention to what he is saying, and the listener during the speech has the task of paying attention to how he is hearing, whether through the discourse he within himself is secretly speaking with God; otherwise the listeners would also have a task in common with God, so that God and the listeners would jointly check on the speaker and pass judgment on him. Such is the relation between the speaker and the listener with regard to the religious address. Or it is the same as the reading of the appointed prayer by a subordinate church worker, who is without *authority*—it is not actually the church worker who is praying. But the listener, who sits in the church and is inwardly before God while he listens to the reading, he is praying. And yet he is not speaking, his voice is not being heard; neither is he saying something else softly to himself but is silently and sincerely praying before God with the audible voice of the one who is reading the prayer aloud and whispering to him what he is to say. The earnestness is not that one person tells another person or dictates to another what he is to say, but the earnestness is that now the other person, speaking of himself, says it himself to God. —Now we presumably agree on this matter, and the requirement is repeated only so that the speaker very vividly thinks privately of the occasion for this discourse.

The discourse is asking you, then, or you are asking yourself through the discourse: *What kind of life is yours; do you will one thing and what is this one thing?* It does not expect you to name something that is one thing only in a presumptuous sense, since it does not intend to address itself to such a person, with whom it would not be able to involve itself also for a reason other than that he had prevented himself from earnestly thinking about the occasion for the discourse. Also for another reason: namely, a person can have an opinion radically different from ours, have the very opposite opinion, and one can nevertheless become involved with him since it is assumed that ultimately there must be a point of unity, an agreement on something universally human, whatever one will call it more specifically. But if he is demented, one cannot become involved with him, because he starts out from the very last point on which one might hope ultimately to agree with him. A person can dispute with someone, dispute to the extreme, as long as it is assumed that ultimately there is something common, a unity in something universally human, in paying attention to oneself. But if in his secular striving he in despair starts out like one demented, by despising himself, even brazenly boasting of it and priding himself on his disgrace, one cannot become involved with him in dispute, because like one demented, and even more terribly, he starts out from the very last point on which one might hope ultimately to agree with him.

The discourse therefore assumes that you will the good and now asks you *what kind of life is yours; do you will one thing in truth?* It does not inquisitively ask about your occupation in life, about how many workers are in your service, about how many subordinates you have in your department if you have a government position. No, the discourse is not inquisitive. It asks you first and foremost, before anything else, whether you are living at all in such a way that you could truthfully answer the question, that the question truly exists for you. Before being able to answer this earnest question earnestly, a person must already have chosen in life, chosen the invisible, the internal; he must live in such a way that he has hours and periods in which he collects his mind so that his life can attain the transparency that is a condition for being able to submit the question to himself and to answer it—if what I suppose is correct, that for this it is required that one must know whereof one speaks. Someone who is only busy with his secular job and the rest of the time is shouting with the crowd—it would be foolishness to prompt him by such a question to new foolishness—in the answer.

So the discourse now asks you: *Are you living in such a way that you are conscious of being a single individual?* The question is not the inquisitive kind such as one asks about the individual with regard to distinction, the person whom admiration and envy are united in singling out. No, it is the earnest question about what each person is according to his eternal destiny, about what he is to be conscious of being, and when is this question more earnest than when before God he considers his life?

VIII 220

This consciousness is the fundamental condition for willing one thing in truth, because the person who even to himself is not a unity, is even to himself not something altogether definite, the person who exists only in an external sense—as long as he lives a number in the crowd, a fraction in a worldly complex—indeed, how would it even occur to such a person to occupy himself with the thought: to will one thing in truth! Yet the question must be asked about this consciousness; likewise the discourse does not ask in general but asks you as a single individual, or rather, you ask yourself about it, my listener, whether you have this consciousness, whether you very vividly think of the occasion for this discourse. Outside the crowd is making noise; one person makes noise by being at the head of the crowd, the majority by being along in the crowd. But the Omniscient One, even though he surely can maintain an overview better than anyone else, does not want the crowd. He wants only the single individual, wants to become involved only with the single individual, *no matter* whether the single individual ranks high or low, is eminent or wretched.

Each human being, as a single individual, must account for himself to God; and while no third person dares to intrude into this settling of accounts between God and the single individual, the speaker dares to and ought to remind us with his question that this is not forgotten, remind us that the most pernicious of all evasions is—hidden in the crowd, to want, as it were, to avoid God's inspection of oneself as a single individual, avoid hearing God's voice as a single individual, as Adam once did when his bad conscience fooled him into thinking that he could hide among the trees. [124] It may be more comfortable and more convenient and more cowardly to hide in the crowd this way in the hope that God would not be able to tell one from another. But in eternity everyone as a single individual must make an accounting to God, that is, eternity requires of him that he must have lived as a single individual. And eternity will bring out before his consciousness everything he has done as an individual, he who had forgotten himself in noisy delusion; and in eternity he, the single individual, will be dealt with very scrupulously, he who thought he was in the crowd, where things are not done very scrupulously. Everyone must make an accounting to God as an individual; the king must make an accounting to God as an individual, and the most wretched beggar must make an accounting to God as an individual—lest anyone be arrogant by being more than an individual, lest anyone despondently think that he is not an individual, perhaps because in the busyness of the world he does not even have a name but is designated only by a number.

VIII
221

What else, indeed, is the accounting of eternity than that the voice of conscience is installed eternally in its eternal right to be the only voice! What else is it than that in eternity there is an infinite silence in which the conscience speaks only with the single individual about whether he as an individual has done good or evil, and about his not wanting to be an individual while he lived! What else is it than that in eternity there is infinite space, so that everyone as an individual is by himself with his conscience, because in eternity there is no crush, no crowd, no hiding place in the crowd, no more than there is rioting or disorder in the streets! Here in temporality the conscience already wants to make each one separately into the single individual, but here in temporality, in the restlessness, in the noise, in the crush, in the crowd, in the jungle of evasions, alas, yes, here even the terrible thing happens that someone completely deafens his conscience—*his* conscience, since he does not get rid of it; it still is his or, rather, he belongs to it. At this point, however, we are not discussing this terrible matter, but even in the better person it all too easily happens that the voice of conscience becomes merely one voice among many others, and then the solitary voice of the conscience, as is usual with the solitary voice, is so easily outvoted—by the majority. But in eternity the conscience is the only voice heard. It must be heard by the single individual, because the single individual has become the eternal echo of this voice. It must be heard; there is no place to escape it, because in the infinite there is no place; the individual himself is the place. It must be heard; the individual looks around in vain for the crowd. Alas, there seems to be a world between himself and the next single individual, with whom in turn the conscience is speaking about what he as a single individual has said and done and thought— good or evil.

Are you now living in such a way that you are aware as a single individual, that in every relationship in which you relate yourself outwardly you are aware that you are also relating yourself to yourself as a single individual, that even in the relationships we human beings so beautifully call the most intimate you recollect that you have an even more intimate relationship, the relationship in which you as a single individual relate yourself to yourself before God?

If you are bound to another human being by the holy bonds of marriage, do you in this intimate relationship consider that even more intimate relationship to yourself as a single individual before God? The discourse does not ask you whether you really do love your wife; it hopes so. It does not ask if she really is the delight of your eyes and the desire of your heart; it wishes that for you. It does not ask what you are doing to please your wife, about how you two have arranged your domestic life, about what beneficial advice you may have received from others, or what harmful influence others might have had upon you. It does not ask whether your marriage is now just like most other marriages, whether it is more praiseworthy than that of many others, whether it is perhaps regarded by some as

VIII
222

an example worthy of imitation. No, the discourse does not ask about all that; neither does it question you flatteringly or pumpingly or observingly or excusingly or comparatively. It asks you about the ultimate, whether you in that most intimate relationship to yourself as a single individual are aware of the responsibility you have, not before your wife, not before other people, not in comparison with other people, but as a single individual before God, where you are not asked whether your marriage was in conformity with that of others, with custom and use, or was better than that of others, but where you as a single individual are asked only whether it was in conformity with your responsibility as a single individual.

Custom and use change, and any comparison limps or is only half truth; but eternity's custom, which never becomes obsolete, is that you are a single individual, that even in the intimate relationship of marriage you should have been aware of this. Truly, it is not a divorce that eternity has in mind, nor is it a divorce that eternity does away with the distinction between man and woman. Your wife will not have occasion to grieve because you bear in mind that most intimate relationship of yours with God, and if she were foolish enough herself to want only earthly things, or foolish enough also to want to weigh you down in an earthly way—nevertheless, a woman's foolishness will certainly not be able to change eternity's law, and in eternity it will not be asked whether it was your wife who seduced you (eternity will discuss that with your wife), but you will only be asked as a single individual whether you allowed yourself to be seduced.

If your marriage is blessed in such a way that you see a family growing up around you, then in your relationship, your intimate relationship, to your children, are you aware that you have an even more intimate relationship as a single individual to yourself? You share the responsibility with your wife, but therefore eternity will indeed ask her as a single individual about her share of the responsibility, because in eternity there is no complication at all that could make the accounting difficult and the evasion easy. Eternity does not ask whether you brought up your children the way you saw others doing it but asks you as an individual how *you* brought up your children. It does not speak with you as you are able to speak in an intimate way with a friend—alas, this intimacy can also very easily make you accustomed to evasions, because even the most intimate friend still speaks as a third person, and by much intimacy of this kind a person can easily become accustomed to speaking of himself as a third person. But in eternity you are a single individual, and conscience, when it speaks with you, is no third person, no more than you are a third person when you are speaking with the conscience, because you and the conscience are one; it knows everything you know, and it knows that you know it. With regard to your children's upbringing, you can deliberate on alternatives with your wife and your friends, but ultimately the action and the responsibility are yours alone as the single individual; and if you refrain from acting, if you hide from yourself and from others in the thicket of deliberation, then you alone as the single individual have the responsibility you have thereby taken upon yourself. Yes, in temporality, where we are cross-questioned about one thing and another, in the multifariously compounded complexity of interaction we certainly would think it a delusion, a figment of the imagination, that each one of these countless millions of people could separately be convinced, accurately down to the very least detail, of what constitutes his life; but in eternity it can be done, because each one separately becomes the single individual.

VIII
223

And that is the way it is in every one of your relationships. If you do not live in an out-of-the-way spot in the world, if you live in a heavily populated city and you then turn your attention outward, sympathetically give heed to people and events, do you bear in mind, every time you relate yourself in this way to an outside world, that in this relation you are relating yourself to yourself as a single individual with eternal responsibility? Or do you filter yourself into the crowd, where the one blames another, where at one moment there are, as they say, *a great many*, and where at the next moment, every time responsibility is mentioned, there is *no one*? Do you judge as the crowd judges, in the capacity of the crowd? You are not obliged to have an opinion about something that you do not understand.

No, on the contrary, you are eternally exempted, but as an individual you are eternally obliged to make an accounting of your opinion, of your judgment. And in eternity you will not be pryingly and busily asked, as by a journalist, whether there were a great many who had the same—wrong opinion, but only whether you had it; whether you have pamperingly accustomed your soul to judge light-mindedly and unthinkingly along with the others because the crowd judged unthinkingly; whether you perhaps have corrupted the better part in you by boasting along with the crowd that you were many and that you were justified because you were many, that is, you were many who were wrong. In eternity you will be asked whether you perhaps have harmed a good cause because you also judged along with those who did not understand how to judge but who had the crowd's considerable power in a temporal sense, negligible power in eternity's sense.

VIII
224 In temporality there is counting and they say, "One more or less is of no consequence"—and a person says this to himself, about himself! In temporality there is counting and they say, "One person against hundreds—what does that amount to?" So one cowardly gives in to numbers—and untruth usually is numbers; truth is content with being a unity. But one gains by this cowardly giving in; one does not gain a place in the infirmary, no, one gains the strange result of becoming the strongest, because the crowd is indeed always the strongest. Eternity, however, does not count; the single individual is continually only one, and the conscience keeps close watch on the single individual. In eternity you will look around in vain for the crowd; you will listen in vain to hear where the uproar and the throng are so that you, too, can run there; in eternity you also will be abandoned by the crowd. And this is terrible, because to be abandoned by the crowd in temporality is blessed when the eternal comforts, since the pain is only a jest.

What, then, does the conscience want to emphasize by means of the awareness that you are a single individual? It wants to teach you that if you pass judgment (for in a great many cases it will keep you from passing judgment) your judgment is then your own responsibility, so that with a sense of shame as before one who is dead you test what you understand and what you do not understand. It wants to scare you away from seeking the brilliant escape into that rubbish that you are many, because many fools do not make one wise man, and the crowd is a dubious recommendation for a cause. The bigger the crowd, the more likely that what it praises is foolishness, the less likely that it is truth, and the least likely that it is any eternal truth, because eternally, of course, there simply is no crowd at all. It is not the nature of truth to please a light-minded crowd immediately—and basically it never does that. To a multitude like that the truth must just look foolish. But the person who judges with eternal responsibility by being aware as a single individual is slow to form judgments about what is more un-usual, because it may be a lie and deception and mirage and vanity, but it also may be the truth. He recalls what that simple wise man of old said, "That a person's eyes cannot see by the light by which most people see can be due to the fact that he is accustomed to the dark; but it can also be due to the fact that he is accustomed to an even brighter illumination, and if that is the case this is not ludicrous."[125] No, this is not ludicrous, but it is ludicrous, or it is sad that light-minded people laugh at a person—because he is wiser or better than they are—because laughter, too, requires a rational basis, and if this is lacking the laughter is the ludicrous. But here in temporality, in the world's appalling prodigality with human beings, here num-ber tempts, here counting is tempting, to count oneself along in the crowd; here one easily becomes dizzy with round num-bers. Yes, here in temporality perhaps no single individual will ever succeed—even if he in truth willed the good, he will never succeed in splitting up the crowd.

But eternity can do it; eternity takes hold of each one sep-arately with the strong arms of conscience, encircles him as the single individual, sets him apart with his conscience. And woe to him if this alone judges, for in that case eternity sets him apart with his conscience, *there* where hardship certainly is, but not as in temporality, where the hardship is the excuse, yes, is the victory—no, *there* where the hardship is to be alone, with-out excuses, to be alone and to be lost. The royal psalmist declares that while the heathen make a big noise God is in heaven and laughs at them.[126] I dare not believe this. One might rather say: While the crowd makes a big noise and up- roar and triumphs and jubilates; while one individual after the other hurries to the crowd's arena, where it is said to be good to be if one is seeking oblivion and indulgence from the eternal; while the crowd seems to be shouting mockingly at God, "All right, see if you can get hold of us!" since in a throng it is of course always difficult to see the individual, difficult to see the trees if one is looking at the forest—then the earnestness of eternity calmly waits. And if all the generations that have lived on earth rose up and united into one crowd in order to charge against eternity and to coerce it also with their enormous ma- jority, eternity splits them up as easily as the imperturbability of the cliff that, without moving from the spot, disperses the foaming surf, as easily as a storm wind in its advance scatters the chaff. Just as easily, but not in the same way, because the wind blows away the chaff only to pile it in drifts again; eter- nity disperses the crowd by giving each person separately an infinite weight by making him heavy—as the single individ- ual. There the same thing that is the highest blessedness is the highest earnestness; there the same thing that is the most bliss- ful comfort is also the most dreadful responsibility.

In eternity there are plenty of rooms;[127] there is exactly one for each one, because where there is a conscience, and this is and must be in everyone, there is in eternity a solitary prison or a delightful room of eternal happiness. This awareness of being a single individual is the basic consciousness in a human being because it is his eternal consciousness.

VIII
226

But the person who bears in mind that he is a single individ- ual, that he is alone with himself in the ultimate and highest responsibility because as a third person even the most intimate friend must of necessity omit from his judgment what is cru- cial: to be the one involved, the one to whom the conscience in this matter says *Du*,[128] whereas it says *Du* to the friend only with respect to how he advises—the person who bears this in mind becomes slow to judge, is reluctant to pass judgment on very much, and this helps him to will one thing. He does not consider it to be exactly an advantage of life in the populous big cities that, given the speed of the means of communication, almost everyone can easily have a hasty and superficial opinion on everything possible. On the contrary, he regards this easiness as a temptation, a trap, and learns earnestness in order to be concerned as a single individual about his eternal responsibility. "Even a fool would be a wise man if he could keep silent," says the proverb,[129] and this is true not merely because he would not betray his foolishness but also because this self-control would help him to become aware of himself as a single individual, would prevent him from quickly accepting the opinion of the crowd or, if he himself had an opinion, from quickly getting a crowd to accept it. The vision of the person who is aware of himself as a single individual is formed to see everything reversed. His mind becomes intimate with eternity's true thought—that everything in life appears reversed, that even in the very next moment, to say nothing of eternity, the purely momentary is vanity and futility, just as desire's fiery moment (and what is so powerful at the moment as lust!) is nauseating to recollection, just as the fiery moment of anger and revenge and passion, the gratification of which seems an obsession, is a horror to recollect. The angry person, the vengeful person, the passionate person *is asserting himself*, so he thinks, in the moment of passion; but in the moment of recollection, when he recollects the revenge committed, he is nauseated by himself, because he perceives that in the moment of revenge he *lost himself.* The purely momentary seems a gain, which, however, already in the very next moment proves to be a deception and, eternally understood, engenders regret. So it is with everything momentary, also with the opinion of the crowd and going along with the crowd insofar as the opinion and sympathy are the momentary.

Are you now living, my listener, in such a way that you are clearly and eternally aware of being a single individual? This was the discourse's question, or this is the question you ask yourself if you are very vividly thinking of the occasion of this discourse. The discourse will not be able to tell you what indeed only disturbs, whether or not many people are convinced

VIII
227

that a person ought to live in this awareness. But it makes no difference whether all, *each one separately*, have this conviction, or no one has. Neither will the speaker try to win you over to this conviction, that is, if it is really his—thus he does not need you any more than you need him if you have this conviction: the lofty earnestness of the eternal wants the recommendation neither of the majority nor of eloquence. One thing only the discourse does not dare to promise you—it does not wish to insult you either—it does not dare to promise you earthly advantages if you accept and in appropriation adhere to this conviction. On the contrary, if adhered to it will make your life strenuous, many a time perhaps burdensome; if adhered to it will perhaps expose you to ridicule by others, not to mention that adherence might ask even greater sacrifices from you. It goes without saying that the ridicule will not disturb you, that is, if you hold fast to the conviction; the ridicule will even be of advantage to you also by convincing you even more that you are on the right path. Therefore the opinion of the crowd does have its significance; a person must not haughtily remain ignorant of it—no, he should become aware of it. Then if he just takes care to do the opposite, he usually will hit it right; or if he originally does the opposite and then is so lucky as to have the opinion of the crowd manifest itself as contrary, then he can be fairly sure that the right position has been taken. He has, then, not only profoundly examined and tested his conviction by himself, but he also has the advantage of having it tested once again—with the help of ridicule, which possibly wounds but by the wound shows that he is on the right path, the path of honor and of victory—just like the soldier's wound when it is on the chest, where both the wound and the medal of honor should be.

You undoubtedly have noticed that the boy who is regarded as a jolly good fellow by his schoolmates is the one who is not afraid of his father, who dares to say to the others, "Do you think that I am afraid of him?" But if they detect in one of their peers that he actually and literally is afraid of his father, they usually will ridicule him a little. Alas, in the motley crowd of frightened people (why, indeed, does a person run to join the

crowd unless he is frightened!) it is also a jolly good thing not
to be afraid, not even of God. And if it is detected that there is a
single individual outside who actually and literally is afraid,   VIII
not of the crowd but of God, then they usually will ridicule   228
him a little. They gloss over the ridicule and say: A person is to
love God. Yes, indeed, God knows it is a person's greatest
comfort that God is love and that he dares to love God; but let
us not become haughty and foolishly, yes, blasphemously
abolish what has been handed down from the fathers, what
God himself devised: that one quite actually and literally is to
fear God. And the person who fears God is one who is aware of
being a single individual and thereby aware of his eternal responsibility before God, because he knows that even if he could
make it through life rather well with the help of evasions and
excuses, even if he could gain the whole world along this leaf-
shaded path, there nevertheless is a place hereafter where there
is no more evasion than there is shade in the burning desert.

The discourse will say no more about this; it only asks you
repeatedly: Are you now living in such a way that you are
aware of being a single individual and thereby aware of your
eternal responsibility before God; are you living in such a way
that this awareness can acquire the time and stillness and liberty
of action to penetrate your life relationships? You are not asked
to withdraw from life, from an honorable occupation, from a
happy domestic life—on the contrary, that awareness will support and transfigure and illuminate your conduct in the relationships of life. You are not to withdraw and sit brooding over
your eternal accounting, whereby you only take on a new
responsibility. You will find more and more time for your
duties and your tasks, while concern for your eternal responsibility will keep you from being busy and from busily taking
part in everything possible—an activity that can best be called a
waste of time.

This was the main question, because just as only one thing is
needful and just as the discourse is about willing one thing, so
the awareness of being a single individual with eternal responsibility before God is the one thing needful. The discourse now
goes on to ask: *What is your occupation in life?* The discourse does

not ask pryingly whether it is great or small, whether you are king or only a laborer; it does not busily ask whether you are earning a lot of money or acquiring great prestige—that is what the crowd asks and talks about. But your occupation, be it great or small, is surely such that you dare to think of it together with the responsibility of eternity, such that you dare to acknowledge it at this moment and at any other time.

Suppose something terrible happened, suppose the city in which you live suddenly perished like those cities in the far south and everything was suspended, with everyone standing in his once-chosen walk of life but without the excuse of possible conformity with contemporary use and custom, appraised by a later generation—would that you then might not be put to shame! Or what if one of those persons of distinction, whose memory the crowd commemorates, as crowds do, with noisy celebration and shouting, what if he, and this is much more earnest, came to you, visited you—face-to-face with him, with his probing look, would that you then might dare to admit to your occupation!

Are you not familiar with such thoughts, for it is indeed in this way that those transfigured ones might wish to be beneficial after their death by visiting the single individual, since in their blessed abode they must surely be revolted if they became aware of such things when a thoughtless crowd treats the glorified dead as only a live fool can wish to be treated—making noise and clapping hands to their honor. Do not think that the transfigured one has become exclusive; on the contrary, he has become more humble, more humanly involved with every human being. Therefore, when he goes traveling like a superior official on a visit to the single individuals, he does not reject the lowliest occupation if it has genuine integrity. There in eternity where he is, all petty diversities are forgotten; but the glorified one, like eternity, does not want the crowd, he wants the single individuals. Therefore, if you might ever feel almost ashamed of your lowly occupation because it is so inferior in the world's diversity, the transfigured one's visit to you as an individual will definitely give you bold confidence. The transfigured one's visit to you as an individual will specifically give you bold confidence—what am I saying, for if you are very vividly thinking of the occasion of this discourse you are standing as an individual before someone even higher, who nevertheless thinks more humanly—about the lowliness of the occupation, but also infinitely more purely about what true integrity is.

In the course of your occupation, what is your frame of mind, how do you perform your work? Are you convinced that your occupation is your calling so that you do not reinterpret it according to the results and think that it is not still your calling if the results are unfavorable and your efforts do not succeed? Alas, this vacillation is incalculably weakening. Therefore stand fast; by God's help and by your own faithfulness something good will surely come of the poor beginning. There is a beginning everywhere, and the good beginning is everywhere where you begin with God; and no day is an unlucky day to begin, not even the unlucky day, if you begin with God.

Or have you allowed yourself to be deceived into regarding something as your calling because the results were favorable, because it was an immediate success,[130] perhaps even an extraordinary success? Alas, that kind of thing is indeed said in the world, sometimes even by those who think that they are speaking devoutly: "The proof that one's occupation is justified is that one is able to do it." Therefore if someone could harden his mind so that, unmoved, he *could* practice any and all cruelty, this would be what he was to do. Therefore if a brazen person could bring himself to consider the most loathsome crime so he *could* execute it, then this would be what he was to do! No, an unfavorable result can no more refute the believer's conviction that he is in his calling than a propitious result can summarily demonstrate that one is in one's calling.

VIII
230

Have you made up your mind about how you want to perform your work, or are you continually of two minds because you want to be in agreement with the crowd? Do you stick to your bid, not defiantly, not despondently, but eternally concerned; do you, unchanged, continue to bid on the same thing and want to buy only the same thing while the terms are variously being changed? Do you think that the good is just like gold, that it can be purchased at too high a price? Is there any profit you could not do without for its sake, any distinction you could not renounce, any relationship you could not give up; is there any acclamation from above that is still more important to you—or perhaps acclamation from below? But if you think that the good must be bought at any price, do you become envious when you see others buying at a lower price what you have to purchase dearly—but what, do not forget, is worth any price? If your endeavor succeeds, are you then aware that you are an unworthy servant,[131] and when it fails, are you then aware that you are an unworthy servant—so that the reward does not change you, as if you were more profitable because you received a reward, and adversity does not change you, since it only expresses what you shamefacedly admit, that you have nothing to claim? Are you hiding nothing suspicious in your soul, so that you would still wish things were different, so that you would dare robber-like to seize the reward for yourself, would dare to parade it, would dare to point to it; so that you would wish the adversity did not exist because it constrains in you the selfishness that, although suppressed, yet foolishly deludes you into thinking that if you were lucky you would do something for the good that would be worth talking about, deludes you into forgetting that the devout wise person wishes no adversity away when it befalls him because he obviously cannot know whether it might not indeed be a good for him, into forgetting that the devout wise person wins his most beautiful victory when the powerful one who persecuted him wants, as they say, to spare him, and the wise one replies: I cannot unconditionally wish it, because I cannot definitely know whether the persecution might not indeed be a good for me. Are you doing the good only out of fear of punishment, so that you scowl even when you will the good, so that in your dreams at night you wish the punishment away and to that extent also the good, and in your daydreams delude yourself into thinking that one can serve the good with a slavish mind? Oh, the good is not a hard taskmaster who wants one thing one day and tomorrow something else; the good always wants one thing and always the same thing. But it is scrupulous and can be that; it requires sincerity and can see whether it is there!

[132]*And now the means that you use.* What means do you use to perform your work; is the means just as important to you as the end, just exactly as important? If not, you cannot possibly will one thing; in that case the indefensible, the irresponsible, the self-serving, the heterogeneous means enters in, disturbing and defiling. Eternally understood, the means is one thing, the end is one thing, the means and the end are one and the same. There is only one end: the good in truth, and only one means: to will to use only the means that in truth is the good means— but the good in truth is indeed the end.

Temporally and mundanely the two are separated and the end is considered more important than the means; the end is considered primary. It is required of the one striving that he achieve the end; he may be less scrupulous about the means. But this is not the case, and to have an end in this way is an ungodly impatience. In the eternal sense, the relation between end and means is rather the reverse. If a person sets himself an end for his striving here in life and does not achieve it, he may possibly be altogether without guilt in the eternal sense, yes, is even to be praised. After all, he can be prevented by death or by adversities that are not under his control; in that case he is entirely without guilt. He can even be prevented from achieving the end by refusing to use means other than what is admissible according to eternity's understanding, that is, by renouncing the impatience of passion and the devices of sagacity—in that case he is even to be praised. Thus he is not eternally responsible for achieving his end in temporality, but he is unconditionally eternally responsible for which means he uses. When he wills to use or uses only the means that truly is the good means, he is, eternally understood, at the end. If achieving the end is meant to be the excuse and the defense for using the inadmissible, the dubious means—alas, suppose he died tomorrow. In that case the sagacious person would be trapped in his folly; he had used the inadmissible means, but he died without achieving his end. Achieving the end comes at the conclusion, but using the means comes at the beginning. To achieve the end is like hitting the target with one shot, but using the means is like taking aim, and yet taking aim is a more reliable testimony to the marksman's goal than the on-target shot, because a shot can also hit the target accidentally, and the marksman may also be guiltless if the gun failed to go off, but taking aim allows for no irregularities.

VIII
232

To the temporal and earthly passion the end is unconditionally more important than the means, and therefore this is the passionate person's torment, which at its highest presumably might make a person insomniac and then mad: that he does not have time under his control, that he always can come too late, even if it were only half an hour. And since earthly passion unfortunately is the universal passion, it can truthfully be said that it is not wisdom that saves most people from becoming mad but sluggishness. On the other hand, the eternal's blessed comfort, which is like a rest, like "the cold of snow in the time of harvest,"[133] is that the person who wills the eternal never comes too late—if the means is to him unconditionally just as important as the end. Eternity is not temporally inquisitive and impatient about the result, and for that very reason or for the reason that the means is unconditionally just as important as the end. To the earthly and secular passion, this point of view must seem shocking and procrastinating, and the conscience must seem the most procrastinating of all. It is indeed "a blushing spirit with a sense of shame that creates a commotion in a person's interior and fills it with difficulties," because to this spirit the means is unconditionally just as important as the end.

So, then, my listener, as you do your work, which is assumed to be something good and honorable, is the means unconditionally just as important to you as the end? Or does your thought become dizzy, so that because of the magnitude of the end you see the dubious means as a diminutive triviality—alas, what eternity is least of all is dizzy; it is clear and transparent! Do you think that the magnitude of the enterprise precludes asking questions about a petty wrong, that is, you think that any wrong whatever would be something trivial, when as guilt it is indeed something infinitely more impor-

tant than the greatest enterprise! Do you think that the masterpiece is indifferent to the way in which it came to be! Well, yes,
the masterpiece can perhaps be indifferent, but do you think
that the master dares to be indifferent to the question of
whether he devoutly dedicated his powers in sacred service or
whether amid glittering sins and bolstered up by despair he
perhaps created—a masterpiece? And if your thought does
not become dizzy in this way, if you are definitely sober and
alert, are you altogether scrupulous in the use of the means?
If a young person (and he is of course a blushing, innocent
spirit) came to you, would you dare unconditionally to let him
know everything? Is there not anything at all in your entire
conduct—yes, how shall I describe it; I could use many words   VIII
to describe it, but I would rather say it briefly this way: any-   233
thing that you, if you spoke of it to adults, people of your own
age, might be fairly certain they would almost admire for its
sagacity and cunning, but that a youth, strangely enough,
would blush at (not because you could be so sagacious but
because you did not have the nobility to scorn acting so
sagaciously)—namely, that by flattery you had gained this one
and that one, by suppressing something you had gained this
and that advantage, by a little lie you had made a brilliant
transaction, by a false alliance you had advanced your cause;
that you had won victories by uniting with the admiration of
misunderstanding, had gained wealth and power by *sagaciously*
scheming to enter into the *most tender* association. Is there not
anything at all in your whole conduct, open or secret, that you
would at no price have the heart to let a young person find out
(and it is of course beautiful that you love the youth this way
and wish to preserve his purity!)—anything that you, in opposition to yourself, nevertheless could still have the heart to
allow yourself to become guilty of? Anything that you at no
price could have the heart to allow a young person to find out—
yet, what am I saying?—if you very vividly think of the occasion of this discourse, then you stand before a higher judge
who judges infinitely more purely than the purest youth's innocence, a judge to whom you do not refrain from divulging
your guilt out of a sense of consideration because he knows it.

And what is your frame of mind toward others? Are you in harmony with everyone—by willing one thing? Or are you divisively in a faction, or are you at loggerheads with everyone and everyone with you? Do you want for everyone what you want for yourself, or do you want the highest for yourself, for yourself and for yours, or that you and yours shall be highest? Do you do to others what you want others to do to you—by willing one thing? This willing is the eternal order that orders everything, that brings you in harmony with the dead and with the people you never saw, with strange people [134]whose language and customs you do not know, with all the people on the whole earth, who are blood relatives and eternally related to divinity by eternity's task to will one thing. Do you want a different law for yourself and for yours than for others; do you want to have your comfort in something different from that in which every human being unconditionally can and will be comforted? If a king and a beggar and one of your peers came to you at the same time, would you in their presence dare with bold confidence to assert what you want in the world, with bold confidence to assert wherein you seek your comfort, positive that His Royal Majesty would not disdain you even though you are an inferior, positive that the beggar would not go away disheartened as if he could not have the same comfort, positive that your peer would rejoice in your bold confidence!

VIII
234

Alas, there is something in the world called an alliance; it is a dangerous thing, because all alliances are divisiveness. It is divisive when the alliance excludes the commoner, and when it excludes the nobleman, and when it excludes the government worker, and when it excludes the king, and when it excludes the beggar, and when it excludes the wise, and when it excludes the simple soul—because all alliances are divisiveness in opposition to the universally human. But to will one thing, to will the good in truth, to will as a single individual to be allied with God—something unconditionally everyone can do—that is harmony. If you sat in solitary confinement, removed from all human beings, or if you were banished to a desert island with animals for company—if you will the good in truth, if you are allied with God, then you are in concordance with all people. If something terrible happened (since godly upbuilding should not, like a woman's indulgent finery, be intended for a grand occasion), if you were buried alive, if when you awakened in the coffin you had recourse to your familiar comfort, then also in this solitary torment you would be in harmony with all human beings.

Is this your frame of mind now? Have you no advantage, no gift, no preferential treatment in life that you separately or in alliance with others have conceitedly taken, so that you comfort yourself with it and do not dare to tell the uninitiated the source of your comfort? So even if you indeed give the pauper alms for his comfort, you treasonably still have a final comfort for yourself, indeed have a comfort for poverty but comfort yourself with the assurance that your wealth guarantees you against ever becoming poor. Even if you indeed help the simple soul, you traitorously still have a final comfort for yourself, that your mental endowment is so outstanding that it could never happen to you that you would wake up tomorrow and be the most obtuse person in the nation. Even if you will indeed counsel the youth, you still do not have the heart to initiate him into your life because you have a private secret, because you are a traitor who cheated the youth out of the highest with your secret and cheated yourself out of the highest—with your secret!

And now a question concerning the *one who is suffering*. The question is not about how he feels—alas, the discourse does not sympathize in that way. But if you very vividly think of the occasion for this discourse, then by your being before God you are lifted above human sympathy, then you do not abjectly need it. Then you can, if it manifests itself just as you would wish it, which certainly happens rarely enough, then you can with bold confidence give thanks for it, but you are not to give thanks for it bent down like a suppliant—God will surely prevent that. If sympathy is denied you, if people are scared and in selfish cowardice avoid you, yes, almost loathe you because they do not even dare to imagine your sufferings, then you must be able to do without sympathy. You are not to miss it bitterly—God will surely see to that. The discourse then asks

VIII
235

you, or you ask yourself by way of the discourse, whether you are now living in such a manner that you are willing one thing in truth. The discourse does not presume to want to pass judgment. On the contrary, it judges no one, and if even Holy Scripture has a predilection for the unfortunate, it surely behooves an upbuilding meditation just out of respect to address the sufferer in exactly the same way as one addresses the powerful, the eminent, in the world. The discourse does not inquisitively and busily ask the name of your unusual suffering or how many years it has lasted, does not ask what the physician or psychologist thinks, whether or not they hold out an earthly hope. Alas, sufferings, too, can be taken in vain this way as a mark of distinction that draws the attention of others to itself. Therefore, you ask yourself questions by way of the discourse. When the sufferer speaks with himself in solitude, asks himself what constitutes his life, whether he is willing one thing in truth, then there is no temptation to a long-winded narrative about what he himself indeed knows best, no temptation to comparison—and all comparison is damaging, indeed, it is evil.

Do you now will one thing in truth? You know, if you will only one thing so that you alone will be free from the suffering, then you do not will one thing in truth. But neither do you will one thing in truth if you could make yourself so obtuse that the wish vanished, so that in the pain of the wish you no longer maintained a connection with what it is to be human in the happier sense, loving what it is to be human, loving the one who is happier. What is your condition now in this suffering (the physician and the psychologist ask you how you feel, but eternity makes you responsible for your condition); is it such that in the fever of impatience it does not light-mindedly and superstitiously fluctuate, that in depression it is not a sluggish absence of pain but is such that you patiently will to suffer everything and therefore allow the eternal to comfort you? How does your condition change as time goes by? Did you perhaps begin well but became more and more impatient, or were you perhaps impatient in the beginning but learned patience from what you suffered?[135] Alas, perhaps your suffering continued unchanged over the years, and if it changed, this is of course a matter for the physician or the psychologist to describe. Alas, perhaps the unchanged sameness of your suffering seems like slow death to you. But while the physician and the psychologist and your friend know of no change to speak of, the discourse asks you whether an infinite change has taken place beneath the weight of this unchanged sameness—not in the suffering (after all, even if it can be changed it can only be changed finitely) but in you, an infinite improvement in you from better to better?

VIII
236

If the discourse were to describe your changed condition over the years, would it dare to use the apostolic words for that and say of your life in the unchanged suffering, "Suffering taught him steadfastness, steadfastness taught him experience, and experience taught him hope"?[136] Would the discourse dare to say beside your grave, "He won the hope that will not put to shame"? Instead of despondently muttering words of thanks at your grave because you were dead, would the discourse one day dare to say cheerfully and with bold confidence, as beside a hero's grave, "The content of his life was suffering, and yet his life put that of many to shame"? In eternity there will be no question about your suffering, as little as about the king's purple, just as little; in eternity you will be asked as a single individual only about your faith and about your faithfulness. There will be no question at all about whether you were in charge of much or little, whether you were given many pounds to work with[137] or were given a hundredweight to bear—but only about your faith and your faithfulness. In temporality other kinds of questions are asked; a person is asked particularly about how much he is in charge of, and if it is very much, one forgets in worldly astonishment to ask about faithfulness; but if it is very little, one does not care to hear anything about it at all, neither about the burden nor about the faithfulness. Eternity asks only about the faithfulness, asks the king about it just as earnestly as it asks the most wretched sufferer. To be in charge of little is no excuse,[138] nor is it an answer to the question that simply and solely asks about faithfulness, the question that in eternal compassion knows that sufferings can tempt a person but also that they can be a guide, "because grief is better than laughter, for when the countenance looks sad the heart can be changed for the better" (Ecclesiastes 7:3)—and this is of course the change eternity asks about and not about the changelessness of the suffering. This is the way eternity questions. If you yourself very vividly think of the occasion for this discourse, you ask yourself about this, and if the change has not taken place, then this question, if it is asked in truth, will certainly be helpful to you in the change. Human sympathy, even though it questions you ever so diligently, cannot by the question change the changelessness of the suffering; but eternity's question, if you address it to yourself in truth before God, already contains the possibility of change. But I am speaking almost as if for upbuilding. The discourse has scruples, as if out of respect, about urging the question, but you yourself know best that if you pose the question it is the question of the accounting: Are you now living in this way?

VIII
237

These were the discourse's questions. But now if, as single individuals, you, my listener, and I are obliged to confess to ourselves that we are far from living in such a way, far from the purity of heart that wills only one thing in truth, are obliged to confess to ourselves that the questions certainly demanded an answer and yet in another sense, simply in order to avoid every illusion, did not need any answer, since they rather were indictments against ourselves, which despite the form of a question nevertheless changed into a cry—should then, as single individuals, you, my listener, and I unite in saying, "Our lives are probably just like everyone else's"? What, must we then begin all over from the beginning and again have to speak about the evasion in being many, for where there are many there are externality and comparison and indulgence and excusing and evasions! Having come to understand the perniciousness of this evasion, must we nevertheless in turn end by having recourse to it, must we console ourselves with a collective failure! Alas, already here in temporality a collective failure is a poor comfort, and in eternity there is no collective failure.

Indeed, in eternity the single individual, you, my listener,

and I, will be questioned [139] as an individual, alone by himself
as an individual, and about the particulars in his life. If I have
spoken erroneously in this discourse, you, my listener, will not
be asked about it, nor any person from whom I could have
learned it, because if he has presented something false he will be
asked about it and I will be held responsible for having learned
the false teaching from another, nor anyone with whom I may
have had association, because if his association was pernicious
he will be asked about that, but I will be held responsible for
having sought or not having avoided association with him, and
for letting myself be corrupted. No, if I have spoken erroneously, and insofar as I have spoken erroneously, I will be
asked about it as a single individual and without any excuses. In
eternity there is not the remotest thought of any collective
failure. In eternity the single individual, you, my listener, and
I, will be questioned as the single individual, alone by himself
as an individual and about the particulars in his life. If it is
the case that I have spoken truthfully in this discourse, I will not
be questioned further about this, not about whether I have won
people (on the contrary, the question would probably be
whether I dared to do the least thing to win them), not about
whether I have had earthly advantage from it (on the contrary,
the question would probably be whether I dared to do the least
thing to gain it), not about what results I have produced, or
whether I produced no results whatever, or whether loss and
the ridicule of others were the only results I have produced—
no, eternity will exempt me from all foolish questions.

VIII
238

In temporality things can become so confused that a person
does not know which is which, which question is earnest and
which is frivolous—especially when the frivolous question is
heard a thousand times while the earnest question is heard
once. Eternity, however, is very able to distinguish—of course
that does not make the matter easier; the earnest question becomes only more earnest. In eternity there is not the remotest
thought of any collective failure. In eternity the single individual, you, my listener, and I, will be questioned as a single
individual, alone by himself as a single individual, and about
the particulars in his life. [140]If it is the case that in this discourse

there is contained a true observation on life, if it is the case that I have been granted the capability and the opportunity to be able to present this, but if it is also the case (which we could assume to be so) that the circumstances under which this was to be delivered did not seem favorable—eternity would not become inquisitively involved in a prolixity of details about the circumstances but would hold me responsible as a single individual if I remained silent. In temporality, when the task is to be sagacious to one's own advantage, when worldly sagacity judges and evaluates, then unfavorable circumstances are not merely a defense for silence, but silence is admired as sagacity, whereas favorable circumstances are an invitation for all to put in a word. Eternally, however, the fact that the circumstances are difficult makes it doubly obligatory to speak—the difficulty is the summons. Eternally the single individual will be asked only if he knew that they were unfavorable and whether in that case he dared to remain silent and then by his silence, yes, as the saying goes, by his consent, as a single individual made his contribution so that the circumstances became even more unfavorable to the truth. Eternally, there will be no hiding place and no evasion for him in the circumstances, because he will be questioned as a single individual, and the difficulty of the circumstances will be as a double indictment against him. In other words, remaining silent is not like sleeping, in the sense that the one who is sleeping does not sin, inasmuch as the single individual has incurred shocking guilt in the world —by remaining silent. The guilt was not that he did not get the circumstances changed; the guilt was that he remained silent, not out of a sober-mindedness that remains silent when it is proper to remain silent, but out of a sagacity that is silent because it is the most sagacious.

But what, then, should we do when the questions sound like indictments? Above all, each one separately is to become a single individual with his responsibility before God; each one separately is to endure this rigorous judgment of singularity. Or is this not the purpose of the confession? The number of confessors does not create a kind of company any more than "the number of the dead creates a kind of company" in that quiet garden—not even the king needs to go separately to confession so as not to enter into the inferior company of others, because those who are confessing are not together in company. Each one is alone as a single individual before God; husband and wife, even though they go together *to* confession, nevertheless do not confess together, because the person who is confessing is not in company; he is as a single individual alone before God. And when he as a single individual admits to himself that the questions that he addresses to himself with the help of the whispering of an insignificant one are indictments, then he is confessing. A person does not confess merits and exploits, but he confesses sin. And when he is confessing, he perceives that he has no merits, that merits and exploits are delusions and illusions that belong where one is among the crowd or at least is associating with others—and therefore that the person who never became conscious of himself as the single individual is easily tempted to become to himself a very meritorious person. But the purpose of the confession is certainly not that a person should become aware of himself as the single individual in the moment of confession and otherwise live without this awareness. On the contrary, in the moment of confession he should as a single individual make an accounting of how he has lived as a single individual. If the same consciousness is not required of him for everyday use, the confession's requirement is a self-contradiction. It would be equivalent to requiring of an ordinary man that every once in a while he must as king make to himself and to God an accounting of how he had lived as king—he who had never been king. And so it is also with requiring of a person that he as a single individual must make an accounting of his life if he is allowed to live his life without this awareness.

My listener, do you recollect now how this discourse began, or may I remind you of it? Of the temporal it holds true that it has its time, but the eternal must always have time. And if this has not happened in a person's life, then the eternal comes again under another name and must again always have time—it is repentance. Since no human life is conducted in perfection but each one in weakness, Governance has given humankind two

VIII
240

attendants along the way. The one calls forward, the other back, but repentance's call is always at the eleventh hour. Therefore confession is at the eleventh hour, but not in the sense of the sudden, because the confession is a holy act, which requires a collected mind. A collected mind, that is, a mind that has collected itself from all distraction, from every relation, in order to concentrate on its relation to itself as the single individual who is responsible before God; a mind that has collected itself from all distraction and thus also from all comparison, whether it tempts to earthly and incidental despondency because the person comparing must himself confess that he is behind many others, or whether it tempts to arrogance because he, humanly speaking, seems to be further ahead than many others. That the person making the confession is beyond comparison, that he has withdrawn from every relation in order to concentrate on his relation to himself as a single individual and by doing this become eternally responsible for every relation he is in ordinarily—this is a new expression for the true extremity of the eleventh hour. The more comparison there is, the more it seems that there is still plenty of time; the more comparison, the more indolent and the more paltry a person's life becomes. But when all comparison infinitely ceases, he is as the single individual confessing before God—and he is guilty *beyond comparison*, just as the requirement that requires purity of heart is beyond all comparison. God requires of him purity of heart, and the person confessing requires it of himself before God—alas, this is indeed why he confesses sins. However difficult the act and the hour of confession can be, the one confessing nevertheless wins the eternal: that he is confirmed in the consciousness that he is a single individual and in the task to will one thing in truth.

This consciousness is the strait gate and the narrow way.[141] It is not the way as such that is narrow, although quite a few people walk along it single-file; no, the narrowness is simply that each one separately must become the single individual who must press forward through this narrow pass along the narrow way where no comparison cools, but also where no comparison kills with its insidious chill. The broad way, on the other hand, is broad because many are walking on it. The way of the crowd is always broad. There the gorgeous poisonous flower of excuses blooms; the beckoning hiding places of excuses are there; the chilling breezes of comparison are there— that way does not lead to life. Only the single individual can will the good in truth, and even if he, with all the questions as accusers against him not only in the eleventh hour of the confession but also for everyday use in repentance, works encumbered—the way is nevertheless the right one; he is still in relation to the requirement that requires purity of heart by willing one thing.

VIII
241

If you, my listener, know much more about confession than has been said here, as indeed you do, know what follows the confession of sins, this delaying discourse may still not have been in vain, provided it actually has *halted* you, has *halted* you by means of something that you know very well, you who know even much more. But do not forget that surely the most terrible thing of all is "to go on living deceived, not by what might appear fashioned to deceive, alas, and for that very reason dreadfully deceived—deceived by much knowledge." Bear in mind that in these times it is most likely a temptation for speakers to abandon the specific as soon as possible in order to get everything possible said, lest someone suspect that the speaker did not know what everyone in a Christian country knows; alas, only God knows *how* the single individual knows this. But of what good is it to a person if he goes further and further and it must be said of him, "He is continually going further," when it must also be said of him: There was nothing that halted him. Halting is not indolent resting; halting is also movement. It is the heart's inward movement, it is self-deepening in inwardness; but merely to proceed further is the course straight ahead on the surface. On this road one does not arrive at willing one thing. Only when the person who at some time is decisively halted goes further and again halts before going further, only then can he will one thing; but purity of heart was to will one thing.

Father in heaven! What is a human being without you! What is everything he knows, even though it were enormously vast and varied, but a disjointed snippet if he does not know you;

what is all his striving, even though it embraced a world, but a job half done if he does not know you, you the one who is one and who is all! Then may you give the understanding wisdom to comprehend the one thing; may you give the heart sincerity to receive the understanding; may you give the will purity through willing only one thing. Then, when everything is going well, give the perseverance to will one thing, in distractions the concentration to will one thing, in sufferings the patience to will one thing. O you who give both the beginning and the completing,[142] may you give to the young person early,

when the day is dawning, the resolution to will one thing; when the day is waning, may you give to the old person a renewed remembrance of his first resolution so that the last may be like the first, the first like the last, may be the life of a person who has willed only one thing. But, alas, this is not the way it is. Something came in between; the separation of sin lies in between; daily, day after day, something intervenes between them: delay, halting, interruption, error, perdition. Then may you give through repentance the bold confidence again to will one thing. Admittedly it is an interruption of the usual task; admittedly it is a halting of work as if it were on a day of rest when the penitent (and only in repentance is the burdened laborer quiet) in the confession of sin is alone before you in self-accusation. Oh, but it is indeed an interruption that seeks to return to its beginning so that it might rebind what is separated, so that in sorrow it might make up for failure, so that in its solicitude it might complete what lies ahead. O you who give both the beginning and the completing, may you give victory on the day of distress so that the one distressed in repentance may succeed in doing what the one burning in desire and the one determined in resolution failed to do: to will only one thing.

Part Two

WHAT WE LEARN FROM THE LILIES
IN THE FIELD AND FROM THE BIRDS
OF THE AIR[1]

THREE DISCOURSES

PREFACE[2]

Although this little book is without the *authority* of the teacher, *a superfluidity, insignificant* like the lily and the bird—oh, would that it were so!—yet by finding the only thing it seeks, a good place, it hopes to find the *significance of appropriation* for that single individual,[3] whom I with joy and gratitude call *my* reader.

S. K.

PRAYER

Father in heaven! From you come only good and perfect gifts. It must also be beneficial to comply with the counsel and teaching of whomever you have appointed as a teacher of human beings, as a counselor to the worried. Grant, then, that the one who is worried may truly learn from the divinely appointed teachers: the lilies in the field and the birds of the air! Amen.

I

[To Be Contented with Being
a Human Being]

**THIS HOLY GOSPEL IS RECORDED BY MATTHEW
CHAPTER 6, VERSE 24 TO THE END**[4]

[5]No one can serve two masters, for he must either hate the one and love the other or be devoted to the one and despise the other. You cannot serve God and mammon. Therefore I say to you, do not worry about your life, what you will eat and what you will drink, nor about your body, what you will wear. Is not life more than food, and the body more than clothing? Look at the birds of the air; they sow not and reap not and gather not into barns, and your heavenly Father feeds them. Are you not much more than they? But who among you can add one foot to his growth even though he worries about it? And why do you worry about clothing? Look at the lilies in the field, how they grow; they do not work, do not spin. But I say to you that not even Solomon in all his glory was clothed as one of these. If, then, God so clothes the grass of the field, which today is and tomorrow is cast into the stove, would he not much more clothe you, you of little faith? Therefore you should not worry and say, "What shall we eat?" or "What shall we drink?" or "What shall we wear?" The pagans seek all these things; your heavenly Father knows that you need all these things.

> But seek first God's kingdom and his righteous-
> ness; then all these things will be added to you.
> Therefore do not worry about tomorrow: tomor-
> row will worry about itself. Each day has enough
> trouble of its own.

Who has not known this Holy Gospel from earliest childhood and often rejoiced in the joyful message! And yet, as a matter of fact, it is not simply a joyful message; it has an essential quality that actually makes it into a Gospel—namely, it addresses itself to those who are worried. Indeed, in every line of this solici-tous Gospel it is clear that the words are being spoken not to the healthy, not to the strong, not to the happy, but to the worried; it is clear that the message is itself doing what it says God does: it takes upon itself the worried and has solicitude for them—in the right way. Ah, how necessary this is, because anyone who has cares, especially the more deeply and the longer they pene-trate into the soul or the longer they penetrate it deeply, is perhaps also tempted to be impatiently unwilling to hear any human words about comfort and hope. The person in distress is perhaps wrong, is perhaps too impatient when it seems to him that no human being can speak appropriately to his cares. The happy person does not understand him, the strong person seems to rise above him just when comforting him, and the worried person only increases the cares for him by his con-tribution. When this is the case, it is best to look around for other teachers whose words are not a misapprehension, whose encouragement does not contain any hidden blame, whose glance does not judge, whose comfort does not agitate instead of calm.

    To such teachers this solicitous Gospel refers the person with cares: to the lilies in the field and the birds of the air. With these inexpensive teachers, whom one pays neither with money nor with humiliation, no misapprehension is possible, because they are silent—out of solicitude for the worried person. All

misapprehension, after all, stems from speech, more specifically from a comparison that is implicit in talking, especially in
conversation. For example, when the happy person says to one
who is worried: Be glad, the remark also implies: as I am glad;   VIII
and when the strong person says: Be strong, it is tacitly under-   251
stood: as I am strong. But silence respects the worry and respects the worried one as Job's friends did, who out of respect
sat silent with the sufferer and held him in respect.[6] And yet
they did look at him! But that one person looks at another
implies in turn a comparison. The silent friends did not compare Job with themselves—this did not happen until their respect (in which they silently held him) ceased and they broke
the silence in order to attack the sufferer with speeches, but
their presence prompted Job to compare himself with himself.
No individual can be present, even though in silence, in such a
way that his presence means nothing at all by way of comparison. At best, this can be done by a child, who indeed has a
certain likeness to the lilies in the field and the birds of the air.
How often has not a sufferer experienced and movingly sensed
that when only a child is present there is still no one present.
And now the lily in the field! Even if it has a good livelihood, it
does not compare its prosperity with anyone's poverty; even if
it is free from care in all its loveliness, it compares itself neither
with Solomon nor with the most wretched of persons. And
even if the bird soars lightly up in the sky, it does not compare
its buoyant flight with the heavy steps of the worried person;
even if the bird, richer than the one whose barns are full, does
not store up food, it does not compare its rich independence
with the indigent person who gleans futilely. No, out where
the lily blooms so beautifully, in the field, up there where the
bird is freely at home, in the heavens, if comfort is being
sought—there is unbroken silence; no one is present there, and
everything is sheer persuasion.

Yet this is so only if the person in distress actually gives his
attention to the lilies and the birds and their life and forgets
himself in contemplation of them and their life, while in his
absorption in them he, unnoticed, by himself learns something

about himself—unnoticed, since there is indeed sheer silence, no one present. The worried person is free of any and all co-knowledge, except God's, his own—and the lilies'.

In this discourse, then, let us consider how by properly looking at the lilies in the field and at the birds of the air the worried person learns:

to be contented with being a human being.

"*Look at*[7] *the lilies in the field*," look at them—that is, pay close attention to them, make them the object—not of a fleeting glimpse in passing but of your consideration. This is why the term used is one that the pastor ordinarily uses in the most earnest and solemn context when he says: Let us in this hour of devotion consider this and that. The invitation and request are that solemn. Maybe there are many who live in the big city and never see lilies; maybe there are many who live in the country and indifferently pass by them every day. Alas, how many are there indeed who really look at them according to the directions in the Gospel!

The lilies in the field—since here it is not a matter of the rare plants that a gardener raises in his garden and that are looked at by experts. No, go out to the field, out there where no one is solicitous about the abandoned lilies and where it nevertheless is so clear that they are not abandoned. Should not this request be appealing to the worried person? Alas, he, too, is like the abandoned lily—abandoned, unappreciated, disregarded, without human solicitude, until he, by properly considering the lily, understands that he is not abandoned.

So the worried one goes out to the field and stops beside the lilies. Not as a happy child does, or a childlike adult, who runs around to find the most beautiful lily in order to gratify his inquisitiveness by finding the rare specimen. No, with quiet solemnity he considers them standing there in profuse, multicolored abundance, the one just as fine as the other—"*how they grow.*" Well, he actually does not see how they grow, for it is certainly true, as the proverb says, that one cannot see the grass grow, but nevertheless he does see *how* they grow, or just

VIII
252

because it is incomprehensible to him how they grow he sees that there must be one who knows them just as intimately as the gardener knows the rare plants, one who attends to them every day, morning and evening, just as the gardener attends to the rare plants, one who gives them growth. Indeed, it could well be the same one who gives growth to the gardener's rare plants, except that these, because of the assistance of the gardener, can very easily prompt a misapprehension. The abandoned lilies, however, the common lilies, the lilies in the field, do not prompt the observer to any misapprehension. There where the gardener is visible, there where no trouble or expense is spared to promote the growth of the rich man's rare plants, it may seem more understandable that they grow; but out there in the field, where no one, no one, no one cares for the lilies—how can they grow out there? And yet they do grow.

But then the poor lilies themselves certainly must work all the harder. No, *they do not work*; it is only the rare flowers that require so much work to get them to grow. Out there, where the carpet is richer than in the halls of kings, there is no work. As the observer's eyes are delighted and refreshed by the sight, his soul will not be troubled by the thought of how the poor little lilies have to work and slave to make the carpet so beautiful. It is only with the products of human skill that the eyes, while dazzled by the fineness of the work, are filled with tears at the thought of the sufferings of the poor lace-maker.

VIII
253

The lilies *do not work, do not spin*; they actually do not do anything but adorn themselves or, more correctly, be adorned. Just as in the Gospel text earlier, where it says of the birds, "They sow not and reap not and gather not into barns," allusion is made to the man's work to support himself and his family, so these words about the lilies (they do not work or spin) make an allusion to the woman's work. The woman stays in the house, does not go out to seek the necessities of life; she stays at home, sews and spins, tries to keep everything as neat as possible: her daily occupation, her diligent labor, is most closely associated with adornment. So also with the lily: it stays at home, does not leave the place, but it does not work, it does not spin—it only adorns itself or, more correctly, it is adorned.

If the lily were to have any worry, it would not be about livelihood, which, however, the bird might seem to have since it flies far and wide and gleans its food—no, the lily's worry might femininely be about whether it was truly lovely and was adorned. But it is without worry.

Adorned it is, that is certain. Indeed, the observer cannot hold back—he stoops down to a particular lily; he takes the first one he comes to—"*I tell you, not even Solomon in all his glory was clothed as one of them.*" He examines it closely, and if his mind was restless—as restless, alas, as a human mind can be— and if his heart beats violently—as, alas, a human heart can— he becomes altogether calm just in order to look at this lily. The more closely he looks, the more he wonders at its loveliness and its ingenious formation; it is true only of the products of human skill that on closer inspection one discovers defects and imperfections; it is true that if you sharpen your vision with an artfully ground glass you see the coarse threads in even the most delicate human tapestry. Ah, it seems as if the human being to his own humiliation has made the discovery of which he is so proud: when he discovered how to grind glass artfully so that it magnifies the object, he discovered by means of the magnifying glass that even the finest human work is coarse and imperfect. But the discovery that humiliated the human being honored God, because by means of the magnifying glass no one has ever discovered that the lily became less lovely, less ingenious; on the contrary, it proved the lily to be more and more lovely, more and more ingenious. Indeed, the discovery honored God, as every discovery is bound to do, because it holds true only of a human artist that the one who knows him intimately, close up and in ordinary life, sees that he is not so great after all; of the artist who weaves the carpet of the field and produces the beauty of the lilies, it holds true that the wonder increases the closer one comes, that the distance of adoration and worship increases the closer one comes to him.

So the worried person who went to the lilies with his cares stands among them in the field and is filled with wonder at the beauty of the lily he is looking at. He has taken the first one he came to; he has made no choice. It does not enter his mind at all

VIII
254

that there would be any single lily, no more than there would be a blade of grass in the field, of which it would not be true that not even Solomon in all his glory was clothed as one of them. Suppose that the lily could speak—would it not say to the worried one, "Why are you so filled with wonder at me; should it not be just as glorious to be a human being; should it not hold true that all of Solomon's glory is nothing in comparison with what every human being is by being human, so that in order to be the most glorious thing he is and to be conscious of this Solomon must strip off all his glory and just be a human being! Should not what holds true of poor me hold true of being a human being, who, after all, is creation's wonderwork!" The lily, however, cannot speak, but simply because it cannot speak, simply because there is utter silence out there and no one is present, simply for this reason the worried one, if he speaks and if he speaks with the lily, is in the situation of speaking with himself. Indeed, little by little he discovers that he is speaking about himself, that what he says about the lily he says about himself. It is not the lily that is saying it; the lily cannot speak. It is not some *other* human being who is saying it to him, since with *another* human being the agitated thoughts of comparison come so readily and promptly. Among the lilies the worried one is only a human being—and is contented with being a human being.[8]

In exactly the same sense as the lily is a lily, absolutely in the same sense, this person, despite all his worries as a human being, is a human being, and exactly in the same sense as the lily, without working and spinning, is more beautiful than Solomon's glory; exactly in the same sense, this person, without working, without spinning, without any meritoriousness, is more glorious than Solomon's glory by being a human being. And the Gospel text does not say that the lily is more glorious than Solomon—no, it says that the lily is better clothed than Solomon in all his glory. But, alas, in daily association with people, in the multifarious diversity and its various connections, one forgets through the busy or the worried inventiveness of comparison what it is to be a human being, forgets it because of the diversity among individuals. But in the

VIII
255

field with the lilies, where heaven arches high as over a sovereign, free as breathing is out there where the cloud's great thoughts drive away all small-mindedness—out there the worried one is the *only* human being and learns from the lilies what perhaps could not be learned from any *other* human being.

"Look at the lilies in the field." How brief, how solemn, how impartial are these words about the lilies. There is not a trace of an intimation, it is not hinted in the slightest way, that there could be any distinction among the lilies. The words refer to all of them and to each single one; they refer to all of them impartially: the lilies. Someone may think that it would be odd and too much to ask that human language should involve itself with diversity among lilies and their possible worries occasioned by diversity. Someone may think, "It is not worth paying attention to diversities and worries of that sort." Let us understand each other. Is the idea that it is not worthwhile for the lilies to pay attention to such worries, that is, that the lilies ought to be sensible enough not to pay attention to such things, or is the idea that it is beneath the dignity of a human being to bother himself about the possible worries of lilies because a human being is a human being and not a lily? In other words, are such worries in themselves foolish, and therefore not worthy of attention, regardless of whether simple lilies or sensible people have them, or is essentially the same worry something different when the lily has it from when the human being has it, so that it is foolish of the lily to worry about such things but not foolish for a human being? That is to say, if the lilies actually had such worries and the speaker thought that essentially the same worry was of great importance in relation to a human being, then it would indeed not be wisdom and sympathy but human self-love that could speak so tersely and so deprecatingly about the poor lilies, so superiorly about the lilies' trifling cares, so superiorly by calling them trifling cares not worthy of receiving attention. Just suppose that there were diversities among the lilies that in their little world corresponded to human diversities; suppose that these diversities occupied and worried the lilies just as much as they do human beings—and then suppose that what was said was really true: it

VIII
256

is not worth paying attention to such diversities and such worries.

Let us consider this issue more closely, and since the worried person who went out to the lilies in the field desired specifically to avoid all comparison with other human beings, since he was so loath to have any *other* human being speak to him about his worry, the discourse will respect his worry, and I shall not speak about any human being, or about any worried human being, but prefer to speak about *the worried lily*.

Once upon a time there was a lily that stood in an isolated spot beside a small brook and was well known to some nettles and also to a few other small flowers nearby. The lily was, according to the Gospel's truthful account, more beautifully clothed than Solomon in all his glory and in addition was joyful and free of care all the day long. Imperceptibly and blissfully time slipped by, like the running water that murmurs and disappears. It so happened that one day a little bird came and visited the lily; it came again the next day, then stayed away a few days before it came again, which struck the lily as odd and inexplicable—inexplicable that the bird, just like the flowers, did not remain in the same place, odd that the bird could be so capricious. But as so often happens, the lily fell more and more in love with the bird precisely because it was capricious.

This little bird was a naughty bird. Instead of putting itself in the lily's place, instead of delighting in its loveliness and delighting in its innocent bliss, the bird would show off in its feeling of freedom by making the lily feel its lack of freedom. Not only that, but the little bird was also chatty and talked fast and loose, truthfully and untruthfully, about how in other places there were entirely different gorgeous lilies in great abundance, places where there were a rapture and merriment, a fragrance, a brilliance of colors, a singing of birds that were beyond all description. This is how the bird talked, and it usually ended its story with the comment, humiliating to the lily, that in comparison with that kind of glory the lily looked like nothing—indeed, it was so insignificant that it was a question whether the lily actually had a right to be called a lily. VIII 257

Then the lily became worried. The more it listened to the

bird, the more worried it became; no longer did it sleep calmly at night and wake up joyful in the morning. It felt imprisoned and bound; it found the purling of the water tiresome and the day long. Now in self-concern it began to be preoccupied with itself and the condition of its life—all the day long. "It may be all right to listen to the purling of the brook once in a while for the sake of change," it said to itself, "but forever to hear the same thing day in and day out—that is much too boring." "It may be pleasant enough once in a while to be off in a secluded spot alone," it said to itself, "but to be this way all one's life, to be forgotten, to be without companions or to have nettles as companions, which certainly are no society for a lily—this is not to be endured." "And then to look as inferior as I do," said the lily to itself, "to be as insignificant as the little bird says I am—oh, why did I not come into existence some other place, under other conditions, why did I not become a Crown Imperial!" The little bird had told it that of all the lilies the Crown Imperial was regarded as the most beautiful and was the envy of all other lilies. To make matters worse, the lily noted that it was becoming exhausted from its worry but then it talked sensibly to itself, yet not so that it banished its worry from its mind, but talked in such a way that it convinced itself that the worry was proper. "After all, my wish is not a foolish wish," it said. "After all, I am not asking for the impossible, to become what I am not, a bird, for example. My wish is only to become a gorgeous lily, or even the most gorgeous."

Amidst all this, the little bird flew back and forth, and with every visit and every separation the lily became more agitated. Finally it confided everything to the bird. One evening they agreed that the next morning there would be a change and an end would be made to the worry. Early the next morning, the bird came; with its beak it pecked the soil away from the root of the lily so that it could become free. Having done this, the bird took the lily under its wing and flew away. The decision was that the bird should fly with the lily to the place where the gorgeous lilies blossomed and then in turn help the lily to be planted down there in the hope that with the change of place and with the new surroundings the lily might succeed in be-

coming a gorgeous lily in the company of all the others, or   VIII
perhaps even a Crown Imperial, envied by all the others.   258

Alas, on the way the lily withered. If the worried lily had been contented with being a lily, it would not have become worried; if it had not become worried, it would have remained standing where it stood—where it stood in all its loveliness; if it had remained standing there, it would have been the very lily the pastor talked about on Sunday when he repeated the Gospel text: "Look at the lily; I tell you not even Solomon in all his glory was clothed as it is." The Gospel text can certainly not be understood in any other way; whereas it is lamentable, indeed, almost terrible if true, that an interpreter of Holy Scripture, like the little bird, has found occasion in the passage about the lilies to point out that the Crown Imperial grows wild in that region[9]—as if we could then better understand that the lily in its loveliness surpasses Solomon, as if we could then better understand the Gospel, which then would take no notice of the unimpressive lily.

So this is what happened to the worried lily whose worry was to become a gorgeous lily or even a Crown Imperial. The lily is the human being. The naughty little bird is the restless mentality of comparison, which roams far and wide, fitfully and capriciously, and gleans the morbid knowledge of diversity; and just as the bird did not put itself in the lily's place, comparison does the same thing by either putting the human being in someone else's place or putting someone else in his place. The little bird is the poet, the seducer, or the poetic and the seductive in the human being. The poetic is like the bird's talk, true and untrue, fiction and truth. It is indeed true that there is diversity and that there is much to be said about it, but the poetic consists in maintaining that diversity, impassioned in despair or jubilation, is the supreme, and this is eternally false. In the worry of comparison, the worried person finally goes so far that because of diversity he forgets that he is a human being, in despair regards himself as so different from other people that he even regards himself as different from what it is to be human, just as the little bird thought that the lily was so unimpressive that it became a question whether the lily actually was a lily. But the supposedly reasonable defense for the worry is always this—that one does not, after all, ask for anything unreasonable, such as to become a bird, for example, but only to become that specific thing that one is not, even if this specific thing may in turn seem utterly trivial to other worried people. Thus when the comparison with the bird's movement to and fro has incited the passion of worry and has managed to tear the worried one loose from earthboundness, that is, from willing to be what he is intended to be, it looks for a moment as if the comparison were coming to take the worried one to the desired goal; it certainly does come and fetch him, but only as death comes to fetch a person—it lets the worried one perish in the suspension of despondency.

Now, if a person, not without smiling, can think about the lily's anxiety to become a Crown Imperial, think about its dying on the way—oh, may that person bear in mind that it is rather something to weep over that a human being is just as foolishly worried, just as foolishly—but, no, how do I dare to leave things undecided this way, how do I dare in earnest to accuse the divinely appointed teachers, the lilies in the field, this way. No, the lily is not worried this way, and this is why we should learn from it. And if a human being, like the lily, is contented with being a human being, he does not become sick with temporal worries; and if he does not become worried about temporal things, he remains in the place assigned to him; and if he remains there, then it is true that he, by being a human being, is more glorious than Solomon's glory.

So what does the worried person learn from the lilies? He learns to be contented with being a human being and not to be worried about diversity among human beings; he learns to speak just as tersely, just as solemnly, and just as inspiringly about being a human being as the Gospel speaks tersely about the lilies. And this is indeed also the human custom, especially on the most solemn occasions. Let us consider Solomon. When he puts on his royal purple robes and sits majestically on his throne in all his glory—well, then there is also ceremonial address, and the one speaking says: Your Majesty. But when the most solemn term of address is to be used in the

VIII
259

eternal language of earnestness, then we say: Man! We use the very same term of address for the lowliest person when he, like Lazarus, is sunk, almost unidentifiable, in poverty and wretchedness—we say: Man! And in the decisive moment in a person's life when the choice of diversity is enjoined, we say to him: Man! And in the decisive moment of death when all diversities are abolished, we say: Man! Yet this does not mean that we are speaking disdainfully. On the contrary, we are using the highest term of address, because to be a human being is not lower than the diversities but is raised above them, inasmuch as this, the essentially equal glory among all human beings, is certainly not the sad equality of death, any more than it is the essential equality among all the lilies, which is their equality in loveliness. VIII
260

All *worldly* worry has its basis in a person's unwillingness to be contented with being a human being, in his worried craving for distinction by way of comparison. One does not, however, dare to say directly and summarily that *earthly* and *temporal* worry is an invention of comparison, because in actual straitened circumstances a person does not discover his need for food and clothing by way of comparison; the one who lived in solitude among the lilies in the field would also discover it. Worry about making a living, or, as it is more commonly put in a sorrowful plural, worries about making a living are not exactly an invention of comparison. It is nevertheless another matter whether in countless ways comparison does not equivocally play a part in the definition of what is to be understood by worry over making a living, whether there should not be . . . . . but, no, in order to avoid comparison the worried person will be very reluctant to have any *other* human being talk to him about it. Very well, then, let us put it this way: Should one not be able to learn a lot from the birds about this worry.

We shall now consider: *how the one whom worry about making a living causes distress learns to be contented with being a human being by properly paying attention to the birds of the air.*

"*Look at the birds of the air.*" Look at them, that is, pay close attention to them—in the same way as the fisherman comes in the morning to look at the line that has been out all night, in the same way as the physician comes and looks at the patient, in the same way as the child stands and looks when the adult is doing something the child has never seen before. This is how one must pay close attention to the birds—not with a divided mind and distracted thoughts, but with concentrated attention and reflection, if possible in wonder. If someone were to say: One sees a bird so often; there is certainly nothing remarkable about that—well, then he has not understood the invitation in the Gospel text about the birds of the air.

"*The birds of the air*," or, as it says somewhere else, "the birds under the heavens."[10] Of course, we do indeed see birds down near the earth, see them on the ground, but if we are really to benefit from looking at them we must see them under the heavens or at least continually bear in mind that they are at home under the heavens. If by continually seeing a bird on the earth anyone could forget that it was a bird of the air, he would have prevented himself from understanding the Gospel about the birds of the air.

VIII
261
"*They sow not and reap not and gather not into barns.*" Indeed, how could that sort of thing be done up there where the birds have their haunts—under the heavens, there where they live without temporality's foresight, unaware of time, in the moment. The person of foresight on earth learns from time to use time, and when he has his barn full from a *past* time and is provided for in the *present* time, he still takes care to sow seed for a future harvest so that in turn he can have his barn full for a *future* time. This is why three words are used to describe the work of foresight. It is not said tersely as about the lilies—they do not work. These three words suggest the time category that underlies foresight. "*And yet your heavenly Father feeds them.*" The heavenly Father, yes, it clearly must be he who does it if the observer attends to the birds—under the heavens—because there where morning, noon, and night the farmer comes out and calls the birds together and gives them food, there the observer can easily make a mistake and think that it is the

farmer who feeds the birds. But out there where there is no farmer—out in the field, there where there is no storehouse—under the heavens, up there where the carefree birds, without sowing or harvesting or gathering into barns, and without worrying about making a living, soar lightly over forest and lake: there it certainly must be the heavenly Father who feeds them. "He feeds them," or should we perhaps foolishly say what many a foolish farmer has no doubt said, "The birds steal," so it is still actually the farmer who feeds the birds because they steal—namely, from him. Ah, if a person's thinking has sunk so deeply into wretched paltriness that in annoyed seriousness he could think anything like that, how indeed could he learn loftiness from the birds of the air, how could it help him to look at the birds of the air! And yet it certainly should help him if only he would *look at them*, that is, pay close attention to them, learn all over again, learn to forget the wretched sensibleness that inhumanly made his soul so small-minded. No, the heavenly Father feeds the birds and does so even if they do not sow or harvest or gather into barns—that is, the heavenly Father also feeds the creatures who do sow and harvest and gather into barns, and therefore the one who supports himself should learn from the birds of the air that it nevertheless is the heavenly Father who feeds him. But the one who possesses nothing, nothing at all, on earth, the one who in this way also lives "under the heavens," the one who sorrowfully perceives that he is quite close to joyful kinship with the birds of the air—that person learns that the heavenly Father feeds them.

"Look at the birds of the air—your heavenly Father feeds them." How brief, how solemn, how impartial these words are. All the birds are mentioned, not a single one is forgotten in the discourse, which states that the heavenly Father, he who opens his gentle hand and satisfies with blessing everything that lives,[11] does not forget a single one. In the Gospel about the birds there is not the slightest hint of any difference, that perhaps the one was richly supplied, the other meagerly, that perhaps the one had provision for a somewhat longer time, the other only the necessities of the moment, that once in a while a

VIII
262

particular one had to wait, wait in vain, perhaps had to go to bed hungry—no, it speaks only about the birds and that the heavenly Father feeds them.

Yet perhaps someone says, "If a bird gets too little to eat once in a while, if a bird also dies of hunger—that really would not be so awful." How would a human being have the heart to talk about birds that way! Is not worry about making a living essentially the same whether a bird has it or a human being? Would a human being superiorly disregard this worry if only birds were familiar with it and human beings were exempted? Or would it be unreasonable of the bird to be worried about such trivialities but not unreasonable of the reasonable human being to be worried about the same trivialities? Just suppose that the life of birds is not unfamiliar with the diversity related to making a living, something that unfortunately is such an issue among human beings; just suppose that this diversity occupies and worries the birds in the same way it worries human beings.

In the same way—if this is assumed, then the discourse can avoid what the worried person loathes, that *another* person speaks to him about his worry—then the discourse can stay out in the field with the birds and speak about *the bird's worry*.

Once upon a time there was a wood-dove; it had its nest in the scowling forest, out there where wonder lives in apprehension among the secluded tall trees. But not far away, where smoke rises from the farmer's house, lived some of its distant relatives, some tame doves. It met a pair of them occasionally. The wood-dove sat on a branch that stretched out over the farmyard; the two tame doves sat on the ridge of the roof; yet the separation was not so great that they could not exchange ideas in conversation. One day they talked about the condition of things at the time and about making a living. The wood-dove said, "Up until now I have made my living by letting each day have its own troubles, and in that way I get through the world." The tame dove had listened closely, not without feeling a certain pleasurable movement throughout its whole body that is called preening, and then replied, "No, we manage differently; with us, that is, with the rich farmer with whom we live, one's future is secure. When harvest time comes, I or my mate, one of us, sits up on the roof and watches. Then the farmer drives one load of grain into the barn after the other, and when he has driven in so many that I lose count I know that there is provision enough for a long time. I know it from experience." Having said this, it turned, not without a certain self-satisfaction, to its mate sitting close by as if to say, "We two are well provided for, aren't we, my little mate."

The wood-dove went home and pondered this matter. It was promptly struck by the thought that it must be very pleasant to *know* that one's living was secured for a long time, whereas it was miserable to live continually in uncertainty so that one never dares to say that one *knows* one is provided for. "Therefore the best thing," it said to itself, "is to see if you cannot manage to gather a greater stockpile that you could store here or there in a very safe place."

The next morning the wood-dove woke earlier than usual and was so busy gleaning and hoarding that it scarcely had time to eat or to eat its fill. But a fate seemed to hang over it, that it would not be allowed to accumulate abundance, because every time it had collected a little supply and hidden it away in one or another of the presumably safe places—it was gone when the wood-dove came to look for it. Meanwhile there was no essential change about making a living. Every day it found its food just as before, and if it helped itself to a bit less, that was because it wanted to collect and because it did not take time to eat— otherwise it was richly supplied as before. Yet, alas, it had undergone a big change; it was far from suffering actual need, but it had acquired an *idea* of need in the future. It had lost its peace of mind—it had acquired *worry about making a living*.

From now on the wood-dove was worried. Its feathers lost their iridescence; its flight lost its buoyancy. Its day was passed in a fruitless attempt to accumulate abundance; its dreams were fancy's impotent plans. It was no longer joyful—indeed, it was almost as if the wood-dove had become envious of the wealthy doves. It found its food each day, ate its fill, and yet it was, so to speak, not full, because in its worry about making a living it hungered for a long time. It had trapped itself in a snare in which no fowler could trap it, in which only the free can trap

VIII
264

himself: in the idea. "Quite true," it said to itself, "quite true, if I get as much as I can eat every day, I do indeed make my living; the big stockpile I wish to gather I could not eat at one time, and in a certain sense one cannot do more than eat one's fill, but it would be very pleasant to be freed from this uncertainty that makes one so dependent." "It may well be," it said to itself, "that the tame doves pay dearly for their secure living; it may well be that when all is said and done they have many worries from which I have been free until now, but this security for the future keeps running in my mind. Ah, why did I become a poor wood-dove and not one of the wealthy doves!" It noted that it was becoming exhausted from cares, but then it talked reasonably to itself, yet not so reasonably that it expelled worry from its thoughts and put its mind to rest but in such a way that it convinced itself that its cares were legitimate. "After all, I am not asking for something unreasonable," it said, "or for something impossible; I am not asking to become like the wealthy farmer but merely like one of the wealthy doves."

Finally it contrived a scheme. One day it flew over and sat between the tame doves on the ridge of the farmer's roof. Then it observed that there was a place where the two flew in, and it also flew in, because surely the storeroom had to be there. But when the farmer came in the evening and shut the dovecote, he immediately discovered the strange dove. It was placed in a little box by itself until the next day, when it was killed—and delivered from its worry about getting a living. Alas, the worried wood-dove had not only trapped itself in worry but had also trapped itself in the dovecote—unto death.

If the wood-dove had been contented with being what it was, a bird of the air, it would have had its living, the heavenly Father would have fed it; in the state of uncertainty it would have remained where it belonged, out there where the secluded tall trees are in melancholy harmony with the cooing trill of the wood-dove. Then it would have been the bird about whom the pastor spoke on Sunday when he repeated the words of the Gospel: Look at the bird of the air; it sows not and reaps not and gathers not into barns, yet your heavenly Father feeds it.

The wood-dove is the human being—but no, let us not
forget that only out of respect for the worried one has the
discourse let the wood-dove be the victim. Just as when a royal
child is brought up there is a poor child who takes the punishment instead of the prince, so the discourse has let the wood-
dove pay for it all. And the wood-dove has willingly put up
with it, because it knows very well that it is one of the divinely
appointed teachers from whom we should learn, but the
teacher sometimes does this in order to demonstrate personally
the error he wants to caution against. The wood-dove itself is
free from cares—indeed, it actually is the bird of which the
Gospel speaks. So the wood-dove is the human being. When he,
like it, is content with being a human being, he understands—
something he learns from the bird of the air—that the heavenly
Father feeds him. But if the heavenly Father feeds him, then he,
of course, is free from worry about making a living, then he
lives not only as the tame doves do with the rich farmer but
lives with him who is richer than all. He actually lives with
him, since heaven and earth is God's house and property, and
thus the human being is indeed living with him.

This means: to be contented with being a human being, with
being the humble one, the created being who can no more
support himself than create himself. But if a human being
wants to forget God and support himself, then we have worry
about making a living. It is certainly praiseworthy and pleasing
to God that a person sows and reaps and gathers into barns, that
he works in order to obtain food; but if he wants to forget God
and thinks he supports himself by his labors, then he has worry
about making a living. [12]If the wealthiest man who has ever
lived forgets God and thinks he supports himself, he has worry
about making a living. Let us not talk foolishly and narrow-
mindedly by saying that the wealthy man is free from worry
about making a living and the poor man is not. No, only that
person is free who is contented with being a human being and
thereby understands that the heavenly Father feeds him—and
this, of course, the poor can understand just as well as the
wealthy.

Worry about making a living is therefore the snare in which no external power, no *actuality* can trap a person, but in which only he can trap himself, the rich as well as the poor—if he is unwilling to be contented with being a human being. If, namely, he is unwilling to be contented with that, what is the something more that he demands? The something more is: to be himself his own providence for all his life or perhaps merely for tomorrow; and if that is what he wants, then he walks— *cunningly*—into the snare, the wealthy as well as the poor. Thus he wants to entrench himself, so to speak, in a little or large area where he will not be the object of God's providence and the supporting care of the heavenly Father. He may not perceive, before it is too late, that in this entrenched security he is living—in a prison. He himself is doing what the farmer did with the dove—he is shutting the dovecote and thinks that now he is secure, and now he is in fact trapped or, to put it another way, now he is in fact excluded from the care [*Omsorg*] of providence and abandoned to worry about making a living [*Næringssorg*]. Only that person is trapped and shut out who in the thought of supporting himself has shut himself in with his much or his meager possessions; and only that person is free and without worry about making a living who with his much or his meager possessions, yes, in poverty, understands that the heavenly Father feeds him. And from the spiritual point of view, that person who in the presumptuous sense has cunningly shut himself in and thereby trapped himself, has in fact, like the wood-dove, trapped himself unto death.

VIII
266

Thus it already becomes apparent that worry about making a living is produced by comparison—here, namely, in the terrible way that the human being is not contented with being a human being but wants to compare himself to God, wants to have a security by himself, which no human dares to have, and therefore this security is in fact—worry about making a living.

But it is apparent also in other ways that worry about making a living is produced by comparison, insofar as the worry about making a living is not the actual pressing need of the day today but is the idea of a future need. The comparison is again produced by a person's unwillingness to be contented with

being a human being. The poor bird of the air compared itself
with the rich birds and through this comparison discovered
worry about making a living. What it means to be hungry and
to find food it had known for a long time, but never before did
it have worry about making a living. Since these categories,
rich and poor, are now not separated from each other by a
chasmic abyss, since on the contrary they have contact in continual association and constant boundary disputes, and since,
moreover, the different view accordingly changes the concept,
as a result the third category of comparison can be very different. Worried about making a living, the worried person is
unwilling to be contented with being a human being but wants
to be different or to have diversity, wants to be rich, indepen-
dently wealthy, prosperous, fairly secure, etc. In other words,
he does not look at the bird of the air—away from the diversity
of human life—but he looks comparingly at others, at the
diversity, and his worry about making a living is a relation of
comparison.

Even if in making comparisons the worried person does not
fix his attention on degrees of difference and does not regard as
worry about making a living *that* which is more a worldly   VIII
concern (since to be concerned about having just as much as   267
this one and that one is certainly not worry about making a
living), even if this is not the case, comparison nevertheless lies
at the root of the worry about making a living, insofar as this
does not manifest the actual need but the imagined need. Why
is it that the bird does not have worry about making a living?
Because it does not compare one day with another, because in
accord with the words of the Gospel it lets each day have its
own trouble. But even if the worried person does not compare
his condition with anyone else's and in this sense "keeps himself unstained from the world"[13] (alas, comparison is perhaps
one of the most corrupting kinds of defilement)—yet, if he
anxiously compares one day with another, if on the day he has
rich abundance he says: But tomorrow! and if on the day he
feels the pinch of scarcity he says: Tomorrow will be even
worse—then he certainly is making comparisons.

Now, if such a worried person would read this and would

not become impatient with the speaker! I have no objection to doing what a pagan wise man did out of respect for the subject of the discourse: he covered his face.[14] Thus out of respect for the worry I shall willingly cover my face, so that I see no one but speak only about the bird of the air. Indeed, it was through this kind of comparison that the wood-dove discovered worry about making a living in worry's sorrowful association with itself day after day. It did admit that it had its living, but the uncertainty saddened it; it seemed to become so dependent— upon God. It grieved because it never dared to speak with certainty about the next day. But let us not forget that in a godly sense it dared to speak with certainty when it said: The heavenly Father will surely feed me tomorrow. Let us not for- get that it spoke with the greatest certainty about the following day if in all sincerity it restricted itself simply to thanking for today! Is this not the way it is? If a girl in love said to her beloved when he came to visit her, "You will come again tomorrow, won't you?"—there would still be some anxiety in her love. But if, without mentioning tomorrow, she threw her arms around his neck and said, "Oh, thank you for coming today"— then she would indeed be altogether assured about tomorrow. Or if there were two girls, and the one said to her beloved, "You will come again tomorrow, won't you?" and the other said, "Oh, thank you for coming today"—which of the two would be more convinced that the beloved would come again tomorrow?

A useless and perhaps futile conflict goes on often enough in the world when the poor person says to the wealthy person, "Sure, it's easy for you—you are free from worry about mak- ing a living." Would to God that the poor person would really understand how the Gospel is much more kindly disposed to him, is treating him equally and more lovingly. Truly, the Gospel does not let itself be deceived by the illusion of visible diversity, does not let itself be deceived into taking sides with anyone against someone else, with someone who is wealthy against someone who is poor, or with someone who is poor against someone who is wealthy. Not to have worry about making a living is truly well pleasing in God's eyes. Should, then, the wealthy summarily have this advantage and the poor be shut out? Indeed not. If the poor person would really be contented with being a human being and learn from the birds of the air to be without worry about making a living, he would in simplicity raise himself above the apparent diversity; he might sometime be prompted to say: The poor wealthy person, he really does have worry about making a living. What human being can legitimately and truthfully say these words, "I have no worry about making a living"? If the rich person points to his wealth as he says it, I wonder if there is a trace of sense in his words! Is he not simultaneously and scandalously contradicting himself, he who clutches his worries about making a living at the same time that he is keeping them away by means of his treasure, and in his worry about making a living cares for it and increases it! Indeed, if the rich person were to give away all his possessions, throw away his money and his worry about making a living, and say: I have no worry about making a living—then and only then would there be any sense in his words. And this is indeed the situation of the poor man when he, who owns nothing and thus has nothing to throw away, casts his worry about making a living upon God[15] and says: I have no worry about making a living. Is it not so that the wealth must go if there is to be any possible sense in the words? Would it not be a scandalous contradiction for someone who owned a costly collection of excellent medicines that he used every day to say as he pointed at the medicines: I am not sick!

Among individuals in the world, the conflict of discontented comparison is frequently carried on about dependence and independence, about the happiness of being independent and the difficulty of being dependent. And yet, yet human language has not ever, and thought has not ever, invented a more beautiful symbol of independence than the poor bird of the air. And yet, yet no speech can be more curious than to say that it must be very hard and heavy to be—light as the bird! To be dependent on one's treasure—that is dependence and hard and heavy slavery; to be dependent on God, completely dependent—that is independence. The worried wood-dove foolishly feared to be completely dependent on God and therefore ceased to be

VIII
269

independent and to be the symbol of independence, ceased to be the poor bird of the air that is completely dependent on God. Dependence on God is the only independence, because God has no gravity; only the things of this earth, especially earthly treasure, have that—therefore the person who is completely dependent on him is light. So it is with the poor person when he, contented with being a human being, looks at the bird of the air, looks up at it under the heavens, as indeed one who is praying always looks up, one who is praying—no, he, the independent person, is indeed one who gives thanks.

To be contented with being a human being. This was what the discourse was about, and how the worried one learned this from the lilies in the field and the birds of the air, how, on the other hand, comparison generated worldly worries, and how it generated worry about making a living. It was, to be sure, a human being who spoke, but assisted by the lilies and the birds he spoke about the lilies and the birds. Thus, that he is the speaker involves no comparison with any other human being, as if he had any advantage by being the speaker. [16]No, here again there is equality in relation to the divinely appointed teachers: the lilies in the field and the birds of the air.

II

[How Glorious It Is to Be
a Human Being]

If it is so that cares and worry, especially the longer and the more deeply they penetrate into the soul or the longer they penetrate it deeply, also become fixed all the more firmly, then it is surely beneficial to think of a diversion for the worried person, although not in the sense the world too frequently and foolishly recommends the wild tempo or noisy anesthesia of empty diversion. When the worried one feels abandoned and yet, through a self-contradiction in his cares, does not want sympathy because, pinching and pressing, it comes too close to him, so that he winces almost as much from the sympathy as from the pain—then one leads him into surroundings where nothing reminds him of his cares, not even of sympathy, sur-roundings where sympathy is and yet is not, so to speak, sur-roundings that have the moving intimacy of sympathy, insofar as it is somewhat present, and also the soothing distance of sympathy, insofar as it still is not sympathy.

So the Gospel read earlier leads the worried one out into the field, into surroundings that will weave him into the great common life, that will win him for the great fellowship of existence. But since worry has become firmly fixed in him, it is a matter of doing something to get his eyes and his mind away from it. To that end, the Gospel recommends two helpful movements. When the worried one "looks at the lily" at his feet, he is looking *downward*; and when he is looking down at the lily, he does not see the worry. It is certainly possible that in his cares he ordinarily walked with his head down and looked at his worry, but if he looks down in order to look at the lily, then he is looking away from the worry. If he, in compliance with the instructions of the Gospel, looks at the bird of the air, then he is looking *upward*, and if he is looking up at the bird, he does not see the worry. It is certainly possible that in his cares he also sometimes looked upward when he sent a troubled sigh up to God and gazed after it with a worried look, but if he is looking upward in order to see the bird of the air, he is looking away from the worry. How would one better characterize the firm fixations of the worry in a person's soul than to say that it is like the *staring* of the eyes. When the eyes are staring, they are looking fixedly ahead, are continually looking at one thing, and yet they are not actually seeing, because, as science explains, the eyes see their own seeing. But then the physician says: Move your eyes. And thus the Gospel says: Divert your mind—look down at the lily and quit staring at the worry; look up at the bird and quit staring at the worry. Then when the tears stop while the eyes are looking down at the lily, is it not as if it were the lily that wiped away the tears! When the wind dries the tears in the eyes that watch the bird, is it not as if it were the bird that wiped away the tears! Even if the beloved sits with one and wipes away one's tears if the worried person still keeps on crying—is this really wiping away the tears? But the one who brings the worried person to stop crying—that one wipes away the tears.

This is what we dare to call a *godly diversion*, which does not, like the empty and worldly diversion, incite impatience and nourish the worry, but diverts, calms, and persuades the more devoutly one gives oneself over to it. Human sagacity has invented a great deal to entertain and divert the mind, and yet the law for this kind of invention ridicules the useless effort by its self-contradiction. The artifice itself is in the service of impatience; it teaches how to compress the multitude of diversions more and more impatiently into the fleeting moment. The more this sagacity increases, the more it works against itself, since the diversion turns out to cover a shorter and shorter time as the artifice increases.

Let us take an example in which the empty and worldly diversion manifests itself as fragile and self-contradictory as it is. The fireworks exhibitor certainly wants to delight the eye and divert the mind by igniting the artificial flaring transiency in the darkness of the night. Yet the spectator becomes weary if it lasts just an hour; if there is just a little moment between each new firing, the spectator grows weary. Thus the task of sagacity is to finish it off faster and faster; the ultimate, the consummate thing to do would be to fire off the whole lot in a few minutes. [17]But if diversion is designed to pass away the time, the self-contradiction is clear: namely, the diversion, when it is most highly perfected in refinement, can pass away the time for only a few minutes—then the more appallingly it becomes patently clear how long the time is. For a fee one purchases the opportunity to wait in impatient tension for the beginning of the entertainment, and at the very same moment it is over. Just as that delusive flare flashes and instantly vanishes into nothing, so also must be the soul of one who knows only this kind of diversion—in the minute of the diversion he despairs over the length of time.

How different it is with the godly diversion! Have you ever looked at the starlit sky, and have you ever really found a more dependable sight! It costs nothing, and so there is no incitement of impatience; nothing is said about this evening, even less about ten o'clock sharp. Oh no, it waits for you, although in another sense it does not wait for you—the stars now twinkling in the night have done so, unchanged, for centuries. Just as God makes himself invisible—ah, perhaps this is why many never really become aware of him—so also the starry heaven makes itself insignificant, so to speak—ah, perhaps this is why there are many who have never really seen it. Divine majesty disdains the visible, the falsely conspicuous; the solemnity of the starry heaven is more than unpretentious. Ah, but if you stand still, if perhaps with no purpose in mind you went out there where it is visible, unnoticed year after year, if you by chance halted and looked upward—you surely have sensed it: the persuasion mounts with every instant; more and more movingly it steals the temporal from you; with every moment you continue to contemplate it, that which ought to be forgotten sinks into deeper and deeper oblivion. O godly diversion, you do not perfidiously and traitorously call yourself a diversion while at the same time with empty noise, with darting

VIII
272

impatience, you are in league with boredom, into which you
plunge people deeper and deeper—by means of diversion. No,
you are in league with the eternal, and therefore only the beginning is difficult; when that is made, then the stillness of diversion grows, and in that stillness grows the persuasion.

[18]Everything in nature is like this; it seems insignificant and
yet is so infinitely rich. Therefore, if you go hurrying along
your way on an important errand and the road takes you along
the seacoast, watch out! True, there is no one who is calling to
you, no invitation is heard, neither the barker's voice nor the
cannon's thunder as at human entertainments; and yet, watch
out, make haste, lest by standing still for a moment you perhaps discover in the undulating waves the persuasion of uniformity. So it is also with the lily in the field and the bird of the air.
If you are hurrying "to your field, to your business, to your
wife,"[19] and a bird flies past you, do not look after it, because
then you might stand much too long watching the bird. If it is
work time, during which one should tend to one's job, if the
reaper dexterously whets his scythe and swings it against the
grain, let him not look at the lily at his feet lest it so persuade
him that both the lily and the reaper are left standing there.

But the worried one, he is not warned. On the contrary, the
Gospel urges him to go out to the field and then to stand still in
order to look at the lily and the bird, so that this godly diversion might cause the fixedly staring eyes to move, might divert
the mind in which the worry has become firmly fixed. Look at
the lily, see how lovely it is there at your feet; do not disdain
it—after all, it is waiting for you to delight in its loveliness! See
how it sways to and fro, shakes off everything in order to go on
being lovely! See how it regales itself in the wind, exercises as it
were, so that, calm once again, it may rejoice in its happy
existence! See how gentle it is, always willing to jest and to
play, whereas by yielding it is victorious over the most violent
storm and endures it! Look at the bird under the heavens. See
how it flies; perhaps it is coming from far away, from distant,
distant happier realms—so they do, after all, exist! Perhaps it is
flying away, far away to distant, distant realms—so let it take
your worry with it! This it does without detecting the burden,

provided you just keep on watching it. See how it is now standing still; it is resting—in that infinite space. Thus it is resting there where no rest seems possible! See how it finds its path, and what path through all the hardships and adversities of human life is as difficult, as unfathomable as "the bird's mysterious path through the air!" Thus there is a path and a path to be found where a path seems an impossibility.

Yet, since all diversion is not only to pass the time but is to serve primarily to give the worried one something else to think about, we shall now consider how the worried person who looks at the lily and the bird with the help of the godly diversion [*Adspredelse*] that disperses [*sprede*] the fogs has something other than the worry to think about, how by forgetting the worry in the diversion he is led to consider: _{VIII 274}

how glorious it is to be a human being.

"*If, then, God so clothes the grass of the field . . . . . would he not much more clothe you, you of little faith!*" Hence God clothes the grass, or the grass is clothed. The beautifully shaped spathe of the stalk, the delicate lines of the leaves, the lovely shades and blends of colors, the whole opulence, if I may put it this way, of ribbons and bows and finery—all this belongs to the lily's clothing, and it is God who clothes it this way. "Would he not much more clothe you, you of little faith?" "*You of little faith.*" This is the admonition's gentle reproach; this is how love speaks to someone who is in the wrong when it does not have the heart to speak rigorously. It shakes its finger reproachfully at him and says, "You of little faith," but says it so gently that the reproach does not wound, does not distress, does not depress, but instead lifts up and gives bold confidence. If a child came distressed to the adult and asked for something the child did in fact have and had had for a long time but was not aware of and therefore thought that it should ask for it in order to get it instead of giving thanks for having it, I wonder if the adult might not gently reproach the child and say, "Yes, my dear child, you will surely have it tomorrow, you of little faith!" That is, once you come to a better understanding, you surely will appreciate that you have it, that you have always had it, and that it was therefore a kind of ingratitude, although excusable, indeed, becoming to a child, for you to ask for—what you had.

But if this is what the words mean, then the Gospel text declares not only that the human being is clothed as the grass is clothed but that he is clothed far more gloriously. With the help of the added reproach (you of little faith), what is actually said is: Would God not much more *have* clothed you. Thus the text is not about the new dress one would like to have for Sunday, or about the new dress coat one needs so badly, but about ingratitude's wanting to forget how gloriously the human being is clothed from God's hand. Would there not be a discrepancy in the text if the first statement was that the lily is more gloriously clothed than Solomon and the last was: Would God not much more clothe you? Would it not be a discrepancy if the last part was to be interpreted to mean the few pieces of clothing a person may need?

VIII
275

Let us consider this matter properly. The lily is said to be clothed, but this of course must not be understood to mean that the lily's existence is one thing and having clothes on is something else—no, to be a lily is its clothing. Taken this way, would not the human being be much more gloriously clothed? Or would the human being, in his anxiety over articles of clothing, be allowed to forget the first clothing totally? You of little faith, you ingrate with your imaginary need, you worried one, even if your need is so great that you totally forget how God has clothed you—learn from the ant to become wise, but learn from the lily how glorious it is to be a human being, how gloriously you are clothed, you of little faith.

Worldly worry always seeks to lead a human being into the small-minded unrest of comparisons, away from the lofty calmness of simple thoughts. To be clothed, then, means to be a human being—and therefore to be well clothed. Worldly worry is preoccupied with clothes and the dissimilarity of clothes. Is this not like the child who comes distressed and asks for what it has and to whom the adult with gentle reproach says: You will surely have it tomorrow, you of little faith? The Gospel wants first of all to remind even a destitute person not to forget completely how gloriously he is clothed by God.

Moreover, we all are far from being needy in the more serious and strict sense of the word. But we all are perhaps much too inclined to worry about clothes and ungrateful enough to forget the first thoughts—and the first clothing. But by looking at the lily the worried one is reminded to compare his clothing with the lily's—even if poverty has clothed him in rags.

Should not, then, the invitation to learn from the lilies be welcome to everyone just as the reminder is useful to him! Alas, those great, uplifting, simple thoughts, those first thoughts, are more and more forgotten, perhaps entirely forgotten in the weekday and worldly life of comparisons. The one human being compares himself with others, the one generation compares itself with the other, and thus the heaped-up pile of comparisons overwhelms a person. As the ingenuity and busyness increase, there come to be more and more in each generation who slavishly work a whole lifetime far down in the low underground regions of comparisons. Indeed, just as miners never see the light of day, so these unhappy people VIII never come to see the light: those uplifting, simple thoughts, 276 those first thoughts about how glorious it is to be a human being. And up there in the higher regions of comparison, smiling vanity plays its false game and deceives the happy ones so that they receive no impression from those lofty, simple thoughts, those first thoughts.

To be ruler. Yes, what conflict there is about that in the world, whether it is about ruling over kingdoms and countries, over thousands, or about having at least one human being to rule over—besides oneself, over whom no one cares to rule. But out there in the field with the lilies, where every human being who in stillness and solitude suckles the milk of those first thoughts is what every human being is divinely destined to be, is a ruler—indeed, out there no one wants to be a ruler! To be a prodigy. Ah, what efforts are made in the world to achieve this envied position, and what efforts envy makes to prevent it! But out there in the field with the lilies, where every human being is what God has made him to be, is the wonder of creation; indeed, out there no one wants to be a prodigy!

The better individual would no doubt smile, and the strident laughter of the crowd would ridicule the fool who could talk in this sense about being a ruler and about being a prodigy. And yet what can the preacher mean with the words, "that God isolated the human being in order to see whether he would regard himself as a beast"?[20] The person who is unwilling to be calmed, comforted, built up, and uplifted in isolation by the unconditional character of those first thoughts, who wants to devote himself to disappearing and perishing in the futile service of comparisons, regards himself as a beast, no matter whether by way of comparison he was distinguished or lowly. This is why God isolated the human being, made every human being this separate and distinct individual, which is implied in the unconditional character of those first thoughts. The individual animal is not isolated, is no unconditionally separate entity; the individual animal is a number and belongs under what that most famous pagan thinker has called the animal category: the crowd.[21] The human being who in despair turns away from those first thoughts in order to plunge into the crowd of comparisons makes himself a number, regards himself as a beast, no matter whether he by way of comparison became distinguished or lowly.

But with the lilies the worried one is isolated, far away from all human or, perhaps more correctly, inhuman comparisons between individuals. Indeed, not even the one who has turned his back on the largest city in the world has left behind him such a motley crowd, such a confused and enormous multiplicity, as the person who turned his back on inhuman comparisons—in order, as a human being, to compare his clothing with the lily's.

VIII
277

By clothing, then, must be understood, as indicated here, what it is to be a human being. Even a pagan was aware of this.[22] He did not understand attributing everything to God, but he believed that it was the soul that, like a weaver, as he ingeniously put it, itself wove the body, which is the human being's clothing. And now in utter wonder[23] he praised the ingenious creation of the human body and its glory, with which no plant or animal could sustain any comparison. In his thoughts he brought into existence, so to speak, what is the distinguishing mark of being human: the upright walk, and as he simulated it in his thinking his mind was uplifted. He wondered over the ingeniousness of the human eye and even more over expression in the eyes, because the animal has eyes but only the human being has expression in the eyes. This is also why in the beautiful native language of that man of wonder the human being is called the upright, yet in such a way as to suggest a double meaning—first, that the human frame is erect and upright like the straight tree trunk and, next, that the erect and upright being directs his vision upward. Even though the straight tree trunk rises higher, with the aid of vision the erect and upright one proudly lifts his head higher than the mountains. The human being, then, stands erect and—commanding; and this is why it seemed so glorious to that man of wonder that the human being is the only creature that has hands, for the ruler, after all, stretches out his hand when he commands. Thus in many ways that man of wonder knew how to speak gloriously about the human being's glorious clothing.

Many perhaps have spoken more learnedly, more insightfully, and more scientifically about this, but, wondrously enough, no one has spoken with a greater sense of wonder than that noble wise man [Socrates], who did not begin with doubting about everything, but, on the contrary, when he had become old, when he had seen and heard and experienced much, he really began *to wonder*, to wonder about that *simple first thought*, to which no one ordinarily pays attention, not even the scholars and scientists, since such people do not occupy themselves with this—as an object of wonder. But this discourse on wonder is imperfect inasmuch as it assigns the clothing to the soul. Most imperfect of all, indeed, simply foolish, is the discourse that so utterly forgets the solemn first thought that it summarily and thoughtlessly regards being a human beingas if it were nothing, empties it, and promptly commences the foolishness about pieces of clothing, about trousers and jackets, about purple and ermine. But also imperfect is the discourse that, although aware of the first thought, is not really aware of God. No, if a human being is going to compare himself to the lily, he has to say: All that I am by being a human being— VIII
278

that is my clothing. I am responsible for none of it, but glorious it is.

Now, how should we speak about this glory? We could go on speaking for a long time without ever finishing, but this is not the place for that. Let us therefore speak briefly instead and concentrate everything on that one single verse that Scripture itself uses with authority: *God created the human being in his image*,[24] but again for the sake of brevity let us understand this verse with regard to only one thing.

God created the human being in his image. Must it not be glorious to be clothed in this way! In praise of the lily, the Gospel declares that it surpasses Solomon in glory. Must it not be infinitely more glorious to resemble God! The lily does not resemble God—no, it does not do that. It bears a little mark by which it reminds one of God; it has a witness, since God has not let himself be without witness in anything created, but the lily does not resemble him.

When a person sees his image in the mirror of the ocean, he sees his own image, but the ocean is not his image, and when he departs the image disappears. The ocean is not the image and cannot keep the image. Why is this, except for the reason that the visible form by its very visibility is powerless (just as the physical presence makes it impossible to be omnipresent); therefore it cannot reproduce itself in another in such a way that the other keeps the image when the form departs. But God is spirit, is invisible, and the image of invisibility, of course, is in turn invisibility. Thus the invisible Creator reproduces himself in the invisibility, which is the qualification of spirit, and the image of God is explicitly the invisible glory. If God were visible, well, then no one could resemble him or be his image, because the image of all that is visible *does not exist*, and in all that is visible there is nothing, not even a leaf, that resembles another or is its image. If that were the case, then the image would be the object itself. But since God is invisible, no one can *visibly* resemble him. The lily does not resemble God, precisely because the glory of the lily is visible, and therefore the pagan spoke imperfectly about the human being even when he spoke very consummately about the glory of the human body but said nothing about the invisible God's creation of every human being in his image.

To be spirit, that is the human being's invisible glory. Thus when the worried one out in the field stands surrounded by all the witnesses, when every single flower says to him, "Remember God!" he replies, "I will indeed do that, my children—I will worship him, and you poor little ones cannot do that." Consequently the erect, upright one is a worshiper. The upright gait is the sign of distinction, but to be able to prostrate oneself in adoration and worship is even more glorious; and all nature is like the great staff of servants who remind the human being, the ruler, about worshiping God. This is what is expected, not that the human being is to come and assume the command, which is also glorious and is assigned to him,[25] but that worshiping he shall praise the Creator, something nature cannot do, since it can only remind the human being about doing that. It is glorious to be clothed as the lily, even more glorious to be the erect and upright ruler, but most glorious to be nothing by worshiping!

To worship is not to rule, and yet worship is what makes the human being resemble God, and to be able truly to worship is the excellence of the invisible glory above all creation. The pagan was not aware of God and therefore sought likeness in ruling. But the resemblance is not like that—no, then instead it is taken in vain. It truly is only within the infinite diversity,[26] and this is why to worship is likeness with God just as it is the excellence above all creation. The human being and God do not resemble each other directly but inversely; only when God has infinitely become the eternal and omnipresent object of worship and the human being always a worshiper, only then do they resemble each other. If human beings want to resemble God by ruling, they have forgotten God; then God has departed and they are playing the rulers in God's absence. This was paganism; this was human life in the absence of God. This was why paganism was still like nature, and the most grievous thing that can be said about it is that it could not worship— even that noble, simple wise man, he could be silent in wonder, but he could not worship. But the ability to worship is no

VIII
279

visible glory, it cannot be seen, and yet nature's visible glory sighs; it pleads with the ruler, it incessantly reminds the human being that whatever he does he absolutely must not forget—to worship. Oh, how glorious to be a human being!

But then in his diversion with the lilies the worried one had acquired something quite different from his worry to think about; he began to consider properly how glorious it is to be a human being. If in a worldly way he again forgets this amid the crisscrossing of comparisons and the clash of diversities among individuals, it is not the fault of the lilies; then it is rather because he has forgotten the lilies, forgotten that there was something he should learn from them and something he absolutely must remember to do for them. If worldly worry is to be defined with a single phrase, would we not have to say that it is worry about clothes, worry about appearances. For that very reason the upbuilding in the invisible glory is the loftiest lifting up above worldly worry—to worship is the glory and also a service that is rendered to the lily.

So it is with the lilies' teaching. We shall now consider how the worried one learns from the **bird** *how glorious it is to be a human being.*

"*The bird sows not and reaps not and gathers not into barns*"; the bird has no worries about making a living. But is this actually a perfection? Is it a perfection to be careless in danger when one does not recognize it, does not know it exists; is it a perfection to take assured steps because one is walking blindly, to walk confidently because one is sleepwalking! No, then it is certainly more truthful to say that it is a perfection to recognize the danger, to face up to the danger, to be awake, to say that it is a perfection *to be able* to have worry about making a living—precisely in order to conquer this fear, in order to let faith and trust drive out this fear so that in faith's freedom from care one truly is without worry about making a living. Only faith's freedom from care is, divinely speaking, the soaring whose beautiful but imperfect symbol is the bird's easy flight. This is why we also speak of rising on the wings of faith, and in the divine sense this wing-stroke is something perfect, the bird's wing-stroke a feeble and metaphorical suggestion. Yes, just as the weary bird slowly sinks to earth with exhausted wing-strokes, so even the proudest flight of the most daring bird is no more than earthly and temporal weariness compared with the high soaring of faith, is a slow sinking compared with faith's easy ascent.

We shall now examine this more closely. Why does the bird not have worry about making a living? Because it lives only in the moment, because there is nothing eternal in the bird. But is this indeed a perfection! On the other hand, how does the possibility of worry about making a living arise—because the eternal and the temporal touch each other in a consciousness or, more correctly, because the human being has consciousness. In his consciousness he is eternally far, far beyond the moment; no bird flew so far away, and yet for this very reason he becomes aware of the danger the bird does not suspect—when eternity came into existence for him, so also did tomorrow. By means of consciousness he discovers a world that the most widely traveled bird does not know: the future; and when this future is taken back into the moment by means of consciousness, then the worry unknown to the bird is discovered, because however far it flew and from however far away it flew back, it never flew to the future and never returned from it.

Since, then, the human being is consciousness, he is the place where the eternal and the temporal continually touch each other, where the eternal is refracted in the temporal. Time can seem long to the human being because he has the eternal in his consciousness and measures the moments with it, but time never seems long to the bird. This is why the human being has a dangerous enemy that the bird does not know—time, an enemy, yes, an enemy or a friend whose pursuits and whose association he cannot avoid because he has the eternal in his consciousness and therefore has to measure it. The temporal and the eternal can in many ways touch each other painfully in the human consciousness, but one of the especially painful contacts is worry about making a living. This worry seems infinitely remote from the eternal. This is not a matter of filling up time with some glorious accomplishment, some great idea, some uplifting feeling, as in the hours described as being lived for eternity. Alas, no, this is only a matter of lowly work in the hours that quite literally are lived for temporality, the lowly labor of producing the means of temporal subsistence. Yet the ability to have worry about making a living is a perfection and is simply suppression's expression for the loftiness of the human being, because just as high as God lifts up he also presses down just as low, but to be deeply pressed down therefore also means to be loftily lifted up. God lifted the human being high above the bird by means of the eternal in his consciousness; then in turn he pressed him down, so to speak, below the bird by his acquaintance with care, the lowly, earthly care of which the bird is ignorant. Oh, how noble it seems for the bird not to have worry about making a living—and yet how much more glorious it is to be able to have it!

Therefore the human being can certainly learn from the bird, can in fact call the bird his teacher, yet not in the highest sense. Just as the bird is without worry about making a living, so also, after all, is the child—ah, who would not willingly learn from a child! When in worry the actual or fancied need makes a person despondent, discouraged, dejected—then he is eager to find relief, eager to learn from a child, eager in his secret, grateful mind to call the child his teacher. But if the child were to start speaking and speak as a teacher, the adult would no doubt gently say, "Yes, my dear child, but this is something you do not know about." If the child kept on speaking, the adult would then call it a naughty child and perhaps not hesitate to smite—the teacher, and perhaps justifiably do that. Why? Because in an earnest sense the adult is the child's teacher and the child is the adult's teacher only in the beautiful sense of jesting earnestness. But in that case to be able to have worry about making a living is still a perfection, and the human being is by far the superior, even though, following the Gospel's instructions, he is willing to learn from the bird and in his secret, grateful mind calls it his teacher.

The bird, then, which is free from worry about making a living, is indeed a prototype for the human being, and yet, by being able to have worry about making a living, a human being has a perfection the prototype does not have. This is why he never dares to forget that the one who referred him to the bird of the air, as if for initial, childish instruction, is the very one who in earnestness and in truth is the actual prototype, that he is the very one who is the prototype of the essential human perfection. When it is said that the birds have nests and the foxes have holes, but the Son of man has no place to lay his head,[27] this is about a state that is more helpless than the bird's and is also conscious of this. But then, with the consciousness of being without a nest, without a place of resort, in that situation to be free from care—indeed, this is the divine prototype of the lofty creation, of the human being.

For the bird, this prototype does not exist, nor for the child, but therefore to be able to worry about making a living is a perfection. Is this not the case? Do we really say that it is a perfection in the woman that she, as the weaker sex, cannot go to war, that it is a perfection in the prisoner that he cannot come out and risk his life, that it is a perfection in the sleeper that he sleeps through the danger, or do we really say that it is a perfection to be barred from daring to name as one's prototype him who was lifted up on high! But why, then, do we speak differently with regard to worry about making a living, as if the woman were more fortunate because it is primarily the husband who must earn a living, as if the prisoner were fortunate because the state takes care of him, as if the person who slept himself into wealth were fortunate, or as if the most fortunate of all might be the person who perhaps by his wealth was barred from naming the God-man as his prototype!

But out there with the bird the worried one cannot talk this way. He attends to the bird; he completely forgets his imagined worries; for the moment he forgets even the actual need. His mind is eased—indeed, he is built up. But if the bird dared to speak words of instruction, he presumably would answer, "My little friend, this is something you do not know about." That is, he would become conscious of its being a perfection to be able to worry about making a living.

"The bird sows not and reaps not and gathers not into barns," which means that the bird does not *work.*

But then is this a perfection, not to work at all; is it a perfec-

VIII
283

tion to steal the time of day in the same sense as sleep steals the time of night! Admittedly the bird awakens early for song, and yet, yet when it has slept it actually awakens to dream; even its most beautiful song is a dream about an unhappy love affair, and thus it sleeps and dreams life away, a happy or a sad jest. But is this indeed a perfection? Is it a perfection in the child that it plays and becomes tired—as the man from work—and sleeps and plays again! It is lovable in the child—ah, who would not gladly learn from a child! And if at times the adult does his work but has no joy in it, yes, perhaps is even annoyed—ah, then he is eager to be put at ease by the child, eager to learn from it, is eager in his secret, grateful mind to call the child a teacher. But if necessary he would not hesitate to reprimand the teacher, and the adult would justifiably do that. Why? Because in an earnest sense the adult is the child's teacher, and the child is the adult's teacher only in the beautiful sense of jesting earnestness.

The bird does not work; its life in an innocent sense is vanity, and in an innocent sense it even takes life in vain. Is this really a perfection? If so, perhaps it is then an imperfection on God's part that he works, that he has worked until now![28] Is it a perfection on the part of the bird that in hard times it sits and dies of hunger and knows of nothing at all to do, that, dazed, it lets itself fall to the ground and dies? Usually we do not talk this way. When a sailor lies down in the boat and lets matters take their course in the storm and knows of nothing to do, we do not speak of his perfection. But when a doughty sailor knows how to steer, when he works against the storm with ingenuity, with strength, and with perseverance, when he works himself out of the danger, we admire him. When late in the forenoon we see someone who gets up late, slothful and yet hungry, waiting to obtain food by chance, we certainly do not commend this; but when we get up early in the morning and see the good workman, or even if we do not see him but early in the morning see that he has already been there, that the fisherman has already been out to his nets, that the farmhand has already tethered the cows, we commend the fisherman and the farmhand. To work is a human being's perfection. By working,

VIII
284

human beings resemble God, who indeed also works. When a human being works for his food, we will not foolishly say that he is supporting himself; expressly to call to mind how glorious it is to be a human being, we prefer to say: He is working together with God for his food. He is working together with God—that is, he is God's co-worker.[29] As you can see, the bird is not; sure enough, the bird gets its food, but it is not God's co-worker. The bird gets its food just as a tramp gets his subsistence out in the country, but the servant who works for his food is called a co-worker by the master of the house.

The bird does not work—and yet it gets food. Is this a perfection in the bird? Usually we say that the person who will not work does not receive food either, and God also says this.[30] When God makes an exception of the bird, the reason is that the poor bird cannot work. The poor bird cannot work—do we talk that way about a perfection? The perfection, then, is to work. It is not, as it has been poorly stated, a dire necessity to have to work in order to live. Oh, no, it is a perfection not to be a child all one's life, not always to have parents to take care of one while they are alive and also when they are dead. The dire necessity—which, incidentally, still specifically acknowledges the perfection in the human being—is needed merely to force the person who himself is unwilling freely to understand that to work is a perfection and therefore refuses to go to work gladly. Therefore even if there were no so-called dire necessity, it would still be an imperfection for a human being to cease working.

It is said of the honorary medals a king may award that some wear the medal to their honor and others honor the medal by wearing it. Allow us, then, to mention a great example who actually can be said to have honored what it means to work—the Apostle Paul. If anyone at all might have wished the whole day to be twice as long—then certainly Paul; if anyone at all could have given every hour great meaning for many—then certainly Paul; if anyone at all could easily have been supported by the congregations—then certainly Paul; and yet he preferred to work with his own hands![31] [32]Just as he humbly thanked God that he enjoyed the honor of being flogged, persecuted, and insulted, just as he, humble before God, proudly calls his chains a matter of personal honor,[33] so he also considered it an honor to work with his own hands. An honor, so that with regard to the Gospel he dared to say with a woman's beautiful and an apostle's holy sense of shame: I have not earned one penny by proclaiming the Word,[34] I have not married money by becoming an apostle. An honor, so that with regard to the most insignificant person he dared to say: I have not been exempted from any arduousness of life, nor have I through preferential treatment been barred from any of its advantages— I, too, have had the honor of working with my own hands!

Oh, in the desperate, glittering, or miserable wretchedness of worldly comparisons, where as little is known about what honor is as about perfection, there people cravenly or traitorously speak in another way. But out there with the bird the worried one knows how glorious it is to work and thereby how glorious it is to be a human being. What makes the difference is not whether one person works for riches and another for bread, whether one person works in order to pile up a superabundance, another in order to ward off poverty; no, what makes the difference is—that the bird cannot work.

But then in this diversion with the bird the worried one had acquired something quite different from his worry to think about; he began to consider properly how glorious it is to work, how glorious it is to be a human being. If in turn he forgets it in the midst of work—ah, then that beloved teacher, the bird, will perhaps fly by him and remind him of what he forgot—if he will just look at the bird.

III

[What Blessed Happiness Is Promised in Being a Human Being]

If it is true that cares and worry, especially the longer and the more deeply they penetrate into the soul or the longer they penetrate it deeply, also give the strength of worry, then it is indeed probable that the comforting friend may get the worst of it in the struggle. In other words, what is carried on between the worry and the comfort is a kind of struggle; they regard each other as enemies in the same sense as sickness and medicine; they cannot tolerate, they cannot bear each other—at least not at the outset. Who has not experienced what powers worry can give a person, how he both cunningly and powerfully knows how to defend himself against the comfort, how he is able to do what no commander is ordinarily able to do—to lead the very same defense briskly into the struggle again in the very same moment his worry's defense is disarmed! Who has not experienced how the passion in worry can provide a person with such a power of thought and expression that the comforter himself almost becomes afraid of it! Who has not experienced that scarcely anyone desiring something can speak as ingratiatingly in order to win over another as a worried person can speak fascinatingly in order to convince himself once again—and his comforter—that there is no comfort! But when this is the case, when the worried one has become the stronger, at times perhaps only apparently because of his stubbornness, at times, alas, actually the stronger because of the magnitude of his affliction, is there then nothing at all to be done? Certainly there is. In that case one tries to prompt the worried one to enter into someone else's suffering, and the person who is himself unwilling to accept comfort from another person is often willing to share in another's cares, to become worried

with someone else and on behalf of someone else. In this way
the struggle is forgotten. While the worried one sadly suffers
with another, his mind is set at ease. The person who armed
himself against comfort is now disarmed; the person who was
like a fortified city is now like a city that has surrendered; by
grieving with someone else, he himself finds comfort.

VIII
287

In this way the Gospel text leads the worried one out to the
field, and he who, alas, simultaneously weak and strong,
thought he was victor over all human comfort now stands in
completely different surroundings. Look at the grass; *"today it
stands, tomorrow it is cast into the stove."*[35] Ah, what a poor,
miserable life! What sheer futility! And even if it is not cast into
the stove, "the sun rises with its heat and withers the grass, and
its flower falls off, and the beautiful form that was seen de-
cays."[36] So the grass withers, and no one knows its place anymore. No, no one, no one knows its place anymore, no one
asks about it, and if anyone asked he could not possibly find it.
What a wretched life—to be, to have been, and then to be
forgotten that way!

Look at the bird! *"Are not two sparrows sold for a penny?"*[37]
Alas, one sparrow has no value at all—there must be two if the
buyer is to give one penny. What a change: so joyful, so
happy—and now not worth a penny. This is how the bird dies.
How hard to die this way! [38]When the first swallow returns in
the spring, we all greet it joyfully, but whether it is the same
one that was here last year, well, no one knows that; no one
knows it, and therefore no one can recognize it!

There is indeed beauty and youthfulness and loveliness in
nature, there is indeed multifarious and teeming life, and there
is rapture and jubilation. But there is also something akin to
profound, unfathomable cares of which none of those out there
has any inkling, and precisely this, that none has any inkling, is
the sadness in the human being. To be lovely this way, to
blossom this way, to dart around this way, to build with the
beloved this way: to live this way—and to die this way! Is this
life or is this death? When the patient lies in the critical moment
of his illness, we ask: Is it life or death? But then, of course, we
also see the perilousness, see it before our own eyes, and see it

with a shudder. But in nature, where everything smiles invitingly and appears secure! Yet the life of nature is always in this tension: Is it life or death? Is it life, which, eternally young, renews itself, or is it decay, which perfidiously conceals itself in order not to be seen for what it is, the decay that deceives with the loveliness of the lily and the field, with the carefreeness of the bird, while underneath the decay itself is perfidiously only waiting to reap the deception. Such is the life of nature: short, full of song, flowering, but at every moment death's prey, and death is the stronger.

So the worried one sinks into sadness, things darken before his eyes, nature's beauty pales, the bird's song becomes as silent as the grave, decay will swallow everything—and yet he cannot forget the bird and the lily. It seems as if he wanted to rescue them from death by his recollection, rescue them for a longer life by recollecting them. Precisely this is the basis of the sadness. But is death's earnest reminder of death really more gripping than that of the sadness contained in these words: Is it life or death? What death says is more horrible: It is all over; but what sadness says is more gripping: Is it life or death? Death's shape is more abominable, he, the pale reaper; but it is more gripping when death, like the lily, is clothed in loveliness. So the worried one, in being gripped by sadness, becomes weakened like a woman, becomes mollified like a city that has surrendered—and comfort finds admission.

Let us now reflect on how the worried one, through his sadness out there with the lily and the bird, acquires something different from his worry to think about in the earnest sense, how he is led to consider properly:

what blessed happiness is promised in being a human being.

"No one can serve two masters, for he must either hate the one and love the other or be devoted to the one and despise the other. You cannot serve God and mammon."[39] But are these also words of the Gospel? They certainly are. This is how the Gospel text about the lilies in the field and the birds of the air begins. But are they spoken to a worried person? Certainly, they are spoken to a

worried person, to whom a high value is attributed, and for
this very reason the words are rigorous. The more rigorously
the authority speaks to a worried person, the more it also
admits to him; the more it requires of the worried one, the
more it also admits to him—the rigorousness and the requirement are the admission. Is this not so? When the physician sees
that everything is over with the sick person, one can promptly
hear it in the physician's voice; he speaks casually half aloud,
evasively. But, on the other hand, when the physician sees that
there is much to be done, in particular that the sick person

VIII
289

himself can do a great deal, then he speaks rigorously: the
rigorousness is the admission. Therefore what we sometimes
hear is not at all dubious, that instead of pleading for gentleness
a person has said, "Just speak rigorously to me." And the
Gospel's rigorous words, are they not akin to the earnest father's saying to his child, "I do not want to hear any whining"?
Does that mean that the earnest father is unconcerned about his
child's troubles? Far from it, he specifically wants the troubles
to be legitimate, but toward foolish troubles he is like a consuming fire. So also with the Gospel. One can speak in many
ways about the lilies and the birds; one can speak gently, movingly, ingratiatingly, fondly, almost as a poet speaks, and a
human being also may speak this way, may coax the worried
one. But when the Gospel speaks authoritatively, it speaks
with the earnestness of eternity; then there is no more time to
dwell dreamily over the lily or longingly to follow the bird—a
brief, an instructive reference to the lily and the bird, but then
the eternal requirement of earnestness. And just as it holds true
of diversion that it mitigatingly gives the worried one something else to think about, so it also holds true of the rigorous
words of earnestness that in earnestness and truth they give the
worried one something different from his worry to think
about.

"No one can serve two masters." Here there can be no doubt
about which two are referred to. That is why the worried one
was taken out into the field, where the question cannot be
about human relationships, about serving a master as his ap-
prentice or a wise person as his adherent, but only about serv-

ing God or the world. Nature does not serve two masters; there is no vacillating or double-mindedness in nature. The poor bird of the air and the humble lily of the field do not serve two masters. Even though the lily does not serve God, it still serves only to God's honor. It does not spin, it does not work, it does not want to be anything at all itself or to have anything for itself, have it as plunder. The bird does not serve two masters. Even though it does not serve God, it exists only to God's honor, sings to his praise, does not demand at all to be anything itself. So it is with everything in nature; that is its perfection. But that is also its imperfection, because there is therefore no freedom [*Frihed*]. The lily standing out there in the open field [*i det Frie*] and the free bird of the air are nevertheless bound in necessity and have no choice.

"*He must either hate the one and love the other or be devoted to the one and despise the other*"—therefore love of God is hatred of the world and love of the world hatred of God; therefore this is the colossal point of contention, either love or hate; therefore this is the place where the most terrible struggle carried on in the world must be fought, and where is this place? In a person's innermost being. This may be why the person who sensed this struggle in his own inner being often paused and sought diversion in watching the raging of the elements and the battle of nature, because he felt this struggle is indeed like a game, since it makes no difference whether the storm wins or the ocean. Yes, why is it really that the storm and the ocean struggle, and over what is it really that they are struggling! The terrible struggle in a person's inner being is something different. Whether the struggle is over millions or a penny, the struggle is a matter of someone's loving and preferring it to God—the most terrible struggle is the struggle over the highest. The penny seems to be nothing, the struggle seems to be over nothing, over a penny, and yet the struggle is over the highest and everything is at stake. Or is it more insulting to a girl that the beloved prefers a million dollars to possession of her instead of preferring a penny?

Now the sadness is indeed forgotten in the terribleness of the struggle, but then we come to the glorious thing: *that the human*

VIII
290

being is granted a choice. What blessed happiness is promised
hereby to the one who rightly chooses.

A choice. My listener, do you know how to express in a
single word anything more glorious! If you talked year in and
year out, could you mention anything more glorious than a
choice, to have choice! It is certainly true that the sole blessing
is to choose rightly, but certainly choice itself is still the glorious condition. What does the girl care about an inventory of
all her fiancé's excellent qualities if she herself may not choose;
and, on the other hand, whether others praise her beloved's
many perfections or enumerate his faults, what more glorious
thing could she say than when she says: He is my heart's choice!
A choice—it is indeed the glorious treasure, but it is not intended to be buried and concealed, because an unused choice is
worse than nothing, is a snare in which the person trapped
himself like a slave who did not become free—by choosing. It
is a good you never can get rid of, it stays with you and, if you
do not use it, as a curse. A choice, not between red and green,
not between silver and gold—no, a choice between God and
the world. Do you know anything greater to place together for
a choice! Do you know any more overwhelming and humbling
manifestation of God's complaisance and indulgence toward
human beings than that in a sense he places himself on the
straight line of choice with the world just in order that the
human being can choose; that God, if language may be used
this way, proposes [*frie*] to the human being, that he, the eternally strong one, proposes to the weak human being, for the
strong one, after all, always proposes to the weaker one. Compared with this choice between God and the world, how insignificant is even the girl's choice between suitors! —A choice,
or is it perhaps an imperfection in the choice under discussion
here that a human being not only *can* choose but that he *must*
choose? Would it not be to the young girl's advantage if she had
an earnest father who said, "My dear girl, you have your freedom [*Frihed*], you yourself may choose, but you must choose";
would it be better that she had the choice but coyly picked and
picked and never really did choose!

No, a person *must* choose, for in this way God holds himself in honor while he also has fatherly solicitude for humankind. If God has lowered himself to being that which *can be chosen*, then a person indeed *must* choose—God is not mocked. Thus it is truly the case that if a person avoids choosing, this is the same as the blasphemy of choosing the world.

The human being must choose *between God and mammon*. This is the eternal, unaltered condition of the choice; there will be no escape, never in all eternity. No one will be able to say, "God and mammon, they are not so unconditionally different—they can both be combined in the choice"—because this is to refrain from choosing. When there is a choice between two, then to want to choose both is "to one's own destruction to shrink from"[40] choosing. No one will be able to say, "One can choose a little mammon and then God also." No, no, it is presumptuous blasphemy for someone to dare to believe that only the person who insists on having much money chooses mammon. Alas, the person who insists on having a penny without God, a penny he wants to have all for himself, chooses mammon. A penny is enough, the choice is made, he has chosen mammon; that it is little makes no difference. If someone disdains one girl and chooses another, and the second girl is nothing compared with the first one, who was like the Queen of the Orient—has he therefore not disdained the girl? If someone buys a toy with the money with which he could buy the highest, has he not therefore disdained buying the highest? Is it really an excuse that instead of buying the highest he has bought what even in the sense of nothingness is nothing at all! If anyone does not understand this, the reason is that he is unwilling to understand that God is present in the moment of choice, not in order to watch but in order to be chosen. Therefore it is deceitful talk if someone says that God is so lofty that he cannot lower himself to being chosen, because then the choice is abolished. And if the choice is abolished because God is not present as the object of choice, then mammon is not an option either. It is God's presence in the choice that poses the choice between God and mammon. And God's presence in order to be chosen is what gives eternal earnestness to the decision of choice, because neither what has been granted to a

VIII
292

human being nor how he chose shall ever be forgotten. But that kind of talk, which through loftiness would prevent God from letting himself be chosen, is blasphemy, which in a polite way tries to get God put outside, which, instead of humbly being content with what God wants, superiorly wants to be aware of the difficulty that, so to speak, must be involved with being God. To place a crown of thorns on his head and spit on him is blasphemy, but to make God so lofty that his existence becomes a delusion, becomes meaningless—that, too, is blasphemy.

Therefore the human being must choose. The struggle is terrible, the struggle in a person's inner being between God and the world. To have the choice is the glorious perilousness of the condition, but what, then, is the eternal happiness that is promised if the choice is rightly made or, what amounts to the same thing, what should a person choose? He should choose God's kingdom and his righteousness.[41] For this he should give up everything, no matter whether this everything is millions or a penny, because also the person who chooses a penny in preference to God chooses mammon. Only when the human being, although he works and spins, is just like the lily, which does not work or spin, only when the human being, although he sows and reaps and gathers into barns, is just like the bird, which does not sow and reap and gather into barns—only then does he not serve mammon.

"*Seek first God's kingdom and his righteousness; then all these things will be added to you.*"

God's kingdom—that, then, is the name of the blessed happiness that is promised to the human being; it is at this name and before the glory of this name that all nature's beauty and its peace pale and vanish. Whereas sadness with downcast eyes sees nature sink in decay, the eyes of faith seek the invisible glory. Just as Noah, rescued, saw the destruction of a world, so also sadness sees the destruction of the visible world, sees all that decline whose life is fused with the visible, whereas faith, rescued, sees the eternal and the invisible.

VIII
293
Seek first God's kingdom—"*which is above in the heavens.*" The bird is not seeking anything. However far it flies, it is not

seeking: it is migrating and is drawn, and its longest flight is a migration. But the person in whose soul the eternal is implanted seeks and aspires. If the visible does not deceive him, as the person is deceived who grasps the shadow instead of the form, if temporality does not deceive him, as the person is deceived who is continually waiting for tomorrow, if the temporary does not deceive him, as the person is deceived who procrastinates along the way—if this does not happen, then the world does not quiet his longing. Then it helps him only by means of repulsion to seek further, to seek the eternal, God's kingdom, which is above in the heavens—that high the bird has never gone; the bird that flies the highest of all still flies under the heavens.

Seek first God's kingdom—"*which is within you.*"[42] The flower does not seek anything; if the flower is to obtain anything, that anything must come to it; the flower waits, and even this it does without longing. But the person whom the visible did not deceive by anesthetization, the person whom temporality did not lull to sleep with monotonous uniformity, the person whom the temporary did not spellbind with delusion—that person the world does not satisfy; it only helps him, by painfully keeping him awake and expectant, to seek, to seek the eternal, God's kingdom, which is within a human being. The flower does not know such an invisible inner glory; what it has it is obliged to betray immediately; the bud quickly breaks the silence, betrays the glory, which in fact is soon gone.

Seek *first* God's kingdom. This is the sequence, but it is also the sequence of inversion, because that which first offers itself to a person is everything that is visible and corruptible, which tempts and draws him, yes, will entrap him in such a way that he begins last, or perhaps never, to seek God's kingdom. But the proper beginning begins with seeking God's kingdom first; thus it begins expressly by letting a world perish. What a difficult beginning! How this earthly life begins for a human being we cannot say for sure; it was begun unnoticed, and a human being avoids the difficulty of the beginning. But living for the eternal begins with seeking God's kingdom first. There is no time to amass a fortune beforehand, no time to deliberate on this question; there is no time to lay up a penny beforehand, because the beginning is: to seek God's kingdom first. If a person has something that he knows must be done first each morning, then he also knows that there can be no thought of doing anything else that could be done beforehand; he knows that even if at another time of the day he did what was prescribed, it would be wrong, because this should have been done first. Yet it certainly would also be possible that an earthly task could be done at another time of the day, but it holds true of seeking God's kingdom that this must be done first; that is unconditionally the only way in which it can be done. The person who thinks of doing it at another time of the day, at some other hour, has not even arrived at the beginning, which, after all, is to seek it first. The person who does not seek it first is not seeking it at all, regardless, absolutely regardless of whether he is seeking a penny or millions.

"*God's kingdom and his righteousness.*" The last word describes the first, because God's kingdom is "righteousness, peace, and joy in the Holy Spirit."[43] Therefore it is not a matter here of starting out on a search to find God's kingdom, since God's kingdom is righteousness. Even if in describing you had all the intense longings of desire, even if you could bring the world's ordinarily busy metropolis to a standstill, because everyone listened to your discourses, in so doing you would not come closer to God's kingdom, not a single step, because God's kingdom is righteousness. You can live so hidden in the great mass of people that not even the authorities know your name and address; you can be the one and only, the absolute monarch of all kingdoms and lands—you would not thereby be one step closer to God's kingdom, because God's kingdom is righteousness.

But what is righteousness, really? It is to seek God's kingdom first. Righteousness is not extraordinary abilities, because it is expressly of them that righteousness will demand an accounting when it requires righteousness of you. Neither is righteousness earthly obscurity, because no human being is so lowly that he can do no wrong, and just as no coin is too small to carry the image of the emperor, so is no human being too lowly to carry the image of God. Neither is righteousness power and dominion, because no human being stands so high that he is higher than righteousness, so high that he would need to lay down his crown in order to have the opportunity to practice righteousness.

Righteousness is to seek God's kingdom first. If you do to people what is right and just but forget God, are you then practicing righteousness? Is not practicing righteousness in this way like the thief's doing what is right and just with the money he has stolen? To forget God—is not this the same as stealing your whole existence! But if you first, before you do anything else, seek God's kingdom, then you will not practice unrighteousness toward any human being, and you will not forget God either, since how would one be able to forget that which at all times is the first thing one seeks.

The beginning is to seek God's kingdom first, and righteousness is to seek God's kingdom first. See, this was why we said that it is not a matter of starting out on a search to find God's kingdom. On the contrary, you remain in the place where you are and that is assigned to you; any searching away from this place is already unrighteousness. If it were the case that you should first seek elsewhere before beginning to seek the kingdom of God, then it would indeed not be true that you should *first* seek God's kingdom. Thus while the world of the visible perishes and sinks in decay, you nevertheless remain in your place, and the beginning is to seek God's kingdom first. From an earthquake one flees to safer places; from a forest fire one flees to bare ground; from a flood one flees to higher ground. But if it is the case that the world of the visible is sinking in decay, then a person of course has no other place to which he can flee, and for that very reason he remains on the spot and seeks God's kingdom first. If the whole world of the visible does not perish, then God's kingdom will be for him like another place upon the earth and he will start out on a search to find God's kingdom, and in his fruitless and self-contradictory search he will either find out that he is not finding it or he will be deceived if he thinks he has found it.

But if a person seeks God's kingdom first—"*then all these things will be added to him.*" They will be *added* to him, since

VIII
295

there is only one thing that is to be *sought*: God's kingdom. Neither wealth's thousands nor poverty's penny is to be sought; this will be added to you.

"*All these things,*" or as it is written in another Gospel: the rest.[44] Oh, what blessed happiness God's kingdom must be! If you take everything the bird and the lily have, every glorious thing that nature has, and think of all this together, it is all contained in the word: the rest, all these things. Therefore God's kingdom must be valued so highly that in comparison with it one can speak in such a way about the former, can speak so disregardingly, so slightingly, so loftily. When a man has accumulated a very great fortune but may still have some outstanding claims he could legitimately make, he says: No, never mind the rest. When a man called to a high position in a foreign country goes away and takes with him everything that is dear and important to him but there is still a good deal left, he says, "No, all these things I shall not take with me!" Alas, the sum total of what the bird has is "the rest"; the whole glory of the lily is "all these things"—oh, what a blessed happiness God's kingdom must be!

But then in his sadness out there with the lily and the bird the worried one did indeed acquire something other than his worry to think about; he began to consider what blessed happiness is promised in being a human being. Then let the lily wither and let its loveliness become indiscernible; let the leaf fall to the ground and the bird fly away; let it become dark on the fields—[45]God's kingdom does not change with the seasons! So let the rest be needed for a long time or a short time, let it come abundantly or sparingly; let all these things have their moment when they are lacking or possessed, their moment as a subject of discussion until in death they are eternally forgotten—God's kingdom is still that which is to be sought first but which ultimately will also last through all eternities, and "if that which will be abolished was glorious, that which remains will be much more glorious,"[46] and if it was hard to live in want, then it must indeed be only an easier separation to die to want!

Part Three

THE GOSPEL OF SUFFERINGS

CHRISTIAN DISCOURSES

These Christian discourses (which in more than one respect are not, and thus for more than one reason are not called, *sermons*) are not intended "to fill an idle moment for inquisitiveness." If, however, just one single sufferer, who perhaps is also going astray in many thoughts, should by means of them find a heavy moment lighter, should find in them a trail leading through the many thoughts, then the author will not regret his intention with them.[2]

It is "The Gospel of Sufferings," not as though the subject were exhausted by these discourses but because each discourse is a draught of this, praise God, inexhaustible supply, not as though the particular discourse were exhaustive but because each discourse still drinks deeply enough to find the joy.

S. K.

I

[What Meaning and What Joy There Are in the Thought of Following Christ]

You who yourself once walked the earth and left footprints that we should follow; you who from your heaven still look down on every pilgrim, strengthen the weary, hearten the disheartened, lead back the straying, give solace to the struggling; you who will come again at the end of time to judge each one individually, whether he followed you—our God and our Savior, let your prototype stand very clearly before the eyes of the soul in order to dispel the mists, strengthen in order to keep this alone unaltered before our eyes so that by resembling you and by following you we may find the right way surely to the judgment, since every human being ought to be brought before the judgment—oh, but may we also be brought by you to the eternal happiness with you in the life to come. Amen.

[3]LUKE 14:27: WHOEVER DOES NOT CARRY HIS CROSS AND COME AFTER ME CANNOT BE MY DISCIPLE.

Guidance enough is indeed offered on life's way, and no wonder, since every error passes itself off as guidance. But even though errors are numerous, truth is still only one, and there is only one who is "the Way and the Life,"[4] only one guidance that in truth leads a person through life to life. Thousands upon thousands carry a name by which it is indicated that they have chosen this guidance, that they belong to the Lord Jesus Christ, after whom they call themselves Christians, that they are his bond-servants, whether they be masters or servants, slaves or freeborn, men or women. *Christians* they call themselves, and they also call themselves by other names, and all of them designate the relation to this one guidance. —They call themselves *believers* and thereby signify that they are pilgrims, strangers, and aliens[5] in the world. Indeed, a staff in his hand does not identify a pilgrim (many a person, after all, could carry a staff without being a traveler) as definitely as calling oneself a believer publicly testifies that one is on a journey, because faith simply means: What I am seeking is not here, and for that very reason I believe it. Faith expressly signifies the deep, strong, blessed restlessness that drives the believer so that he cannot settle down at rest in this world, and therefore the person who has settled down completely at rest has also ceased to be a believer, because a believer cannot sit still as one sits with a pilgrim's staff in one's hand—a believer travels forward. — They call themselves *"the communion of saints"*[6] and thereby signify what they should be and ought to be, what they hope sometime to become when faith is laid aside and the pilgrim staff laid down. —They call themselves *cross-bearers* and thereby signify that their way through the world is not as light as a dance but is heavy and hard, although faith for them is still also the joy that conquers the world. Just as the ship as it lightly proceeds at full sail before the wind at the same time deeply cuts its heavy path through the ocean, so also the Christian's way is light if one looks at the faith that overcomes the world, but hard if one looks at the laborious work in the depths. —They call themselves *"followers of Christ,"* and this is the name we will ponder at this time as we consider:

> *what meaning and what joy there are in the thought of following Christ.*

When the bold warrior bravely advances and with his breast intercepts all the arrows of the enemy but also protects his squire who is following behind, can we then say that this squire is following him? When the fond wife believes that in what she cherishes most in the world, in her husband, she has the beautiful prototype of what she wished to attain in life and then as a woman walks along at his side (for woman was taken from man's side[7]), leaning on him, can one then say that this wife is following her husband? When the undaunted teacher calmly stands in his place, surrounded by ridicule, persecuted by envy, when every attack is aimed only at him but never takes aim at the adherent who endorses him, can one then say that this adherent is following him? When the hen sees the enemy coming and therefore spreads her wings to cover the chicks that are walking behind her, can one then say that these chicks are following the hen?

No, one cannot talk this way; the relation must be changed. The bold warrior must step aside so that it can now become manifest whether his squire will indeed follow him, follow him in the actuality of danger when all the arrows are aimed at his breast, or whether he will cravenly turn his back on the danger and lose his courage because he lost the courageous one. The noble husband, alas, he must step aside, leave her, so that it can now become manifest whether the grieving widow, without his support, will follow him or whether, deprived of his support, she will indeed abandon the prototype. The undaunted teacher must hide himself or must be hidden in a grave so that it can be disclosed whether the adherent will follow him, will persevere in that place surrounded by ridicule, persecuted by envy, or whether in his lifetime he will shamefully desert the place because the teacher in death honorably left it.

To follow, then, means to walk along the same road walked by the one whom one is following; it means, therefore, that he is no longer visibly walking ahead. It was therefore indeed necessary for Christ to go away, for him to die, before it could become manifest whether the disciple would follow him. It is many, many centuries since this happened, and yet this is continually still happening. There is a period when Christ almost visibly walks by the child's side, goes ahead of it, but then there also comes a time when Christ is taken away from the eyes of sensate imagination, so that it can now become manifest whether the adult will follow him in the earnestness of decision.

When the child is permitted to hold onto its mother's dress, can one then say that the child is walking the same road *just as* the mother is? No, one cannot say that. First the child must learn how to walk by itself, to walk alone, before it can walk the same road as the mother and just as the mother walks it. And when the child learns to walk by itself, what must the mother do then? She must make herself invisible. That her tenderness remains the same, remains unchanged, yes, that it probably increases at the very time the child is learning how to walk by itself—of this we are well aware. Perhaps, however, the child may not always be able to understand it.

But what it means for the child to have to learn to walk by itself and to walk alone is, spiritually speaking, the task assigned to the person who is to be someone's follower—he must learn to walk by himself and to walk alone. How strange! Almost jestingly and always with a smile we talk about the child's worry when it must learn to walk by itself, and yet language has perhaps no stronger or more gripping or truer expression for the most profound trouble and suffering than this: to walk by oneself and to walk alone. We are well aware that heaven's solicitude is unchanged, yes, is even more concerned in this dangerous time, if that were possible, but it may not always be understood while one is learning.

To follow, then, means to walk by oneself and to walk alone along the road that the teacher walked—to have no visible person with whom one can take counsel, to have to choose by oneself, to scream in vain as the child screams in vain since the mother does not dare to be of visible help, to despair in vain since no one can help and heaven does not dare to be of visible help. But to be helped invisibly means to learn to walk by oneself, because it means to learn to conform one's mind to the mind of the teacher, who is, however, invisible. To walk by oneself! Indeed, there is not one, not a single human being who can choose for you or in the ultimate and decisive sense counsel you about the one and only important issue, counsel you decisively about your salvation, and even if ever so many are willing, it would only be to your harm. Alone! When you have chosen, you will surely find fellow pilgrims, but in the decisive moment and every time there is mortal danger you will be by yourself. No one, not one, hears your ingratiating appeal or heeds your vehement complaint—and yet there is help and willingness enough in heaven. But it is invisible, and to be helped by it is to learn to walk alone. This help does not come from outside and grasp your hand; it does not support you as a kind person supports the sick one; it does not lead you back by force when you have gone astray. No, only when you completely yield, completely give up your own will, and devote yourself with your whole heart and mind—then help comes invisibly, but then you have indeed walked alone.

We do not see the powerful instinct that leads the bird on its long journey. The instinct does not fly ahead and the bird behind. It looks as if it were the bird that found the way. Likewise we do not see the teacher but only the follower, who resembles the teacher, and it looks as if the follower himself were the way, just because he is the true follower who walks by himself along the same road.

This is the meaning of the thought: to follow [*følge efter*] someone. But to *follow Christ* means to take up one's cross or, as it says in the text just read, to carry one's cross. To carry one's cross means to deny oneself, as Christ explains it when he says, "If anyone would come after me, let him deny himself and take up his cross and follow me" (Matthew 16:24). It was also "this mind that was in Christ Jesus, he who thought it not robbery to be equal with God but humbled himself and became obedient unto death, even to death on the cross" (Phil. 2:5ff). As was the prototype, so must the imitation [*Efterfølgelsen*] also be, even though it is a *slow and difficult task* to deny oneself, a heavy cross to take up, a heavy cross to bear, and one that, according to the prototype's instructions, is to be carried in obedience unto death, so that the imitator [*Efterfølger*], even if he does not die on the cross, nevertheless resembles the prototype in dying "with the cross on."[8]

VIII
309

One good deed, one noble resolution, is not to deny oneself. Alas, this is perhaps what we learn in the world, because even this is so rarely seen that on the rare occasion it is greeted with astonishment. But Christianity teaches otherwise. Christ did not say to the rich young man, "If you want to be perfect, then sell all your property and give it to the poor."[9] Many would surely find even this requirement extreme and eccentric; we might not even admire the young man if he did it but would smile at him as an eccentric or pity him as a fool. Christ, however, speaks in another way and says: Go, sell what you have and give it to the poor "and come, take up the cross and follow me" (Mark 10:21). Thus to sell one's property and give it to the poor is not to take up the cross, or it is at most the beginning, the good beginning, in order to take up the cross and follow Christ. To give all to the poor, that is the first step; it is (since the language allows an innocent kind of ingenuity) *to take up the cross*; the next step, the protracted continuation, is: *to carry one's cross*. It must take place daily, not once and for all, and there must not be anything, anything at all, that the follower would not be willing to give up in self-denial. Whether what he is unwilling to deny himself involves a mere trifle, as we say, or something big, makes no essential difference at all, because the mere trifle becomes infinitely significant as guilt through the misrelation to the required self-denial. Perhaps there was someone who in the hope of doing the utmost was willing to do what the rich young man did not do and who still did not become a follower, because he stopped, "turned around and looked back"[10]—at his great achievement; or if he went ahead he still did not become a follower, because he thought that he had done something so grand that trifles did not matter. Alas, why is it that to deny oneself in trifles is the most difficult of all? I wonder if it is not because a certain kind of refined self-love apparently is able to deny itself in great matters. But the smaller, the more insignificant, the more petty the requirement, the more insulting it is to self-love, because in relation to such a task it is completely abandoned by its own and others' grandiloquent conceptions, but so much the more humble is the self-denial. Indeed, why is it hardest of all to deny oneself if one lives alone and as though in a remote place? I wonder if it is not because a certain kind of refined self-love is also capable of apparently denying itself—when many people are watching admiringly. But just as little as any difference is made by what differences are involved in an individual person's denying himself according to his situation—thus a beggar unconditionally

VIII
310

can deny himself just as well as a king—so also no essential difference is made by what differences are involved in a person's refraining from self-denial, because self-denial is the inwardness to deny oneself. This is a heavy and difficult task. It is true that self-denial is a matter of casting off burdens and thus far might seem to be easy enough, but it is indeed hard to have to cast off the very burdens that self-love is eager to carry, yes, so eager that it is even very difficult for self-love to understand that they are burdens.

To follow Christ means, then, to deny oneself and means to *walk the same road* Christ walked in the lowly form of a servant, indigent, forsaken, mocked, not loving the world and not loved by it. Therefore it means *to walk by oneself,* since the person who in self-denial renounces the world and all that is of the world renounces every connection that ordinarily tempts and captures. "Thus he does not go to his field; neither does he bargain and trade nor take a wife."[11] The person who, if need be, certainly does not love his father and mother, sister and brother less than before but loves Christ so much more that he can be said to hate these others[12]—that person indeed walks by himself, alone in the whole world. Indeed, in the crisscrossing busyness of life it seems to be difficult, impossible, to live in this manner, even impossible to judge whether anyone actually is living in this manner.

But let us not forget that it is eternity that will judge how the task was accomplished and that the earnestness of eternity will call for the silence of a sense of shame with regard to everything of the world, about which there was perpetual talk in the world. In eternity you will not be asked how large a fortune you are *leaving behind*—the *survivors* ask about that; or about how many battles you won, about how sagacious you were, how powerful your influence—that, after all, becomes your *reputation for posterity.* No, eternity will not ask about what *worldly things* remain *behind you* in the world. But it will ask about what riches you have gathered in heaven, about how often you have conquered your own mind, about what control you have exercised over yourself or whether you have been a

VIII
311

slave, about how often you have mastered yourself in self-denial or whether you have never done so, about how often you in self-denial have been willing to make a sacrifice for a good cause or whether you were never willing, about how often you in self-denial have forgiven your enemy, whether seven times or seventy times seven times,[13] about how often you in self-denial endured insults patiently, about what you have suffered, not for your own sake, for your own selfish interests' sake, but what you in self-denial have suffered for God's sake.

And the one who will ask you, the judge, from whose verdict you cannot make an appeal to someone higher, was not a military commander who conquered kingdoms and countries, one with whom you could talk about your worldly exploits; his kingdom was specifically not of this world.[14] He was not robed in purple, someone with whom you could find select company, since he wore the purple only in ridicule.[15] He was not powerfully influential, thus could not wish to be initiated into your worldly secrets, since he was so scorned that the distinguished man dared visit him only in the secrecy of the night.[16] Ah, but it is always a comfort to be with like-minded people—if one is cowardly, then not to be forced to face a tribunal of warriors; if one is selfish and worldly-minded, then not to be forced to be judged by self-denial. This judge does not merely know what self-denial is, he does not merely know how to judge in such a way that no malpractice can hide itself—no, his presence is the judging that makes everything that looked so good, which was heard and seen with admiration in the world, become silent and turn pale; his presence is the judging, because he was self-denial. He who was equal with God took the form of a lowly servant,[17] he who could command legions of angels,[18] indeed, could command the world's creation and its destruction,[19] he walked about defenseless; he who had everything in his power surrendered all power and could not even do anything for his beloved disciples but could only offer them the very same conditions of lowliness and contempt; he who was the lord of creation constrained nature itself to keep quiet, for it was not until he had given up his spirit that the curtain tore and the graves opened and the powers of

VIII
312

nature betrayed who he was:[20] if this is not self-denial, what then is self-denial![21]

This was the meaning of the thought of following Christ, but now let us consider the *joy in this thought*.

My listener, if you imagine a young man standing on the threshold of his life, where many roads lie open before him, and asking himself which career he would like to follow, is it not true that he would make careful inquiries into where each particular road leads or, what amounts to the same thing, try to find out who has walked this road previously. Then we mention to him the famous, the eulogized, the glorious names of those whose memory is preserved among the people. At first we perhaps mention many names so that the choice can be proportionate to the young man's possibility, so that the wealth of instruction offered can be abundant. But then he himself, driven by an inner need, narrows the choice, and finally there remains only one, a single one, who in his eyes and according to his heart is the most excellent of all. Then the young man's heart beats violently when he enthusiastically mentions this name, to him the one and only name, and says: Along this road I will walk, because he walked along this road!

Now, we shall not distract our attention or waste time mentioning such names, because there is indeed but one name in heaven and on earth, only one single name, and therefore just one road to choose—if a person is to choose in earnest and choose aright. There must be several roads, since a person is to choose, but there also must be just one to choose if the earnestness of eternity is to rest upon the choice. A choice in which it makes no difference what is chosen does not have the eternal earnestness of the choice. There must unconditionally be everything to gain and everything to lose in the choice if the choice is to have the earnestness of eternity, even if, as said before, there must be a possibility of choosing something else, so that the choice can actually be a choice.

There is only one name in heaven and on earth, only one road, only one prototype. The person who chooses to follow Christ chooses the name that is above every name, the proto-

type that is supremely lifted up above all heavens, but yet at the
same time is human in such a way that it can be the prototype
for a human being, that it is named and shall be named in
heaven and on earth, in both places, as the highest name.[22]
There are prototypes whose names are mentioned only on
earth, but the highest name, the one and only name, must of
course have this excluding quality that in turn identifies it as the
one and only name—that it is named both in heaven and on
earth.

This name is the name of our Lord Jesus Christ. But is it not
then joyous to dare to choose to walk the same road he walked!
Unfortunately, in the confused and confusing jargon of the
world, whatever is simple and earnest almost sounds at times
like a jest. The person who certainly has exercised the greatest
power ever exercised in the world proudly calls himself Peter's
successor [*Efterfølger*]. But to be Christ's follower [*Efterfølger*]![23]
Indeed, that does not tempt to pride; it is the equal opportunity
for the mightiest and the lowliest, for the wisest and the
simplest—that is the blessedness of it. Is it really so glorious to
become *the* superior person no one else can become; is it not
disconsolate instead! Is it so glorious to dine on silver when
others starve, to live in palaces when so many are homeless, to
be the scholar no ordinary person can become, to have a name
in the sense that excludes thousands and thousands—is that so
glorious! If this, the *envious* [*misundelig*] diversity of *mortal life*,
were supreme, would it not be inhuman, and would not life be
unbearable for the fortunate! How different, on the other hand,
if the only joy is to follow Christ. Indeed, there can be no
higher joy than this: to be able to become the highest; and this
supreme joy cannot be made more confident, more blessed,
more secure than it is by means of the joyful thought, *heaven's
merciful* [*miskundelig*] thought: that this every human being
can do.

So the person who chose to follow Christ goes forward on
the road. Then when he, too, must learn to know the world
and what is to be known in it, the world's strength and his own
weakness, when the battle with flesh and blood becomes
alarming, when the road becomes difficult, the enemies nu-

merous, and the friends nonexistent—then his pain will surely force him to sigh: I am walking by myself. My listener, if a child starting to learn to walk were to come crying to the adult and say: I am walking by myself—would not the adult say: That is just splendid, my child! So, too, with following Christ. Along this road it is not only true, as we usually say, that when the need is greatest help is nearest—no, here on this road the greatest suffering is the closest to perfection. Do you know any other road where this is the case? Along any other road the reverse is true: There, if sufferings come, the weight of them is predominant—indeed, predominant to such an extent that it can mean that one took the wrong road. But on the road along which a person follows Christ, the greatest suffering is the most glorious; when the pilgrim sighs, he really considers himself blessed. When a person takes any other road, he must become familiar in advance with the precariousness of that road; things may go well and without mishap, but many obstacles can also rise up so that he cannot press his way ahead. But on the road of self-denial, of following Christ, there is eternal road safety; along this road are the "road signs" of suffering, the joyous signs that one is going ahead on the right road. But what greater joy is there than to dare to choose the best road, the road to the highest; and what joy in turn is as great as this, except the joy that in all eternity the road is secure!

But there is still one final blessed joy contained in the thought of following Christ. Admittedly, as has been shown, he does not walk along with the follower, nor is he visible before him, but he has gone *ahead*,[24] and this is the follower's joyful hope: that he is to follow him. It is indeed one thing to follow him on the road of self-denial, and this also would be joyful; it is something else to follow him into eternal happiness. When death has separated two lovers and then the survivor dies, we say: Now she has followed him—he went ahead. In the same way Christ went ahead, and not only that, he went ahead *in order to prepare a place for the follower*.

When we speak of a human predecessor, it perhaps holds true that by going ahead he has made the road easier for the one who follows him, and if the road referred to pertains to the

VIII
315
earthly, the temporal, the imperfect, then it may be the case that the road has even become utterly easy for the follower. But this is not the case with the Christian or with the perfect road of self-denial; essentially this road is equally difficult for every follower. But then in an utterly different sense it holds true of Christ that he went ahead. He did not prepare the way for the follower by going ahead, but he went ahead to prepare a place in heaven for the follower. A human predecessor can sometimes justifiably say: Now it is quite easy to go afterward, since the road has been cleared and prepared and the gate is wide. Christ, on the other hand, must say: Behold, everything is prepared in heaven—if you are prepared to walk through the narrow gate of self-denial and along its hard road.

Amid the busyness of the world, this place in the hereafter perhaps appears to be very unsure, but the person who in self-denial renounced the world and himself must surely have convinced himself that there is such a place. After all, a person who exists must be somewhere; he must have a place of resort somewhere. But he cannot have his place in the world he has given up—therefore there must be another place—indeed, there must be in order for him to be able to give up the world. How easy this is for a person to understand if he has actually denied himself and the world! And it is also easy to test his personal life in this respect to see how really sure he is that there is such a place in the life to come if one has actually assured one's life eternally.

The Apostle Paul declares (I Corinthians 15:19), "If we hope only for this life, we are the most miserable of all." This is indeed the case, because if there were no eternal happiness in a life to come, the person who for Christ's sake renounces all the world's goods and bears all its evils would be deceived, dreadfully deceived. If there were no eternal happiness in the life to come, it seems to me that just out of compassion for a person like that it must come into existence. If, then, a person does not hanker after worldly things and a life of ease, does not strive for earthly advantage, does not even grasp it when it is offered, if he chooses toil and trouble and the thankless task, whatever it may be, chooses it because he chose the best cause; if he, when he must do without the things of this world, does not even have the consolation of knowing that he has done his very best to acquire them—then he is, of course, a fool in the eyes of the world; he is the miserable one in the world. If, then, there were no eternal happiness in the life to come, he would indeed be the most miserable of all; his very self-denial would make him miserable, him who had not even tried to acquire the things of this world but voluntarily gave them up. If, however, there is an eternal happiness in the life to come, then he, the miserable one, is still the richest of all. It is one thing to be the most miserable one in the world if the world is to be supreme; it is something else to be the most miserable one in the world if there is an eternal happiness, or to be that if there were not an eternal happiness. That there is this eternal happiness is most gloriously demonstrated by Paul, for there can be no doubt whatever that without it he would have been of all men the most miserable. If, on the other hand, a person tries to secure himself in this world, seeks to assure himself of the advantage of this world, then his assurances that there is a blessed happiness in the life to come are not exactly convincing; they hardly convince others, and they have hardly convinced him himself. But of this let no one judge, or each person only himself, since wanting to judge someone else in this regard is only another attempt to secure oneself in this world; otherwise he would certainly see that both judgment and eternal happiness belong to the other world.

VIII
316

Over the years, alas, it has happened again and again, and the repetition continues, that someone goes ahead, someone for whom another person longs, whom he wishes to follow, but never has any human being, never has any loved one, never has any teacher, never has any friend gone ahead—in order to prepare a place for the one following. Just as the name of Christ is the one and only name in heaven and on earth, so also is Christ the one and only predecessor who has gone ahead in this way. Between heaven and earth there is only one road: to follow Christ. In time and eternity there is only one choice, one single choice: to choose this road. There is only one eternal hope on this earth: to follow Christ into heaven. There is one blessed joy in this life: to follow Christ; and in death there is one final blessed joy—to follow Christ to life!

II²⁵

[But How Can the Burden Be Light If the Suffering Is Heavy?]

MATTHEW 11:30: MY YOKE IS BENEFICIAL, AND MY BURDEN IS LIGHT.

Of the Pharisees it is said (Matthew 23:4), "They bind heavy burdens, hard to carry, and lay them on men's shoulders, but they themselves will not touch them with a finger." Unfortunately this behavior is repeated often enough in this world. It is repeated in the circumstances in which there seems to be justification for the distinction that one party is to carry the burden and the other to be free—even if this is truly not the case, because the one is to carry the burden of the master, the other of the subordinate; the one the burden of the teacher, the other of the pupil; and thus everyone is to carry his burden, no one is to be exempted, not even the independent person, who must carry the burden of responsibility when the dependent person carries the burden of duty. The same pharisaical behavior repeats itself even in the circumstances in which two are to be equally yoked and pull together, so that the one partner is so inclined to wanting to lay the burdens on the other that the husband demands everything of the wife, and the wife demands everything of the husband, so that in the relationship of friendship and unity one person refuses to do like for like but demands everything of the friend, of the fellow worker, and to be free himself. Indeed, not only this crops up, but what is even more lamentable, that a person by ingratitude, lack of appreciation, fickleness, and by additional difficulties makes the burden difficult to carry, so that one selfishly demands that the other must carry the burden and then even makes the burden difficult for him to carry.

This is no disgruntled and malicious picture of the world as it   VIII
is at present; on the contrary, it is an old and seasoned experi-   318
ence, verified in the most diverse times by the most diverse
people. This is the way the human race [*Slægt*] is, certainly
related [*i Slægt*] to the divine,[26] but it is also more or less
degenerate [*vanslægtet*]. This is best seen when one considers
the prototype of the race. If the human race were not related to
God, there could be no such prototype for it; but on the other
hand, when one looks at the prototype, the corruption shows
up in stronger colors; when one looks at the prototype and its
purity, the shadow of corruption is so much darker. This prototype is the Lord Jesus Christ. He came "not to be served,"[27]
not to lay burdens upon others; he carried the burdens, the
heavy burden that all, each one separately, would preferably
shove away: the burden of sin; the heavy burden that not even
the human race itself could carry, the sin of the human race.
And it was made difficult for him to carry it—he was forsaken,
despised, persecuted, insulted, he was handed over to death by
sinners; he was regarded as an enemy by sinners and continues
to be—because he is "the friend of sinners."[28] Yet he carried the
burden that the human race had laid upon him or that he took
upon himself, and not only this, but his whole life, and every
moment in it, was devoted to carrying the burdens of others.
He was heard to say, "Come here, all you who labor and are
burdened" (Matthew 11:28); but no one ever heard him say:
No, I have no time today; I would rather not do it today since
I've been invited to have a good time; I do not feel like it today,
because I have my own concerns; today I have lost patience
with people, since I have been deceived so often. No, words
like that are not heard from his mouth—if so, there would have
been guile on his lips,[29] something Scripture denies and at
which faith shudders—for in his heart he would not really have
meant it. There was no human suffering so dreadful that he
wished to remain ignorant of it lest it disturb his joy or increase
his sorrow, because his only joy was to provide the suffering
one with rest for his soul, and his greatest sorrow was when the
suffering one would not let himself be helped. Wherever you
encountered him, in a remote spot in order to find solitude, or

in the temple and the marketplace in order to teach, he was willing at once; he did not excuse himself by saying that he was seeking solitude; he did not excuse himself by saying that he was occupied. When those who were his next of kin, so to speak, wanted to misuse this relationship, wanted to make demands upon his time, he did not recognize them,[30] but if there was someone who was suffering, he acknowledged him. He came when a ruler sent a messenger for him,[31] and when in passing a woman touched the fringe of his garment[32] he did not say: Do not stop me—no, he stopped, and when the disciples wanted to hold back the crowd, he prevented them.

VIII
319

Ah, if it were wisdom—as we are all too prone to think it— that everyone is closest to himself, then Christ's life was foolish, since his life was such sacrifice that it seemed as if he were the closest to everyone else but the furthest from himself. But if he is unconditionally and eternally the prototype, then let us learn from him as he himself requests (Matthew 11:29): "Take my yoke and learn from me"—let us learn from him to carry burdens, our own and those of others.

Pharisaically to lay the burden on others is truly easy, but it is hard to carry it oneself. In a high-minded moment to promise to carry the burden is easy, but carrying it is hard. Who understands this better than the sufferer, who suffers by carrying burdens. If someone wishes to hear sighing and complaining and whining, this is heard often enough from those who suffer. But it also holds true that it is easy enough to whimper and complain and moan even about trifles. A sufferer does not need to learn this, because pain itself is the first inventor of that, and pain has the scream readily available. But to remain silent and endure, or even to find joy in the bitterness of the suffering, find it not only in the hope that the suffering will sometime cease, but find it in the suffering as we ordinarily speak of it, that sorrow is mixed with joy—this is surely worth learning.

But this teaching is the very content of the Scripture passage: My yoke is beneficial and my burden is light. And it is just as it says, even though for the sufferer it may seem difficult to understand, as if these gentle words were hard words—hard, that is, to grasp. Thus the sufferer exclaims in wonder and asks:

But how can the burden be light if the suffering is heavy?

Let us then—not with the unbelieving wonder that hides denial in its cry, but with the believing wonder that affirms and, only praising God, makes it doubtful in order once again to wonder blessedly—let us with this wonder of faith consider this question. It certainly was not Christ's intention to lead people out of the world into regions of paradise where there is no need or wretchedness at all or by magic to make mortal life into worldly delight and joy. This would be only a Jewish misunderstanding, a sensate, frivolous misunderstanding. No, he wanted to teach what he demonstrated by his example, that the burden is light even if the suffering is heavy. Thus in a certain sense the burden remains the same, since the burden is the suffering, the heavy suffering, and yet the burden becomes light. A person's lot here on earth has not become different from before because Christianity entered into the world. A Christian can come to suffer exactly the same as was suffered before—yet the heavy burden becomes light for a Christian. We shall consider this first and then examine in particular what light burden the Christian particularly has to carry.

When we speak of carrying burdens, ordinary language makes a distinction between a light burden and a heavy burden. We say that it is easy to carry the light burden and hard to carry the heavy one. But the discourse now is not about that; it is about something much more solemn—that the one and the same burden is heavy and yet light. The discourse is about this marvel, for is it really a greater marvel to change water into wine than for the heavy burden to continue to be heavy and yet be light! We do, however, indeed speak this way sometimes. When someone is on the verge of collapsing under the heavy burden he carries, but the burden is the most precious thing he owns, he declares that in a certain sense the burden is light. We see this in the world. We see it with loathing when the miser almost slaves to death with the treasure he carries, although he

VIII
320

considers this heavy burden light, because his treasure is everything to him. We see it and are quietly uplifted when someone
carries what in the noble sense is dearest in the world to him,
and the burden is certainly heavy but nevertheless light. When
in distress at sea the lover is just about to sink under the weight
of his beloved, whom he wishes to rescue, the burden is most
certainly heavy, and yet—yes, ask him about it—and yet so
indescribably light. Although they are both in peril of their
lives, and the other one is the heavy weight, he still wants only
one thing, he wants to save his life. Therefore he speaks as if the
burden did not exist at all; he calls her his life, and he wants to
save his life. How does this change take place? I wonder if it is
not because a thought, an idea, intervenes. The burden is
heavy, he says, and he halts, but then a thought, an idea intervenes, and he says, "No, oh no, it is actually light." Is he
double-tongued to speak this way? Oh no, if he is speaking this
way in truth, then he is truly in love. Therefore it is with the aid
of the thought, of the idea, of being in love that the change
takes place.

VIII
321

"*My yoke is beneficial.*" If a person is, as they say, a lucky fellow
or, rather, if he is also a happy-go-lucky fellow, he can easily
toss his head proudly and carry it high. But when a person
walks bowed down under the heavy yoke of suffering, it presumably would be someone who knew nothing else than to
sink under the weight; so he walks with bent head, silent in
inarticulate, thoughtless desolation. Thoughtless—yes, because the error is simply that he does not have one single
thought that could at least help him lift the burden. There must
be a thought—if it is always necessary, then surely it is especially so here—in order to distinguish a person as being above
the beast. Thus it is a beautiful and uplifting statement by a
noble man who, when speaking of the earthly struggle, asks
for just one thing: Give me a great thought.[33] Thus there can be
many glorious and valuable thoughts that, even though unable
to make the burden light, yet can help lift up the burden. There
can be the thought of better times in the past or better times
coming, the thought of a person one loves or of a person one

admires, the thought of what one owes to another person or the thought of what one owes to oneself. But in the main there is still only one thought, one single thought, that can determine the issue, one thought that contains faith's transformation from the heavy burden into the light burden—this thought is that it is beneficial, that the heavy suffering is beneficial.

But that the heavy suffering is beneficial—that must *be believed*; it cannot be seen. Later it perhaps can be seen that it *has been* beneficial, but in the period of suffering it cannot be seen, and neither can it be heard, even though ever so many people ever so lovingly keep on repeating it: it must be believed. Faith's thought must be there, and the inward, trusting, repeated utterance of this thought to oneself, for if it is true that the word is the binding power, that with a word one binds oneself forever, then it is also true that the word is the releasing power that loosens the yoke of thralldom so that the believer walks freely under the yoke, loosens the tongue ligaments so that the muteness ends and the voice returns with adoration. It must be believed. To see joy when one sees nothing but joy all around is not difficult; indeed, the language itself almost mockingly shows how superficial this empty saying is. But if one sees nothing but misery all around, then in faith to see joy—yes, this is quite in order. It is quite in order with respect to the use of the word "faith," because faith always pertains to what is not seen,[34] be it the *invisible* or the *improbable*; and it is quite in order that a human being is a believer.

It is said of faith that it can move mountains.[35] But even the heaviest suffering cannot be heavier than a mountain. The most powerful expression language has is just the reverse: The suffering rests on a person heavily like a mountain. But if the sufferer still believes that the suffering is beneficial to him— yes, then he does move mountains. So the person who with every step he makes moves a mountain does move mountains every day he lives. In order to move the mountain, one must get under it. Alas, this is the way the sufferer gets under the heavy burden; this is the heaviness. But faith's perseverance *during* the suffering, the faith that it is beneficial—this lifts the mountain and moves it. A sufferer, touched and moved, can

VIII
322

perhaps listen to another's loving, sympathetic, heartening words: It is beneficial to you—but he still cannot move the mountain. A prisoner can listen tearfully to his beloved's voice outside, but he still does not become free—sometimes it makes his imprisonment more oppressive. The sufferer can hear these voices, but if he does not hear the same voice in his inner being he cannot move the mountain. In his despair he can even refuse to listen to these voices, but that helps him even less to move the mountain. But if he believes that it is beneficial to him, then he moves the mountain. It is quite true, is it not, that this huge mountain blocks his way, and he would very much like to go around by another road or have the mountain removed, but if it is beneficial to him, then of course the road is laid out, and then the mountain is on his road. The beneficialness, if I may put it this way, gives the mountain feet upon which to walk. That ingenious pagan said: Give me a place to stand outside the world and I will move the world;[36] that noble man said: Give me a great thought—ah, the former cannot be done, and the latter does not quite suffice. There is only one thing that can help, but it cannot be given by someone else: Believe, and you will move mountains!

VIII
323

Believe that the yoke is beneficial to you. This beneficial yoke is Christ's yoke. But what, then, is the yoke? Well, it can differ radically, but only the yoke that the sufferer believes is of benefit to him is Christ's yoke. Therefore it is not true that the Christian is exempted from human sufferings as we know them in the world; no, but the person who bears the suffering in such a way that he believes the yoke is beneficial to him is carrying Christ's yoke. No new suffering, humanly speaking, has been added, but neither has any old suffering been removed. To that extent everything is unchanged, and yet it has now been given, this great thought, and yet the place has been found outside the world: faith. It is not an invention of sagacity, not its petty and garrulous busyness about benefits and benefits; no, it is the faith of few words, the faith that believes in the benefit. By means of sagacity one can worm one's way through the world, wriggle out of many adversities, talk one's way out of some, hit upon a remedy for some; but all this is faith as little as it is—moving mountains.

Thus when faith clings to the beneficialness and moves the mountain, faith's joy is so great that the yoke is actually light. The very idea of its heaviness makes the yoke light when it can be done with the help of faith. When someone lifts up a feather, he says: It is light. But when someone goes over to a heavy weight and at the sight of it despairs of his own strength but nevertheless tests the weight and succeeds in lifting it, he becomes so joyful that in joy's wonder at the change he exclaims, "It is light." Has he therefore become rash; has he therefore forgotten that he despaired of his own strength; has he therefore taken the divine help in vain? No, indeed, it is precisely in faith's blessed wonder that he speaks this way.

If a girl femininely has just one single wish, alas, but hidden in hopelessness, she can then say: It is impossible. This utterance can signify that she has become apathetic, that she wants to go to bed, wants to sleep off her wish, to sleep herself into oblivion; it can signify that she no longer wants to hide [*gjemme*] her wish in hopelessness but wants to forget [*glemme*] it in hopelessness. But if she femininely holds fast to the wish with all her heart in hope against hope and it is then fulfilled, she will surely exclaim on that joyful day: It is impossible! She will surely welcome the certainty with that happiest greeting of most blissful wonder: It is impossible! It may take some time before she can persuade her heart to say: It is certain, because it is indescribably more precious for her to greet the certainty every day with these words: It is impossible! Is she then a light-minded person who trifles with certainty? Is she an ingrate who does not know how to value certainty? No, she is discriminating, because it is indeed discriminating to begin each day of certainty again in wonder; she is humble and humbly believing. Her wonder is the wonder of faith, and her continuing to wonder is faithfulness to the power that made the impossible possible.

See, the foolish bridesmaids[37] are a symbol of foolish expectancy; but let us change the parable somewhat. Think of the five wise bridesmaids who kept the lamp of expectancy lit and came in with the bridegroom. Then, when the door was closed, if they immediately said: Now everything is certain and decided—I wonder if in another sense their lamps may be said to be put out? But faith keeps the lamp lit. If it is a matter of expectantly waiting, it keeps the lamp lit until the end; and if fulfillment has come, then faith keeps the lamp lit and never forgets that it was impossible. However, the person who impatiently found the yoke heavy only while it was heavy—when the yoke is made light for him, he becomes his old self again; he becomes a faker, a paltry faker who now can easily understand what he could not possibly understand.

One must, however, wait for the fulfillment of an expectation, but for the beneficialness of suffering one does not need to wait—that is, if one does not insist on seeing it (which is a defect) but will believe: This can be done at once. Therefore, faith that the heavy suffering *is* beneficial is far more perfect than the expectation of a happy ending. The happy ending can fail to come, but the believer believes that the suffering *is* beneficial to him—thus the benefit cannot fail to come—when it *is*. The believer humanly comprehends how heavy the suffering is, but in faith's wonder that it is beneficial to him, he devoutly says: It is light. Humanly he says: It is impossible, but he says it again in faith's wonder that what he humanly cannot understand *is* beneficial to him. In other words, when sagacity is able to perceive the beneficialness, then faith cannot see God; but when in the dark night of suffering sagacity cannot see a handbreadth ahead of it, then faith can see God, since faith sees best in the dark. When sagacity consoles a sufferer, it proceeds like this. It says, "It will turn out all right and after a while will be beneficial." Meanwhile sagacity uses the moment to leave. It is similar to the physician's visiting the patient and saying, "After a while"—and then leaving. The patient can never get hold of the physician and hold him to his words as a deceiver, because the physician sneaks away. But when faith comforts a sufferer, it sits down with him and says, "The suffering *is* beneficial to you—just believe it. This is something that can be understood *immediately* by faith. Therefore I would like to stay with you so that you can vent your anger upon me if I am speaking untruthfully. I do not need any marginal time, as if I were running aimlessly;[38] I do not need any time to run away, as if I were a trickster; no, it *is* beneficial to you. Just let the suffering increase; it is beneficial to you. The beneficialness *is* just as I *am*— I, faith." This is the way the beneficialness is for faith, and the beneficialness *is* even when faith goes through spiritual trial, when it seems as if faith has fallen from God's grace, as if it only exasperated him so that he made the test harder and harder as faith increased, so to the believer in discouragement it seems as if he should regret his faith, as if that person were fortunate who goes on living carelessly and never really becomes involved with God but comfortably walks the broad road or, admired, walks the popular middle road and under the yoke never presses forward on the narrow road of faith. But whoever lives in this way is no Christian, whatever else he is, because for the Christian the yoke is beneficial—that is, he believes it. One person carries an iron yoke, a second person a wooden yoke, a third person a gilded yoke, a fourth the heavy yoke, but only the Christian carries—the beneficial yoke.

"*My burden is light.*" What else is meekness [*Sagtmodighed*] except to carry the heavy burden lightly, just as impatience and sullenness are to carry the light burden heavily.

There is in the language a marvelous word that also fits readily in many a connection but never intensely in any connection except with the good. It is the word *courage* [*Mod*]; wherever there is good, courage is also present there; whatever happens to the good, courage is always on the side of the good. The good is always courageous, only the evil is cowardly and afraid, and the devil always trembles.[39] This is how strong this word is, which never turns its back on danger but always faces it, takes pride in itself and yet is very flexible when it is a matter of fitting beautifully in the intense connection with the diversity of the good. This strong word is very repellent to everything evil but very faithful in solidarity with the diversity of the good. There is courage [*Mod*], which bravely defies dangers; there is high-mindedness [*Høimod*], which proudly lifts itself

VIII
326

above grievances; there is patience [*Taalmod*], which patiently bears sufferings; but the gentle courage [*sagte Mod*] that carries the heavy burden lightly is still the most wonderful compound. It is not wonderful with iron strength to deal harshly with what is the hardest of all, but it is wonderful to have iron strength and be able to deal gently with what is weakest of all, or deal lightly with what is heavy.

Yet it is to meekness [*Sagtmodighed*] that Christ summons his followers: Learn from me, for I am meek and lowly of heart.[40] Yes, he was meek. He did indeed carry lightly the heavy burden that far exceeded the powers of a human being, indeed, of humankind. But when someone, at the same time as he himself is carrying this heaviest burden, has the time and willingness and sympathy and self-sacrifice to concern himself unceasingly with others, to help others, to heal the sick, to visit the miserable, to rescue the despairing—is he not carrying the burden lightly! He carried the heaviest burden of solicitude, solicitude for fallen humankind; but he carried it so lightly that he did not quench a smoking wick or break a bruised reed.[41]

As the prototype was, so also ought the follower to be. If someone carries a heavy burden, but then he also seeks the help of others and lays some of it upon them, or if he carries a heavy burden but he also has enough to think about just in carrying his burden—then he certainly is carrying the burden partially or totally, but he is not carrying it lightly. If someone must focus all his powers, if he has not one single thought, not one single moment, to give to others, if he carries his burden with extreme effort, he certainly is carrying it, but he is not carrying it lightly. He may be carrying it patiently, but he is not carrying it meekly. Courage [*Mod*] makes a noise, high-mindedness [*Høimod*] holds its head high, patience [*Taalmod*] is silent, but meekness [*Sagtmod*] carries the heavy weight lightly. Courage and high-mindedness can be seen, and patience can be seen in the effort, but meekness makes itself invisible—it looks so light, and yet is so heavy. That courage resides within is seen in the eyes, that there is high-mindedness is seen in the posture and glance, that there is patience is seen on the mouth, which is silent, but meekness cannot be seen.

What, then, is the light burden of meekness? Well, it is the
heavy burden that is carried lightly. But what, then, is the
heavy burden of meekness? Well, there can be enormous differences, but it is not these differences that determine the matter
but rather the meekness. There can also be enormous differences among the light burdens of impatience, but it is not these
differences that determine the matter but rather the impatience
that makes it into the heavy nonpatience that is not related to
courage and belongs to the family only in the way a degenerate
does. But it is actually true that through meekness the heavy
burden becomes light in a divine sense, just as it is a sad truth
that through impatience the light burden actually becomes
heavy. The beneficialness is the light yoke, and meekness is the
light burden. Never in all eternity can there be any doubt that
what is beneficial is light to carry; therefore doubt directs itself
against something else. It *can* superbly understand that what is
beneficial is light, but it *refuses* to believe that the heavy suffering is what is beneficial. Never in all eternity can there be any
doubt that meekness is a light burden; therefore doubt directs
itself toward something else. It *can* superbly understand that
meekness is light, but it *refuses* to understand that through
meekness the heavy weight becomes the light burden, that the
burden actually becomes light, which it nevertheless does.

Thus, if the one who does not know today what he is going
to have to live on tomorrow, if he, in accordance with the
Gospel text (since Christ did not come into the world *in order to*
abolish worry about making a living by bringing prosperity),
does not worry about tomorrow,[42] then he is indeed carrying
the heavy burden lightly. Alas, while there certainly are never
very many who can be said to have enough for their lifetime, it
can seem to a worried person, whose eyes are confused by
seeing too far ahead, as if his worry about making a living
stretched even beyond his lifetime. If so, then he carries the
heavy burden heavily. But if he patiently resolves to carry the
burden as long as this is required of him, then he still is not
carrying it lightly.

The most cunning and strongest enemy is time, especially
when it concentrates for the attack and is called the oncoming,

the future, because then it is like the fog that cannot be seen close up but the farther away it is seen the more terrible it appears. When patience feels the weight of the future with the eye, one sees how heavy it is, but gentle courage is not worried even about tomorrow. Meekness quickly turns the eyes inward and thus does not see the infinity of the future. It calls the future tomorrow. Tomorrow is indeed the future, but it is the future seen as close up as possible. So quietly does it proceed; so delicately does meekness deal with the future. But close up we cannot see the fog that takes on a threatening shape if one gives the eyes free rein, and close up one cannot see the future either. This is why meekness is not worried even about tomorrow. Is this not carrying lightly the burden of time, the burden of the future?

VIII
328

Thus, if someone who is born a slave, if he, according to the apostle's fervent admonition[43] (for Christ did not come *in order to* abolish slavery, even though that will follow and does result from it) is not concerned about freedom and only if it is offered chooses to be free—then he is carrying the heavy burden lightly. How heavy the burden is the unfortunate one knows best, and human sympathy shares his knowledge. If he sighs under the burden, as humanity does along with him, he is carrying the burden heavily. If he resigns himself patiently to his fate and patiently hopes for freedom, he still is not carrying the burden lightly. But the meek person who has the courage really to believe in the freedom of the spirit carries the heavy burden lightly—he neither gives up his hope of freedom nor does he expect it. The question that is justifiably called the decisive question, the question of freedom, the question that for a born slave surely must be called a question of life and death, to be or not to be—this death-dealing or life-giving question the meek person treats as lightly as if it did not pertain to him, and yet in turn so lightly that in a way it does pertain to him, he says: It does not trouble me to be born a slave, but if I can become free, then I will rather choose that. To bite at the chain is to bear it heavily, to scorn the chain is also to bear it heavily, to bear the chain patiently is still not bearing it lightly, but for the born slave to bear the chain of thralldom as a free man is able to bear a fetter—that is bearing it lightly.

So it always is with meekness. Just as we at times see with amazement what thriftiness can do with a penny, so gentle courage is good at doing things little by little and thus making light that which is heavy. Just as a doubter in apprehensive reticence hardly dares to take a step, dares not deny or affirm anything lest he go too far, so also the meek person has the reticence of eternity. But he is not apprehensive because on the contrary he is boldly confident; he does not doubt but strongly believes. In his faith he breathes soundly and freely, and yet his courage is so meek that what he has to bear looks like a mere trifle. VIII 329

It is indeed the case that every state of mind produces what is outside itself, shapes the task in its own likeness. We cannot say: Wherever there is great danger there is always a person of courage, but instead say: Wherever there is a person of courage, there is sure to be great danger—in other words, he needs it, he demands it, courage's instinct for self-preservation in the person of courage needs it. The task becomes something different through its relation to the person who accomplishes it. The same danger that may be surmounted by the disheartened becomes visibly greater when the one who surmounts it is a person of courage. The same wrong that is borne by an ambivalent individual becomes visibly larger when the righteous person bears it. The same leap made by a fugitive driven by anxiety becomes visibly greater when a ballet dancer does it with lightness. Thus courage makes the danger great and surmounts it, high-mindedness makes the wrong shabby and rises above it, patience makes the burden heavy and carries it, but meekness makes the burden light and carries it lightly.

Therefore it is, humanly speaking, unrewarding to be meek. Meekness walks so quietly that no one becomes aware of the heavy weight; not even the person who lays the burden on the meek really comes to know that. Courage gets paid with the visibility of the victory, high-mindedness with the pride of the glance, patience with the marks of suffering, but meekness is unrecognizable. The meek slave, for example, conceals his master's wrong with his meekness, because it looks as if the slave had a very good life with the master, and so he has—with the aid of meekness. Thus if a traveler saw how slaves groan under the chains, he would become aware, his sympathy would be aroused, and he would give a vivid description of the dreadfulness of slavery. But he would not become aware of the meek slave; he might even believe that it was the master who was the good one. When, for example, the quiet woman meekly bears all her husband's difficulties and moods and indignities, perhaps his unfaithfulness, does it not look—but of what use is it to speak of how it looks—after all, it cannot be seen. If she bears it patiently, then it perhaps can be seen, but if she is to be found anywhere, this meek woman, there is to be seen only a happy marriage, only a beloved husband and a wife who is happy in her home, happy with her husband. Yes, blessed is she—if she is not happy in her husband, she nevertheless is blessed in her meekness.

"Learn from me, for I am meek and lowly of heart." Yes, Christ was meek. If he had not been meekness, he would not have been the one he claimed to be either. But if he had not been meekness, he would not have suffered so much either, since the world itself would have shuddered at the wrong it did him, but his meekness concealed the world's guilt. He did not assert his rights; he did not plead his innocence. He did not talk about how they were sinning against him; he did not point out their scandalous guilt with a single word. Even in his last moment he said: Father, forgive them, they know not what they do.[44] Does not his meekness here conceal their guilt, which becomes as if far, far less than it is by his speaking of it this way, whereas in another sense it becomes even more terrible by their sinning against meekness. When Peter had denied him three times[45] and Christ only looked at him meekly, does not this meekness conceal Peter's guilt and make it something far less! Just listen to the cry in the words: to deny his Lord three times at the very moment he is being betrayed, in the hands of the enemy, insulted and mocked! You shudder as you become aware of it, not through the description of it but merely through the utterance. Christ's meekness, however, keeps one from becoming aware of how deep this fall was.

This meekness we ought to learn from him, and this meekness is the Christian's most specific mark. "If anyone strikes you on the right cheek, turn to him the other also" (Matthew 5:39). Not to strike back is not meekness; nor is it meekness to put up with being wronged and accept this for what it is. But it is meekness to turn the left cheek. High-mindedness also bears the wrong, but as it lifts itself above the wrong it actually makes the wrong seem greater than it is. Patience also bears the wrong, but it does not make the wrong less than it is. Only meekness makes the wrong less, because if one does not take something for what it is, and this something is wrong, injury, insult, then one indeed makes the wrong less. Imagine this happening before our eyes. At the moment the first blow is struck, is it not true that your attention stops at the wrong, and you see it in the person of high-mindedness, and you see it in the person of patience. But as the person of meekness calmly turns the left cheek, you are kept from becoming aware—he bears the wrong so lightly that you almost become less indignant with the perpetrator. To forgive your enemy is not meekness, but to forgive seventy times seven times[46]—that is meekness. Or *this*: that the meek person is so solicitous to forgive that it almost seems as if he were the one who needed forgiveness, or that the meek person who humbly knows how heaven's forgiveness of him depends on his forgiveness actually *needs* to forgive his enemy.

VIII
331

So meekness carries the heavy burden lightly, and the heavy burden of injury so lightly that it is as if the guilty party's fault became less. This meekness paganism does not know. In a Christian sense, this meekness has one glorious quality: it has no reward on earth; and yet another glorious quality: that its reward is great in heaven.[47]

We have now discussed how the Christian carries the heavy burden lightly, how he is not different from others by being exempted from the burden but is Christian in carrying it lightly. The one who carries the beneficial yoke, and the one who, heavily burdened, carries the light burden—that one is a Christian.

But when Christ speaks of the light burden, when he says *my* burden, there can also be quite particularly the thought of a burden that he has laid upon his followers. He has indeed laid it upon them to carry human burdens lightly, but then in addition a light burden that is specifically for the Christians. What is this? Let us first ask this question: Of all burdens, which is the heaviest? Certainly the consciousness of sin; that is beyond dispute. But *the one who takes away the consciousness of sin and gives the consciousness of forgiveness instead*—he indeed takes away the heavy burden and gives the light one in its place.

But why a burden, even if it is called light? Yes, if someone will not understand that forgiveness is also a burden that must be carried, even though a light burden, he is taking forgiveness in vain. Forgiveness is not to be earned—it is not that heavy; but neither is it to be taken in vain and it is not that light either. Forgiveness is not to be paid for—it is not that costly and it cannot be paid for; but neither is it to be taken away as nothing; it is bought at too high a price for that.[48]

See, here again meekness pertains to having faith, to carrying the light burden of forgiveness, to bearing the joy of forgiveness. Flesh and blood may find it difficult to carry the light burden, but if the light burden becomes heavy to carry, then it is the rebellious mind that refuses to believe; if, however, the light burden becomes so light that it cannot be called a burden at all, then light-mindedness has taken it in vain. Forgiveness, reconciliation with God, is a light burden to carry, and yet it is exactly like the light burden of meekness. For flesh and blood it is the heaviest burden, even heavier than the consciousness of sin, because it is conducive to offense. Therefore, just as the Christian will always be recognizable by meekness, so also the essentially Christian is of such a nature that it can be believed only in meekness. Every extreme, of heavy-mindedness or of light-mindedness, is promptly a sign that faith is not really present. Christ did not come into the world in order to make life light in the sense of light-mindedness or to make it heavy in the sense of heavy-mindedness but to lay the light burden upon

VIII
332

the believer. The light-minded person wants to let everything be forgotten—he believes in vain; the heavy-minded person wants to let nothing be forgotten—he believes in vain. But the person who has faith believes that everything is forgotten but in such a way that he carries a light burden—because does he not carry the recollection that it is forgiven him! The light-minded person wants even this recollection to be forgotten—everything to be forgiven and forgotten. But faith says: Everything is forgotten, but remember that it is forgiven. One can indeed forget in many ways. One can forget because one gets something else to think about; one can forget thoughtlessly and light-mindedly; one can think that everything is forgotten because one has oneself forgotten. But eternal justice can and will forget in only one way, through forgiveness—but then, of course, the believer must not forget either, but he must steadfastly recollect that it is forgiven him. The heavy-minded person does not want to forget; he does not want to recollect that it is forgiven him; he wants to remember the guilt—and therefore he cannot believe. But *from* forgiveness a new life will spring in the believer, and as a consequence forgiveness cannot be forgotten. No longer is the Law the only disciplinarian [to lead us] to Christ,[49] but forgiveness through Christ is the gentle disciplinarian who does not have the heart to remind us of what has been forgotten but still reminds us of it to the extent of saying: Just remember that it is forgiven. It is not forgotten but is forgotten in forgiveness. Every time you recollect the forgiveness, it is forgotten; but when you forget the forgiveness, it is not forgotten, and then the forgiveness is wasted.

But is this not a light burden? If you know of any other way to explain it, my listener, then explain it to me. I know of no other way than the simplicity of faith, which nevertheless pertains to a difficult saying, because a saying is always difficult that places together such different words as: "light" and—"burden." It is a difficult saying—ah, but human life does have difficulties. But the difficult saying can be understood, and life's difficulty can be borne, indeed, borne lightly by the Christian—because for him the yoke is beneficial and the burden light.

VIII
333

III

[The Joy of It That the School of Sufferings Educates for Eternity]

We best learn to know children when we watch them play, and young people when we hear them wish—what they wish to be in the world or wish from the world. To choose is the earnestness of life. Even the foolish choice at which one can hardly keep from smiling is earnestness, lamentable earnestness; but wishing, like guessing, is a jest; yet we come to know the young person best through his wish. The choice, as the actual, is also restricted in many ways by actuality; the conditions of the choice are perhaps limited, the chooser inside the many narrower stipulations of actuality, cramped by but also supported by a multitude of considerations. In the wish, however, everything adapts itself to the young person. The deceitfulness of the possible obeys him unconditionally but thereby beguiles him into betraying his inner being; in the wish he is totally himself, and the wish is the most accurate representation of his inner being. That the young person then betrays his inner being in the wish is, of course, something innocent and can even be beneficial to him in learning to know himself and his immaturity. The danger is that the wish, hidden inside, may later turn traitor against him; by really being disclosed the wish does no harm, but by being concealed it can easily turn traitor.

If one imagined a crowd of young people, each one wishing, one would find out by means of the wishes to what extent there was something deeper in the individual's soul, because there is no mirror as accurate as the wish. Although in other respects a mirror sometimes flatters the person looking into it, shows him different from what he actually is, we must say that the wish, aided by possibility, flatteringly beguiles him to disclose himself entirely as he is, beguiles him to look exactly like himself. We shall not pursue this further but simply assume that among these young people there was also one who said, "No, I do not wish for power or wealth or honor or the happiness of love; the only thing I wish for is struggle and danger and difficulties and sufferings; only this inspires my soul." This is how he spoke, and one can always be sure that what an unspoiled youth says contains wisdom if one just interprets it a bit differently from the way it is said.

So, then, there was a young man who wished to suffer in the world. But I wonder if he expressed altogether accurately what he wished, since he obviously did not exactly wish to suffer but, on the contrary, wished to struggle. That there was depth in his soul, we shall not deny him. He did not want to sleep his life away in pleasure, to scintillate with advantages gained without any effort, to parade cravenly in the flabbiness of preferential treatment. He wanted to struggle; he did not even want to struggle for the sake of honor, advantage, or power, but he wanted to struggle for the sake of struggling. But wanting to struggle for the sake of struggling is by no means wanting to suffer—indeed, it is the opposite, but, please note, it is also the opposite with the greatest resemblance. Whereas someone else wishes to know that he is the stronger and wishes the proof of it implicit in the honor and esteem and power gained by struggling, our youth wanted continually to renew his self-esteem by being the stronger in the struggling, the continued struggling for the sake of struggling. He did not want to settle down in peace and quiet—his soul was too aspiring for that; he did not want to hear any news that the struggle was over now. No, just as the bowstring's self-esteem longs for only one thing, to be stretched in battle, and is distressed by only one thing, by having to be put away slackened, no matter how many victories it had won, so he wanted to live and die in the struggle and on the day of battle, first and last in the tension of exertion, in the vortex of battle.

So it was a misunderstanding, a deception, an illusion for the young man to use the wise words "to suffer," "to wish sufferings." If one were to repeat his words to him and say, "Yes, you made the right choice," and now explained to him what they

implied, that aggressive young man who, wishing, challenged
the world to battle, would perhaps lose courage; instead of
falling in the struggle, he perhaps would sink under suffering.
Alas, to want to suffer and to choose sufferings—that is a wish
that never arose in any human heart.[50] The person who thinks
that is deceiving only himself. In order to grasp the thought of
suffering and the joyous gospel of suffering, in order to endure
the suffering and actually have benefit from it, in order to be
able to choose suffering and in order to believe that this actually
is wisdom leading to eternal happiness, a human being needs
divine guidance. It can never occur to the natural man to wish
for suffering. The most profound change must first take place
before a person can believe this secret of sufferings. He must
first be gripped by and then be willing to learn from the only
one who went out into the world with the purpose of willing to
suffer, with the choice of willing to suffer and with insistence
upon it. He went out into the world, but he did not go out the
way a youth goes out from his paternal home. He went out
from the Father in Heaven; he relinquished the glory he had
before the foundation of the world was laid[51]—yes, his choice
was eternally free, and he came into the world—in order to
suffer.

VIII
336

It is said of him, the Lord Jesus Christ: **Although he was a
son, he learned obedience from what he suffered** (Hebrews
5:8). This is the text we shall examine as we consider that even if
no human being, as he is by nature, can wish sufferings, this is
the joy of it:

that the school of sufferings educates for eternity.

When we say of someone that he has learned from what he
suffered, this statement simultaneously contains something inviting and something deterring. The inviting thing is: he
learned. People are not unwilling to learn; on the contrary,
they are eager to learn and especially eager to *have* learned
something. They prefer to learn *everything very quickly*, but if
some effort must be made, they are also willing to make some
effort. But if it is a matter of learning *a little, slowly*, but of

course thoroughly, they are already impatient, and if a long time is required they become, as the language sarcastically puts it, thoroughly [*tilgavns*, of benefit] impatient. But if suffering is to be the teacher, be the schooling, then they completely lose their zeal for learning and think that they are already wise enough, and wise enough to perceive that one can indeed buy wisdom at too high a price, because they cannot promptly, with a commonsense estimate, think through the suffering and understand its beneficialness. If, namely, the suffering is not greater, not more serious, not heavier, not more difficult than can be grasped in its benefits by common sense, then suffering is not the schooling, then it is the schooling that has its arduousness, its suffering, which, of course, is an entirely different matter.

People are eager to learn, and if they hear about a great teacher they hurry to him. Then they are quickly prompted to teachability, then they are eager to buy schooling for money and for admiration. Indeed, they compete to come to him, because it flatters the vanity to have learned from the admired teacher, the one they pay by means of money and admiration, while they also cash in on him and are themselves paid for having learned—from the admired teacher. But if the teacher is unwilling to deceive them, is unwilling to take either their money or their admiration, if he knows only one truth and wants to know only one, the truth that he has by no means invented himself and in which he himself is only a learner— that through sufferings, by himself in sufferings, a person will with the help of God learn the highest truth—then they become impatient and almost indignant with the teacher. The same young man who wanted only one thing, to admire the teacher, who wished for only one thing, in the capacity of the first loyal adherent to proclaim the admired one's praise in the world, becomes indignant when he hears that sufferings are to be the teacher to whom everyone is to be directed. How strange that the young man would so eagerly and admiringly need the teacher and be deceived; on the other hand, he is angry at having to do without the teacher and through sufferings to

VIII
337

be in the truth. How strange that the most coveted good in the world is independence and that there nevertheless is almost no one who covets the only way that truly leads to it: sufferings.

People are eager to learn something, to learn something by which they could amount to something, to learn something that could be of benefit to them, or to learn something of which the knower dares to say that by knowing it he knows a great deal. But when it comes to learning to know oneself through sufferings, then they lose the courage or the ability to comprehend, then they easily see, so they think, and believe that the outcome bears no relation to the arduousness. —Alas, it must indeed be said that, instead of learning something, every human being must *learn* first what is most important to learn. And this first, this most fundamental schooling underlying all other, which is the schooling of sufferings—this is the last to be sought.

"*He learned obedience from what he suffered.*" Imagine if you will, my listener, a very lowly person. He lives in a remote place; his capacities are very limited. Is it not true that the world will say of him: What would he be able to learn? And yet, yet there is one thing he is able to learn—he is able to learn obedience. Indeed, if he were even more limited than he is, yet, yet there is one thing he is able to learn—he is able to learn obedience. But why is it so difficult to learn obedience: is it not because one must learn first of all that obedience is truly worth learning, that far from being what is busily called a waste of time obedience means to gain the eternal? Why is this so difficult to believe? "Because it is so difficult to obey." And why is it so difficult to learn to obey? Because we must learn first that obedience is eternally worth learning.

All the knowledge allied with inquisitiveness, thirst for knowledge, natural talent, the self-seeking passion, all the knowledge the natural man promptly understands to be worth learning is also basically and essentially easy [*nem*] to learn, and aptitude [*Nemme*] is involved here from first to last. Therefore people are willing enough when it is a matter of *learning more*, but when it is a matter of *learning anew* through sufferings, then learning becomes hard and heavy, then aptitude does not help,

VIII
338

but on the other hand no one is excluded even though he is ever so lacking in aptitude. The lowliest, the simplest, the most forsaken human being, someone whom all teachers give up but heaven has by no means given up—he can learn obedience fully as well as anyone else.

This was the first part, that you, my listener, imagined the lowliest human being. But now imagine that the one who Holy Scripture says learned obedience from what he suffered—that it was he who was with the Father from eternity, that it was he who came in the fullness of time,[52] that it was he who finished what the Father had begun, who completed creation and transformed the shape of the world.[53] Holy Scripture speaks of him as of the lowliest of men, says nothing about who he was, about what he was, about what he was able to do, about what he accomplished, nothing about his work, which is beyond all human thought—it only says: he learned obedience from what he suffered! Alas, he who knew everything, he whose thought encompasses everything, he who therefore needed to learn nothing because what he does not know simply does not exist—of him it says: He learned obedience from what he suffered.

Christ *learned* obedience. Surely his will from eternity was in harmony with the Father's; his free decision was the Father's will. But when he came in the fullness of time he learned obedience from what he suffered—what he suffered when he came to his own and they knew him not,[54] when he went around in the lowly form of a servant[55] and carried God's eternal plan although his words seemed futile, when he, the only one in whom there is salvation, seemed superfluous in the world, when he achieved nothing, nothing, when no one paid attention to him or, what surely was even harder, when he was an object of the vile pandering of inquisitiveness. Ah, even when wickedness rose up against him in ferocious rebellion and carried him, the Holy One, to death—this is not as horrifying as the time when he was an object of inquisitiveness, when the Savior of the world was capable of nothing in the lost world but only of gathering the inquisitive, the idlers around him, so that the workman left his task to stare at him, the merchant ran

VIII
339

out of his shop, and even the person hurrying by cast an inquisitive look at him. Vinegar could not have been a more acid
drink[56] for the Holy One than the scatterbrained attention of
the idlers and the nauseating sympathy of inquisitiveness when
one *is the Truth!* Sin's presumptuousness against the Holy One
was not as bitter as to be taken in vain by inquisitiveness!

Yes, he learned obedience from what he suffered—what he
suffered when he who possesses the blessing was like a curse
for everyone who came near him and for everyone who
avoided him, an affliction for his contemporaries, like an affliction for those few who loved him, so that he had to wrench
them out into the most terrible decisions, so that for his mother
he had to be the sword that pierced her heart,[57] for the disciples
a crucified love; an affliction for the vacillators, who basically
perhaps in the hiddenness of a secret desire grasped the truth of
his words but did not dare to join him but for that very reason
also kept a thorn in their souls, a split in their inner being, a
painful mark of having been his contemporaries; an affliction
for the wicked, that he by his purity and holiness had to expose
their hearts and make them guiltier than ever. What heavy
suffering: to have to be the stumbling stone in order to be the
Savior of the world![58]

He learned obedience from what he suffered, what he suffered when he himself indeed sought but also, as it were, had to
seek the scorned company of sinners and tax collectors, when
no one dared to own up to knowing him, when inquisitiveness
gravely shook its head and conceited sagacity mockingly said,
"The fool," and compassion shrugged its shoulders in pity,
when pride looked judgingly at him when he came along and
cowardice sneaked away, when everyone of high standing
avoided him in order not to be suspect, when even the better
one made his relationship to him ambiguous in order not to
lose too much, when the person who had backed away early
enough counted himself fortunate, when no one felt any oblig-
ations to him but thought anything allowable as self-defense
against him, when even the beloved disciple denied him.[59]

He learned obedience from what he suffered, what he suffered when Pilate said: See what a man![60] It is not the ferocious

rebellion, not the blinded raging mob that derisively shouts this way; no, it is a distinguished man robed in purple who compassionately speaks this way. Judas sold him for thirty pieces of silver,[61] but Pilate wanted to sell him at an even lower price, wanted to make him a poor wretch of a man, an object of pity for the compassion of the raging mob.

Therefore his entire earthly life was the heaviest suffering, heavier than any mortal being's can ever be, heavier than any human being can imagine, heavier than any language can express. But for that very reason the suffering was also in the highest sense such that obedience could be learned from it. When someone who is guilty suffers, there is not only no reason, which there never is, but there is not even any apparent occasion for losing faith in God, just as there is not any merit if he patiently suffers his punishment. But when someone suffers innocently, there is opportunity to learn; the opportunity is there, but that does not mean that obedience is learned. But Christ learned *obedience* from what he suffered. He said, "If it is possible, Father, let this cup pass from me; yet not my will be done but yours."[62] That he said this is the first part of obedience, and that he emptied the bitter cup is the second. If he had emptied the bitter cup without saying this, his obedience would not have been perfect. Part and parcel of obedience, and the first part, is also the praying question and the questioning prayer: whether it is the Father's will, whether another way is possible. Therefore his life was obedience, obedience unto death, unto death on the cross.[63] He who was the Truth and the Way and the Life, he who needed to learn nothing, he still learned one thing—he learned obedience. Obedience is so closely related to the eternal truth that the one who is Truth learns obedience.

Now, if it were the case that obedience follows suffering directly, there surely would be someone who would have the courage to choose suffering and someone who, if suffering came to him, would have the courage to count himself fortunate. Ah, but such is not the case, it is not that easy to learn. Humanly viewed, the suffering itself is the first danger, but the second danger, even more terrible, is: failing to learn obe-

dience! Suffering is a dangerous schooling, for if one does not
learn obedience—ah, then it is terrible, just as when the most
powerful medicine has the wrong reaction. In this danger, a
person needs help, needs God's help; otherwise he does not
learn obedience. And if he does not learn obedience, then he
may learn what is most corrupting—learn craven despon-
VIII   dency, learn to quench the spirit, learn to deaden any noble
341   fervor in it, learn defiance and despair. Yet, because the schooling of suffering is so dangerous, we justifiably say that this
school educates for eternity; this danger does not exist in any
other school, but then there is not the gain either: the greatest
danger and the greatest gain, but the greatest gain is the eternal.

A person can learn a great deal without actually coming into
a relation to the eternal. If, namely, a person in learning turns
outward, he can come to know very much, but despite all this
knowledge he can be and continue to be a riddle to himself, an
unknown. Just as the wind drives the mighty ship but does not
understand itself, just as the river drives the wheel but does not
understand itself, so a human being can achieve amazing
things, encompass a multifariousness of knowledge without,
however, understanding himself. Suffering, on the other hand,
turns a person *inward*. If this happens, a person will not in
despair mount a resistance, seek to drown himself and forget
the suffering in the world's distractions, in amazing enter-
prises, in extensive indifferent knowledge; if this happens, the
schooling within begins. Just as we ordinarily say that school
life must be kept out of contact with the world, must be kept
fenced in and entrenched, kept quiet, out of the way, so also is
this utterly true of this school of sufferings, because the school
of sufferings is in the inner being, where suffering teaches,
where God is the one who hears the lessons, where obedience is
the test that is required. Admittedly, suffering often comes
from the outside, but it is not until the suffering is taken into
the inner being that the schooling begins. Many sufferings can
assault a person, and in turn he may also manage to assault in
order, as it is called, to keep his sanity; that is, he may manage
to keep himself from beginning the schooling of suffering.
Worldly sagacity also knows many remedies for sufferings, but

all these remedies have the dismal quality that they save the body but kill the soul; worldly sagacity also knows many encouraging remedies for the sufferer, but all of them have the dismal quality that they invigorate the body but distress the spirit; worldly sagacity also knows how to give a desperate zest for life through sufferings, but only inwardness in sufferings gains the eternal.

When a person suffers and wills to learn from what he suffers, *he continually comes to know only something about himself and about his relationship to God; this is the sign that he is being educated for eternity.* Alas, it is certainly true that through sufferings a person comes to know a great deal about the world, how deceitful and treacherous it is, and much else like that, but all this knowledge is not the schooling of sufferings. No, just as we speak of a child's having to be weaned when it no longer is allowed to be as one with the mother, so also in the most profound sense a person must be weaned by sufferings, weaned from the world and the things of this world, from loving it and from being embittered by it, in order to learn for eternity. Therefore the school of sufferings is a *dying to* and quiet lessons in *dying to.* In this school the lessons are always quiet; here the attention is not dispersed by many subjects, because here only the one thing needful[64] is taught. The attention is not disturbed by the other learners, because here the learner is alone with God. The instruction does not dubiously hinge upon the teacher's competence, because God is the teacher. Only one thing is learned: obedience. Without sufferings one cannot learn obedience, because the suffering is the very guarantee that the attachment is not self-willfulness, but the person who learns obedience learns everything. Ordinarily we say that one must learn to obey in order to learn to be master, and this is indeed true, but one learns something even more glorious by learning obedience in the school of sufferings—learns to let God be master, to let God rule.[65] But what is all eternal truth except this: that God rules; and what is obedience except this: to let God rule; and what other connection and harmony are possible between the temporal and the eternal than this—that God rules and to let God rule! And

VIII
342

where is this to be learned except in the school of sufferings,
when the child is weaned and self-willfulness dies and the suffering one first learns the difficult lesson that it is indeed God
who still rules, until he learns in joyful obedience to let God
rule! Everything that a human being knows about the eternal is
contained primarily in this: it is God who rules, because whatever more a person comes to know pertains to *how* God has
ruled or rules or will rule. But this eternal truth is expressed in
the language of obedience in this way: to let God rule. It is one
and the same, except that in obedience the humble assent, the
confident, strengthening yes of devotedness is heard. If the fear
of the Lord is the beginning of wisdom,[66] then learning obedience is the consummation of wisdom; it is to be promoted in
wisdom by being educated for the eternal. Indeed, if you, disci-
plined by sufferings, have ever subjected yourself in perfect, in
unconditional obedience, then you have also discerned the
presence of the eternal within you, then you have found the
peace and rest of the eternal. Wherever the eternal is, there is
rest; but there is unrest where the eternal is not present. There
is unrest in the world, but above all there is unrest in a person's
soul when the eternal is not present in it and he is only "full of
unrest."[67] But if diversions, under the guise of driving out this
unrest, increase it, then sufferings, under the guise of increasing it, drive it out. At first the rigorous earnestness of sufferings is like a discipline that increases the unrest, but if the
sufferer will learn, then he is educated for the eternal.

VIII
343

To find rest is to be educated for the eternal. On the whole there is
only one way in which rest is to be found: to let God rule in
everything; whatever more a person comes to know pertains to
how God has willed to rule. That there is a reconciliation for the
person who is brokenhearted—there is rest in that, but he
cannot find rest in this eternal thought if he does not first find
rest in the thought of obedience: that God must rule [*raade*] in
everything, because reconciliation is indeed God's plan [*Raad*]
for the salvation of humankind. That satisfaction has been
made for guilt—there is rest for the penitent in that, but he
cannot find rest in this eternal thought if he does not first rest in
this: to let God rule in everything, because making satisfaction

is indeed God's plan from eternity. That God will forgive you—there is rest in that, but you cannot find rest in this eternal thought if you do not rest in the thought that God is to rule in everything. Otherwise God's grace would become your merit, and it would not be God who gives both to will and to do,[68] gives the growth and gives the completion, something that all your own effort cannot achieve; it adds not one foot to your stature,[69] not an inch, something that all your own self-concern cannot do, because it only distresses the spirit and delays growth. But faith and faith's obedience in sufferings love forth the growth, because the object of all faith's work is to get rid of egotism and selfishness in order that God can actually come in and in order to let him rule in everything. The more suffering there is—provided something is learned from the suffering—the more all that is selfish is removed, rooted out, and the more obedience replaces it as the receptive soil in which the eternal can take root. You cannot take the eternal, you can only appropriate it; but you cannot appropriate what belongs to you, only what belongs to another; and this in turn you cannot legitimately appropriate if he is unwilling to give it to you. On the other hand, if he is willing to give it to you, then the appropriation is the inward deepening, but in relation to God and the eternal the appropriation is obedience, and in obedience there is rest. There is rest in the eternal. This is the eternal truth, but the eternal can rest only in obedience—this is the eternal truth for you.

VIII
344

Therefore, as soon as unrest begins, the cause is that you are unwilling to obey; but suffering will help you to obey. Therefore, when there is suffering, but also obedience in suffering, you are being educated for eternity; then there is no impatient hankering in your soul, no restlessness, neither of sin nor of sorrow. Just as the cherubim with the flaming sword stood guard to keep Adam from returning to paradise,[70] so also suffering is the guardian angel who keeps you from slipping out again into the world. Suffering is the school that will also keep you in school so that you may be properly educated for eternity. And just as one of the ancient prophets has said that the idol-worshiper carries his god but the true God carries his

believers,[71] so also is the "Let God rule in everything" of obedience the true knowledge about the only true God, but what
else is it to be educated for eternity! Whereas the idol-worshiper,
whatever his idol may be, crawls to his death in disobedience and
self-willfulness by willing to carry his god, the one who learned
obedience from what he suffered is lightly carried by God,
lightly, as lightly as he alone is who is educated for eternity.

The school of sufferings educates for eternity. We ordinarily speak in
another way about schooling; we say that one school educates
for science, another for art, a third for a specific occupation,
and so on. We thereby say that school has its day but in turn
there comes a time when one is to have benefit from what one
learned in school. But when the school of sufferings makes
slow progress for the sufferer, he perhaps heaves a sigh and says:
This school attendance just never ends, and he presumably
believes that in this sigh is contained the heaviest suffering.

But is this actually the case? The experts assume that the
length of the growing period is directly related to the quality of
the creature. The lowest forms of animal life are born in an
instant and die in almost the same instant; the lower animals
grow very fast. Of all creatures the human being grows most
slowly, and the experts demonstrate from this that he is the
most elevated creature in creation. We speak the same way
about school. The one who is destined to serve only in a lowly
occupation goes to school for only a short time; but the one
who is destined for something higher must go to school for a
long time. Therefore the length of the school period has a
direct relation to the significance of what one is to become. If,
then, the school of sufferings continues for a whole lifetime,
this demonstrates that this school must educate for the
highest—indeed, that it is the only one that educates for eternity, because no other school period continues so long. Truly,
if a temporal wisdom were to think that one should attend its
school for a whole lifetime, the learner would justifiably become impatient and say: When am I going to have any benefit
from what I have learned in this school! To itself and to the
learner, only eternity can justify making his whole lifetime into

VIII
345

a school period. But if eternity is to conduct a school, then it has to become the most select school, but the most select is the very one that lasts the longest. As a teacher ordinarily says to the young pupil who prematurely finds the school period too long: Now, just do not become impatient; after all, you have a long life ahead of you—so eternity more justifiably and trustworthily says to the sufferer: Now, just do not become impatient; there is time enough—after all, there is eternity. When eternity speaks, there is no guile in its mouth as there is in the teacher's well-meaning words, for how can the teacher vouch for the long time that is supposed to lie ahead for the youth. But eternity must surely know that it is, and if it is, then there is, of course, time enough.

The longest school educates for the highest; the school that continues just as long as time can educate only for eternity. The yield of the school for life appears in time, but suffering's life-school educates for eternity. It educates for eternity. It is also distinguished by this, that although one ordinarily grows older in going to school, and that is just as it should be, in eternity's school one becomes younger, and that is just as it should be. The eternal life is rejuvenation. Should there not, then, be time enough for the learner to have all the benefit and joy from what he learned? What is it that produces impatience about the all-too-long school period if it is not that one becomes older every year, and therefore one legitimately fears that the school period will continue too long. But if one becomes younger with each year! Can there be any more alleviating thought; it is indeed mighty enough to make the longest school period into the shortest! When the shortest school period has lasted just one year, the learner has become one year older; but when the longest school period has lasted seventy years and the learner has become younger each year, then this schooling is obviously even shorter than the shortest.

The idea that the eternal life is rejuvenation is truly a very beautiful, blissful, and upbuilding thought. Yet I shall not develop it further, because in my opinion it is so beautiful that it is almost dangerous and can very easily become a deception if, precisely when it manifests itself in all its beauty to someone, it

VIII
346

fascinates his imagination instead of giving him the momentum to strive—as if rejuvenation occurred by magic, as if rejuvenation did not in another sense take a long time. Indeed, a person must have learned a great deal and learned very profoundly in the school of sufferings before he can, actually to his own upbuilding, associate with such an elevated thought. If it is ordinarily the case that one must crawl before one can walk, then here it holds true that one must walk before one begins to fly—and this thought indeed has the lofty flight of eternity. That is why I always prefer to speak about lowlier things, about the beginner's slow and laborious gait, because this kind of talk cannot deceive anyone; and, on the other hand, the person who has come so far that to his own upbuilding and progress he is refreshed by the thought of rejuvenation, that person needs no other person's words, least of all mine—on the contrary, I need to learn from him.

But even if I myself do not want to speak on this, I shall nevertheless in conclusion—in order to carry out the task of this discourse: the *joy of it* that the school of sufferings educates for eternity—call to mind what one of the oldest teachers of the Church, one of the apostolic fathers, has so beautifully depicted. In a section of his books called *Visiones*,[72] he tells how God granted him three visions. In addition to their significant content, these visions had the singularity that the person who showed them to him and explained them was a very old woman the first time, the second time she appeared younger and more joyful to look at but still had the old woman's hair and wrinkled skin, but the third time she was young, joyful, yet as earnest as eternity's youthfulness is. He explains this in more detail, but among other things also adds, "They who honestly do penance shall become younger." In this way he restrains the powerful thought, lest it become a high-flying mirage, so that the learner does not only not become younger but, what is even worse than becoming older, is deceived. This discourse also exerts a restraining influence in the same way, because it is only the school of sufferings that educates for eternity. If any such thing is to be granted to a person, it must happen to him in the school of sufferings.

Yet the joy still remains; at the end it remains as it remains the end here: that no other school continues as long as the school of sufferings, and that therefore no other school educates for eternity, and that in the school of eternity it can turn out that the learner is rejuvenated. No proficiency, no knowledge, nothing except suffering, provided one learns obedience from it, educates for eternity as truly as the One who was and is the Truth, the One who knew everything yet learned one thing but nothing else, *learned* obedience from what he suffered. If it were possible for a human being to learn obedience to God without sufferings, then Christ as man would not have needed to learn it from sufferings. What he learned from sufferings was human obedience, because the eternal harmony of his will with his Father's will is indeed not obedience. The obedience belongs to his abasement, as it says: He abased himself and became obedient.[73] But to be a human being is indeed his abasement; therefore, for a human being in his relation to God it holds true that obedience is learned only from sufferings; if this holds for the pure one, how much more then for the sinful human being! Only suffering educates for eternity, because eternity is in faith, but faith is in obedience, but obedience is in suffering. Obedience is not apart from suffering, faith is not apart from obedience, eternity is not apart from faith. In suffering obedience is obedience, in obedience faith is faith, in faith eternity is eternity.

IV

[The Joy of It That in Relation to God a Person Always Suffers as Guilty[74]]

When we hear a beautiful, upbuilding, gripping true saying, we usually also ascertain who said it, on what occasion, in what situation; that is, we ascertain to what extent the true saying was truth in the one speaking—something we fervently wish both for his sake and our own. A pompous saying devoid of truth is "like a tree that bears lovely but useless fruit" (Wisdom 10:7);[75] and a true saying that does not have its truth in the speaker is disheartening, like a blessing that curses the one who is blessing. But a true word that has truth in the speaker is in the most beautiful sense a good word in the right place, is like a golden apple in a silver bowl.[76] It is as if the saying were of greater value and therefore is compared to the golden apple, whereas the speaker is only the costly vessel of hallmarked silver in which the true is authentically set in truth. In a way the saying does have the greater value; it goes out into the world and is acted upon by others, who have not said it but only acted upon it. Every time, however, that the saying is confirmed in its truth, we are piously reminded of its noble original setting. If, for example, a king declares that earthly wealth and power and might are sheer vanity, we rejoice that the speaker is indeed a king, because he has surely had the opportunity to experience it. He is not like someone whom all such things dazzled at a distance in the hankering of desire, because he has seen them at very close range. When someone who owned very much, yes, as if everything, but also only as if everything, in order really to feel it when he lost everything—when he says, "Blessed be the name of the Lord,"[77] we are assured and gladdened, because he was indeed the tested one. Many a splendid saying is preserved in this way, and many a speaker is called to mind, but among them is also a robber. This cannot disturb us; on the contrary, in another sense we would miss such a person if he were not there, because in the world of truth there is no difference between a king and a robber; *there* the only questions asked are whether what he said is truth and whether it was truth in him.

According to the narrative of the holy evangelists, two robbers were crucified with the Lord Jesus. The robber's words are spoken from the cross at the moment of death—truly an occasion that surely must guarantee the truth of the words in him, for who indeed speaks more sincerely than a dying person when he concentrates his soul in one single word! The wise saying of a king wearied with vanity is no more worthy of attention than the humble words of a penitent robber at the moment of death. There were two robbers, but only the one is remembered, the one whom everyone recognizes when we say: The words of the robber on the cross. Which of the robbers it was is not stated, neither by name nor by any other specification, whether, for example, it was he who hung on the right side or on the left. Of course, this makes no difference at all, even if it can childishly satisfy an innocent thirst for knowledge to assume that he was the one on the right side, since it is to those on the right side that it will at some time be said: Come, O blessed of my Father, inherit the kingdom prepared for you before the foundation of the world[78]—and the same one who will say those words did in fact say to this robber: Today you will be with me in paradise.[79] The other robber mocked to the very last, hardened himself even upon the cross—he presumably hung on the left side.

The Gospel writer Luke has preserved the robber's words on the cross (Luke 23:41).

We are receiving what our deeds have deserved, but this one has done nothing wrong.

VIII
350

We shall at this time make these words the subject of our consideration as we consider:

the joy of it that in relation to God a person always suffers as guilty.

Guilty? Not guilty?[80] This is the earnest question in legal proceedings. This same question is even more earnest in concern about oneself, for if the authorities force their way into the most hidden nooks of the house in order to apprehend the guilty person, concern about oneself forces its way further than any judge does in order to find the guilt, into the heart's most secret nook, where only God is the judge.

As long as the judgment is human and the relation is between human beings, we all of course agree that to be innocent is the only thing to be desired, that innocence is the mighty stronghold that no human injustice and lack of appreciation can capture or demolish, that innocence is the purity that not even rape can violate, the invulnerability that not even death can mortally wound.

Yet this is not always the case, and it actually is the case only as long as the main tension of the relation is a relation between two, because in love's most fervent and tender relation between human beings love's highest possible wish is to be in the wrong, yes, to be the guilty one. Humanly we speak of unhappy love as the heaviest suffering, but in turn there is the heaviest, the most agonizing suffering in an unhappy love when the object of love is such that it essentially cannot be loved; yet the only thing the lover wishes with all his heart is that the object of love be loved. If, namely, the object of love can still essentially be the object but only the possession is denied, then the unhappy love is less unhappy, less agonizing. Then the possession is denied, but the object is not lost; on the contrary, it has all the essential perfection that blissfully satisfies love's requirement. There is indeed a requirement; hidden in all love, not selfishly but deeply and eternally grounded, there is a requirement that is the very being of love.

Let us imagine such an unhappily loving girl and her suffering. Is it not true that she would say: "Whether I am in the right or in the wrong is a trifle; I can still live with that, for if I am in the wrong he will readily forgive me; but if he is in the wrong, if he is guilty, if he is the kind of person who cannot be loved, then this is my death, then I have lost everything. I have only one single object of my love; it is he, he alone in the entire world, and he, alas, cannot become the object of love. Ah, it is not an external obstacle, for then he would still be the beloved and I less unhappy, but there is an obstacle in his essential

VIII
351

nature, or the obstacle is that his nature lacks depth of heart, and I am most unhappy." Consequently she would much rather be in the wrong herself, indeed, be the guilty one if only the beloved might be in the right. What does this mean? It means that this girl truly loves; she does not quarrel, not even about right and wrong; so there are still two. No, she has truly become one with her object and therefore does not feel the loss of him until he is lost essentially—by becoming unessential or essentially someone else, not when he is lost incidentally—by becoming someone else's. If only he were in the right, if she were guilty—then she considers her love saved. But if he were in the wrong, then she considers her love dreadfully lost. This is truly the way it is, because the person who is the perfect one but is that for someone else than me is not essentially lost and I can go on loving him just the same, but the person whose essential nature is lost is essentially lost.

But when a human being relates himself to God and the question there is about being in the right or in the wrong, I wonder if any human being has actually ever managed to think the dreadful thought that in the relationship to God there could be a question of unhappy love due to God's being unable to become its object! God is not lost or lost to a person if for seventy years, if so be it, God makes a person's life harder than any other person's life ever was and leads him in such a way that he comprehends nothing, nothing at all of this riddle. But if the slightest thing happened that could demonstrate or could even merely appear to demonstrate that God was not love— well, then all would be lost, then God would be lost, for if God is not love, and if he is not love in everything, then God does not exist at all.

Oh, my listener, if you have experienced a human life's heaviest moment, when it all became dark for your soul, as if there were no love in heaven or as if he who is in heaven were nevertheless not really love, when it seemed to you as if there were a choice you had to make, the dreadful choice between being in the wrong and gaining God or being in the right and losing God—is it then not true that you have found the blessedness of heaven in choosing the former, or rather in this, that it

really was not a choice, that on the contrary it was heaven's
eternal claim on you, its claim on your soul, that there must be
no doubt, no doubt, that God was love! Alas, whereas many
indefinitely put off the thought of whether God actually is
love, it would truly be better if they made the love in them
blaze just by the thought of the horror that God was not love,
made the love blaze, because if God is love, then he is also love
in everything, love in what you can understand and love in
what you cannot understand, love in the dark riddle that lasts a
day or in the riddle that lasts seventy years. Alas, although
many call themselves Christians and yet may seem to be living
in uncertainty as to whether God actually is love, it would truly
be better if they made the love blaze just by the thought of
paganism's horror: that he who holds the fate of everything
and also your fate in his hand is ambivalent, that his love is not a
fatherly embrace but a constraining trap, that his secret nature
is not eternal clarity but concealment, that the deepest ground
of his nature is not love but a cunning impossible to understand. We are not, after all, required to be able to understand
the rule of God's love, but we certainly are required to be able
to believe and, believing, to understand that he is love. It is not
dreadful that you are unable to understand God's decrees if he
nevertheless is eternal love, but it is dreadful if you could not
understand them because he is cunning.

   If, however, according to the assumption of the discourse, it
is true that in relation to God a person is not only always in the
wrong but is always guilty and thus when he suffers also suffers as guilty—then no doubt within you (provided you yourself will not sin again) and no event outside you (provided you
yourself will not sin again by taking offense) can displace the
joy.

The joy is this: that now and at every moment and at every
future moment it is eternally true that nothing has happened or
ever can happen, even if it were the most sorrowfully contrived
horror of the sickest imagination that became a reality, there is
nothing that can rock the faith that God is love; and the joy is
that if a person refuses to understand this by means of the good

VIII
352

then the guilt will help him to understand it. *If in relation to God a person always suffers as guilty, then at every moment, whatever happens, he is indeed reassured that God is love or, more correctly, at every moment he is prevented from falling into that doubt, because the consciousness of the guilt draws the attention to itself.*

Most people probably have an idea, sometimes a vivid idea, at specific times a fervent feeling, that God is love; and yet there perhaps are many people who live in such a way that it vaguely seems to them that if this or that horrible thing, which they especially dread, were to befall them they would have to give up their faith, let go of God, lose him. But is anything more indefensible than to go on living this way: to vitiate the highest passion in a semidrowsiness between doubt and trust, so that the individual never faces the insidious enemy that sucks the blood of the innermost being, so that, thinking he is not in despair, he never comes to shudder at this condition—because he has dozed off in despair! Alas, God is not the one who loses anything by this, but the sleeper, he who truly is sinning by sleeping, he loses everything, loses that without which life really is nothing. Just as Scripture speaks of suffering the ship-wreck of faith,[81] so also it must be said of the person who gave up his faith in God's love that he is suffering the shipwreck of eternity's joy of living. What more is there, then, to live for! Just let it storm, as long as the ship holds together—that is hard. Let fair weather and fair winds come—that is joyful. But if the ship has a basic defect, of what help or harm is anything else; if the timbers separate, what more is there, then, to expect! But the person who gave up God, who thought that something like this had happened or could happen that might upset his faith in God's love—that person has suffered damage in the innermost joint in a human being. Whether there are any spikes that in particular can be said to hold the ship's structure together, I do not know, but this I do know—that this faith is the divine joint in a human being and that if it holds it makes him the proudest sailing ship, but if it is loosened it makes a wreck of him and thereby makes the content of his whole life futility and miserable vanity.

Now, if it were possible that a person could have even just a

VIII
353

show of right in giving up his faith that God is love, he must *first* be unconditionally pure and be altogether without guilt, not merely, humanly speaking, in this or that, but altogether without guilt before God, because only on this assumption can doubt gain a foothold. Without it, doubt is not merely deprived of a place of resort, is not only built upon sand, but is built over an abyss. *Second*, something must happen that is incompatible with the idea that God is love. But no human being would be able to endure this horror; only once was it endured by him who was the Holy One, by him who *before God* was without guilt.

This is why we should always speak about Christ's suffering with fear and trembling and preferably in worshipful silence, because human thought is as little able as human language to depict or clearly make out the depth of this horror. This is why we should speak with the circumspection of humility or humbly be silent about how Christ suffered, lest we be tempted by the ungodly thirst to search out the secrets of God, which even paganism's perception punished with an eternally burning thirst.[82] This is why we must be especially alert in these days when attempts are made in many ways to frighten life away from faith, as if to believe were to comprehend, as if one could not boldly believe and believe unto salvation because one cannot—brazenly comprehend. *Before God* only Christ was without guilt, and for this very reason he had to suffer the superhuman suffering, had to be led to the border, as it were, of justifiably mistrusting that God is indeed love, when he cried out: My God, my God, why have you abandoned me.[83]

Not so with the robber of whom we speak. While the Savior of the world groans, My God, my God, why have you abandoned me—words that the greatest preacher of our Church and also its most orthodox person, words that Luther, precisely because of his orthodoxy, hardly dared to preach about[84]—the robber at the Savior's side preaches first and foremost to his own upbuilding, as a true preacher does, on the God-fearing thought: I suffer as guilty. Although the profound horror in Christ's suffering cannot become a sermon topic, the theme of the robber is very properly that of a sermon. Under the name of sermon we certainly do hear many insipid and tasteless words about God's love, but these penitent words about sin and guilt are still the only proper beginning after which God's love becomes the ending. Yes, the penitent robber is preaching; if that king is called a preacher,[85] how much more, then, the penitent robber. He is the proper preacher of repentance. A camel's-hair shirt[86] is certainly a tight-fitting piece of clothing, but to be crucified is an even tighter fit; to live in a desert[87] is surely a lowly assignment in life, but to be crucified is still the hardest and heaviest position. And to say "Repent *ye*"[88] is still not as excellent an exhortation to repentance as to say "*I* suffer as guilty," and to say of oneself "I am a prophet"[89] is not as stirring as to say "I am a sinner who is suffering as guilty." The robber is preaching to himself, to the other robber, to all those present, and saying, "You are all sinners; only he who hangs between us, only he is without guilt before God; he suffers as innocent." "In the world," declares this uplifted preacher of repentance, "it is indeed usually the custom that one robber walks between two so-called righteous men, but this custom and this righteousness are a delusion. Here the truth is seen: that the only righteous one, the only one, is crucified between two robbers. See, this is why Scripture says, 'He was reckoned with transgressors'[90]— yet not because we two are robbers and, humanly speaking, greater sinners than others—no, take me down, hang in my place any one of all you here present, and he, the Holy One, as one crucified together with him, is still reckoned with transgressors. Indeed, as soon as the Holy One is reckoned in the human race, he is reckoned among transgressors. I wonder if any human being, even if he were, humanly speaking, persecuted as one who was innocent, sentenced innocent, crucified innocent, I wonder if here at the crucified one's side he would dare say: I suffer as innocent." This is a Christian repentance sermon that reminds even the martyr that *before God* he suffers as guilty; it is a Christian repentance sermon, because the Jews nevertheless hold to the conception that there are holy men who should preach repentance[91] and that by striving one can become holy enough to be a preacher of repentance. In

VIII
355

Christianity, however, an *actual* sinner preaches repentance, and even the holy men, humanly speaking, must put up with an actual sinner's being a preacher of repentance who does not say "Woe unto you,"[92] when he begins, but says "God be merciful to me a poor sinner,[93] I suffer as guilty."

Yet the penitent robber is no preacher of repentance; his sermon is no repentance sermon. If that were the case, it would have nothing to do with the theme of this present discourse: the joy of it that in relation to God a human being always suffers as guilty. But it is precisely on this that the robber preaches to his own comfort and relief. What is upbuilding and instructive in this robber is that in the moment of his most ignominious death he still had enough depth and humility to grasp that suffering as guilty is an alleviation in comparison with the pain of the death suffered on the cross standing in the middle. Through comparison with this suffering, the penitent robber finds comfort and relief in the thought that he is suffering as guilty. Why? Because then the suffering is not at all involved with the troubled question of doubt's anxiety about whether God is love. Thus the robber is no preacher of repentance, except insofar as the Gospel's joyful message is always that; he proclaims the joyful message that is painful and humbling only for the proud. When, for example, in paganism a person was wronged by others, was persecuted for the sake of the good, was sentenced to death for the sake of the good, alas, then he became self-important and said *in relation to God*: I suffer as innocent, and proudly thought that it was easiest—to be in the right. But at Christ's side such a person learns that there is only one who before God suffered as innocent, and this humbles him. In paganism, because one was in the right on one count in opposition to people—well, if this is too little, let us say because one was in the right on all counts in relation to people— one would extend this to God and on one count be in the right in relation to God, before whom one nevertheless is in the wrong on all counts. The pagan was so proud and blind that he did not grasp this horror; he proudly boasted of "his glittering vice"[94] as a virtue.

So the robber finds relief in the thought that he suffers as

VIII
356

guilty. And so it is also in comparison with the superhuman terror of suffering when before God one is without guilt. When a person suffers as guilty and when he acknowledges it, he has God to hope in, God to cling to, then he has, if I may put it this way, rescued God—and what danger should one not be able to endure; indeed, even in God's consuming wrath one still has him—on one's side. But when before God one suffers as one who is altogether innocent, then it seems as if God were against one, then one is—abandoned by God. When one suffers as guilty, then the concern—in which there nevertheless is the comfort of eternity, indeed, the joy of eternity: to admit that God is right—is humbling. But when one, entirely innocent, suffers, then it seems as if it has not yet been quite decided that God is love, seems as if the struggle were about justifying God, something only the conceit of fools and conceited wisdom can regard as the easiest—because for a human being that is really presumptuousness.

What does doubt about God's love want? It wants to reverse the relation, wants to sit quiet and safe, judging, and to deliberate upon whether God is indeed love; it wants to make God the defendant, to make him the one from whom something is required. But along this road God's love will never be found; doubt's striving toward God will be banished from God because it begins with presumptuousness. Faith's eternal happiness, on the other hand, is that God is love. This does not mean that faith understands how God's rule over a person is love. Right here is faith's struggle: to believe without being able to understand. And when this struggle of faith begins, when doubts arise, or when "doubt assaults faith with many wild thoughts,"[95] then the consciousness of guilt comes to the rescue as the relief, as the last reinforcement. One would suppose it to be a hostile power, but no, it specifically wants to help faith, help the believer by teaching him not to doubt God but himself. Instead of the mendacity about thinking through the doubt, which is patently doubt's most dangerous invention, the consciousness of guilt thunders its "Halt!" and leads faith back rescued, rescued because there was no conflict—about whether God is love.

Just as Scripture declares that God has laid everything under sin,[96] so that every mouth shall be stopped,[97] so also this humbling but at the same time rescuing thought stops the mouth of doubts. When doubt's thousands of questions want to assail faith and make it seem as if God could not answer, the consciousness of guilt teaches the believer that it is he who is unable to repay one in a thousand[98]: ergo, God is love. If you cannot grasp the absolute power of this conclusion, faith grasps it. If you cannot grasp the joy in the thought that in this way it is eternally guaranteed that God is love, faith grasps this; faith understands that to make it possible to think through doubt is a delusion, but understands that it is a blessing that it is made impossible to doubt. If it is terrible for a son to be in the right in relation to his father, if it is an upbuilding thought that in relation to his father a son *always* is in the wrong, oh, then it is also a blessing that it is made impossible to doubt that God is love. Let the insipid lauding of God's love fall silent—the true declaration of honor is this: I suffer at all times as guilty—so certain is it in all eternity that God is love. Alas, in paganism the happiest of all thoughts was secured only by one's being able to think that one was in the right in relation to God. In Christianity this is eternally secured. If this, then, is the only joyful thought both in heaven and on earth, if "the joy and again I say joy's"[99] only source is that God is love: then it is also joyful that this stands so firm that no doubt, none whatever, can rock it, cannot even begin to shake it. The consciousness of guilt is the mighty one that guards this treasure; at the very same moment doubt wants to assail him, doubt is doomed; then the mighty one shoves it down into the abyss, down into the nothing from which it came, but at the very same moment faith has its object again—that God is love. Here there is not the talk, not the deceitful talk, about the dubious victory or rather about doubt's assured victory: thinking through doubt; but here is the fully certain talk about doubt's certain death, its certain death at birth. If doubt is to have the least show of a foundation, it must have innocence to appeal to, not innocence in comparison with other human beings, not innocence in this or in that, but innocence *before God*. If it does not have this, which is an impossibility, then it is promptly shattered, destroyed; it is reduced to nothing—alas, this is the very opposite of beginning with nothing.[100]

When it is so, according to the assumption of the discourse, that in relation to God a person always suffers as guilty, *then the joy of it is this, that the fault therefore lies in the individual, and as a consequence of that there must always be something to do, there must be tasks, moreover human tasks,* and along with the tasks a hope that everything can and will improve if he improves, becomes more diligent, more prayerful, more obedient, more humble, more devoted to God, more heartfelt in his love, more fervent in spirit.[101]

Is this not joyful? If it is so that courage rightly says: Where there is danger, there I am also, or turns it around and says: Where I am, there danger is also; and if it is so that loving sympathy rightly says: To sit with a sufferer and have nothing to do is even harder than to be one—then it is likewise so that where there is task there is hope. But if in relation to God a person always suffers as guilty, then as a consequence there is always a task and always hope. Ah, my listener, if you have been tried and tested in life, if you have been so tried and tested that one can speak with you of terrible things because you are acquainted with dangers and horrors other than what mawkishness, cowardice, and softness, like a naughty child, whine about—not getting one's way promptly, having to endure something, not succeeding at once, God's not paying any attention to one's anger—if you have been more earnestly tried and tested, is it not true that then you understood that this had to be the moment of hardest suffering, this halting when it seemed as if there were no task! It was not that the sufferer refused to pick up the burden because it was so heavy; there was something even heavier: there seemed to be no task; not even the suffering could become the task. It was not that the sufferer, who had worked for a long time in vain, now rebelled against God and refused to work any longer. Alas, no, the unspeakably heavier burden was that there did not even seem to be the requirement of any task for him. It was not that the

VIII
359

sufferer, who had made a mistake so many times, had now become weary of starting again from the beginning; no, it was the horror of hopelessness, as if there were nothing to start on, as if with the most sincere will he could not find any task. If we see a horse, perhaps already overstrained, hitched to a too heavy load, if we see its final effort to strain every muscle to drag the load ahead, we have sympathy for the horse, but there is still always the hope that it will succeed. But if you see a painfully suffering horse strain every muscle, but you see no task, no load—would not this sight be something to despair over. Is it really hopelessness to reject the task because it is too heavy; is it really hopelessness almost to collapse under the burden because it is so heavy; is it really hopelessness to give up hope out of fear of the task? Oh no, but this is hopelessness: to will with all one's might—but there is no task. If you ever saw a person in distress at sea, is it not true that you were filled with apprehension about him, that you watched with a shiver of sympathy, but you hoped. But if you saw someone who by mistake had sunk in a bog, is it not true that this sight was something to despair over and that you watched with a freezing shudder. What was lacking was not strength or the will to use the strength—but what was lacking was: task. Whether such an unfortunate person has great strength or little, whether he uses it or does not, he sinks all the same—not under the heavy weight of the task, not under its immensity, but he sinks into the insidiousness that there is no task.

Indeed, when there is nothing to do, when not even the suffering itself is the task, then there *is* hopelessness, then there is a dreadful vacation from work for slowly dying in hopelessness. As long as there is an assigned task [*Opgave*], as long as there is something assigned [*Opgivet*], one is not hopelessly resigned [*opgivet*]. As long as there is an assigned task, there is a means for shortening time, because work and effort shorten time; but if there is nothing to do, if there is no task but only the mockery of deep insidiousness in denying the task—then there *is* hopelessness, and then time is deathly long.

Thus, only if there is nothing to do and if the person who says it *were* without guilt *before God*—for if he is guilty, there is indeed always something to do—only if there is nothing to do and this is understood to mean that there is no task, only then is there hopelessness. That is, if it is said that there is nothing to do, it does not at all follow that there is no task, because patience can certainly be the task. But if there is no task and if the sufferer *were* without guilt *before God*, then and only then is there hopelessness. If in relation to God a sufferer could be in the right, if it were possible that the fault is with God, well, then there would be hopelessness and the horror of hopelessness, then there would be no task. The tasks of faith and hope and love and patience and humility and obedience—in short, all the human tasks, are based on the eternal certainty in which they have a place of resort and support, the certainty that God is love. If it had ever happened to a human being in relation to God that the fault lay with God, there would be no task; if this ever had happened to a single human being, there would be no tasks for the entire human race. It would not be only in this particular case that there was no task; no, if God just one single time had demonstrated that he was not love in the smallest or the greatest, had left the sufferer without a task—then for all humankind there is no longer any task, then it is foolishness and futility and soul-deadening pernicious laboriousness to believe, a self-contradiction to work, and an agony to live. Life issues from the heart, and if a person's heart suffers damage, then by his own fault there is no longer any task for him except the sedulous toil of sin and emptiness; but from the heart of God issues the life in everything, the life in the tasks. If it is so that the creature must die if God withdraws his breath,[102] then it is also true that if God for one single moment has denied his love, then all tasks are dead and reduced to nothing, and hopelessness is the only thing there is.

Alas, most people sometimes feel and admit to themselves that in this or that the fault was theirs, and yet many a one perhaps secretly has the gloomy thought that it could happen and perhaps has happened that a person gets lost, and God nevertheless was to blame for it. So one goes on living, busily engaged with everything else, does not consider oneself to be in despair, is not appalled by this condition, because no light was permitted to penetrate this gloom. Indeed, this is not even obscurely desired, because the darkness there has an uncomfortable presentiment that it would become a troublesome clarity to understand the claim God has on a human soul, a troublesome clarity to understand that there is always a task. But is only that person mortal who is dead, would not the person who is alive be called mortal when death is his certainty; likewise, is not that person in despair who has not even begun to despair because he has not detected that he was in despair! Or when a businessman in drawing up his accounts realizes that he is ruined and despairs, is he any more in despair than the businessman who obscurely realizes that there is something wrong but hopes to sneak through for a time? Is it more desperate to despair over the truth than not to dare to face the truth! Everyone who secretly houses that gloomy thought about God is in despair. In the spiritual sense, one can see it in him, as it were, because in relation to God he is not like someone who drops his eyes in the consciousness of his guilt and of what he owes God,[103] nor is he like someone who humbly lifts his trusting gaze to God—no, he glowers.

Truly, it would be better to dispel the gloom than to glower, to shudder at the thought of this horror that actually belongs to paganism, the horror that God was unable or unwilling to give a person bold confidence. A false god can neither reduce a person to nothing nor make him perceive the nothing that he is—for that the false god is too weak. Neither can a false god give a person bold confidence—he is not strong enough for that. This is why we can say that the false god himself taught the pagan to glower. Even the wisest pagan who has ever lived, however much wiser he otherwise was than the lowliest believer, still has, in comparison with him, a gloominess in his inner being, because when all is said and done the pagan could never be eternally sure and clear whether the fault lay with him or whether it might in a rare case lie with God, whether hopelessness was not a state in which a person can be without guilt because the god himself bears the guilt by leaving him without a task. One can excuse the pagan only by saying that this is so because his god himself is gloomy.

But the Christian's God is clarity. Therefore every human being is without excuse and without any excuse. But when you take away all excuses, yes, when you take away the breeding gloomy torpor that gives birth to the excuses, there is no gloominess, and when you take away all excuses, a person is without any excuse and always without excuse. But if before God he is never pure and is always without excuse, then he is always guilty, even when he suffers. But if he always suffers as guilty, then it is eternally certain that God is love, and then there is the joy that there are always tasks, always things to do.

VIII
362

Is this not joyful? "What," perhaps someone asks, "that in relation to God a person always suffers as guilty?" Yes, if this is rightly understood to mean that it is eternally certain that God is love and that there is always task. See, doubt indolently and with brazen obtrusiveness wants to force itself into the nature of God and demonstrate that God is love. But the demonstration will never in all eternity succeed, because it begins with presumptuousness. When all is said and done, what is doubt really but that gloomy darkness, what else but the source of all excuses and *the excuse* that turns the relation around and doubts about God? But if this is the case, if it is right for a human being to doubt God's love, then the individual is of course excused. If, however, doubting God's love is presumptuousness, then the individual is obviously without excuse, stands accused, guilty, and is always under obligation to a task. This is the law, but there is also the joy that there also is always a task. If doubt is the beginning, then God is lost long before the end, and the individual is released from always having a task, but also from always having the comfort that there is always a task. But if the consciousness of guilt is the beginning, then the beginning of doubt is rendered impossible, and then the joy is that there is always a task.

The joy, then, is that it is eternally certain that God is love; more specifically understood, the joy is that there is always a task. As long as there is life there is hope, but as long as there is a task there is life, and as long as there is life there is hope—indeed, the task itself is not merely a hope for a future time but is a joyful present. The believer who bears in mind that in

relation to God a person always suffers as guilty therefore dares
to say, "Whatever happens to me, there is something to do, and
in any case there is always a task; hopelessness is a horror that
belongs nowhere if a person will not presumptuously give
himself up. So even if the heaviest thing of all happened to me,
something that has never before happened to any human being, if there was nothing, nothing at all to do—the joy still *is*
that there is a task, because then the task is to bear it with
patience. And if even the utmost of patience is required, such as
never before was required of any human being, the joy still *is*
that there is a task, because then the task is not to abandon
patience, not even at the last extremity." The consciousness of
guilt helps make it impossible to begin to doubt that God is
love; therefore it is eternally certain that God is love. But if this
is eternally certain, then there also are always tasks, because all
tasks have their ground in God. If in relation to God a person
always suffers as guilty, then there is always a task. Thus, that
there is always a task and that it is eternally certain that God is
love are one and the same and are contained in this—that in
relation to God a person always suffers as guilty.

VIII
363

    Let us once again recall the penitent robber. Can he now be
said to proclaim the comfort there is in suffering as guilty
because there is always a task? It might seem that the robber
lacked the occasion for this. A person being crucified does not
have many moments left; for a different reason it seems that for
him there can be no question of tasks. Yet this is not the case.
Through comparison with the superhuman suffering of the
other man on the cross, the robber finds comfort and relief in
the thought that he suffers as guilty, and hence he also finds that
there is a task, the final task, but it is indeed also his final hour.
For the very reason that he suffers as guilty, he has the comfort
and relief that there is a task, and the task is to repent and regret.
While the Savior of the world sighs, "My God, my God, why
have you abandoned me,"[104] the repentant robber humbly understands, but still also as a relief, that it is not God who has
abandoned him but it is he who has abandoned God, and,
repenting, he says to the one crucified with him: Remember me
when you come into your kingdom. It is a heavy human suffer-

ing to reach for God's mercy in the anxiety of death and with belated repentance at the moment of despicable death, but yet the repentant robber finds relief when he compares his suffering with the superhuman suffering of being abandoned by God. To be abandoned by God, that indeed means to be without a task. It means to be deprived of the final task that every human being always has, the task of patience, the task that has its ground in God's not having abandoned the sufferer. Hence Christ's suffering is superhuman and his patience superhuman, so that no human being can grasp either the one or the other. Although it is beneficial that we speak quite humanly of Christ's suffering, if we speak of it merely as if he were the human being who has suffered the most, it is blasphemy, because although his suffering is human, it is also superhuman, and there is an eternal chasmic abyss between his suffering and the human being's.

Perhaps the penitent robber had another secret thought also; perhaps he said to himself: Suppose there came at this moment an order from the governor to take down the ones being crucified and grant them life; then I, who have suffered as guilty, have the comfort that for me there are plenty of tasks. But for him, the Holy One, the innocent one, for him there is no task. His task has been a superhuman one; *before God* he has absolutely nothing for which to blame himself; his life was obedience, and yet he was abandoned by God! "See, this is the superhuman suffering," declares the penitent robber. "No human being has suffered this way; no human being can ever suffer this way, because *before God* no human being is without guilt—but then neither has any human being ever been nor can any human being be said to be abandoned by God. A human being, on the other hand, suffers as guilty; God has not abandoned him, there is always a task. And if there is a task, there is hope, and that there is a task and hope is the comfort. This comfort is for everyone who acknowledges that he suffers as guilty, even for me, a lost one, a crucified robber; for me there presumably is nothing to do—alas, the pains of death are already engulfing me—but there is a task, and I was not abandoned by God." Again, this is no repentance sermon except for the defiant individual who does not *want* to know what the terrible is and for whom what is truly joyful is conducive to offense. The person who humbles himself, the person who is so much in the truth that he understands what the terrible is, also comprehends that this robber proclaims joy.

But now, is it really so that in relation to God a person always suffers as guilty [*skyldig*]? Or is the aim of this discourse to incite thoughts to conflict and to confuse the concepts, to deprive the, humanly speaking, innocent [*uskyldig*] sufferer of the comfort that he, humanly speaking, is suffering as innocent, and to grant the person who, humanly speaking, suffers as guilty the mendacious comfort that every human being *in that sense* always suffers as guilty? By no means. The discourse has only one aim, what I venture to call the best aim; it wants only one thing, what I venture to call the best: in every way to make it eternally certain that God is love. Truly, to want this is really to think everything for the best! In whatever way this becomes certain, even if at first glance the way seems difficult and hard—if it nevertheless is achieved, and a greater certainty that God is love—that, then, is the joy. The thought that God is love contains all joy in itself to such a degree that any and every way in which this thought achieves clarity and certainty, every way, even the most difficult, is joyful. The thought that God is love contains all the blessed persuasion of eternity. Then the road, even if it is the most difficult, and the condition, even if it is the most bitter, are unconditionally joyful. Hence, if it were not as we have assumed, that in relation to God a person always suffers as guilty—if it nevertheless is as we have developed, that there is joy in this thought, then a person would indeed have to wish this assumption to be true, then if he is of the truth he would have to say: Since it is clear to me that, if in relation to God I always suffer as guilty, it is eternally certain that God is love, then I will wish only that it may always remain clear and vivid to me that I suffer as guilty.

However, a person does not need to wish it (even if, in order to be understood properly, a person at heart must wish it, because if it is true that inclination actuates work, then there is also the understanding that only the fervency of the wish helps to surmount the difficulties), because it is actually the case that in relation to God a person always suffers as guilty—and eternally certain that God is love. Let others proclaim the pleasure of thinking through doubt. This is beyond my power, and that kind of pleasure is not to my liking. I find joy and the certainty of joy in the upbuilding thought that one can make it impossible to begin to doubt, that the consciousness of guilt safeguards the joy.

So we shall consider more closely what was the assumption of this discourse. We shall not allow ourselves to be disturbed by a robber's having spoken the words just read and spoken them about himself, because with the same words a robber can indeed say something important; but neither shall we hide what in a more specific sense still holds true of the robber—that he suffers as guilty. In other words, we make a proper distinction between being in the wrong and suffering as guilty, since it does not follow that a person suffers as guilty because he is in the wrong. Therefore, there are three categories on which the discourse must dwell: when a person, humanly speaking, is guilty, then he suffers as guilty in relation to God and other people; when a person, humanly speaking, suffers as innocent, then we human beings say of him that in his relation to God he is in the wrong with God; in relation to God a human being always suffers as guilty.

When a person, humanly speaking, is guilty, then he suffers as guilty in relation to both God and other people. This is the robber's situation—he is a criminal who is suffering his punishment. The truth in him is that he himself fully and deeply acknowledges that he suffers as guilty. Even in such cases, unfortunately, we sometimes hear from a guilty person the blasphemous kind of talk that wants to shove the guilt aside, the brazen and presumptuous talk that the criminal tendency was congenital, that his crime was the result of a neglected upbringing, and other things of that kind.

This was the first category. The second is that a person, humanly speaking, suffers as innocent, but yet we say of him in his relation to God that he is in the wrong with God. Thus it is

VIII
366

not the sufferer who is speaking with himself about his relation to God, but it is we others who speak as a third party about such a sufferer's relation to God. This relation is described by a singular phrase—namely, that God is testing a person. Let us name one of those glorious prototypes, a tried and tested person who passed the test—Job. Who would ever think of saying that Job, humanly speaking, suffered as guilty! If this were not blasphemy, it would still be presumptuousness toward that venerable man—Job, who is said to be and has been and is a prototype for the human race. Who in the human race would dare speak that way about him! Even God in heaven speaks, as it were, with a kind of partiality, yes, so humanly; he is, as it were, proud of Job. He even says to Satan, "Have you noticed my servant Job?"[105] This is the way a human being speaks of something magnificent that belongs to him and of which he is proud; this is the way a human being speaks of someone of whom he is so sure that he dares to challenge him with danger just to have the joy of seeing him victorious.

Job, then, suffers as one who is innocent, humanly speaking; he has no blame, no crime for which to upbraid himself. On the contrary, his life and conduct had been in the sight of God, lauded by men, for it was not only on the day of sorrow that Job becomes the prototype; he was that already in his prosperous days and thereby was well prepared to stand the ordeal. Yet Job was continually in the wrong with God. God's thoughts are eternally higher than the thoughts of a human being, and therefore every human conception of happiness and unhappiness, of what is joyful and what is sorrowful, is faulty thinking. By remaining in this circle of conceptions, a person remains continually in the wrong with God, and he gets out of this circle of conceptions only by acknowledging that he is always in the wrong with God.

But when impatience starts to move in the, humanly speaking, innocent sufferer, in the one God is testing, when he, because he, humanly speaking, is in the right, in the right in this or in that, in some way wants to be in the right with God— what then? Is he then to be allowed or is he able to turn the relation around and be in the right with God (this is the reverse relation, because a person always is in the wrong with God; then everything is turned around if for one single time he was in the right in the least little thing). Is the doubter to remain in the right or, what amounts to the same thing, is everything to be lost? No, then something else happens, then the one being tested understands that instead of talking with others he must talk with himself before God; and out of respect for the one being tested the rest of us understand that we dare to say no more, do not dare to make him guilty. So the one being tested talks with himself before God, and then the final reinforcement in the struggle moves in: in relation to God a human being always suffers as guilty.

VIII
367

The fundamental relation between God and a human being is that a human being is a sinner and God is the Holy One. Directly before God a human being is not a sinner in this or in that, but is essentially a sinner, is not guilty of this or that, but is essentially and unconditionally guilty. But if he is essentially guilty, then he is also *always* guilty, because the debt of essential guilt is so extreme as to make every direct accounting impossible. The relation among human beings is such that a person can be in the right in something and in the wrong in something else, can be innocent in one thing and guilty in another, but a relation of that kind between God and a human being is impossible, because if such were the relation, then God would not be God but a human being's equal, and if such were the relation, the guilt would not be the essential.

Yet in daily life a person is not conscious of the fundamental relation every single moment—no human being would be able to endure this; in daily life a person more or less lives in the stipulations of human criteria—whereas the fundamental relation measures him with God. But that does not mean that the fundamental relation is absent; on the contrary, it rests deepest in the soul. Law in a state always exists in the same way, but it is, so to speak, resting. As soon as a crime is committed, however, the law swings into action; it emerges from its rest, so to speak, and asserts its validity. It is like that with a person's fundamental relation to God. When confusion is about to intrude, when impatience wants to stare itself dizzy at a particular thing and thereby finally turn everything around—then the fundamental relation asserts itself. When impatience wants to rebel, as it were, against God, wants to quarrel with God as one quarrels with one's equal by insisting on being in the right, something else happens; then the fundamental relation rebels against the impatient one and teaches him that in relation to God a human being is essentially guilty, thus *always* guilty. The guilt of the person in relation to God is not guilt of this or that—the relation cannot be summed up that way. He is eternally guilty and therefore always guilty; whenever he so wills, God can assert the fundamental guilt, and even if, humanly speaking, a person were in the right in everything, in relation to God he is nevertheless always guilty. This is how God fights. Even the mightiest king, who with the most overwhelming superiority is fighting a rebel, still fights with the aid of the powerful military forces he has on his side; but God in heaven fights by shifting the attack to the side of the attacker. When impatience, like a rebel, wants to attack God, the consciousness of guilt attacks the rebel; that is, the attacker ends up fighting with himself. God's omnipotence and holiness do not mean that he can be victorious over everyone, that he is the strongest, for this is still a comparison; but it means, and this bars any comparison, that no one can manage to fight with him.

This was the third category, the theme of this discourse: that in relation to God a human being always suffers as guilty. Or should the discourse presumably support the view that every time a person suffers he should torture himself with the idea that the suffering was simply punishment for this or that? Not at all. The one who, humanly speaking, suffers innocently is still to believe humbly that with God he is always in the wrong. But if he fails, if he begins to doubt and becomes impatient, then this final thought, the actual clincher, teaches him that the suffering is not simply punishment for this or that specific thing (if that were so, it would follow that he could still be in the right in something), but that he is eternally guilty and therefore always guilty. The untruth is in timidly wanting to link the undeserved suffering as punishment with this or that particular thing—quite as if a person were not otherwise totally guilty, quite as if God were a cruel tyrant who pursued some particular thing, quite as if the person were not always guilty.

See, this most certainly was what Job's friends actually wanted to say to Job: that in relation to God a human being always suffers as guilty. Indeed, that is not untrue either. Their mistake was something else, that they wanted to take it upon themselves or presume to say this to him, since one human being has no right to say this to another. Furthermore, Job's friends did not have any criterion for what it means: to suffer as one who is *innocent before God*. The highest that the Jews knew was a piety such as Job's, and this is why it was doubly arrogant and doubly unjust of the friends to speak in this way to Job. The Christian, however, knows that there is only one, but also that there is one, who before God suffered as innocent. No one dares to compare himself to him or measure himself by his standard; between him and every human being there is an eternal difference. That is why it now applies with renewed clarity that in relation to God a *human being* always suffers as guilty.

The assumption, then, stands firm, but then in turn what was developed from that assumption stands firm—it stands firm that this is the joy, that in relation to God a human being always suffers as guilty. But this joy has its humbling side. Thus, although it holds true that one person is not allowed judgingly to say this to another when the sufferer, humanly speaking, is suffering as innocent, it also holds true that the person who, when he is tried, himself wants to test it will surely experience what joy is contained in this thought. If suspense is always fatiguing, and if it is always disconsolate to be unable to come to any conclusion [*Slutning*], this thought is truly a concluding thought [*Slutnings-Tanke*]. If someone wished to think through doubt, it would, of course, be possible for him at the very moment he thought he was finished to discover that he had forgotten one doubt and thus would have to begin again from the beginning. But this eternal concluding thought is a conclusion because it is the same at the beginning as at the end; it is a concluding thought, indeed, the only one

VIII
369

with which a person can truly begin, and yet it is in turn a concluding thought, the only one with which a person can end. But it is also a strong and powerful thought. This thought is not a soldier of fortune that embarks on an adventure in life and leaves doubtful what is to happen to it or what it is to become. No, this thought is powerfully armed[106] with full gear, and it already *is* what *it should become*, because it is a man's will—and yet this does not say very much—but it is a man's will in covenant with God; it is the will of one who before God is resolved [*besluttet*], who, resolved, is aware of the dangers but, resolved, is also in covenant with the victory.

V

[The Joy of It That It Is Not the Road That Is Hard but That Hardship Is the Road[107]]

There is in authorized language a universal, generally accepted metaphor that compares life to a road. The similarity can indeed be fruitful in many ways, but the inevitable dissimilarity contained in the metaphor is no less worth noting. In a physical sense the road is an external actuality, no matter whether anyone is walking on it or not, no matter how the individual travels on it—the road is the road. But in the spiritual sense, of course, the road cannot be physically indicated; yet in a certain sense it does exist whether anyone walks on it or not, and yet the road first comes into actual existence in another sense, or it comes into existence with each individual who walks on it; the road is: *how* it is walked. We cannot indicate the road of virtue and say: *There* runs the road of virtue. We can only say how the road of virtue is walked, and if anyone refuses to walk in just that way, he is walking another road. It would, however, be unreasonable to define a highway by *how* it is walked. Whether it is the young person who walks it lightly and trippingly in a cheerful frame of mind with his head high or the old decrepit person who struggles along with bowed head, whether it is the happy person hurrying to reach the goal of his wish or the worrier who turned his back on the wish and goes slowly ahead, whether it is the poor traveler on foot or the rich traveler in his light carriage—the road is the same for all; the road is and remains the same, the same highway.

The dissimilarity in the metaphor shows up most clearly when the discussion is simultaneously about a road in the physical and a road in the spiritual sense. For example, when we read the Holy Gospel about the compassionate Samaritan,[108] there is mention of the road between Jericho and Jerusalem.

The story tells of at least three, in fact five, people who walked "along the same road," whereas, spiritually speaking, we have to say that each one walked his own road—the highway, alas, makes no difference; it is the spiritual that makes the difference and distinguishes the road.

The first was a peaceful traveler who walked along the road from Jericho to Jerusalem, perhaps on an errand, perhaps for a devout purpose, in any case a peaceful traveler on a lawful road. The second man was a robber who "walked along the same road"—and yet on an unlawful road. Then a priest came "along the same road"; he saw the poor unfortunate man who had been assaulted by the robber; he perhaps was momentarily moved but went on his usual light-minded road, given to a momentary impression but without depth. Next a Levite came "along the same road." He saw the poor unfortunate man; he walked past unmoved, continuing *his* road. The highway, alas, belonged to none of the travelers, and yet the Levite walking "along the same road" was walking his way, the way of selfishness and callousness. Finally a Samaritan came "along the same road." He found the poor unfortunate man on the road of mercy; he demonstrated by his example how one walks on the road of mercy; he demonstrated that the road, spiritually speaking, is precisely this: how one walks. This is why the Gospel says to the learner, "Go and do likewise." In other words, when you walk the road as the Samaritan did, you are walking the road of mercy, because the road between Jericho and Jerusalem has no advantage with regard to practicing mercy. It all happened on "the same road," and yet it was at one time the road of lawfulness, the second time the road of unlawfulness, the third time the road of light-mindedness, the fourth time the road of callousness, the fifth time the road of mercy. There were five travelers who according to the Gospel walked "along the same road," and yet each one walked his own road.

Thus the spiritual question of "how one walks life's road" makes the difference and the difference of the road. In other words, when life, quite universally understood as living, is compared to a road, the metaphor simply expresses the universal, that which everyone who is alive has in common by being alive; to that extent they are all walking along the road of life and are all walking along the same road. But when living becomes an earnest matter, then the question becomes: How shall one walk in order to walk the right road on the road of life? The traveler does not ask as one usually asks, "Where is the road?" but asks how one walks along the road and about how one ought to walk. Yet just to ask properly requires some consideration, because impatience does not mind being deceived and in fact merely asks where the road is, in the spiritual sense, as if that decided everything in the same sense as when the traveler has found the highway. Worldly wisdom is very willing to deceive by again and again answering the question, "Where is the road?" while the difficulty is omitted, that spiritually understood the road is: *how* it is walked. At times worldly sagacity teaches that the road goes over Gerizim, at times over Moriah,[109] at times that it goes through some science or other, at times that the road is certain doctrines, at times certain external acts. One is unwilling to admit to oneself that all this is a deception, because the road is: how it is walked. It is indeed as Scripture says—two people can be sleeping in the same bed—the one is saved, the other is lost;[110] two people can go up to the same house of worship—the one goes home saved, the other is lost;[111] two people can recite the same creed—the one can be saved, the other is lost. How does this happen except for the very reason that, spiritually speaking, it is a deception to know where the road is, because the road is: how it is walked.

But even the person who has learned to ask properly how one ought to walk still asks about one thing: Where does the road lead? Any praise of the perfection of the road can be meaningless if the road does not lead to perfection—alas, the more perfect the road is, the sadder it is if it still leads to perdition. On the other hand, however difficult and however troublesome it is to walk, if the road is still the road of perfection, it is nevertheless joyful.

How, then, does one walk along the road of perfection? Along the road of pleasure one walks lightly, as in a dance;

along the road of honor one walks proudly, crowned with a wreath; along the indulgent road of happiness one walks indulged in all desires. But how does one walk along the road of perfection? The one who asks earnestly, the one who stands on the road and inquires about the old footpaths, will also get an earnest reply, the old answer: that the road is hard, that a person walks the road of perfection in hardships.

[112]Whether you consult the Scriptures of the Old Covenant or the New, there is only one view on this. There are many replies, but they all say the same thing. The reply is always the same; only the voice is different, so that the reply, by means of this difference, might win different people. So specific and decisive is Scripture's one and only view, that the road of perfection is in hardships, that perhaps on no other theme are so many Scripture passages to be found that all say the same thing: "He who will serve the Lord must prepare his soul for temptations" (Sirach 2:1); "through many hardships we must enter the kingdom of God" (Acts 14:22); "we are destined for hardships" (I Thessalonians 3:3–4), etc.

For this very reason we shall not cite any specific Bible passage but instead find support in the total and integral impression of Scripture's universal teaching that along the road of perfection we walk in hardships, and on that basis we shall, to the upbuilding of a sufferer (for these discourses are, after all, the gospel of sufferings), consider the joy of it:

> *that it is not the road that is hard but that hardship is the road.*

Therefore, the road of perfection is walked in hardships; and the subject of the discourse is: the joy for the sufferer in this thought. At this point, then, the discourse is not an admonishing discourse about how one is to walk on the road of hardships but for the sufferer a joyful discourse on hardship as the *how* that characterizes the road of perfection. In the spiritual sense, the road is how it is walked. What, then, is the road of perfection; that is, how is the road of perfection walked? The walking is done in hardships. This is the first *how*. The second is: how one is to walk along the road of hardship. It is very important that this second *how* must never be forgotten, neither first nor last, but neither has it been forgotten; on the contrary, it is kept in mind—indeed, the sufferer will surely be strengthened for that when he for himself has really found the joy of it that the road of perfection is in hardships—he who precisely by being a sufferer is indeed in hardship.

When hardship is the road, this is the joy: *that as a consequence it is **immediately** clear to the sufferer what the task is and he **immediately** knows this for sure; therefore he does not need to spend any time or waste any energy on deliberating whether the task should not be something else.*

What is it that makes a child, even if a powerful man is taken for comparison, capable of doing what the powerful man is scarcely able to do; what is it that helps the child by giving it the head start? Obviously this—that the child has no difficulty whatever in finding out definitely what the task is, what it has to do—because the child has only to obey. It is up to the parents or the superiors to give thought and consideration to the task; as soon as the child is told what it should do, that is the task. The child has nothing to do with whether it is right or not right; not only should it not, but it dare not, spend a single moment in that kind of deliberation—on the contrary, it must *immediately* obey. Compared with a powerful man, the child is certainly the weak one; but it is also the weak one who has a very essential advantage, the weak one who unconditionally employs all its strength to accomplish the task, and so expediently that not a single moment is wasted on doubting the task, not the slightest bit of energy is lost in dubiousness about the task.

VIII
374

The task is assigned with the accent and trustworthiness of authority. This is the head start, but after that one even gives the child impetus by adding: Do it immediately. Then the child does the amazing thing—indeed a child is capable of doing what even a powerful adult is rarely able to do. Who has not often seen with amazement this wonderful thing: what a child is capable of doing! If the father or mother or just the nanny says, but with authority: Now go to sleep at once—the child goes to sleep. There is a lot of prosaic talk in the world about many an amazing achievement on the part of men, and yet there is only one—he who was called the one and only—who is said to have been able to sleep at will.[113] Take an average adult, even someone more powerful; he is in the same situation as the child who, in the opinion of the parents, needs sleep. He says to himself: It would do you good to sleep; I wonder if he really can do as the child does, who goes to sleep immediately! Alas, as he lays his head on the pillow, probably the opposite happens, that just then the restless thoughts awaken. Perhaps everything becomes confused when he begins to doubt— whether it is right to go to sleep, whether the work is not being neglected and what then must be feared—when he once again wishes to fall asleep but cannot. Finally he becomes impatient and says: What is the use of lying here if I cannot sleep. He gets up again, but not to work, because now he can neither work nor sleep. Inasmuch as one rises strengthened from the rest of sleep, it is at times almost tempting to remain in bed and not get up—it is in another sense indeed difficult to get up again from a vain attempt to sleep, and one indeed gets up even more tired from a vain attempt to sleep.

VIII
375

The difficulty for the adult, in which also the advantage of authority and maturity is certainly contained, is that he must do double work: work to find out the task and get it firmly set and then work in order to carry out the task. The greatest difficulty seems to be just to get the task firmly set or actually to get set firmly on what the task is. Perhaps people are really not unwilling to spend time and energy and are not incompetent either—if only it could become unmistakably clear to them what the task is. But the point is that this communication cannot in any decisive way come to them from the outside; it has to go through the person who is himself involved. The adult is indeed of age; he is to be his own master. But it is the lord and master who is to assign the task, just as parents and superiors do it for the child. Thus the adult is simultaneously master and servant; the one who is to command and the one who is to obey are one and the same. This is unquestionably a difficult situation, that the one giving the command and the one obeying the command are the same. It can so easily happen that the servant meddles in the deliberation about the task, and conversely, that the master pays too much attention to the servant's complaints about the difficulties in carrying out the task. Then, alas, confusion develops; then instead of becoming his own master a person becomes unstable, irresolute, vacillating; he runs from one thing to the other, tears down and builds up and begins again from the beginning. He is tossed about by every breeze, but without moving from the spot. Finally the situation becomes so awkward that all his energy is expended in thinking up ever new changes in the task—just as a plant goes to seed, so he goes to seed in busy trifling deliberation or in fruitless wishing. In a certain sense he uses much time, much diligence, and much energy, and it is all as good as wasted, because the task does not remain fixed, because there is no master, since he, of course, should be his own master.

When a team of horses is to pull a heavy load ahead, what can the driver do for them? Indeed, he cannot pull it himself, and the second-rate driver can whip them—anyone can do that—but the competent driver, what can he do for them? He can help them get on the move pulling the wagon in a single instant with concentrated strength in a single pull. If, however, the driver creates confusion, if he handles the reins in such a way that the horses think that they should only get ready to pull on a given signal—but it was the coachman's idea that they should pull now; or if he pulls unevenly on the reins so that the one horse thinks that it is to pull and the other that the coachman is holding it back so that it can get ready—well, then the wagon does not move from the spot even if the horses have enough power.

But just as we are distressed to see this sight, to see that there is power enough but that the person who is to be the master, the driver, is spoiling things, so also are we distressed to see the same thing happen to a human being. He does not lack power—a person never really does—but he mismanages himself. The person who is to be the master (it is, of course, he himself) ruins it; such a person works with perhaps scarcely a third of his power in the right place and with more than two-

VIII
376

thirds of his power in the wrong place or against himself. Now he gives up working in order to begin to deliberate all over again, now he works instead of deliberating, now he pulls on the reins in the wrong way, now he wants to do both at the same time—and during all this he does not move from the spot. During all this, his life comes to a standstill, as it were; he cannot get the task firmly set, so that it stands firm, so that he is able to tear himself away from this work and have his strength available to carry out the task. The task does not become a burden, but he is swamped with the burdensome muddling with the task in order to get it, if possible, to stand firm. When that is so, he naturally never gets around to carrying the burden; after all, he cannot even get it to stand still; the moment he wants to turn his back, as it were, in order to pick up the burden, the burden seems to tumble down and he has to stack it up again. Ah, if one looks at people's lives, one often must say in sorrow: They do not themselves know what powers they have; they more or less keep themselves from finding that out, because they are using most of their powers to work against themselves.

Let us then think about the subject of this discourse more closely. The sufferer has hardship; now for it, now! If he can just get the task very firmly set, he will succeed in holding out all right; if he immediately knows for sure what the task is, then much has already been won. But doubt wants to prevent this if possible; it wants insidiously to take away all his powers and make them serve in a wrong place, in finding out what the task is, or in thousands of fabrications as to what it could be. If this happens, doubt wins the battle; if it lures him into struggling where he is not to struggle, then he must succumb in the hardship.

VIII
377

Is it not joyful, then, that hardship is the road, for then it is immediately clear what the task is. Doubt wants to trick the sufferer into thinking about whether it would not still be possible that the hardship could be taken away and he could still continue walking along the same road—without hardship. But when hardship is the road, then it is of course impossible to

take away the hardship and have the road still remain the same.
—Doubt wants to trick the sufferer into thinking about
whether it would not still be possible that he had been mistaken
about the road, that the hardship could mean that he is on the
wrong road. But when hardship is the road, then the fact that
there is hardship on the road cannot possibly mean that he has
made a mistake; on the contrary, this is the sign that he is on the
right road. —Doubt wants to trick him into thinking about
whether it would not still be possible to take another road. But
when hardship is the road, then it is of course impossible to
take another road. There can be no doubt, therefore, about
what the task is; not one single moment, not one ounce of
strength should be used in further deliberation; that hardship is
the road firmly sets the task, makes certain what the task is.
Indeed, however severe the hardship, no hardship is as severe
as this hardship of restless thoughts in an irresolute and vacillating soul.

The sufferer perseveres and walks ahead in hardships on the
road of perfection—but the hardship becomes more and more
severe. Now for it, now! But if only the task stands firm and
fixed, much is already won; and far be it from us to help
broadcast the mendacious fable that little by little the hard road
becomes easier, that it is hard only at the beginning. It is just the
opposite—it becomes harder and harder. This can easily be
verified if one is attentive to people and is *willing* to see. A
person who has never made a beginning at willing the good is
perhaps rarely to be found, but most people fall away when it is
apparent that the road becomes harder instead of easier. When
a person has come so far that all his illusions vanish—about
willing the good to a certain degree, that the good to a certain
degree has its reward in this world—when willing the good
becomes a really earnest matter, then the road first becomes
really hard and from now on becomes harder and harder. It is
always best to say this in order not to deceive people with
fabulous talk, to beguile them for a moment and then in the
next moment make them even more impatient. But what contains no deceit, the eternal certainty, is that hardship is the road.

VIII
378

Then not one single moment, not one single ounce of energy is again to be spent on deliberating further—the task stands firm and fixed, hardship is the road.

Therefore, when someone wants to trick the sufferer into thinking that others are walking along the same road so easily, so free of care, without hardships, while he is walking in hardships, the task once again stands fixed and firm; the sufferer has only one answer: Hardship is the road. Far be from us also this hypocritical talk that life is so varied that some are walking along the same road without hardships, others in hardships. It certainly is possible for someone to be walking without hardships, but he certainly is not walking without hardships along the same road as the person who is walking in hardships, because hardship is the road. There is a kind of sagacity that is quite reluctant to make a complete break with the good but is also exceedingly reluctant to renounce the pleasant days of a soft life and worldly advantage. This sagacity is usually very inventive in the kind of fabrication that there is great variety— not in life, for there is no lie in that—but that there is such great variety on the road of perfection. Let us recall what was developed at the beginning of this discourse, that spiritually understood the road is: how it is walked. You see, when a poor traveler, whose feet are perhaps even blistered and raw, when he practically drags himself along the road, wincing at every step, there is much good sense in the thought—even if he never has the right to be envious—of envying the rich man driving past him in a comfortable carriage. The highway is altogether indifferent to the difference in how one travels on it, and thus it is indeed undeniably more pleasant to ride in a comfortable carriage than to walk in such distress. Spiritually, however, the road is: how it is walked, and thus it would surely be odd if on the road of hardship there were the difference that some walked on the road of hardship without hardships. Thus once again the task stands firm and fixed; the sufferer immediately knows with certainty what the task is, because hardship is the road. If someone wants to walk without hardships, he can, of course, do so; but then he also walks along another road— which is his business. But doubt cannot seize hold of the sufferer and make him doubtful with the thought that others are walking *along the same road* without hardships.

If what the proverb says is true, that well begun is half done, then it is also true that the firm setting of the task is half the work, indeed, more than half. But since hardship is the road, then the task is so firm and fixed that not even Satan himself is able to smuggle in a doubt about what the task is. If doubt is to have a free hand, then hardship must be made incidental to the road. For example, when a traveler speaks of a road and says: This road is hard, something incidental can be meant; perhaps there is another road that is easy and leads to the same destination, or the road at other times may be easy but just at this time is hard. When, however, hardship is the road, then every doubt about hardship as the task is a deliberate attempt—to take a wrong road—since there is only one single road, the road of hardship, the road the sufferer is on. Doubt about the task always has its stronghold in the idea that there could be other roads, or that the road could be altered in such a way that the hardship is removed. But since hardship is the road, the hardship cannot be removed without removing the road, and there cannot be *other roads*, but only *wrong roads*.

Is this not joyful, joyful for the sufferer, who is indeed on the road of hardship, joyful because not the slightest deliberation is needed about whether it is the right road, joyful because he can immediately begin on the task, begin with the determination that has all its strength available and concentrated upon persevering in the hardship. When hardship is the road, then it is not something unavoidable in the hopeless sense, not at all; since it is the road, he could not wish to avoid it. With this thought, the sufferer is at once fully under way with perseverance in the hardship. He does not waste so much as a moment or squander a glance on looking around—no, with all his might and main he is in the hardship, joyful in the hardship, joyful in the thought that hardship is the road. To be sure, the task is not actually what supplies the power, because the task is of course what is assigned, and the person to whom it is assigned is to employ his power to carry it out, and yet we can say that the task supplies power. When parents know how to assign the task with authority, when the coachman knows from seasoned experience how to assign the task, it is indescribably helpful. So it is also for the adult when the task is firmly set with the authority of eternity, which is indescribably helpful in carrying out the task. If a child is so unfortunate as to have a father who does not know how to command, or the horses a second-rate driver, it seems as if the child and the horses would not have half of the powers they actually do have. Alas, and when the adult who is a sufferer surrenders his soul to the power of vacillation, he is actually weaker than a child. But then it is indeed also a joy that hardship is the road, because then the task is immediately at hand and stands unshakably fixed and firm.

VIII
380

Hardship is the road—and this is the joy: *that it is not a quality of the road that it is hard, but it is a quality of the hardship that it is the road; therefore the hardship must lead to something; it must be passable and practicable, not suprahuman.* Each of these thoughts contains a more particular upbuilding specification of this joy, and therefore we shall dwell on each one separately.

It is not a quality of the road that it is hard, but it is a quality of the hardship that it is the road. The closer the relation between the hardship and the road is made, the more firm and fixed the task stands also. If we say: The road is hard, the latter is a more particular specification of the road; there are two thoughts: the road—and that it is hard. We then say: This is the way it is; it is an actuality that the road is hard. But since there are still two thoughts, it also seems as if doubt had been granted a little concession, as if it could squeeze in here between the road and its being hard, as if something could still be said for doubt when it wants to trick the sufferer into thinking about whether the road could not possibly exist without being hard, or without being as hard as it presumably is, because doubt whispers: After all, the statement may be broken up as follows: the road, and then, it is hard. But when the hardship is the road, then doubt must breathe its last, then it cannot possibly have a chance. The one term, then, is not superior to the other, the whole statement does not split for conceptualization into a noun and an adjective. No, they are one and the same: hardship is the road and the road is hardship. They belong together so intimately that doubt cannot even get a chance to draw a breath between them, because they are one thought. They belong together so intimately that the relation between hardship and the road is the relation of inseparability. There cannot be a more intimate relation. Remove the hardship, then you remove the road; remove the road, then you remove the hardship. So intimately do they belong together; so fixed and firm does the task stand.

The hardship must lead to something. In other words, one cannot draw an inference such as this: A road is hard; therefore it must lead to something. Insofar as a road is a road, the conclusion holds true that it must lead to something, because the very moment it does not lead to something it ceases to be a road. The conclusion holds true insofar as the road is road, but not because it is hard. For the person who is not as yet firmly established in faith, this adjective almost seems to make it more dubious whether the road can indeed lead to something. When, however, hardship itself is the road, the conclusion follows: therefore it must lead to something, because this is not inferred from its being hard but from its being a road.

VIII
381

These are the Lord's own words: The road is hard that leads to eternal happiness;[114] and if he has said them, then they indeed stand eternally fixed and firm. We certainly do not praise it if someone has gone astray in many thoughts, but if that is the case, we would like to come to his aid with a more imperfect expression for the same thing—more imperfect because it is understood only by someone who is not unacquainted with doubt and thus can also be only temporarily useful to him until he again learns the more perfect expression: to cling solely to the Lord's words. That the Lord has said these words is certainly the best safeguard against doubt, because in obedience to believe has much more security than the security that in thought's understanding it is impossible for thinking to doubt it. Alas, just because it is impossible for thinking, it does not follow that it is impossible for the thinking person; he can will to doubt, despondently or defiantly. But if these are not the Lord's own words—that hardship is the road—they are nevertheless his teaching, for does he not teach that hardship is beneficial? So it is he who guarantees the words. A human being can do this: he can clearly and with clear thoughts develop the implications of a thought, but he cannot guarantee the thought—only the one with authority can do that, and only he who is the one and only authority can guarantee all with authority.

When it is declared that the road is hard that leads to eternal happiness, the thought is this: Well, this is how it is, the road is hard; hardship is an opposition, an obstacle on the road. One must go through it, but then it does indeed lead to eternal happiness. Hardship, then, is an *opposition*, an *obstacle on the road*; yet one must go through it. But when hardship itself is the road, no wonder that one must go through it, no wonder that the hardship leads to something! Doubt very much wants to rob the sufferer of bold confidence, wants to leave him stuck in the hardship, to let him perish in the despondent, indeed, the presumptuous thought that he is forsaken by God, as if he had come onto a road that led only to an inclosure, as if it were in a hopeless sense that the apostle said "that we are destined for hardships" (I Thessalonians 3:3), as if the hardship had no qualification but we were simply appointed to hardship. When, however, the hardship has the qualification of being the road, there is immediately a breath of air, then the sufferer draws a breath, then it must lead to something, because then the hardship is indeed itself the forwarding agent. It is not a difficulty *on* the road that makes, if I dare say so, a new team of horses necessary, but the hardship itself is a team, the very best; if one only lets it rule, it helps one forward, because hardship is the road.

Is it not joyful how the sufferer can breathe in this thought with bold confidence! Not only does he commend himself to God alone and advance against the hardship. No, he says: The hardship itself is a sign to me that I have good references, the hardship is my helper—because hardship is the road. As long as the child is still afraid of the teacher, it surely can learn a great deal, but when trust has driven out the fear and bold confidence has conquered, then the highest level of education begins. So it is also when the sufferer, convinced that hardship is the road, has overcome the hardship, because in the highest sense is it not an overcoming of the hardship to will to believe that hardship is the road, is the helper! The Apostle Paul declares somewhere: Faith is our victory,[115] and in another place says: Indeed, we more than conquer.[116] But can one more than conquer? Yes, if before the struggle begins one has changed the enemy into one's friend. It is one thing to conquer in the hardship, to overcome the hardship as one overcomes an enemy, while continuing in the idea that the hardship is one's enemy; but it is more than conquering to believe that the hardship is one's friend, that it is not the opposition but the road, is not what obstructs but develops, is not what disheartens but ennobles.

The hardship must be passable and practicable. What can be encountered on a road that blocks it so it becomes impassable? It is hardship. But if hardship is the road, then this road is indeed unconditionally passable. If he so pleases, the sufferer can picture the hardship as more and more terrible; this makes no difference in any sense—it is eternally certain that hardship is the road, and thus it is impossible to imagine a hardship that can block this road. From this, too, we can see that hardship must lead to something. Indeed, what else but hardship could keep a road from leading to something, but if this cannot appear as an opposition along this road, then of course this road must lead eternally to something.

Wonderful! The road of hardship is the only road where there is no obstacle, because instead of blocking off the road the hardship itself prepares the road. How joyful this is! For what is more hopeless than for the traveler to have to say: There is no longer any road; and what is more joyful than for the wanderer to dare to say at all times: Here there is always a road!

The hardship is not suprahuman. No, if the hardship were suprahuman, the road would then be blocked, and the hardship would not be the road. The Apostle Paul says: "No temptation has confronted you except the human. God will make both the temptation and the way out such that you can bear it."[117] But has not God made the temptation bearable when he

VIII
383

has from all eternity arranged it in such a way that the hardship itself is the road; then hardship has once and for all been made endurable. And how can it be more sure that there is always a good way out of temptation than to have hardship itself as a way out, because then hardship itself is continually a way out and a good way out of hardship.

The suprahuman temptation will pile up over a person; like the steep mountain that makes the hiker despair, so the suprahuman temptation will frighten the sufferer, transform him into a creeping thing in comparison with the size of the temptation. Just as a force of nature mocks human effort, so suprahuman temptation, haughtily swaggering, will be proud, like mockery at the poor sufferer. But, God be praised, there is no suprahuman temptation; there is only a mendacious fable invented by a pusillanimous or a crafty person who wants to shove guilt away from himself, to minimize his guilt by magnifying the temptation, to justify himself by making it suprahuman. Scripture says the very opposite; it not only says that there is no suprahuman temptation, but in another place where it is speaking of the horror of which the anticipation would make people faint, it says to the believers, "When this happens, raise your heads."[118] Consequently the temptation does not have suprahuman dimensions; on the contrary, when the hardship is most appalling, the believer is a head taller, a head taller—he is indeed taller by the head that he lifts up above the hardship. And if hardship is the road, then the believer is also above the hardship, because the road *upon which* a person is walking admittedly does not go over his head, no, but when he is walking upon it he is stepping on it with his feet.

In this way there is sheer joy in the thought that hardship is the road. The sufferer immediately knows specifically what the task is; he can begin immediately with full power. No doubt can come to slip in between the road and the hardship, because they are eternally inseparable; and therefore it is eternally certain that this road must lead to something, because here no hardship can block the road, which is always passable, just as the hardship is never suprahuman.

But it must surely never be forgotten, it must be repeated

here in the conclusion that the second point still remains: how the sufferer is to walk the road of hardship. Ah, but if it is true that it is of meager benefit for a person with a cold heart to cling to a dead understanding, truly, truly the understanding that makes a person joyful and warm in hardship will also strengthen him for the next, to walk rightly on the road of hardship. Indeed, to believe with a sureness of spirit and without doubt that the hardship one is in is the road—is that not indeed walking rightly on the road of hardship!

VI

[The Joy of It That the Happiness of Eternity Still Outweighs Even the Heaviest Temporal Suffering[119]]

Before a person starts on something, whether it is something to be done or to be suffered, he first makes an estimate as to whether he, acting, can erect the tower[120] and how tall, as to whether he, suffering, has the strength to build the foundation and how deep. Therefore he makes an estimate of his capacities and the relation between his capacities and the task, and then he *deliberates* [*overveie*].[121] "To deliberate" is a transferred expression, but a very suggestive one, and therefore has the advantage a figure of speech always has, that one, as if through a secret door, indeed, as if by a magic stroke of the sudden, from the most common everyday conceptions stands in the middle of the loftiest conceptions, so that while talking about simple everyday things one suddenly discovers that one is also talking about the very highest things.

"To deliberate" is derived from "to weigh [*veie*]"; the scale weighs, or one weighs on the scale. Just what does it mean to weigh? It means to indicate the indifferent relation between two magnitudes, or to indicate this relation indifferently. So it is with the scale. It makes no difference at all to the scale which of the two weighs more; it merely gives the weight and has no preference for the one side or the other. This is what we prize in a scale and why we say, if it is so, that the scale is excellent and accurate. Now, we cannot speak in any other way about a scale, because otherwise we would certainly have to say that to weigh in that manner is not a difficult matter; the difficulty commences when there is preference for the one side or the other, and it is now a matter of—well, let us just use the simple yet so suggestive expression—it is now a matter of keeping one's tongue balanced.[122]

Therefore one weighs [*veie*] on the scale, but a person delib-
erates [*overveie*]; thus he does more than weigh in the same sense as the scale does. He over-weighs [*over-veie*]; he is higher than the weighing; he stands above the weighing—he chooses. We can, then, legitimately say that the word "deliberate," if one just holds tightly to it, ultimately states what is essential about human nature, states its composition and its preeminence. In weighing there must be two magnitudes; therefore the person deliberating, simply in order to be able to weigh, must be so composed that he has two magnitudes. This is also the case; he is composed of temporality and eternity. Spiritually understood, temporality and eternity are two magnitudes that are to be weighed. But in order to deliberate the person in turn must himself be a third party or have a third position in relation to the two magnitudes. This is the choice: he weighs, he deliberates, he chooses. Here, however, there is never any chance that the two magnitudes weigh equally much, which can of course happen with a scale, that it indicates the relation as one of equality. No, praise God, that can never happen, because properly understood the eternal already has a certain overweight and the person who refuses to understand this can never begin really to deliberate.

So a person deliberates before he begins, for example, at the beginning of his life. As yet he does not have much experience or any precise knowledge of temporality; in idea he has only a metaphor for temporality and for eternity, and he chooses between them. Ah, we dare to say, almost with certainty, of every human being that once upon a time in the beginning it was so very clear to him that eternity has the overweight; yes, not only was it clear to him but it moved him deeply, stirred his innermost being, and therefore very often this first choice of the young person is probably not without tears of inwardness.

Yet everything is by no means settled by that, because just as it is of little good to a person to know in an indifferent way the relation between the temporal and the eternal, so this first choice is of little use if it is not repeated again and again—alas,

perhaps will have to be repeated under very changed conditions. The youth has become an adult, life presses upon him,
now he is (let us hasten, however, from the lighter things in
order to be able to dwell longer on what these discourses
should be, the gospel of sufferings) a sufferer. Thus, even
though he does not waste his time and squander his strength on
continual weighing and deliberating, he must weigh again,
must in earnest weigh and deliberate again. He knows now
how heavy temporality is—does eternity indeed have the overweight now? In this way he asks himself questions, but he also
asks other people. Even if he does not waste his time and
squander his strength in chatter with just anybody, he earnestly
does ask the advice of someone who has been tried and tested.
God be praised, such counselors, such witnesses, are still to be
found, if not among the living, then among the dead and departed, and then first and foremost in Holy Scripture. Perhaps
the sufferer reads these words from the Apostle Paul:

VIII
387

**Our hardship, which is brief and light, procures for us
an eternal weight of glory beyond all measure.**
(II Corinthians 4:17)

This time we will make these words the subject for upbuilding as we consider the joy of it for the sufferer:

*that the happiness of eternity still outweighs even the heaviest
temporal suffering.*

But before examining the apostle's words more closely, we
must first make one comment that certainly seems superfluous
inasmuch as what it says is altogether self-evident, but yet, on
the basis of what experience teaches about human life, is perhaps well worth pointing out. That is, it is altogether self-
evident that if there is to be any meaning to this discourse, if a
person is to be assured that the happiness of eternity still outweighs even the heaviest temporal suffering, then he must
weigh it, he must see to it that the counterweight of eternity is
earnestly taken into consideration. Indeed, this is altogether
self-evident, and if it were also self-evident that everyone did
that, then everyone would have to be convinced that the happi-

ness of eternity has the overweight, because if only this thought is properly put on the scale in earnest, it will surely have the overweight. Ah, but how rarely, perhaps, a person weighs [*veie*] correctly in this way. Yet again and again in the world, day in and day out, from morning until night, there is this continual talk about deliberating [*overveie*] and deliberating, and yet it holds true that the person who does not continually have the conception of eternity as the other magnitude in the deliberating deliberates upon nothing—he cannot even deliberate. To deliberate on something temporal versus something else temporal when the eternal is left out is not deliberating. This is being fooled; this is wasting one's time and forfeiting eternal happiness by being fooled with life's childish tricks and games. Here, again, we see how much lies in the simple term "to deliberate." The basic meaning of human deliberating is to weigh the temporal against the eternal; in all other human deliberating this basic meaning must be present. Otherwise, despite all the busyness and pompous importance, the deliberating is baseless and meaningless.

VIII
388

But I wonder if people actually live in such a way that they continually take the thought of eternity earnestly into consideration? There is a busyness, a busy working for and a busy talking about the necessities of life, a busyness that seems totally to have forgotten what the necessary is. Now, if you get involved with these busy people you will hear them talking incessantly about deliberating and deliberating, even though they have totally forgotten the basic meaning of deliberating. And the more fortunate, the more favored person is only all too easily persuaded and beguiled by temporality, until it seems to him that things go so well for him that he does not need anything more; or if it nevertheless seems to him that things do not go so well for him, then he is still beguiled by temporality in such a way that it never occurs to him to look in the right place for the reason. But if you are involved with such a person, you will also hear him incessantly talking about deliberating and deliberating, even though you are quickly convinced that he has totally forgotten the basic meaning of it.

Alas, perhaps many people live this way; they even call

themselves Christians, although what is decisively the basis of all Christianity is just this basic meaning of deliberating. Perhaps many live this way, deceived by temporality. Let me illustrate this situation with a simple picture. When the well-to-do person is riding comfortably in his carriage on a dark but starlit night and has the lanterns lit—well, then he feels safe and fears no difficulty; he himself is carrying along the light, and it is not dark right around him. But just because he has the lanterns lit and has a strong light close by, he cannot see the stars at all. His lanterns darken the stars, which the poor peasant, who drives without lanterns, can see gloriously in the dark but starlit night. The deceived live this way in temporality: busily engaged with the necessities of life, they are either too busy to gain the extensive view, or in their prosperity and pleasant days they have, as it were, the lanterns lit, have everything around them and close to them so safe, so bright, so comfortable—but the extensive view is lacking, the extensive view, the view of the stars.

Surely people like that are themselves deceived, but on the other hand they have no intention of deceiving others with blind guidance or with bedazzling guidance, because this bedazzling lantern-light of temporality is always just as dangerous as blind guidance in the dark. But there are also people of the kind who, presumptuously self-deceived, presumptuously want to teach others the same thing. They want to do away completely with this conception of eternity and the happiness of eternity! With all kinds of clever inventions of comfortability, they want to teach people to make it as bright as possible around them in temporality so that they would no longer be able to see eternity. Or even if they do not want to do away completely with the conception of eternity and the happiness of eternity, they still want to degrade it in such a way that no eternal difference (indeed, can anything be more meaningless) remains between the temporal and the eternal. What difference, then, can remain? It seems to be beyond dispute that just as there is a difference of humanity between a human being and an animal, there must be an eternal difference between the temporal and the eternal. Or is the *difference* supposed to be that they are not *different*; or can eternity in all eternity have any other difference from the temporal than the difference of eternity? Such false teachers presumably cannot be called Pharisees, but what is actually worse: *either* a Pharisee who scrupulously indicates the right road but certainly does not walk it himself, a Pharisee whose words I can trustingly accept and act upon, while I leave it to God to do what can never be my business—to judge the hypocrite; *or* a so-called honest guide who does indeed walk the same road he recommends to others but, please note, changes the road and personally walks along the recommended—road of error?

Now the sufferer. When he does not see to it that this conception of eternity and the happiness of eternity enter earnestly into consideration, when as he weighs the heaviness of his suffering he does not weigh the weight of eternal happiness—what wonder is it, then, that the temporal suffering tips the scales, no wonder that he finds it heavy, dreadfully heavy. Alas, when eternity eventually weighs him, it will surely find him to be too light,[123] because the heavier a person becomes in this way, the closer he comes to being found too light by eternity. Or if the sufferer just once takes this thought of eternity into his hand, so to speak, and weighs it—but finds that it does not weigh much—no wonder that the temporal suffering weighs more! If the very next moment the sufferer again throws away the thought of eternity—and with indifference—no wonder that he finds the suffering still heavier, heavy to the point of despair, when not only the suffering weighs down but he himself adds to the weight of the suffering the presumptuous thought that he might be abandoned by God—because he himself abandoned the eternal! No wonder that a sufferer of that sort finally seeks the last escape of despair and wants to put an end to this agony—by beginning what awaits him in eternity!

VIII
390

After this sad observation, let us turn to a consideration of the apostle's words just read. Paul surely was the man who knew how to weigh and to deliberate; truly, if no guile was found on Christ's lips,[124] neither was a false weight to be found with an apostle.

"Our hardship, which is brief and light, procures for us an eternal weight of glory beyond all measure." So, then, hardship **procures**

an eternal weight of glory beyond all measure. But if *hardship* at every moment, that is, also when the temporal suffering presses down the most, *procures a weight of glory such as that, then the eternal happiness certainly does have an overweight.* That is, what procures something, the means by which something is acquired, is naturally the inferior, the end the superior. This is a thought so easily grasped, so universally accepted, and yet so deeply grounded that it is regarded as the saddest, the most loathsome confusion if someone reverses the relation and makes the end, that which in itself is the end, the means—for example, makes truth a means in the service of avarice or of ambition or of other base passions. The moral order of things, which is concerned with what in itself is the end, teaches that the means is inferior to the end. Indeed, even when the end is something earthly and something else earthly is the means, the means is still inferior to the end, even if the end and the means in another sense are equally inferior because they are both earthly. If, for example, someone procures for himself some earthly good with his money, he regards the money as inferior to the good he provides himself by means of it, although at some other time he may regard the money as the end and another earthly good as the means and as the inferior thing whereby he procures money for himself.

But an *eternal* weight of glory, vast beyond all measure, is no earthly good; this end cannot by chance be the superior and the means the inferior; neither can the relation switch, so that this good is at one time the end and the next time is the means whereby another good is acquired. This end is infinitely superior, is the end in itself. If, then, the suffering *procures* this good, eternal happiness quite simply and directly has the overweight, even when the suffering weighs more. That good is so infinitely superior to the means that even in the heaviest moment of suffering the consciousness that it is procuring an eternal weight of glory, vast beyond all measure, gives eternal happiness the overweight. Whoever refuses to understand and to believe this bears the guilt himself; in the heaviest moment of suffering he allows this consciousness to be extinguished, the consciousness of what the suffering is procuring.

When does temporal suffering weigh most appallingly on a person? Is it not when it seems to him to have no meaning, procures and acquires nothing; is it not when suffering, as the impatient person expresses it, is meaningless and pointless? Does someone who wants to take part in a competition complain even if preparation takes ever so much effort; does he complain even if it involves ever so much suffering and pain? Why does he not complain? Because he, although running aimlessly,[125] understands, or thinks he understands, that this suffering will procure the victory prize for him. Just when the effort is greatest and most painful, he encourages himself with the thought of the prize and that this specific suffering will help to procure it for him. How many sufferings will not a person endure when he understands that he thereby will procure his livelihood, or honor, wealth, the reward of love, or whatever else we want to mention! But the point is that here the temporal understanding is still adequate, or at least the person thinks it is adequate. He understands or thinks he understands that suffering will procure for him what is coveted—alas, *the* coveted, which is so infinitely inferior to the great eternal weight of glory that is beyond measure. If, however, the suffering embraces a person so tightly that his understanding wants to have nothing more to do with it, because the understanding cannot comprehend what the suffering would be able to procure when the sufferer cannot grasp this dark riddle, neither the basis of the suffering nor its purpose, neither why he should be so afflicted more than others nor how this would benefit him— and he now, when powerless he feels that he cannot throw off the suffering, rebelliously casts away faith, refuses to believe that the suffering will procure anything—well, then eternal happiness certainly cannot have the overweight, because it is totally excluded.

However, if the sufferer firmly holds on to what the understanding admittedly cannot comprehend, but what faith, on the other hand, firmly holds on to—that suffering will procure a great and eternal weight of glory—then eternal happiness has the overweight, then the sufferer not only endures the suffering but understands that the eternal happiness has the overweight. The insight that comprehends that the suffering will procure something gives the perseverance of temporality; but the faith, contrary to the understanding, that the suffering, which seems to be utterly evil and useless, will procure a great eternal weight of glory gives the perseverance of eternity. Although at times a sufferer may find endurable the hardship he is in but, worried, has fears about whether in the next moment it could become unendurable, there is opened to every sufferer access to a security—of a kind different from the deceitful security that deceitfully builds upon a human probability— that is, of willing to believe that the heaviest suffering will procure a great eternal weight of glory beyond all measure.

Therefore, even when the temporal suffering is the heaviest, eternal happiness still has the overweight. We shall not examine more closely in what sense the apostle says that suffering will procure that glory; that does not pertain to the subject of this discourse. May it only be kept in mind that in no way can it be understood in the sense of being deserved, for then one would have to be able to comprehend that the suffering will procure eternal happiness, and then in turn one would have to be able to comprehend eternal happiness, since it could be comprehended that it is deserved, but in that case the discourse would definitely not be about an eternal happiness, because the eternal happiness can only be believed—and for that very reason it cannot be deserved either. However, we shall not pursue this any further, but this stands fixed and firm: suffering procures a great eternal weight of glory beyond all measure— therefore the eternal happiness has the overweight.

"Our hardship, *which is brief and light*, procures . . . . . ." But if the hardship is brief and light, then it is very clear that the eternal happiness has an overweight, so not a word more needs to be said, because a brief and light hardship, which moreover procures a great eternal weight of glory, can certainly not counterbalance—indeed, it must rather be said to weigh nothing in comparison with this great weight of glory. Even the most impatient sufferer will surely admit this but will also think that this proves nothing, least of all about his suffering, because his suffering is far from being brief and light—it is indeed indescribably heavy and protracted. If that is the case, then the discourse has really brought itself into an awkward situation. But not so, the apostolic words have to be understood in a special way: Our hardship, which is brief and light. On another occasion,[126] I tried to explain what surely everyone knows, with what accent of truth the Apostle Paul can be called a person tried to the extreme in almost all human sufferings. Here I must be brief and in this connection limit myself and know of nothing more characteristic to say than this: Paul was not a coddled man. The impatient person must not allow himself to be deceived by appearances and think that this is a favorite of fortune who is talking about a little bit of half-hour hardship. The meaning of the apostolic words is therefore not altogether direct but is something like this: "In faith I anticipate such a great eternal weight of glory beyond all measure; for me the happiness of eternity is such a good that in comparison with it I call thirty years of all kinds of suffering a hardship that is brief and light." See, this is apostolic talk. We hear many an insipid eulogy on the happiness of eternity that aims to delude the senses with flamboyant phrases and sentimental description— an apostle does not know about such things, but he does understand that the best eulogy on the happiness of eternity is that it is such a good that in view of it the speaker calls such sufferings a hardship that is brief and light.

So it is the comparison that makes thirty years of sufferings a hardship that is brief and light. But to compare, after all, means to weigh. But the comparison does not weigh in such a manner that it keeps the two magnitudes far apart from each other; instead, it brings them so close together that the presence of the eternal happiness changes the expression about the hardship. Because the thought about eternal happiness is present, because the eternal happiness is present, the apostle speaks this way about the hardship. But this is quite as it should be. Does not the presence of a king make one speak differently from the way one usually does about the same thing! In the king's presence one says of some adversity that would ordinarily annoy and make one grumble at home: Your Majesty, it is a trifling

matter. In the presence of the beloved, we speak differently
from the way we usually do about the same thing. In the presence of the beloved, one says of something that would ordinarily be disturbing: Darling, it is a small matter. To change
one's words this way, and especially one's mind, we call a
subject's respect for the majesty of the king; we call it the
celebration of love in relation to the beloved; we call it solemnity in relation to the highest, and in minor relations we call it
politeness. Politeness is first and last a matter of heeding that
someone is present and who it is who is present. But the happiness of eternity—and when it is present in the thought about
it—alas, how often here a sufferer is rude enough, to put it
mildly, not to pay any attention to it, to pretend as if it were not
present—for in thought it can indeed always be present.

So, then, eternal happiness has the overweight. The sufferer
who does his best to speak the heavenly court language under-
VIII
394 stands that it has the overweight. Luther has said somewhere
that a Christian has to wear the royal court dress of the cross,[127]
but I wonder if a Christian ought not also to be practiced in
speaking, and to practice so as to be able to speak, the heavenly
court language with all his heart. As stated previously, gabbily
to gush about the glory of eternal happiness is empty and
foolish talk, but with closed lips, as it were, instead of speaking
directly about eternal happiness, by speaking in another way
about one's hardships in life, to show that one is speaking about
eternal happiness—that is the language of the royal court.

But it is spoken only with the whole heart, inasmuch as the
heavenly royal court language contains no falsehood in the
sense in which we ordinarily and legitimately speak of the flattering falsity of royal court language; it is no manner of speaking as royal court language ordinarily is—ah, no, it is simply
and solely a manner of thinking. Therefore what the apostle
says is literally true. This hardship of ours is brief and light, or
is then seventy years really an eternity, or is not seventy years
indeed a brief time compared with eternity! And must it not be
light if one is carrying at the same time the expectancy of the
great weight of glory, even if it still is light only insofar as the
great weight makes it light! If the hardship is not light, what

does the heaviest suffering weigh compared with an eternal weight of glory! The question is not about what the heaviest suffering weighs, but about what it weighs compared with an eternal weight of glory.

Consequently eternal happiness has the overweight, and the only requirement for comprehending that it has the over-weight, for speaking unchangingly at every time and in every suffering about the eternally unchanged, is fidelity to this con-ception of the happiness of eternity. The moment the expres-sion is changed, it is not the eternal happiness that has changed but the sufferer. See, the person who will serve a cause only insofar as the cause serves him—his expression is subject to much change; and the person who will love a girl only insofar as it is advantageous to him—his expression varies with the ups and downs. A double-minded person of this sort dishonestly speaks at one time about having the honor to serve this cause and at another time is slyly unwilling to have the shame of serving it; he speaks flatteringly at one time about the honor of being loved and at another time brazenly disclaims—this shame. But the person who humbly and enthusiastically has a cause that he loves understands that it, unchanged, is the same cause he has the honor of serving; he not only does not give up the cause, he not only suffers everything for it—no, he under-stands that he has the honor of suffering for this same cause. He never forgets, as enthusiasm understands, that his relation to the cause is a relation of honor, and whether he wins or suffers has nothing at all to do with this relation. The relation remains unchanged; he has the honor of winning in the service of this cause, or he has the honor of suffering in the service of this cause. How nobly faithful is the courtier who follows an over-thrown emperor into exile and, when his imperial majesty is dressed in rags, still addresses him with the same submissive-ness and homage as he did once in the halls of the palace and says: Your Majesty—because he did not cringingly recognize the emperor by the purple and therefore can now nobly recog-nize him in rags.

So also with the good that is the happiness of eternity. Fidel-ity is thinking and speaking uniformly about it while every-

VIII
395

thing is changing, not speaking ingratiatingly and in lofty tones about this good in temporality's pleasant days and, breaking faith with the eternal and traitor to oneself, changing the language in the day of suffering. Alas, here is the difference: it would grieve the emperor if the courtier changed, but let no one delude himself that the happiness of eternity suffers because a person, breaking faith with it, becomes a traitor to himself. Therefore if a person's life is fairly unacquainted with adversities—well, there is just one thing to say about the eternal happiness of heaven; but if he is tried and tested in all sorts of sufferings, there is still just one thing to say, because this good remains unchanged and is not changed by the suffering, but on the contrary changes the heaviest suffering to a hardship that is momentary and light.

Is not this what is meant by having the overweight—*indeed, is it not to have the overweight in such a way that the suffering actually cannot be weighed on the same scale with the eternal weight of glory* simply because a great weight of the happiness of eternity is not required, but the slightest part of it is a great and eternal weight! This, too, is contained in the apostolic words. Our hardship, that is, temporality's hardship, which is brief and light, procures an eternal weight; but in that case the eternal happiness not only has the overweight, but the relation is of such a nature that the two magnitudes cannot be weighed together. Let us understand each other. The adage has it that a pound of gold and a pound of feathers weigh the same, and this is surely true, but then we add that in another and more important sense the two magnitudes cannot be weighed together. Why not? Because the scale cannot indicate that the one pound is gold and the other pound feathers, that is, because the gold has a special value that makes it meaningless to weigh gold and feathers together. So it is also here with the two stated magnitudes. The distinction is not between happiness and suffering, but between *eternal* happiness and *temporal* suffering. The relation is this misrelation, and that it is a misrelation shows up most clearly in this, that the relation between temporal bliss and eternal happiness is the same misrelation, that temporal bliss amounts to nothing compared with eternal happiness, and it is also the very same with temporal suffering. Temporal suffering and eternal happiness are not only heterogeneous in the essential sense as gold and feathers are but are heterogeneous in the infinitely essential sense; the slightest part of the happiness of eternity weighs infinitely more than the longest earthly suffering.

What an indescribable joy, great beyond all measure! Would that the sufferer might comprehend this, might believe it, might understand that even when the temporal suffering is the heaviest, eternal happiness still has the overweight. Would that the sufferer might weigh properly—indeed, better yet, would weigh so that he not only does not collapse under the weight of the suffering but instead sinks under the overweight of the eternal happiness so that in his presentiment of this eternal happiness he, so to speak, smashes the balance and says: Here there is not even a question of weighing! But how rarely a sufferer like that is to be found! How different it is in the world! We do not say this to disturb the joy that is the theme of this discourse; we say it simply in order, if possible, to disturb the sadness that is the state of all too many people. How many live in such a way that in thoughtlessness they admit that eternal happiness has the overweight, in thoughtlessness admit that an eternal happiness is a magnitude heterogeneous with the temporal—that is, they leave this thought in abeyance, let it stand with its own worth, they do not concern themselves with it at all—the happiness of eternity has become so heterogeneous with the temporal goals of their life! They live in the inert delusion that sure enough we all will be blessedly happy—so heterogeneous has eternal happiness become for them. What a change if it ever were so that the heaviest lifelong suffering seemed to be nothing compared with the happiness of eternity, if it ever were so that the person who not only walked bravely into all the dangers of temporality but walked so bravely that he almost never recognized them as dangers, that in fear and trembling he worked out his salvation![128] Indeed, what is not lost by this change! What made the Romans so brave in battle, if it was not that they had learned to fear things worse than death! But what made the believer brave in life's dangers in quite another way than any Roman was, what else but that he knew a greater danger, but also an eternal happiness! What, then, makes this generation so fainthearted, even in earthly life's dangers, what else but that it does not know the highest danger! What is this generation's greatest guilt, what else but that it does not esteem the happiness of eternity! I wonder how people are going to escape the penalty; does not Scripture say, "How shall we escape (the penalty) if we neglect so great a salvation" (Hebrews 2:3)!

But it is not at all the intention of this discourse to pass judgment; it wishes only that people would judge in a different way. This discourse wants only to proclaim the gospel of sufferings—something the speaker truly has not invented himself, something by whose proclamation he truly does not expect to gain merits—it is too full of joy for that. Someone may gain merit by proclaiming this or that temporal truth, but eternity's truth and the joy of salvation are too joyful to have any room for the wretched bookkeeping of meritoriousness. If in sheer self-sacrifice and in the heaviest sufferings a person were to continue uninterruptedly to proclaim this joy, he would still have no merit, because the joy of it is that when temporal suffering weighs down most heavily, eternal happiness still has the overweight. A temporal truth has to put up with having a current account with its proclaimers; but the happiness of eternity possesses a general receipt that makes current accounts unthinkable, because even when the suffering is heaviest, eternal happiness still outweighs it.

VII

[The Joy of It That Bold Confidence Is Able in Suffering to Take Power from the World and Has the Power to Change Scorn into Honor, Downfall into Victory]

Out of fear of people, out of regard for worldly advantage, to be cravenly and ignobly afraid to own up before the world to the object of one's love is certainly one of the most detestable and contemptible things that can be said of a person; and out of fear of people, out of regard for worldly advantage, to be cravenly and ignobly afraid to own up before the world to one's faith and the object of one's faith—is the most detestable thing that can be said of a person. Therefore, even if it were not so that Holy Scripture most solemnly teaches that the confessors of Christianity are required to confess their faith before the world (indeed, what is required of them is already declared when they are called confessors); even if it were not so that Christ said: Whoever denies me before people I also will deny before my heavenly Father[129]—even if this were not so, it would still follow solely of itself, follow from the inner urge in the Christian, that he would do this. On the other hand, although the confession is commanded and enjoined with the full emphasis of eternity, if the confession is not a consequence of that inner urge, then a confession of that kind is not what is required. Therefore, if someone could presumptuously want to delude himself into thinking that the most sagacious thing, because after all it is required, the most sagacious thing, in view of eternity's judgment, would be to confess Christ: then such a person does not only not confess Christ but blasphemously distorts him, as if Christ were a vain power seeker who craved a great name in the world. No, that was not why Christ required the confession, and that is not the way he required it. On the contrary, he actually required that his followers have such inwardness that confession follows of itself—when it is required. The same inwardness can also be silent and just as pleasing to God, but this same true inwardness surely cannot be silent—when confession is required. Indeed, how could a person's faith be strong enough to believe unto salvation, strong and disregardful enough in this way (alas, this may be just about the most difficult kind of disregard, to pay no attention to one's own fantasies about merit or to the mitigating inventions of one's passions or to the horrifying images of terrified imagination in the consciousness of guilt, but without this disregard one cannot have faith unto salvation) if a person does not have a faith strong and disregardful enough to dare to confess—if it is required.

Every true Christian has therefore always been willing, if required, to confess his faith. He has not vainly and egotistically sought the occasion, and this is commendable, but in sincere concern has instead satisfied himself that, honest before God, he was willing to do it if it was required. This is how it once was when the world all around Christianity was paganism and the Christian was in every way called upon to confess his faith before the world, because *to confess his faith was the same as to proclaim Christianity*. At that time there was also fervor and readiness to confess; it was held in high esteem by the Christians, and therefore, although all were confessors of the same faith, they singled out and called confessors[130] a few who, unlike the martyrs, did not sacrifice their lives but were tried and tested in the many dangers of confession. In those days confession was unconditionally required of everyone, because what the world wanted was to compel the Christians to confess that they were not Christians. Paganism wanted to treat the Christians as criminals, and then (as several of the Church fathers so clearly and penetratingly spelled out) it wanted them to admit and confess, not their guilt, as is otherwise the case with criminals, but on the contrary demanded of the Christian that he confess that he was not a Christian.

But has not the situation changed, now when Christianity has triumphantly prevailed, now when all are Christians, now when the requirement is least of all that one confess that one is not a Christian, but unquestionably the supreme requirement is to confess that one is a Christian. Let us with calmness and self-control consider this matter. If it is God who gives the spirit of power and strength, then it is also the same God who gives "the spirit of self-control,"[131] and even if ignoble cowardice and fear of people are just as detestable in any age, the excesses of eager enthusiasm, "zeal without wisdom,"[132] are no less corrupting and at times are fundamentally just as detestable, just as blasphemous. When a Christian among pagans confesses [*bekjende*] Christ, it is the same as proclaiming Christianity before people who do not know [*kende*] it. That kind of confession does not contain a judgment on the pagans, that they are not Christians, since the pagans do not claim to be Christians. But when the Christian lives among Christians, or among people who all call themselves Christians, then to confess Christ is not the same as proclaiming Christianity (because the people to whom the confession is addressed are, after all, instructed in Christianity and call themselves Christians), but it is judging others, judging those who *call* themselves Christians, that they only *pose* as Christians, thus judging of them that they are not Christians, therefore most leniently judging them for light-mindedness and thoughtlessness, most harshly for hypocrisy.

The two situations are certainly quite different and easy to differentiate, because in the one case the Christian is surrounded by pagans and therefore to be a Christian is exactly the same as to confess Christ. In the other case, the Christian who confesses Christianity is surrounded by Christians who also confess Christianity, and therefore to want to confess Christ to a more eminent degree is to deny the Christianity of others. For the sake of even greater clarity, let me illustrate this point by a simple, palpable example. If there was a kind of food, a dish, that in some way was so important to someone that it involved his deepest emotions (we could imagine a national dish or a dish that has religious significance), and as a consequence that person could not possibly remain quiet if this food was ridiculed or was merely spoken of slightingly—then it would naturally follow that if this happened in his presence he would acknowledge and confess his feelings. Now let us imagine a somewhat different situation. This man is in the company of several others and that particular food is served. When the food is served, each of the guests declares, "This is the most glorious and the most priceless of all dishes." Now, if the man of whom we speak discovers to his amazement, or at least thinks he discovers, that the guests are not eating this dish or let it go by untouched, that they confine themselves to other dishes, although they maintain that that dish is the most glorious and priceless—in such a case is the man called upon to acknowledge his conviction? After all, no one contradicts him, no one says anything else than what he is saying. If on this occasion he solemnly acknowledges his feelings, then *either* there is no meaning to his conduct (inasmuch as all the others are saying the same thing, it is meaningless to *confess* his conviction in agreement with their unanimous conviction, because this, after all, is not confessing but agreeing), *or* he will indeed be judging the others, that they do not mean what they say.

So it is also with confessing Christ among people who call themselves Christians, if we bear in mind the inadequacy of the metaphor—namely, that we can have sensory assurance about whether a person eats or does not eat of the food he so highly praises, but in the spiritual sense only the knower of hearts knows whether a person does not mean what he says. It is very possible that a Christian discovers with amazement, or at least thinks he discovers, that many people, all of whom say that to be a Christian is the highest good and that they themselves are Christians, do not seem to care very much about this highest good; but if he then uses the opportunity to confess Christ, then his confession is not a proclaiming of Christianity but a judging of others. To confess in the way the Bible and the Church use this word presupposes opposition, presupposes that there is someone who speaks against it. But this, of course, was not the case; on the contrary, he thought he had discovered that there were many who contradicted themselves or did not mean what they said. Therefore he is not confessing Christ as opposed to those who deny Christ but as opposed to those who also confess Christ—that is, he judges the others, judges that their confession is an untruth—not that what they say is an untruth, since they say what is true, but that the true statement has no truth in them.

If someone is called upon to confess Christ in such a way as to deny him to others whose statements are nevertheless the same—that is a totally different question, and one cannot appeal directly to earliest Christendom for the answer to that. It is a totally different question, one that everyone surely would do well to consider earnestly. Whatever the answer is, it can never be such that it thereby follows that he should be exempted from doing all in his power to help others go forward in their Christianity. But to teach, to guide, to encourage others with whom one has the essential in common in a universal confession of Christianity is not confessing Christ. In those days when Christianity was contending with paganism, which denied Christ, and when every Christian was called on to confess Christ before the world, it surely never occurred to the Christians to confess Christ in their mutual relations with one another, because the individual Christian who in his relation to Christians will take it upon himself to confess Christ presumes arrogantly to deny that the others are Christians. Therefore it must continually be borne in mind that what is synonymous with proclaiming Christianity, as long as Christianity is surrounded by paganism, very easily becomes sectarian conceit and presumption in Christianity.

It by no means follows, however, from these comments, which contain only a recommendation of the necessary precaution, that the situation could never arise in the middle of so-called Christendom that a man is constrained to confess Christ. But we will decide nothing about that but leave it up to the single individual's earnest self-examination; neither have we advanced this for consideration, as if the theme of the discourse were: On Confessing Christ. No, we call to mind the supreme example of fighting for a conviction, so that from the highest we might learn for the lesser, so that in the fight for a conviction that may be allotted to us we might fight in the right way.

VIII
402

Even if this does not happen, even if the life of a person, as he struggles, is not placed in the difficulty of having to confess Christ, he can, of course, also in other ways be brought to the decision that he is under the necessity and obligation to confirm, definitely and to the last extremity, a view related to and scrupulously connected with his innermost conviction.

But here, too, it holds true that, out of fear of people and regard for worldly advantage, to be cravenly and ignobly afraid to own up to one's conviction is one of the most detestable and contemptible things that can be said about a person. Therefore it is beneficial to be well prepared, to be aware of the difficulties beforehand so that one can be resolute in danger but also intimate with the glad thought of guiding bold confidence. Alas, gradually with the spreading of a certain superficial culture and with the proliferating of peoples' various reciprocal interests, gradually with the spreading infection of the envious and pusillanimous small-mindedness of incessant comparison, it unfortunately seems as if everything is aimed at stifling people's bold confidence. At the same time as there are struggles to overthrow dominions and regimes, there seems to be a supreme effort to develop more and more the most dangerous slavery: the small-minded fear of people who are one's equals. [133]Ah, it is easy enough to overthrow a tyrant (if there is such a person at all, and if this is not an old tale revived for the sake of the heroic exploit of overthrowing him)—he can certainly be overthrown; at least it is possible, indeed easy, to take aim at him. In these days, fear of people in connection with rulers and the mighty is to be regarded as an old story; in any case there are many who in this regard are fighting against the danger—so the danger certainly does not amount to much either. Perhaps an inexperienced person naively concludes that the danger against which a lot of people are fighting must certainly be great because there are so many fighters. But a somewhat more experienced person perhaps more soundly concludes: the danger against which many fight is hardly great—because there are many; where there is a great danger to fight, "many" is what one sees last.

VIII
403

But this evil spirit, the small-minded fear of people in relation to equals and the tyranny of the equal, this evil spirit, which we ourselves conjure up and which does not reside in any individual person and is not any individual person but covertly sneaks around and seeks its prey, insinuates itself into the relation among individuals—this evil spirit, which essentially wants to do away with every individual's relation to God, is very difficult to eradicate.

People are scarcely aware that it is a slavery they are creating; they forget this in their zeal to make people free by overthrowing dominions. They are scarcely aware that it is a slavery; how could it be possible to be a slave in relation to equals? Yet it is rightly taught that a person is also a slave of what he is unfreely dependent upon. But our freedom-loving age thinks otherwise; it thinks that if one is not dependent on a ruler, then one is not a slave either; if there is no ruler, then there is no slave either. One is scarcely aware that it is a slavery that is being created, and just this makes it so difficult to tear oneself away from it. This slavery is not that one person wants to subjugate many (then one would of course become aware), but that individuals, when they forget the relation to God, become mutually afraid of one another; the single individual becomes afraid of the more or of the many, who in turn, each one out of fear of people and forgetting God, stick together and form the crowd, which renounces the nobility of eternity that is granted to each and every one—to be an individual.

In this way, as in so many other ways, a person can become tried and tested in the world, can be brought to the point that he must and should stand by a conviction; but he will never be left without guidance if he only seeks it and in the right place—and where, then, but in Holy Scripture. For example, we read in the Acts of the Apostles that the apostles were forbidden by the council to proclaim Christ. The apostles, however, did not allow themselves to be deterred by that but feared God more than people and proclaimed Christ. Thereupon the council had them seized and would have had them killed if Gamaliel had not advised against it. But the apostles were flogged and then

VIII
404

allowed to go. But now when they had been flogged (we read in Acts 5:41):

> **"Then they went away from the council, joyful because they had been deemed worthy to be scorned for the sake of Christ's name."**

Continually bearing in mind these words, we shall consider the joy of it for everyone who suffers for a conviction:

> *that bold confidence is able in suffering to*
> *take power from the world and has the power to change scorn into*
> *honor, downfall into victory.*

If we imagine a youth who is well instructed in the truth, we are by no means able to deny that he knows the truth. Yet his experience will probably be like that of others before him— that when he has become an adult he has come to know something totally different, although he still knows only the truth. The youth does indeed know the truth but he is ignorant of and without experience of the conditions of actuality, the whole surrounding world, within which truth has to step forward. It is seldom that in this regard a person is helped from earliest childhood by a more obscure intimation. Ordinarily the youth has a credulity, which is lovable, that in turn sometimes does become his ruin. The youth's thirst for knowledge eagerly and willingly appropriates the truth as it is communicated to him; his immature but beautiful imagination then creates for him a picture he calls the world, where what he has learned now unfolds before him as on a stage. In the youth's unspoiled thoughts, they fit each other perfectly: the truth, which he has learned in its purest form, and the world, that is, the stage of the imagination, which he himself creates. So must be the relation between the truth and the world, the youth thinks, and then, confident, he goes out into the world of actuality.

But what does he see there? Now, we will not dwell on all the defectiveness and mediocrity and instability and small-mindedness he now sees in the world around him; we will not pause at the sad discoveries the youth makes about himself,

how he, too, is not the person he had imagined, how he comes
to verify, alas, perhaps to interpret at length this verse: "That he
himself is also beset with frailty" (Hebrews 5:2). We move on
to more powerful dramatic scenes. In other words, the world
can present in two ways the reverse of what an unspoiled youth
had believed. A youth does not see any of these sights without
terror, and even while he is lifted up by the divine glory of the
one sight, he shudders at the first impression of this same sight
[*Syn*]—which is now so uplifting only by way of the God-
fearing inspection [*Eftersyn*].

The youth is instructed in the true and the good, in loving
the good for the sake of truth, and in avoiding even the appearance of evil. But the world now shows him the reverse. There
is a *reverseness* that may be called *brazenness*; there are people
who reverse the concepts and who, as the apostle says, *"place
their glory in their shame," "boast of their disgrace."*[134] A youth
must see this with horror; they not only do evil, but they do
not even hide it; they not only do not hide it, but they do it
openly; they seek the light, although ordinarily we think that
evil shuns the light; they raise their eyes, and by this they are
known, although ordinarily we think that the evil conscience
drops its eyes; they not only do evil openly, but they boast of it
and "commend those who do it."[135]

But the world can in yet another way show the reverse of
what the unspoiled youth believed; there is another reverseness
that certainly contains what is most elevating, even though it is
so terrifying a scene that the youth shudders because it does not
agree with his beautiful ideas. This happens when the good
must suffer in the world for the sake of the truth, when the
world shows itself to be unworthy of the good, when the
righteous has no reward, indeed, is rewarded with scorn and
persecution, when the confusion finally becomes so great that
people think they are doing God a favor[136] by persecuting the
witness to the truth; this happens when the good is compelled
to call the scorn glory, is compelled in the opposite sense and
with the eternal emphasis of truth to place glory in shame.
Such things no doubt rarely occurred to a youth; such things a

VIII
406

youth has rarely been able to imagine; the youth most often and most naturally has that lovable credulity, but it does not comprehend anything like this.

When this happens, when the concepts are shaken in an upheaval that is more terrible than an earthquake, when the truth is hated and its witnesses persecuted—what then? Must the witness submit to the world? Yes. But does that mean all is lost? No, on the contrary. We remain convinced of this, and thus no proof is needed, for if it is not so, then such a person is not a witness to the truth either. Therefore we are reassured that even in the last moment such a person has retained a youthful recollection of what the youth expected, and he therefore has examined himself and his relationship before God to see whether the defect could lie in him, whether it was not possible for it to become, as the youth had expected, something he perhaps now desired most for the sake of the world—namely, that truth has the victory and good has its reward in the world. But when he is reassured that he does not bear the guilt and is reassured that from now on he bears the responsibility if he does not act, then bold confidence rises up in him with supranatural powers, then he reverses the relationship and marvelously transforms shame to honor, places his honor in being scorned by the world in this way, "boasts of his persecutions and his chains," praises God that "it has been granted him to suffer this way."[137] *This reversing is the reverseness of bold confidence*; it is also a reversing of what an unspoiled youth had expected to see in the world. Woe to the one who presumptuously, precipitously, and impetuously brings the horror of confusion into more peaceable situations; but woe, also, to the one who, if it was made necessary, did not have the bold confidence to turn everything around the second time when it was turned around the first time! Woe to him—if it is hard to bear a world's persecution, it is still harder to bear the responsibility for not having acted, to stand ashamed in eternity because he did not through God win the bold confidence to transform shame into honor.

This is what the apostles did, but they did it in **suffering**. At this point let us promptly say what we should repeat again and

VIII
407

again—they did it in suffering; otherwise the discourse would in essence become a presumptuous lie and, if anyone were to act accordingly, would in the result become the most dreadful error. —After the apostles had been flogged, "they went away joyful because they had been deemed worthy to be scorned for the sake of Christ's name."[138]

In this world many horrifying speeches have been heard about the errors and sins of human beings (we need only call to mind the ancient prophets and judges)—ah, but even the most rigorous denunciatory lecture is not so terrifying as this apostolic bold confidence. Even the most rigorous denunciatory lecture still acknowledges having a solidarity with the people it denounces. It is so rigorous simply in order that they might improve; as it denounces, it becomes involved with them. But to be brought to such an extremity that there is only one recourse left: to thank God, to be joyful that it has been granted to one to be scorned—this, compared with even the most rigorous denunciatory lecture, is to speak in tongues. I wonder if anyone can actually think of this situation without shuddering, because if such speech is not madness and in that case is contrary to all rules—then it is either the height of brazenness or a marvel of bold confidence. If one were to characterize the most corrupt and confused age, I wonder if one could characterize it more accurately but also more horrifyingly than to say: The corruption and confusion were such that they compelled the good person to graze the borders of brazenness, compelled him to boast of being scorned! On the other hand, if we wanted to find the most reliable way to express that the good always has the victory, what expression is more reliable than this: In suffering, bold confidence is able to take power from the world and has the power to change scorn into honor, victory into downfall![139] When we say this, we are not saying that the good person is eventually victorious in another world, or that his cause will eventually be victorious in this world. No, he is victorious while he is living; suffering, he is victorious while he is still alive—he is victorious on the day of suffering. If all human opposition mounts up, yes, if a world rises up against him, he is the stronger. Not even the power of language can hold him; he breaks through language, as it were. Through God he presses ahead with bold confidence to force honor out of shame, victory out of downfall. But if it is alarming to see a sleepwalker, who is indeed walking with enormous assurance over the abyss, yet in an incomprehensible way, then it is not without a shudder that we look at this apostolic assurance, which, at the height of madness, through God speaks in tongues with bold confidence.

VIII
408

When the Apostle Paul says, "To be judged by a human court is to me a very small thing,"[140] these are surely strong and powerful words, which truly should not be repeated light-mindedly, because we certainly do need to pay attention to human judgment; but nevertheless these words are more human. But to thank God because one was flogged, to boast that one was scorned—this is shocking and it also means that human judgment is regarded as even less than little, as less than nothing. It is so shocking that in all honesty, with none of the deceptiveness that merely wishes to avoid dangers, we dare to say: We thank God that we were not tried in this way, were not faced with decisions that would take this bold confidence. With the apostles, there is no question of whimpering about trifles, of a few individual corrupt and brazen people, such as there have been in every age, while then again there are many with whom one both wishes to have and does have language and concepts in common. No, the apostles stood alone with a world against them; it was not merely what we call the bad ones; no, it was the whole world that stood against the apostles. And of their relation to this world they had to judge that to be flogged was an honor, to be scorned was something to boast about. The apostles stood alone this way; for them only one thing mattered, and as Paul adds, "All else is loss."[141] Alas, such words are repeated so often and parroted so often that finally we think that by sheer repetition they fit into our common everyday language, from which they are certainly as different as night and day. Yes, how many have the capacity to think the triumphant reverseness of bold confidence that is implied in this statement.

When in actuality a person is just enthusiastic enough to be willing to sacrifice something for a cause, we are already close to regarding him pityingly as a simpleton, to feeling sorry for him as a poor nitwit. Yet his enthusiasm implies only that he loves a cause so much that because of it he is willing to bear the loss of something else, of the world's goods, of money, of reputation. But how far this still is from the apostolic view! The enthusiast does regard the possession of earthly goods as a gain, even if he is willing to give it up and bear the loss—the apostolic view is to regard the possession as loss. If someone is so enthusiastic as to consider all earthly goods to be nothing, well, then the world is close to considering such a person mad. Yet this enthusiasm is not apostolic, because the apostle not only reckons the earthly goods as nothing, he even regards them as loss. Therefore, just as a person ordinarily seeks after wealth, honor, esteem, so an apostle seeks to escape from these goods. In this we all agree with the apostle—we would all like to avoid loss—but again the disagreement is as great as great can be, because by loss we understand exactly the opposite of what the apostle understands by it.

VIII 409

Nevertheless it is joyful, indescribably joyful, that bold confidence has the power to be victorious in this way and is able in this way, despite language and all people, to stamp the concepts, and let us not forget this—with the genuine mark of the divine. Thus to triumphant bold confidence what we simple-mindedly and whiningly call loss is gain, what the world rebelliously calls shame is honor; thus what the world childishly calls downfall is victory; thus the language a whole race speaks in unanimous agreement is still turned upside down, and there is only one single human being who speaks the human language correctly, he whom the whole race is unanimous in thrusting away from itself.

But since it is on account of, and with continual reference to, those words in the Acts of the Apostles that we have called attention to this joy that through God bold confidence has this power, let us then also try to understand the apostles and how the apostles understood themselves on this. Surely such words and such miracles of faith ought to be discussed with bold confidence. Despite all the timorous sagacity that wants to teach people evasions and calculations, the discussion should be boldly confident and unreserved, because from a godly point of view everyone who dares to proclaim worldliness will be eternally responsible. The discussion should, if possible, be such that it must send a shiver through anyone who presumptuously wants to venture out on such roads but also such that it will shockingly remind the rest of us how Christianity has had to struggle in the world, so that we, if more favorable conditions are indeed granted to us, may in humble gratitude praise God but also honor the apostles in the right way, honor them by honestly confessing without any suppression that it is a distinction before God to be favored with such sufferings, but also by honestly confessing without any suppression that the distinction is of such a nature that flesh and blood would rather be exempt from it. It is false talk to speak flatteringly about an apostle's distinction just as if it were something everyone would like to have, such as money or talent—instead of its being the secret of sufferings, so that practically everyone would decline this distinction with thanks when the condition is, as it was indeed, to become in dead earnest what an apostle became, "scum in the world, a spectacle to the world."[142] This is why we say, as we learn from the example of the apostles, that *in suffering* bold confidence is able to perform this marvel; if bold confidence wants to be in action, it is incapable of performing the marvel. But the apostles were indeed continually suffering. They not only had sufferings—someone who is in action can also have them—but their whole procedure was a suffering, their functioning was a submitting. They did not preach rebellion against authority; on the contrary, they acknowledged its power, but in suffering they obeyed God more than people. They did not ask to be exempted from any punishment; they did not grumble at being punished, but, punished, they continued to proclaim Christ. They did not want to force anyone, but, themselves subjugated, they were victorious by letting themselves be subjugated. If the relation is not this, bold confidence cannot perform the marvel either, because the marvel is this—that to all it looks like ruin, whereas to the apostle it is victory. When bold confidence is less than this, it wants to act, wants to be in the right; it wants to force people to acknowledge it. Then it cannot and will not in suffering endure the martyrdom of madness—that what a whole world calls ruin, that what a whole world works on in the belief that it is ruin, that this, for faith's secret with God, is victory; that what a whole world calls disgrace and works on, supposing that it is disgrace, that this, for faith's secret with God, is honor.

"Then the apostles went away, joyful because they had been deemed worthy to be scorned for the sake of Christ's name." This is the apostles' deepest conviction in the heart's intimacy with God; it is not a contrived comment, as when someone seeks to conceal the consuming heat of his passion under the coolness of the language. No, we find no hostile reference to humankind in any remark by an apostle. They are so reconciled with God, with the thought of being sacrificed, and so exclusively concerned with their relation to God that on that account they have entirely forgotten their relation to people. They do not actually struggle with people; what people do to them is actually of no concern to them, and at most only as an occasion to examine the God-relationship in which alone, totally absorbed, they have their lives.

Paul does not judge King Agrippa,[143] does not attack him in his speech, does not wound him with a word. On the contrary, he deals gently with him; his words are gentle and conciliatory when he says: I would to God that not only you but also all who hear me this day might become such as I am—except for these chains. An apostle suffers: he does not struggle with people, not because he proudly and superiorly elevates himself above their attack—by no means, but because he is solely concerned with his own relation to God. This is simultaneously the eternal, sure means of diversion during suffering and also the highest elevation. When the entire world concentrates all its power to attack an apostle, it cannot manage to struggle with him on equal conditions, because an apostle continually has a third, which to him is simply and solely the most important, to him is everything: the relation to God.

See, to be innocent, humanly speaking, and to be put to

VIII
411

death and yet to die with a witticism on one's lips,[144] that is a proud victory, that is paganism's triumph; and it is also the ultimate in human relationships, but please note, when God is left out, when all life and its greatest scene are basically still a game because God is not included in the game, for if he is included, then life is earnest. An apostle, however, leaves out everything else, forgets everything else, does not see it, does not hear it, does not sense it, but has his sights on God alone; and this is why we hear those humble words from a martyr, "I thank God that it is granted me to be deemed worthy to be crucified." Such words are not spoken to ridicule people. No, for this humble martyr people simply are not present, he has nothing to do with them, all their malice and ignorance is of no concern to him, he does not ask to triumph over them, he does not want to show them that he is after all the stronger. Ah, no, he turns to God, even in that final moment not without fear and trembling about whether he has indeed properly fulfilled his task, but also in confidence and devotion, humbly giving thanks that he was deemed worthy of this ignominious death. See, a raging crowd collects around the martyr; it believes that this affair is between them and him, it jeers at him even in the last moment and then waits to hear either wailing or proud words from the suffering one. It is hidden from the eyes of the crowd that someone else is present, and yet it is true, the martyr sees only God and is speaking only with God. His words— well, they do indeed sound like a ridiculing of the deluded crowd, but they are not said in that way. The martyr is speaking with God; he is giving thanks for being deemed worthy of this suffering.

These words perform miracles. He does not descend from the cross, but he does something even more marvelous; he transforms the language by means of bold confidence. When language's most lofty phrases are hardly adequate to describe this martyr's innocence and, for that matter, his merit, humanly speaking, then precisely because he has nothing to do with people but is before God, he feels that he has no merit whatever. He rips to pieces his account book with people; he lets them keep all their wrongs and he humbly thanks God. Just as the rest of us give thanks for the good things, he gives thanks for the favor of being crucified. Marvelous language, marvelous loftiness—at the peak of madness, as it were, to have this bold confidence! Yet consider, my listener, what it means to thank God for the grace and favor of being crucified! And we, who whine and complain if the world goes against us a little, we who are busy getting our rights, are proud of being right, we who consequently, if we want to be honest, have to confess that we are close to calling such a remark madness!

"So the apostles went away joyful" after they had been flogged. They actually were joyful; it was not a false front as long as the world was looking on; they did not do it in order to show to the world how profoundly they despised it. No, they actually were joyful—indeed, no girl has ever been more joyful on her betrothal day than the apostles were on the day of whipping and on every such day which for them was a day of betrothal with God.

The person who acknowledges a triumphal view is of course joyful on the day of victory, not only on account of victory, but because for him the victory is a confirmation that he actually is going along the road he intended to take, because what he was waiting for has now happened. But the person who acknowledges a militant view is joyful on the day of persecution, because what he must be waiting for now indeed happens. This is in harmony with his whole view. The victory in the first instance is not an accidental piece of good luck but is the essential; in the second instance the joy is that the suffering does not come as an accidental piece of bad luck but as the essential. If the victory had failed to come for that first person, he surely would have searched for the fault within himself; if the persecution had failed to come for the second person, he presumably would have searched for the fault in himself. This is very easy to understand for anyone who at least has a conception of what it means to have a view of life and to live by virtue of it and on the contrary is not accustomed to living on the uncertainty of foolish trifling.

VIII
413

And now an apostle! He had seen the Holy One crucified. He had seen the evil and corruption of the whole world disclosed

when the Lord and Master was scorned—with this impression
the apostle went out into the world. If you possibly can, try to
imagine it any other way than that this man had to wish that
this same world would treat him in the same way, that this
man, disheartened and deeply troubled, would have had to
blame himself if he was not persecuted, whereas he could fear
only one thing, whether it still would not be too great an honor
to be crucified! Try it, imagine that he who was to proclaim to
the world this message about the Holy One's being crucified as
a criminal between two robbers, that this man was dressed in
purple and glory, that this man possessed all the world's goods,
this man who was to proclaim a crucified one's teaching that
his kingdom was not of this world—try it, if you can just bear
the attempt, if it is not out of the question because the mere
thought of anything like this has the ring of a presumptuous
mockery of an apostle. But in that case it is quite as it should be
that the apostles in all sincerity before God were joyful over
having been flogged.

Or imagine that the apostolic proclamation of Christianity
had quickly triumphed, as they say. Imagine that an apostle
could have experienced the danger in which later generations
were tried, that power and glory and dominion were offered to
them—not in order to stop proclaiming Christ but in order to
proclaim him. I really wonder if an apostle actually could have
persuaded himself to understand this. I wonder if he would not
have found it inconceivable that the Lord and Master would be
treated as a criminal and the pupil, "who is indeed not above
the teacher,"[145] would attain honor and high position! I wonder if an apostle would ever have changed so much that instead
of affirming a militant view of life and Christianity he would
have affirmed a triumphant view? The triumphant view assumes that on the average most people, the majority of people,
are of the truth; for that very reason the possession of power
and honor is a sign that one is eminently good. But the militant
view teaches that the good must get the worst of it, and therefore its servants are persecuted, insulted, treated as criminals or
as fools—alas, and by this they are known, and for that very
reason they do not wish power and honor, because that implies

VIII
414

a false admission with regard to their view. The only person who with bold confidence can possess honor and power is the one who is convinced that on the average the human race is good, which at some time may be true; then not to want honor and power when one deserves to have them will in turn be a sign of the unhealthy extreme of vehemence.

The apostles were joyful over having been flogged, and they were sincerely joyful. They may also have thought of those words: Every sacrifice shall be salted.[146] There is a danger to which the apostles were perhaps less exposed, for in those days it was a matter of a life-and-death struggle every day and every moment. Nevertheless, let us consider this danger in order to understand better the apostles' joy over being ridiculed and persecuted. Under more peaceable conditions, when everything seems so secure, when people speak of peace and no danger,[147] when temporality seemingly becomes a magic spell—then the danger is only much too close, so that a person is himself inclined to take the spirit in vain and others also help him to do so. Then people will admire, as it is called, the person who is gifted, admire his rare excellence, and forget that it is all God's gift and help the gifted one also to forget. Then people accept honor from one another,[148] play the wonder game,[149] and, admired or admiring, fritter away their lives in the old rut that makes existence insipid because it is without salt, makes existence a confection because it is without earnestness. Just imagine if an apostle had experienced something like this, if he who certainly was highly entrusted as no one else has ever been, but who also always humbly understood that before God he was nothing, just imagine if he had discovered that people wanted to take in vain the gift of grace granted to him and help him to do the same, wanted to bedizen him in purple and finery and forget God—I wonder if in holy wrath he would not have ripped off these chains of lace, I wonder if he would not have sadly thought of the joy he sensed when existence had pith and had flavor, when an apostle went away joyful after having been flogged and truly was bound to be joyful over it!

We have now considered the joy in the thought that bold confidence has this power of victory; we have also called to mind how the apostles understood themselves in this thought. We dare not withhold from anyone the joy, the triumphant joy contained in that thought; we dare not suppress the fact that bold confidence has this power. But neither have we played fast and loose with our words; on the contrary, to the best of our ability we have added the weight of earnest reflections to the joy, in order if possible to exercise a restraining influence. [150]This joyful thought is not like a so-called harmless remedy that can be used in any way without danger and can be used for a light cold, but it is like strong medicine, the use of which involves some danger, but rightly used also delivers from a sickness unto death. Rarely, indeed, will it in our day be the case that a person truthfully dares to say that he suffers for Christ's sake; we repeatedly commend, however, the sobriety that bears in mind that one dare not appeal directly to the apostles' relation to a pagan world. But even though this were to become a greater rarity, it nevertheless can happen often, and it can happen to every human being, provided he does not want "to shrink back to his own destruction,"[151] that he can come to suffer for a conviction. But it is impossible to fight this battle of conviction in the right way without the assistance of bold confidence. It is our hope and our faith that bold confidence is given also from above in proportion to the danger, but bold confidence is required even in the minor dangers. Therefore, whoever you are, if you have anything you call your conviction (it would indeed be sad if you did not have it), and if you are required to fight for it, do not seek the aid of the world or of people. This aid is indeed treacherous, at times in such a way (and this is not exactly the most dangerous) that it disappoints and fails to show up at the most difficult moment, but also at times treacherous in such a way (and this is the real danger) that, when it comes in abundance, it suffocates the good cause. Just as many a cause may have been lost because the world's assistance failed to come, so also is many a cause ruined because the world was allowed to help.

No, seek the bold confidence before God. If you are perhaps suffering for a conviction, or if you are preparing to suffer for a conviction, or if you are seriously considering what can happen to a person, then rejoice for a moment in the joy that was the theme of this discourse; but do not make a mistake, do not indulge in the joy. Instead, earnestly strive to win bold confidence before God and then the joy will come all the more richly to you. A conviction is not something one should rush to bring out in the world. Alas, much confusion has been created and great harm done because an immature person has brought out an immature conviction. No, just allow the conviction to grow quietly, but let it grow together with bold confidence before God. Then, whatever danger befalls you, you will be convinced of what bold confidence is able to do. A spark in some wood shavings is put out with a glass of water, but when a fire has had time to spread slowly through the whole house and then with a deep sigh (so it is in the actuality of the metaphor; so it is also in the actuality of the spirit characterized by the metaphor) bursts into flames all at once—then the firemen say: There is nothing to be done here; here the fire is victorious. It is indeed sad when the firemen say that the fire is victorious, but it is joyful when it is the fire of conviction that is victorious and the enemies say: There is nothing to be done here. If, namely, the fire of conviction has had time to spread slowly through a person until, when the moment has come, with a deep sigh it all at once finds vent in the flames of bold confidence, then bold confidence is able in suffering (and in a certain sense suffering is indeed manifest when zeal for a conviction consumes a person like a fire) to take power away from the world and has the power to transform shame into honor and downfall into victory.

VIII
416

Let each of us hold fast to this precious gem, to the joyous thought of bold confidence that no one takes bold confidence away from us, even though we willingly admit that our striving in the world is but an insignificant matter compared with the cause of those glorious ones who were tried in the greatest decisions—whereas it still is truly no insignificant matter if we, in our insignificant struggle, were to lose bold confidence.

SUPPLEMENT

KEY TO REFERENCES

Marginal references alongside the text are to volume and page [VIII 100] in *Søren Kierkegaard's samlede Værker*, I–XIV, edited by A. B. Drachmann, J. L. Heiberg, and H. O. Lange (1 ed., Copenhagen: Gyldendal, 1901–06). The same marginal references are used in Sören Kierkegaard, *Gesammelte Werke*, Abt. 1–36 (Düsseldorf, Cologne: Diederichs Verlag, 1952–69).

References to Kierkegaard's works in English are to this edition, *Kierkegaard's Writings* [*KW*], I–XXVI (Princeton: Princeton University Press, 1978–). Specific references to the *Writings* are given by English title and the standard Danish pagination referred to above [*Either/Or*, I, p. 109, *KW* III (*SV* I 100)].

References to the *Papirer* [*Pap.* I A 100; note the differentiating letters A, B, or C, used only in references to the *Papirer*] are to *Søren Kierkegaards Papirer*, I–XI^3, edited by P. A. Heiberg, V. Kuhr, and E. Torsting (1 ed., Copenhagen: Gyldendal, 1909–48), and 2 ed., photo-offset with two supplemental volumes XII–XIII, edited by Niels Thulstrup (Copenhagen: Gyldendal, 1968–70), and with index, XIV–XVI (1975–78), edited by N. J. Cappelørn. References to the *Papirer* in English [*JP* II 1500], occasionally amended, are to the volume and serial entry number in *Søren Kierkegaard's Journals and Papers*, I–VI, edited and translated by Howard V. Hong and Edna H. Hong, assisted by Gregor Malantschuk, and with index, VII, by Nathaniel Hong and Charles Barker (Bloomington: Indiana University Press, 1967–78).

References to correspondence are to the serial numbers in *Breve og Aktstykker vedrørende Søren Kierkegaard*, I–II, edited by Niels Thulstrup (Copenhagen: Munksgaard, 1953–54), and to the corresponding serial numbers in *Kierkegaard: Letters and Documents*, translated by Henrik Rosenmeier, *Kierkegaard's Writings*, XXV [*Letters*, Letter 100, *KW* XXV].

References to books in Kierkegaard's own library [*ASKB*

100] are based on the serial numbering system of *Auktionsprotokol over Søren Kierkegaards Bogsamling* (Auction-catalog of Søren Kierkegaard's Book-collection), edited by H. P. Rohde (Copenhagen: Royal Library, 1967).

In the Supplement, references to page and lines in the text are given as: 100:1–10.

In the notes, internal references to the present volume are given as: p. 100.

Three spaced periods indicate an omission by the editors; five spaced periods indicate a hiatus or fragmentariness in the text.

Opbyggelige Taler

i

forskjellig Aand.

Af

S. Kierkegaard.

Kjøbenhavn.

Hos Universitetsboghandler C. A. Reitzel.

Trykt i Bianco Lunos Bogtrykkeri.

1847.

Upbuilding Discourses

In

Various Spirits.

By

S. Kierkegaard.

———————

Copenhagen.

Available at University Bookseller C. A. Reitzel's.

Printed by Bianco Luno Press.

1847.

En Leiligheds-Tale

af

S. Kierkegaard.

Kjøbenhavn.

Hos Universitetsboghandler C. A. Reitzel.

Trykt i Bianco Lunos Bogtrykkeri.

1847.

An Occasional Discourse

By

S. Kierkegaard.

———

Copenhagen.

Available at University Bookseller C. A. Reitzel's.

Printed by Bianco Luno Press.

1847.

Hvad vi lære af Lilierne paa Marken og af Himmelens Fugle.

Tre Taler

af

S. Kierkegaard.

Kjøbenhavn.

Hos Universitetsboghandler C. A. Reitzel.

Trykt i Bianco Lunos Bogtrykkeri.

1847.

What We Learn from the Lilies in the Field
and from the Birds of the Air.

Three Discourses

By

S. Kierkegaard.

———

Copenhagen.

Available at University Bookseller C. A. Reitzel's.

Printed by Bianco Luno Press.

1847.

Lidelsernes Evangelium.

Christelige Taler

af

S. Kierkegaard.

Kjøbenhavn.

Hos Universitetsboghandler C. A. Reitzel.

Trykt i Bianco Lunos Bogtrykkeri.

1847.

The Gospel of Sufferings.

Christian Discourses

By

S. Kierkegaard.

————

Copenhagen.

Available at University Bookseller C. A. Reitzel's.
Printed by Bianco Luno Press.
1847.

SELECTED ENTRIES FROM
KIERKEGAARD'S JOURNALS AND PAPERS
PERTAINING TO
UPBUILDING DISCOURSES IN VARIOUS SPIRITS

From draft of Three Discourses on Imagined Occasions*;
see 94:20–95:16, 86:13–87:2:*

VI
B 161
238

. . . . . Truly, O God, you will say to many a one who has done great deeds in your name: I do not know you—but I do not appeal to such things but to what I experienced in the quiet solitude when nothing distracted, when the best in me sought you—will you also say: It is not you, that you do not know me? Do you not remember the time

VI
B 161
239

(to be completed)

was it not you who took it from me—and I sought you in tears.

I seek and desire nothing in the world; I have renounced it to have fellowship with you. Were you to say to me now: I do not know you, then all is lost.

If I had the choice between being the greatest of human beings without you and being a hair that you count (and truly, before you, I am no more than that and do not wish for new disarrangement in order to be more than any other human being), I would choose the latter. Even though I am only so very little to you, to me this little is infinitely much as well as being nothing at all to you, but everything otherwise is nothing to me, absolutely nothing.—*JP* III 3401 (*Pap.* VI B 161) *n.d.,* 1844–45

See 84:22–24:

When a skipper sails out in his coastal fruit boat, he usually knows the whole course in advance; but a man-of-war puts out to sea and the orders are received only after it is out on the deep.

So it is with the genius. He lies out on the deep and gets his orders. The rest of us know something or other about this and that which we undertake.—*JP* II 1292 (*Pap.* VI A 93) *n.d.*, 1845

See 105:7–106:7:

Suppose that you go to church every Sunday, read devotional books often, and everything you hear and read applies to you, but yet the kind of suffering that you experience every day is never mentioned. Suppose that every time Amen is pronounced it is your solitary upbuilding to say: Would to God that everything mentioned here might be my task. Suppose that horses could have devotional gatherings and that suffering hunger, being cruelly whipped, being kicked in the stall, being tormented, being hunted out in the open in winter are all discussed—but there is one horse among the listeners that goes home saddened every time because everything that is said, everything the other horses intimate to each other when they put their heads together in the harness or confidentially[*] share with each other out in the pasture, this he understands well enough, but what he suffers is never talked about.[**]

In margin: A horse that comes at an eager gallop every time they are assembled in the evening in the pasture, hoping by listening closely to find out something—until, troubled, it turns around again and seeks its own solitary refuge.

[*] *In margin:* or, by neighing call each other together for collective deliberation.

[**] *In margin:* or, as they stand and toss their heads on a dewy summer morning and the meadow looks so inviting.— *JP* II 1990 (*Pap.* VI A 106) *n.d.*, 1845

VI
A 106
42

VI
A 106
43

See 186:6–14:

Walk along the beach and let the movement of the ocean accompany the indefiniteness of your thoughts—but do not stand still, do not discover the uniformity; if you hear it for just a half second, it is already difficult to tear yourself away from

this spell. Sit in a boat and let the lapping of the water commingle confusingly with the keeping of a single thought in
your mind so that sometimes you hear the lapping and sometimes not—but do not let your eyes become enamored of the
motion of the water; if you surrender for only a half second to
its uniformity, nature's persuasion is almost like a vow for
eternity.—*JP* III 2836 (*Pap.* VI A 126) *n.d.,* 1845

It is now my intention to qualify as a pastor.[1] For several
months I have been praying to God to keep on helping me, for
it has been clear to me for some time now that I ought not to be
a writer any longer,[2] something I can be only totally or not at
all. This is the reason I have not started anything new along
with proof-correcting except for the little review of *Two Ages,*[3]
which again is concluding.—*JP* V 5873 (*Pap.* VII[1] A 4) February 7, 1846

Up until now I have made myself useful by helping the
pseudonyms become authors. What if I decided from now on
to do the little writing I can excuse in the form of criticism.
Then I would put down what I had to say in reviews, developing my ideas from some book or other and in such a way that
they could be included in the work itself. In this way I would
still avoid becoming an author.—*JP* V 5877 (*Pap.* VII[1] A
9) February 1846

VII[1]
A 107
54   And yet my ironic powers of observation and my soul derived such extraordinary satisfaction from gadding about on
VII[1]
A 107
55   the streets[4] and being a nobody in this way while thoughts and
ideas were working within me, from being a loafer this way
while I was clearly the most industrious of the younger set and
appearing irresponsible this way and "lacking in earnestness"
while the earnestness of the others could easily become a jest
alongside my inner concerns. Now this is all upset; the rabble,
the apprentices, the butcher boys, the schoolboys, and all such
are egged on. But I will not play to such a public. . . .
VII[1]
A 107
56   And now that I have remodeled my external life, am more
withdrawn, keep to myself more, have a more momentous

look about me, then in certain quarters it will be said that I have changed for the better. Alas, but my idea is not being served as it was then. But then, after all, my writing days are over.—*JP* V 5894 (*Pap.* VII¹ A 107) *n.d.*, 1846

January 20, 1847

VII¹
A 221
143

The wish to be a rural pastor[5] has always appealed to me and been at the back of my mind. It appealed to me both idyllically as a wish in contrast to a strenuous life and also religiously as a kind of penitence to find the time and the quiet to grieve properly over that in which I personally may have offended. I was convinced that I was about to be successful as an author and, this being the case, I thought it right to end that way. It seems perfectly clear, however, *that the situation here at home is becoming more and more confused.*

VII¹
A 221
144

The question now is, insofar as there is any question about the need for an extraordinary in the literary, social, and political situation—and I dare maintain this before God's judgment seat—whether there is anyone in the kingdom suitable to be that except me. When I gave her up,[6] I gave up every desire for a cozy, pleasant life; my personal guilt makes me capable of submitting to *everything*. In this way there is an ethical presupposition here. In the next place, by accepting a specific post in the state as a teacher of religion, I am committing myself to being something that I am not. Because of a guilt I carry, I would have to be prepared at every moment to be attacked on that score. Then, if I am a clergyman, the confusion will take on tragic dimensions inasmuch as I would have kept back something upon entering this profession. My position as author is different. I contract no personal relationship to any person who can make claims upon my example or upon the antecedents in my life; I ride so loosely in the setting that I can be dashed down any time it so pleases God without affecting any other person in the least. This is the second, the more important, ethical presupposition. As far as my intelligence, talents, skills, and mental constitution are concerned, there can be no doubt that I am rightly constructed in every way, and I will bear a huge responsibility if I refuse a task like that. It certainly is true that it seems more humble to retire and become a pastor, but if I do that, there can also be something vain and proud in proudly rejecting the spectacular. On the other hand, from now on I must take being an author to be the same as being at the mercy of insult and ridicule. But to continue along this road is not something self-inflicted, for it was my calling; my whole *habitus* [inner disposition] was designed for this.

There is no doubt that as an author in times like ours I could by strict moral self-discipline be of great benefit. But it by no means follows that I will win. Rather it means that I am prepared to get the worst of it. Strictly speaking, I am not suited for the tasks of a rural pastor. Therefore, I have constantly intended simply to express the universal and that the ethical meaning should consist in my preferring that to the more spectacular. But now and from now on my career as an author is truly not spectacular. It is perfectly clear that I will be a victim. Out of cowardice and envy the aristocrats will continue to keep quiet, letting me push forward and then letting me fall as a victim to rabble-barbarism, and then finally profit from the whole thing. In other words, humanly speaking, my work will be without reward. But I ask nothing else. The fact that I may be temporarily impatient does not prove a thing, for at any suitable moment I am still willing to sacrifice anything and hope that God will give me the strength to bear everything.

If I am unwilling *à la* Mynster[7] to idolize the establishment (and this is Mynster's heresy) and in my zeal for morality eventually confuse it with the bourgeois mentality, if I am unwilling to abolish completely the category of the extraordinary and again *à la* Mynster only understand that there have been such ones, understand it only afterward, then I cannot personally reject what has so clearly been laid upon me as a task.

Although Mynster has a certain goodwill toward me and in his private opinion perhaps even more than he admits, it is clear that he regards me as a suspicious and even dangerous person. For this reason he would like to have me out in the country. He thinks things are all right so far, but anything is to be feared from a man of character, especially in relation to the whole

VIII¹ A 221 145

network in which he wants to keep life imprisoned. Therefore his advice is entirely consistent on his part; from his point of view it is also well-meant for me, inasmuch as he is not particularly scrupulous about a little damage to a man's inner being just as long as he makes good, in his opinion, in the world. Mynster has never been out on 70,000 fathoms[8] of water and learned out there; he has always clung to the established order and now has completely coalesced with it. This is what is magnificent about him. I shall never forget, I shall always honor him, always think of my father when I think about him, and no more is needed. But Mynster does not understand me; when he was thirty-six years old, he would not have understood me, in fact, he would have resisted understanding me in order not to injure his career, and now he cannot understand me.

But for God all things are possible.[9] Humanly speaking, from now on I must be said not only to be running aimlessly[10] but going headlong toward certain ruin—trusting in God, precisely this is the victory. This is how I understood life when I was ten years old, therefore the prodigious polemic in my soul; this is how I understood it when I was twenty-five years old; so, too, now when I am thirty-four. This is why Poul Møller[11] called me the most thoroughly polemical of men.

—*JP* V 5961 (*Pap.* VII[1] A 221) January 20, 1847

VIII[1]
A 221
146

Only when I am writing do I feel fine. Then I forget all the disagreeable things in life, all the sufferings, then I am at home with my thoughts and am happy. If I refrain from it for just a few days, I immediately get sick, overwhelmed, burdened, and my head gets heavy and weighed down. An urge like this, so plentiful, so inexhaustible, which after continuing day after day for five or six years still surges just as copiously, must certainly be a calling from God. To squeeze back this wealth of thoughts still lying in my soul would be torture, a martyrdom, and would render me totally incompetent. And why should it be thrust back? Because I got the idea of wanting to make a martyr of myself by penitentially forcing myself into some-

VIII[1]
A 222
146

thing for which I, as far as I understand myself, am basically not suited.[12] No, God forbid, and God will certainly not leave himself without witness also in the external world. It is hard and depressing to pay out one's own money to be allowed to work harder and more intensely than any man in the kingdom! And in all this work it is hard and depressing to get out of it the persecutions of the cowardly, envious aristocrats and the insults of the rabble. It is hard and depressing to have these prospects: if I work even harder and more intensely, things will get even worse! But I would gladly and patiently put up with all this if I could only succeed in attaining inner assurance that it is not my duty to force myself into a self-chosen martyrdom by taking a position that in a certain sense I could wish for but could neither fill satisfactorily nor be happy in. But becoming an author is not self-chosen; on the contrary it is by virtue of the deepest need and urge of my whole personal being.

VIII¹
A 222
147

God, give me your blessing and assistance, and above all spiritual assurance, spiritual assurance against the spiritual trials that arise within me, for one can always manage to struggle with the world.

The same thing will happen to me this time as earlier with my engagement. Only, God be praised, with this difference: I do not wrong anyone, I do not break any promise, but the similarity is that once again I must steer into the open sea, live in grace and out of grace, utterly in God's power. It is, after all, much more secure to have a steady job in life, an official appointment, it is not nearly so strenuous—but in God's name the other, by the grace of God, is even more secure. But at every moment it takes faith. This is the difference. The majority of people live far too securely in life and therefore get to know God so little. They have permanent positions, never strain themselves to the limit, have the comfort of wife and children—I shall never disparage this happiness, but I believe it my task to dispense with all this. Why should what we read again and again in the New Testament not be allowed. But the trouble is that men have no knowledge at all of what Christianity is, and this is why there is no sympathy for me, this is why I am not understood at all.—*JP* V 5962 (*Pap.* VII¹ A 222) *n.d.*, 1847

January 24
God be praised that all the assaults of rabble-barbarism have come upon me. Now I have gained time to learn inwardly and to convince myself that it was indeed a gloomy thought to want to live out in a rural parish[13] and do penance in seclusion and oblivion. Now I stand resolved and rooted to the spot in a way I have never been. If I had not been put through the mill of insults, this gloomy idea would have continued to pester me, for a certain kind of prosperity fosters gloomy ideas; if, for example, I had not had private means, I would never, with my disposition to melancholy, have reached the point I have sometimes reached.—*JP* V 5966 (*Pap.* VII¹ A 229) January 24, 1847

Not like the former editor, who succeeded in entering into relation with the conversation of the moment—and therefore succeeded in becoming welcome.

VIII¹
B 212
390

I will rather strive to enter into relation with silence

There are too many pages to rummage in—just as students have too many books—therefore one does not read well.
　　The contents will be what, spiritually understood, could be called daily bread.
　　　　　　　Make clear what *harmony* is, the *universal*. What is common to all (the religious touch).
　　Then I will choose a somewhat more difficult thought—and then it will be like the poor invited to a banquet of the distinguished—then a very simple thought, which will be like the distinguished going to a banquet of the poor.

VIII¹
B 212
391

If possible, the reader is to read aloud.[14]
In margin: Politics in particular must be excluded altogether.—*JP* V 5952 (*Pap.* VII¹ B 212) *n.d.*, 1846

Addition to Pap. VII¹ B 212:

No. 1

Public Opinion

No. 2

What one learns from the lilies in the field and the birds of the air[15]

No. 3

On being a good listener[16]

No. 4

The misuse of laughter

No. 5

The difficult situation of distinction in a small country

No. 6

The intrinsic validity of occupation with the spiritual

No. 7

Why Socrates compared himself to a gadfly[17]

No. 8

Solitude and silence as essential ingredients of personal life[18]

No. 9

On the upbringing of children[19]

No. 10

The corruptive and misleading aspects of the now so common use of the statistical in the realms of the spirit.

—*JP* V 5953 (*Pap.* VII¹ B 213) *n.d.,* 1846

Under the title:

The Gospel of Sufferings[20]

I would like to work out a collection of sermons. The texts would be partly from Christ's Passion Story, partly powerful words such as the apostles spoke when, after having been flogged, they went away joyful and thanked God that they were allowed to suffer something,[21] or when Paul calls his chains a glorious honor,[22] or when he says to Herod Agrippa: I wish that every one of you were such as I am, except for these chains.[23] Or the several passages in the Epistle to the Corinthians, where there is one oxymoron after the other: Ourselves poor, we make all rich;[24] or Rejoice and *again* I say rejoice.[25] Also the passage in the Epistle of James that we should count it all joy when we are tried in various sufferings.[26]

Alongside this should then follow three short but delightful discourses:

What We Learn from the Lilies in the Field
and from the Birds of the Air[27]

There is a scrap of paper [*Pap.* VII¹ A 248] pertaining to this in the old case for my Bible.—*JP* V 5945 (*Pap.* VII¹ A 160) *n.d.*, 1846

See 177:29–37:

Just as the Gospel about the lilies[28] contains a warning to the poor against worry about making a living [*Næringssorg*], it also has a word for the corresponding kind of worry that the rich in particular usually have. "No one can add one foot to his stature."[29] Hypochondriac worry that one's heart is not beating properly, that one is constipated, etc.—*JP* I 99 (*Pap.* VII¹ A 248) *n.d.*, 1845–47

Literary Review
Magister Adler
A Psychological Study from Nature
That Is, Based on His Writings[30]
by
S. Kierkegaard
—*JP* V 5936 (*Pap.* VII² B 242) *n.d.*, 1846–47

All the last four books[31] are to be published in one volume under the title:

Minor Works by S. Kierkegaard
—*JP* V 5954 (*Pap.* VII¹ B 214) *n.d.*, 1846

Addition to Pap. VII¹ B 214:

Minor Works[32]
by
S. Kierkegaard
—*JP* V 5955 (*Pap.* VII¹ B 217) *n.d.*, 1846–47

Addition to Pap. VII¹ B 217:

Contents
I. Discourse on the Occasion of a Confession.
II. Literary Review.   Adler.
III. What One Learns from the Lilies in the Field and from the Birds of the Air. 3 Discourses.
IV. The Gospel of Sufferings.
—*JP* V 5956 (*Pap.* VII¹ B 218) *n.d.*, 1846–47

Addition to Pap. VII¹ B 214:

VII¹
B 216
392

Preface.

That I am working against myself, I know indeed; therefore no one needs to tell me that, because I perhaps still know what he does not know—why I do it. Instead of the large, closely printed books, fruits of an indisputably rare diligence, expensive enough for me to pay, I should rather publish small parts at one mark[33] splendidly provided with many blank pages and with drawings; then I would enjoy esteem in my day, and my efforts would be esteemed with money. But I am hopeful, because working against myself and at the same time working very strenuously means, according to the dialectic of the idea, to serve [*tjene*] an idea, which in my simple thinking is something different from earning [*tjene*] money and esteem. This reduplication, in working to work against myself, signifies a pure idea-relation, guarantees that one's striving is neither a wind- nor a water-mill that is driven by the wind or the water of the moment.

VII¹
B 216
393

Respectfully,
S. K.
—*Pap.* VII¹ B 216 *n.d.*, 1846–47

From sketch:

Preface

VII¹
B 219
393

Each of these parts is so capable of being read separately that I, to indicate this appropriately, have arranged it so that each can be purchased separately. But the one who, without forgetting their upbuilding aspect and that this is of first and last importance, conjointly engages in taking into account the differences within the whole sphere of religiousness, that person will devote himself in particular to the juxtaposition of and the comparison between these three pieces. Nor will he look in vain, even if what is done in the discourses to illuminate this is also hidden, because something like that lends itself only to the person or persons who themselves in self-activity emulatingly act to produce it.

VII¹
B 219
394

S. K.

—*Pap.* VII¹ B 219 *n.d.*, 1846–47

From draft of preface to proposed "Minor Writings":

Although by their very difference in both essence and structure,* the different parts of this work have a relation to one another that will be able to occupy someone who happens to have the time and talent and wish to think about such things, yet each particular part so lends itself to being read separately for upbuilding that in order to suggest this I have arranged it in such a way that each part can be purchased separately. Something that is supposed to serve for upbuilding must never contain a split, as if there were one kind of upbuilding for the simple and another for the wise. I have perceived, however, the relational unity in such a way that what the simple can understand should covertly contain what can engage the wise and more educated. Consequently, it ought to be present but concealed so that only reflective self-activity itself can generate it again, because to be more educated, more developed, is still something accidental—the upbuilding is essentially the same for all.

*for reflective comparison

—*Pap.* VII¹ B 220 *n.d.*, 1846–47

From final copy; see title page:

Upbuilding Discourses
in
Various Styles and Spirits
By
S. Kierkegaard
[*Changed from:* Godly Discourses
by
S. Kierkegaard]

Copenhagen 1846
Available at Reitzel's. Printed by Bianco Luno
—*JP* V 5934 (*Pap.* VII¹ B 192:1–2) *n.d.*, 1846

From draft; see title page:

"Three Occasional [*changed from:* Confessional] Discourses"
by
S. Kierkegaard
—*JP* V 5919 (*Pap.* VII¹ B 136) *n.d.*, 1846

See 4:

VII¹
A 176
112 To the Dedication
"That Single Individual"
in the occasional discourse the following piece
should really have been added.

Dear Reader,
[34]Please accept this dedication. It is offered, as it were, blindly, but therefore in all honesty, untroubled by any other consideration. I do not know who you are; I do not know where you are; I do not know your name—I do not even know if you exist or if you perhaps did exist and are no more, or whether your time is still coming. Yet you are my hope, my joy, my pride, in the uncertainty of you, my honor—because if I knew you personally with a worldly certainty, this would be my shame, my guilt—and my honor would be lost.

It comforts me, dear reader, that you have this opportunity, the opportunity for which I know I have honestly worked. If it were feasible that reading what I write came to be common practice, or at least pretending to have read it in hopes of getting ahead in the world, this would not be the opportune time for *my* reader, because then the misunderstanding would have triumphed—yes, it would have beguiled me to dishonesty if with all my powers I had not prevented anything like that from happening—on the contrary, by doing everything to prevent it I have acted honestly. No, if reading what I write becomes a dubious good (—and if with all the powers granted me I contribute to that, I am acting honestly), or still better, if it becomes foolish and ludicrous to read my writings, or even better, if it becomes a contemptible matter so that no one dares to acknowledge it, that is the opportune time for *my* reader; then he seeks stillness, then he does not read for my sake or for the world's sake—but for his own sake, then he reads in such a way that he does not seek my acquaintance but avoids it—and then he is *my* reader.

I have often imagined myself in a pastor's place. If the crowds storm to hear him, if the great arch of the church cannot contain the great throngs and people even stand outside listening to him—well, honor and praise to one so gifted that his feelings are gripped, that he can talk as one inspired, inspired by the sight of the crowds, because where the crowd is there must be truth, inspired by the thought that there has to be a little for some, because there are a lot of people, and a lot of people with a little truth is surely truth—to me this would be impossible! But suppose it was a Sunday afternoon, the weather was gloomy and miserable, the winter storm emptied the streets, everyone who had a warm apartment let God wait in the church until better weather—if there were sitting in the empty church a couple of poor women who had no heat in the apartment and could just as well freeze in the church, indeed, I could talk both them and myself warm!

I have often imagined myself beside a grave. If all the people of honor and distinction were assembled there, if solemnity pervaded the whole great throng—well, honor and praise to

VIII
A 176
113

one so gifted that he could add to the solemnity by being prompted to be the interpreter of the throng, to be the expression for the truth of sorrow—I could not do it! But if it was a poor hearse and it was accompanied by no one but a poor old woman, the widow of the dead man, who had never before experienced having her husband go away without taking her along—if she were to ask me, on my honor I would give a funeral oration as well as anyone.

I have often imagined myself in the decision of death. If there was alarm in the camp, much running in to inquire about me—I believe I could not die, my old irascible disposition would once more awaken and I would have to go out once again and contend with people. But if I lie secluded and alone, I hope to God I may die peacefully and blessedly.

There is a view of life that holds that truth is where the crowd is, that truth itself needs to have the crowd on its side. There is another view of life that holds that wherever the crowd is, untruth is, so that even if all individuals who, separately, secretly possessed truth, were to come together in a crowd (in such a way, however, that the crowd acquired any deciding, voting, noisy, loud significance), untruth would promptly be present there. But the person who recognizes this latter view as his own (which is rarely enunciated because it more frequently happens that a person believes the crowd lives in untruth, but if it only accepts his opinion everything is all right) confesses that he himself is the weak and powerless one; moreover, how could one individual be able to stand against the crowd, which has the power! And he would not possibly wish to have the crowd on his side—that would be ridiculing himself. But if this latter view is an admission of weakness and powerlessness and thus perhaps seems somewhat uninviting, it at least has the good point of being equable—it insults no one, not one single person; it makes no distinction, not of one single person.

To be sure, the crowd is formed by individuals, but each one must retain the power to remain what he is—an individual. No one, no one, no one is excluded from being an individual except the person who excludes himself—by becoming many. On the contrary, to become part of the crowd, to gather the crowd around oneself, is what makes distinctions in life. Even

VIII
A 176
114

the most well-intentioned person talking about this can easily insult an individual. But then once again the crowd has power, influence, status, and domination—this is also a distinction in life that, dominating, disregards the individual as weak and powerless.—*JP* V 5948 (*Pap.* VII[1] A 176) *n.d.*, 1846

From draft; see 5:1:

> *To the typesetter:*
> the smallest possible brevier
>
> *Preface*
>
> . . .
>
> May 5, '46   S. K.
> —*JP* V 5925 (*Pap.* VII[1] B 150) May 5, 1846

See 5:17–33:

> *From a Possible Preface to My Occasional Discourses*[35]

. . . . . I wonder if a woman who embroiders a cloth for sacred use does not make every stitch as carefully as possible and perhaps begin over again many times. Yet I wonder if it would not distress her if someone viewed it in the wrong way and looked at the pearl-stitch embroidery instead of at the altar cloth, or saw a defect instead of the altar cloth? She found her priceless joy in doing everything as carefully as possible simply because this work has no meaning and ought to have none; the needlewoman is unable to stitch the meaning into the cloth— the meaning lies within the beholder.—*JP* I 811 (*Pap.* VI A 25) *n.d.*, 1845

From draft; see 5:30–6:6

> *Preface*

. . . This meaning lies in the beholder. And in comparison with it everything else, the artistry and the defect, the costli-ness, the poverty, is nothing, nothing at all. Therefore her wastefulness was precious to her, because it does not as usual draw attention to itself but leads attention away from itself [*essentially the same as 5:34–6:1*] her part—but it would be impermissible, it would be an offense against God and the needlewoman if anyone paid attention to it.—*Pap.* VII¹ B 137 *n.d.*, 1846.

Addition to Pap. VII¹ B 137:

And in comparison with it, everything else, the artistry and the defect, the costliness and the poverty, is nothing, nothing at all. No, nobody is wasted in this way, for otherwise the wastefulness would become obvious; here it must not even be seen.—*Pap.* VII¹ B 138 *n.d.*, 1846

Addition to Pap. VII¹ B 137:

In a worldly sense, it makes a great difference whether someone is dressed in gold and jewelry—religiously, it makes absolutely no difference, none at all. When the king wears it, everyone sees and admires it; when a servant of the Church does it—no one dares to see it, because there he sees amiss.— *Pap.* VII¹ B 139 *n.d.*, 1846

From draft; see 7:3–8:3:

Father in heaven! [*essentially the same as 7:3–11*]. But what lies in between them, between this first and this last.[*] Every time the mind feels the urge to seek you in repentance, grant that there may be no interruption, that repentance's sorrowing for you might make up for failure and be a continuation in willing one thing.

[*]*In margin:* delay, halting, interruption, error
                                                    —*Pap.* VII¹ B 140 *n.d.*, 1846

Addition to Pap. VII¹ B 140:

VII¹
B 141
342   But, alas, what intervenes between them, between this first and this last, delay, halting, interruption, error, perdition;[*]

may you give repentance the strength to conquer and in repentance to will again only one thing, to repent with all one's soul, and in repentance the bold confidence to will again one thing. Admittedly it is an interruption, a halting, when the penitent in the confession of sin seeks you, but it is indeed an interruption that will be a connection by making up, in godly grief, for failure and by winning, in trust in you, a continuation. A person seeks you at different hours of the day, but every time he, repenting, seeks you it is always at the eleventh hour.

[*]*In margin:* what is daily committed and what accumulates from day to day.

—*Pap.* VII¹ B 141 *n.d.,* 1846.

VII¹
B 141
343

Addition to Pap. VII¹ B 141:

And there is indeed an opportunity for that, there is indeed an urge in the human being that is a call from God. God's call is issued to a person in many places and at many times, but the call to seek him in the confession of sin is always at the eleventh hour. Whether he is young or old, whether he has sinned much or little, it is the eleventh hour—repentance understands this.—*JP* IV 4947 (*Pap.* VII¹ B 145) *n.d.,* 1846

In margin of Pap. VII¹ B 145:

First of all comes the lightly armed wish and wants to capture the world—but retreats in terror. Then comes the manly strength of resolution and wants to venture battle—but must fall back. Now it is the eleventh hour—then comes repentance.—*JP* IV 4948 (*Pap.* VII¹ B 146) *n.d.,* 1846

From draft; see 8:4–28:

> Ecclesiastes 3:9 (What benefit from all his striving does he have who exerts himself ?)

Everything has its time, says Solomon—
There is even that which has its time of preparation, but does this hold true of the confession of sin; is not this view

all too slow in relation to the speed of repentance, in relation to what is to occur in that very moment.—*JP* III 3786 (*Pap.* VII¹ B 147) *n.d.*, 1846

Deleted from final copy; see 20:25–31:

The forest does not want to become involved with him. Therefore it returns his word without change, without sympathy; its echo is like a no, and even though it re-echoes many times, it is still only a repeated no. If the forest wanted to speak with him, it presumably would answer; if the forest were in sympathetic understanding with him, it would certainly retain his word, keep it unchanged.—*Pap.* VII¹ B 192:8 *n.d.*, 1846

Deleted from margin in final copy; see 24:5:

when the consciousness of sin sharpens the desire for the one thing needful, when the earnestness of the passage strengthens the will in holy resolve, when the presence of the Omniscient One makes self-deception impossible, bear in mind this admonition: . . . . . —*Pap.* VII¹ B 192:9 *n.d.*, 1846

From draft; see 24:21–122:2:

VII¹
B 173
356

The arrangement of the whole discourse, which is to be noted as follows with letters and numbers.

    I. If a person is to will one thing in truth, he must will the good [p. 24].

VII¹
B 173
357

  II. If he, when he wills the good in truth, is to will one thing, he must will the good in truth [p. 36].
     A. The definition of double-mindedness.
    1. The person who wills the good for the sake of reward is double-minded [p. 37].
    2. _____ _____ out of fear of punishment [p. 44].
    3. _____ _____ in order that it be victorious [p. 60].

4. The multifarious double-mindedness that wills the good *to a certain degree* [p. 64]
    B. The definition of unity [p. 78].
1. He must will to do everything [p. 79].
2. He must will to suffer everything [p. 99].
      Lyric over purity of heart, which is compared to the ocean [p. 121].
III. The form of the confessional discourse is to be used [p. 122].

                —*Pap.* VII¹ B 173 *n.d.*, 1846

From draft; see 24:21–122:2:

I.   If it is to be possible for a person to be able to will one thing, he must will the good [p. 24].

II. If a person is really to will one thing in truth, he must will the good in truth [p. 36].
    A. If a person is to will the good in truth, he must make up his mind to will to renounce all double-mindedness [p. 36]

        1.   [p. 37].
        2.   [p. 44].
        3.   [p. 60].
        4.   [p. 64].

    B. If a person is to will the good in truth, he must will to do everything for the good or will to suffer everything for the good [p. 78].
        1. If a person is to will the good in truth, he must will to do everything for the good [p. 79].
        2. If a person is to will the good in truth, he must will to suffer everything [p. 99].

III. It was on the occasion of a confession [p. 122].

                —*Pap.* VII¹ B 174 *n.d.*, 1846

Deleted from final copy; see 24:20:

. . . . .although the whole discourse, because it is not at any actual confession but is only on the occasion of a confession,

VIII¹
B 174
357

VIII¹
B 174
358

is not a confessional discourse but a preparatory meditation.
—*Pap.* VII¹ B 192:10 *n.d.*, 1846

Deleted from final copy; see 30:17; 121:8–37:

When the ocean lies still, deeply transparent, we extol its purity and delight in this sublime picture. So also with a person's soul—when the low and finite and multifarious in it are in motion, it is like muddied water, is murky, opaque, has no depth, but when it is quietly deep in willing only one thing, it is pure as the transparency of the ocean. Therefore we compare the soul to water, and the image is appropriate: stillness is purity, when all that is impure sinks; purity is transparency, transparency is depth.—*JP* IV 4434 (*Pap.* VII¹ B 192:12) *n.d.*, 1846

See 33:16–34:11

VII¹
A 22
12

When a person misguided to the point of perdition is about to go under, his last utterance and the signal is: Yet something better goes down with me. Like bubbles rising from a drowning man, this is the signal—then he sinks. Just as inclosing reserve can become a person's downfall because he will not articulate what is hidden, so also is the uttering of that word: "downfall." The uttering is precisely the expression of his having become so objective to himself that he dares to speak about his own downfall as one speaks about something that has been decided and may now be of psychological interest to a third party. The hope that there still might be something better in

VII¹
A 22
13

him which should have been used in silence to work for his rescue, this hope is expended and used as material for the funeral oration he delivers over himself.—*JP* IV 4591 (*Pap.* VII¹ A 22) *n.d.*, 1846

Deleted from final copy; see 34:24:

When the ocean rages in storm and the sky is hidden, when ocean and sky blend as one in the turmoil, we do not say that the ocean is pure, however terrifying this drama is. Not until they are distinguished in peace, when the sky arches high over the ocean, which deeply reflects it, not until then do we say that it is pure. Purity is not in the blending-into-one of the raging storm but in distinction. Therefore we compare the soul to the ocean. When in the unity of confusion it arrogantly breaches the distinction between good and evil, it is riled and impure, but when the good like the fortress of heaven arches high over the soul, which deeply reproduces this oneness, we say it is pure. Distinction between good and evil is simplicity, confused unity is doubleness—ask a child about it if wisdom no longer is able to understand what a child understands simply! It is an image we use—is it perhaps inappropriate because the distinction between good and evil is not physical like the distinction between ocean and sky,* or is it inappropriate because the sky is, after all, not the good and the ocean, the evil; if, however, the distinction is there and it is in a person's power to commingle it in the unity of confusion or humbly fortify the distinction in the purity of his heart—then the metaphor is indeed appropriate!

In margin: *but spiritually, therefore invisibly, hidden in the soul's invisibility.

—*JP* IV 4435 (*Pap.* VII^1 B 192:13) *n.d.*, 1846

From draft; see 46:19–29:

Indeed, would a slave soul also be able to will one thing? When there is fear, fear of something else than the good, there is always double-mindedness. To fear is like humbling oneself; anyone who does not humble himself before God becomes the slave of people despite all his pride, because humility before God is the true pride.—*Pap.* VII^1 B 153:2 *n.d.*, 1846

From draft; see 48:12–50:20:

It has been said that by the holy sign of the cross one can stop the evil spirit, but with regard to double-mindedness is not this "if" the same. Is not such a person double-minded, and does

fear help him to will the good in truth? By no means, it makes
everything worse, as when sickness sets in. Therefore, is not
hypocrisy the most dangerous of all sicknesses? And I wonder
if it helps him in God's eyes. Does Scripture teach that only the
sensualists and robbers and murderers and the shameless are
unable to inherit God's kingdom; does it not also say: nor the
timorous?[36] Is not a slave soul just as certainly shut out from
eternal happiness if this is freedom?—*Pap.* VII¹ B 153:4 *n.d.*,
1846

From final draft; see 49:16–50:9:

Fear is a dry nurse for the infant, a bloodless disciplinarian
for the youth, an envious sickness for the adult, a horror for the
old. The good does not favor the person who wills the good
only out of fear of punishment—*Pap.* VII¹ B 162:2 *n.d.*, 1846

From draft; see 51:27–30:

VII¹
B 153:5
346

Voluminous and learned books have been written to justify
God's management of the world. As soon as a government has
to be justified in print, it can run to a lot of words, but the
relationship is still not quite the same between God and man,
because God, to be sure, has the Creator's right to require faith
and obedience from the created, as well as that every creature

VII¹
B 153:5
347

may in his heart think only pleasing thoughts about him. On
the other hand, God is certainly not an elective king who could
be set aside at the next assembly—if he does not adequately
justify himself. The matter is quite simple. The punishment is
devised by the loving God for the sake of transgressions. But
just as in a large household where there are many children the
innocent sometimes share a little bit of it, too, so also in a great
household where there are so many millions . . . . . no, not
this way, the reason this happens in a household where there
are many children is that the father or the teacher is still only a
human being; but God is certainly well able to survey the
whole scene, things do not get confused for him who counts
the hairs on a person's head and sees to it that no sparrow falls
to the earth prematurely. Therefore it is not so that under the

management of God the innocent share some of the punishment, too—that is, are regarded as guilty, but the innocent may well share some of the suffering. But as soon as the innocent sufferer turns to God and asks if it is punishment, he promptly gets the answer: No, my dear child, it is no punishment; you certainly know that. Therefore instead of justifying God, a striving that is double-minded because it simultaneously wants to get to the same place by two roads, what is needed is to will only one thing in truth and then everything is in order. He says to himself: The most abominable thing of all would be to let yourself insult God even in your most secret thoughts, to think that he did wrong. What does it matter to me if someone wants to write a big book to justify or accuse God—I believe. Where I seem to be able to understand his management, I still prefer to believe, for faith is more blessed, and as long as a person lives in this world, understanding so easily becomes a matter of delusion and comradely obtrusiveness; and where I cannot understand—well, then it is blessed to believe.—*JP* III 3629 (*Pap.* VII¹ B 153:5) *n.d.*, 1846

From final draft; see 60:12–20:

—Woe to the person who moves the boundary line, as double-mindedness does when it wills the good—out of fear of the world's punishment!—*Pap.* VII¹ B 163:3 *n.d.*, 1846

Deleted in margin of final copy; see 60:21–64:11:

N.B. III [3] must be reworked again; the two forms;
  impatience and willing to be the instrument must
  be kept more decidedly separate from each other.
              —*Pap.* VII¹ B 192:17 *n.d.*, 1846

From draft; see 64:28:

  Nysgjerrighed I write with an *e*
  Anstrængelse with an *æ*. Molbeck [*sic*] writes: *e*.[37]
              —*Pap.* VII¹ B 194 *n.d.*, 1846

From draft; see 95:25–96:14:

And he knows this to the nth degree—in order not to do it—indeed, no double-minded one can have as much sagacity as he uses in the service of the good merely in order to preclude all disappointments and all illusion, lest he in an unlawful manner gain advantage from the good—money, distinction, admiration—and so that no one is fooled by a delusion, an appearance of the good.—*Pap.* VII[1] B 155:10 *n.d.*, 1846

Deleted from final copy; see 98:5:

. . . . . he gets public opinion against him. Possibly, for it will no doubt go with him as that simple wise man[38] so ingeniously has described his life; it will no doubt go with him as with a physician if he is accused by a cook or a confectioner and a bunch of children were to judge between them, because the cook or confectioner has a childish understanding of what is delicious and flattering and a shrewd understanding of making what is unhealthful taste good; the physician knows only about the bitter-tasting and healthful. He does not accomplish anything, ... —*Pap.* VII[1] B 192:21 *n.d.*, 1846

From draft; see 99:17–100:14:

Double-mindedness with regard to sufferings is recognizable in the constant peering for an unforeseen help, the superstitious tension that seeks relief everywhere, the pusillanimity that would rather let itself be corrupted by temporality's wretched grounds of comfort than be eternally healed. Is it not sad that a person is satisfied in this way; is it not strange that we so often speak in such a way to those who are suffering that we offer them silver when we have gold in abundance. Temporality's comfort is silver, indeed, less than silver—but eternity is better than the finest gold. And yet it often seems as if the suffering ones shrank from receiving the highest comfort and the ones speaking were ashamed to offer the highest comfort. Eternity's comfort is not only the highest comfort, but temporality's comfort is a dubious matter—"it lets," as a thinker[*] has expressed it, "the wound close although it is not healed, and yet the physician knows that recovery sometimes comes through keeping the wound open." No, the person who truly wills to suffer everything disdains temporality's relief and thus is comforted eternally.[**]

In margin: So one comforts the sufferers and tells them things will get better; one urges patience, and that is indeed beautiful, but why [*essentially the same as 115:16–24*] that it will surely get better—see, this is gold, and why, then, give silver!

This is to be used later[39]

[*]*In margin:* Johannes Climacus, *Concluding Postscript* [*KW* XII.1, p. 85, *SV* VII 66].

[**]*In margin:* "He must refuse to accept release" (Hebrews 11:35).

—*Pap.* VII¹ B 157:2 *n.d.*, 1846

From draft; see 100:2–14:

But the wish and the suffering along with it are flexible (dialectical) in proportion to the *essentiality of the wish*, and in proportion *to the hiddenness of the wish*, and in proportion to the *length of time*, which works in reverse on human sympathy, which diminishes in time, whereas the suffering becomes heavier and heavier.—*Pap.* VII¹ B 157:3 *n.d.*, 1846

From draft; see 104:7:

On earth Abraham possessed only a burial place, and yet he was God's chosen one; yet a burial place is the least a person can possess.—*Pap.* VII¹ B 157:5 *n.d.*, 1846

In margin of draft; see 105:7–106:7:

Journal 228 [*Pap.* VI A 106]

—*Pap.* VII¹ B 157:6 *n.d.*, 1846

Deleted from margin of final draft; see 105:13:

. . . . . or when it has an accident during its brief allotted time to eat and has got its head out of the nose-bag and stands there hungry with food right in front of it and no one thinks of helping it, but it looks so distressed—*Pap.* VII¹ B 164 *n.d.*, 1846

From draft; 116:37–117:20:

But wherever the good is truly victorious, the victory is essentially equally great. Here again is the blessed equality of the eternal.—*Pap.* VII¹ B 160 *n.d.*, 1846

From draft; see 139:20–31:

. . . . . because you are able to do it. (Adler: the one and only proof is that one *is able* to do it.[40])—*Pap.* VII¹ B 158:8 *n.d.*, 1846

In margin of draft; see 141:3–143:38:

Is it approval from above you cannot do without, or approval from below.

. . . . . with a sense of shame before a young person—so you would not dare to have the heart to let a young person find out how you live but certainly would dare to live that way; so you shrink only from the thought of a young person's getting to know such a thing, but you do not shrink from doing it yourself.—*Pap.* VII¹ B 158:9 *n.d.*, 1846

From draft; see 144:10–13:

. . . . . whose language you do not know, with all the people on the whole earth, despite the different manners and customs and language.
    The suffering one
                                —*Pap.* VII¹ B 158:10 *n.d.*, 1846

From draft; see 147:36:

. . . . . since this does not excuse his lack of faithfulness.
                                —*Pap.* VII¹ B 169:1 *n.d.*, 1846

From draft; see 149:1–150:31:

. . . . . alone as an individual, and will not be asked about what happened to the whole human race, or the neighbor and the neighbor opposite, but will be asked as an individual.— *Pap.* VII[1] B 169:2 *n.d.,* 1846

From final draft; see 149:38–150:8:

. . . . . if I refrained from speaking

Eternally, the fact that the circumstances are difficult makes it even doubly obligating to do it.
                            —*Pap.* VII[1] B 171 *n.d.,* 1846

From draft; see 155:

What We Learn from the Lilies in the Field
and from the Birds of the Air
[*changed from:* the Birds under the Heavens]

3 Discourses

by

S. Kierkegaard
                 —*Pap.* VII[1] B 175 *n.d.,* 1846

In margin of final copy; see 157:1:

To the typesetter:
This is to be set in the smallest possible brevier.
                            —*Pap.* VII[1] B 192:25 *n.d.,* 1846

In margin of final copy; see 159:7–160:5:

This to be printed in the same
type as the altar book.   —*Pap.* VII[1] B 192:26 *n.d.,* 1846

Deleted from final copy; see 165:24:

If the worried one out there with the lilies learns to speak about himself in the same way as human language talks about the lilies, he also is essentially healed.—*Pap.* VII¹ B 192:27 *n.d.*, 1846

From draft; see 182:19–21:

VII¹
B 177:4
358

It is especially difficult for *another* person to speak appropriately concerning worry about making a living. Surely the place of honor as speaker always ought to be granted to the son of

VII¹
B 177:4
359

poverty if he speaks appropriately about poverty. But the mind of one who has been tried in life is perhaps sometimes embittered and unfree, so that by speaking he does not convey cheerful confidence but communicates troubled concern. When this is the case, the inexperienced one may also be permitted to speak if he has learned inwardly to speak appropriately. May God grant that the right words may find their proper place; if this happens with one who is poor, then he is of course undeniably more excellent than the speaker.—*JP* III 3472 (*Pap.* VII¹ B 177:4) *n.d.*, 1846

See 185:6–10:

Time is not merely appalling to a human being but is also mitigating, not merely that which makes life so strenuous (for what strenuousness can be compared to this: an eternal spirit living for years, for weeks, and for hours) but also that which alleviates. If you have ever broken God's commandments, you certainly did not dare at the time to think about God, not even penitently. But after an interval of time in which you did not sin again, you gained the courage; it was as if your guilt had diminished somewhat because it was some time ago and during that time you had not sinned very often. For an eternal spirit this specious semblance does not exist.—*JP* IV 4793 (*Pap.* VIII¹ A 75) *n.d.*, 1847

From draft; see 199:37–200:11:

. . . . . just as he, humble before God, proudly wore his chains as another wore the ribbons of an order[*]; just as he even in death considered it too great an honor to be crucified and requested to be put to death by the sword,[**] so he also considered it an honor to work with his own hands.

[*]*In margin:* proudly wore honor's—chains
[**]*In margin:* had the honor of being crucified.

—*Pap.* VII¹ B 178:2 *n.d.*, 1846

See 202:24–27:

The Most Horrible Collision

imaginable would be a bird, for example, a swallow, in love with a girl. The swallow would be able to *know* the girl (as distinguished from everyone else), but the girl would not be able to tell the swallow apart from any of the 100,000 other swallows. Imagine the swallow's torment when upon its arrival in the spring it said, "Here I am," and the girl answered, "I do not know you."

As a matter of fact, the swallow has no individuality. We see from this that individuality, this difference of separateness, is the presupposition for loving. Because of this, most people are not truly able to love because the distinctiveness of their individualities is too slight.

The greater the distinctiveness of individuality, the more pronounced the individuality, the more distinctive marks there are, and the more there is to know.

In this far deeper sense one sees the significance of the Hebraic expression—to know one's wife,[41] something that was said about the difference between the genders, but the same thing is far more profoundly true about the psychical (*Sjælelige*), the imprint of individuality.—*JP* II 2003 (*Pap.* VIII¹ A 462) *n.d.*, 1847

VIII¹
A 462
205

VIII¹
A 462
206

From draft; see 212:27–37:

The kingdom of God does not change with the seasons! So let the rest be needed for a long time or a short time, let it come abundantly or sparingly, let all these things come and go, be lacking or possessed: The kingdom of God . . . . .

In margin: The kingdom of God is still the first that is to be sought and ultimately lasts in all eternity.

it ultimately also lasts through all eternities.

"If that which will be abolished was glorious, that which remains will be much more glorious" (II Corinthians 3:11).—
Pap. VII¹ B 178:4 *n.d.*, 1846

Deleted from draft; see 215:1–15:

Preface

These Christian discourses* were not [*changed from:* are not] intended to fill an idle moment for some inquisitive people. If, however, just one single sufferer** should, in reading them, find a heavy moment lighter,*** then the author will not regret his intention with them.

S. K.

*(which in more than one respect are not and thus for more than one reason are not called *sermons*)

**who in his suffering is also going astray in many thoughts,

***should find a trail leading through the many thoughts
Pap. VII¹ B 190 *n.d.*, 1846

See 225:10

The following passage was removed from the preface to "The Gospel of Sufferings":

These are Christian discourses, because the life-expression of the discourse, as I understand it, is the essential and the essentially correlative form for Christianity, which is a matter of faith and conviction: Christianity certainly is a fact but the kind of fact that can only be believed, with the result that it can only be talked about or preached about—witnessed not to its being true (for this is the relation of secular wisdom to its various objects), but witnessed to the fact that one *believes* it is true.—*JP* V 5964 (*Pap.* VII¹ A 224) *n.d.*, 1847

In margin of draft; see 217:19–20:

The text lines are to be printed at the beginning in only the first two discourses and not later, partly because the two first ones are Christ's words, partly because in one of them there is no text line.—*Pap.* VII¹ B 193 *n.d.*, 1846

From draft; see 225:2:

For a person to have everything within his power and then to give up all power, and to give it up in such a way that he cannot himself do the least thing, yes, cannot even do anything for his adherents, and to maintain it so rigorously that he even constrains creation, nature, which will betray something—if this is not self-denial, then what is self-denial. Here is the place for a person who denied himself, and just as a warrior may long to be gathered together with the heroes, where only wounds and battles and dangers and victories are talked about, so also the imitator [*Efterfølger*] may long to be away from the confused opinions of the world to a place where all that is talked about is the suffering that is endured, lack of appreciation, terror, mockery, and mortal danger—in short, the experiences of the one who takes up his cross and imitates Christ.—*JP* III 3740 (*Pap.* VII¹ B 181:2) *n.d.*, 1846

Deleted from final copy; see 230:1

II.

Prayer

You who descended from God in heaven to humankind on earth in order to take away the heavy burden of sin, you our

Savior and Redeemer, grant also that we, grateful and humble, may joyfully carry the light burden that you yourself have laid upon your followers. Amen.—*Pap.* VII[1] B 192:34 *n.d.*, 1846

In margin of draft; see 262:22:

Hermae Pastor.
Visiones, Visio III, ch. XI, XII.
—*Pap.* VII[1] B 181:7 *n.d.*, 1846

See 289:5–305:9:

What is the essentially Christian and the point in the fifth of the "Christian Discourses" is specifically that the authority of the Bible is affirmed, that it is not something one has thought out but something commanded, something with authority, the requirement that hardship is the task. Consequently the analogy of the child of whom the parents require something is continually used: in the same way the Bible, God's Word, commands the elders. In an upbuilding discourse [*opbyggelig tale*], I could not so rigorously maintain that the Bible says this.—*JP* I 207 (*Pap.* VIII[1] A 20) *n.d.*, 1847

See 306:6–320:28:

The essentially Christian, the point in the sixth discourse, is specifically that it does not enter into a development of the temporal and the eternal, that when placed together they must yield the concept "suffering"; instead, the presentation is strictly from the apostolic word. An upbuilding discourse, which functions with the aid of reflection, could never be structured in this way.—*Pap.* VIII[1] A 21 *n.d.*, 1847

See 306:12:

Most likely no one is aware now that the word "deliberations" [*Overveielser*] is already a cue word in the introduction to one of the "Christian Discourses," No. VI.—*JP* V 6054 (*Pap.* VIII[1] A 308) *n.d.*, 1847

From draft; see 326:23–327:8:

And a power-hungry tyrant, if there is such a person at all, can easily be overthrown, but this evil spirit, which we ourselves conjure up, this evil spirit, which does not reside in any individual person and is not any individual person but covertly sneaks around and continually seeks its prey, this evil spirit of pusillanimous deference is very difficult to get eradicated again.—*Pap.* VII[1] B 188:2 *n.d.*, 1846

From draft; see 340:8–12:

We remain convinced that as soon as and wherever confessing Christ is not exactly the same as proclaiming Christ, then the actual requirement to confess Christ militantly is not met, so that on the contrary it is sectarian exaggeration to want to confess Christ if this means exactly the same as judging others. But no one can say whether such a situation could develop anywhere in which confessing Christ is proclaiming him.

VII[1]
B 188:4
362

VII[1]
B 188:4
363

But where this is not the case, there nevertheless remains this joyful thought about the power of bold confidence as a supreme comfort. For example, one can possess a weapon that one relies upon for use in the most extreme danger; consequently, although one does not use it because it is not needed, one still knows that because one has this weapon no extreme danger will arise, so that one would have to despair.—*Pap.* VII[1] B 188:4 *n.d.*, 1846

See 159:1–212:37:

The structure of the three discourses about the lilies and the birds is as follows: the first is esthetic, the second ethical, the third religious.—*JP* V 5970 (*Pap.* VIII[1] A 1) *n.d.*, 1847

Despite everything people ought to have learned about my maieutic carefulness, by proceeding slowly and continually letting it seem as if I knew nothing more, not the next thing— now on the occasion of my new upbuilding discourses they will probably bawl out that I do not know what comes next,

VIII[1]
A 4
5

VIII[1]
A 4
6

that I know nothing about sociality. The fools! Yet on the other hand I owe it to myself to confess before God that in a certain sense there is some truth in it, only not as people understand it—namely, that continually when I have first presented one aspect clearly and sharply, then the other affirms itself even more strongly.

Now I have my theme of the next book. It will be called: Works of Love.
—*JP* V 5972 (*Pap.* VIII¹ A 4) *n.d.*, 1847

See 215:3–10:

VIII¹
A 6
6

The Difference *between a Christian Discourse and a Sermon*

A Christian discourse deals to a certain extent with doubt—a sermon operates absolutely and solely on the basis of authority, that of Scripture and of Christ's apostles. Therefore, it is neither more nor less than heresy to deal with doubt in a sermon, however well one might be able to deal with it.

VIII¹
A 6
7

The preface to my "Christian Discourses," therefore, contains the phrase: if a sufferer who is also *going astray in many thoughts.*

A sermon presupposes a pastor (ordination); a Christian discourse can be by a layman.—*JP* I 638 (*Pap.* VIII¹ A 6) *n.d.*, 1847

VIII¹
A 15
10

The Relations of the Three Parts of *Upbuilding Discourses in Various Spirits*

1. Part One
   The design is essentially ethical-ironic and thereby upbuilding, Socratic.
   The most ironic category (which, please note, is also the absolutely moral category) is singleness, that single individual [*hiin Enkelte*]. The single individual [*den Enkelte*] can in fact denote every person and in an eminent way every person who morally-ideally wills to be the highest. The relation is not such

that anyone is excluded by differentiation from eminently being the single individual, and yet it probably is the case that there is no single individual living. This is the relation between facticity and ideality, which is simultaneously just as much moral and ethical as it is ironic.

Incidentally, in order to give maieutic support, in the pseudonymous writings I always used "that single individual" [*hiin Enkelte*] in the sense of differentiation, because of course differential presuppositions are required in order to pursue dialectical developments completely. In the upbuilding discourses, however, the category "the single individual" [*den Enkelte*] has been used strictly in the moral sense and in the sense of equality.

The category of the single individual is just as ironic as it is moral and definitely both, and then again it is decidedly upbuilding (in the religiousness of immanence) in that it completely abolishes the differences as illusion and establishes the essential equality of eternity.

Note. At times the tone of discourse borders on the comic, yet with ironic pathos. If anyone wants to test it, he will see that wherever in this confessional discourse he is moved to laughter, he laughs ironically. For example, when it says: A crowd of friends of the good, or of good friends, attach themselves to him—it is true that they believed they were also attaching themselves to the good, but that certainly must be a misunderstanding, since he himself went around on the side.[42] Or: They erected a building; it was a tie-beam structure [*Bindingsværk*] (of course it took many to do it)[43]—and so on in many passages.

This comic tone is absolutely essential.

2. Part Two is humorous.

The dialectic in the concept: to learn means that the learner relates himself to the teacher as to his more ideal *genus proximum* [nearest genus]. As soon as the teacher takes a lower position within the very same genus and stands below the learner, the situation becomes humorous. For example, to learn from a child or from a dolt, because the child or the dolt can only humorously be called the teacher.

VIII¹
A 15
11

But the situation becomes even more humorous when the teacher and the learner do not have even the same genus in common but in qualitative heterogeneity are related inversely to one another. This is the definitely humorous relation. The lilies and the birds.

The presentation is upbuilding, mitigated by the touching jest and the jesting earnestness of the humorous. The reader will smile at many points but never laugh, never laugh ironically. The tale of the worried lily,[44] which is also a parable, is clearly humorous. So also is the entire discussion about being clothed.[45] On the whole, the humorous is present at every point because the design itself is humorous.

The three discourses are again related to one another esthetically, ethically, religiously.

See p. 175.[46]

3. Part Three

See this book, p. 179.[47]
—*JP* V 5975 (*Pap.* VIII¹ A 15) *n.d.*, 1847

About the Three Discourses 1847

It is not by chance that the fairy tale is used in the first discourse, for this is the way life is, especially when habit takes over—so far from the ideal that the ideal requirement must sound like a fairy tale. —Furthermore, all comparisons are avoided this way.

Some may find that these discourses lack earnestness. They think that earnestness in this situation is to make financial contributions, think up public works, start a new collection campaign, etc., all of which may be very praiseworthy but in the strictest sense is not earnestness. The world, however, has become so prosaic that the only care conceded to be reality [*Realitet*] is worry about making a living and that again in a vexatious sense as emphasized for provocative purposes by agitators who make money on the poor. Love, repentance, etc., are regarded as chimeras, but money, money, money—

I pledge myself to read these three discourses aloud sometime in eternity, and I am convinced that they will be listened to with pleasure, also by those who here object to them and perhaps insult me. Cares are here gently modified in the childlike and pious way in which a happy spirit will remember them. Whether a person here in time is able to act in this way, I will not decide; but if he is so vexed that he defiantly and insultingly turns away from pure evangelical gentleness, then he is not earnest at all but rebellious. Even the sufferer ought to be able to listen sympathetically to an almost childlike but moving interpretation.

Incidentally, Holy Scripture speaks far more severely. Luke 21:34: Do not be weighed down with dissipation, drunkenness, or cares of this life.

When the apostles say to the paralytic: Gold and silver have I none, but what I have I give you: Stand up and walk[48]—it is said very exaltedly, because a miracle, after all, is more than gold and silver. But if they had said: We have only an idea, an eternal and blessed thought, to offer you—would that not have been a good way to phrase it? In the same way I have neither silver nor gold but a mitigating, moving, truly upbuilding meditation.

In the first discourse we see how the rich birds actually corrupt the poor ones. An almost comic light falls on the rich doves that strut around and also an ethical accent, that they are the very ones who have the worry about making a living.—*JP* V 5976 (*Pap.* VIII¹ A 16) *n.d.*, 1847

In all likelihood the wiseacres who know how to rattle off everything will charge my Christian discourses[49] with not containing the Atonement. Consequently, after five years of having the chance to learn from me how maieutically I proceed, they have remained every bit as wise—will probably go on being that. First the first and then the next. But these confounded people muddle into one speech all that I develop piece by piece in big books, always leaving behind in each book one stinger that is its connection with the next. But the insipidness of the speculators and of some clergy is incredible.—*JP* V 5991 (*Pap.* VIII¹ A 49) *n.d.*, 1847

Absolutely right. My *Upbuilding Discourses in Various Spirits* met with approval, especially the last ones,[50] and why? Because they are short and because the whole book, compared with what I usually come out with, is small. See, this is the heart of the matter. Pamphlet literature. I have held back the big book about Adler, and now people have been deluded into becoming profound critics—they see but one little book, ergo, I have spent all my time on that, ergo, it has been written with painstaking care. —I am actually obliged to disguise my capabilities. If I let them see the actual wingspread, the gossip that I scamp my work will start all over again. Wretched market town! And Heiberg[51] and his kind take part in this nonsense—because he himself is a pamphlet author and therefore has to maintain that as a rule a large work is slovenly, especially since it took such a short time.—*JP* V 6014 (*Pap.* VIII¹ A 164) *n.d.*, 1847

If Prof. Heiberg[52] had published at Christmastime a little book entitled "What One Learns from the Lilies in the Field and the Birds of the Air, Three Discourses"—designed in such a way that there was very little on a page, and organized and arranged in such a way that one could also obtain copies with gilded edges, indeed, some with a silk ribbon so that they could be hung on the Christmas tree—the book would have been sold out in the course of a week. The whole city would have been agog as if something were really going on; the mass of coaches driving to congratulate the professor would be so great that for several days it would be unthinkable for a pedestrian to cross on Knippelsbro.[53] Professor Heiberg would have been the man for that!—*Pap.* VIII¹ A 389 *n.d.*, 1847

VIII¹
A 504
227

Instructions for "States of Mind in the Strife of Suffering"[54]

These discourses are presented in such a way as to be continually tangential to the consciousness of sin and the suffering of sin—sin etc. are another matter: these discourses come to the subject of sin. Because the consolation lyrically rises as high as possible over all earthly need and misery, even the heaviest, the horror of sin, is continually shown. Thus, another theme is cunningly concealed in these discourses: sin is the human being's corruption.

In the ordinary sermon this is the confusion: need and adversity are preached together—with sin.

Thus, the category for these discourses is different from "The Gospel of Sufferings," which left the suffering indefinite. Here the distinction is made: innocent suffering—in order thereafter to approach sin.—*JP* V 6101 (*Pap.* VIII¹ A 504) *n.d.*, 1848

VIII¹
A 504
228

N.B.   N.B.

May 11, 1848

VIII¹
A 649
295

Most people (if at an early age it is indicated that they must bear some suffering or other, some cross or other, one of those mournful curtailments of the soul) begin to hope and, as it is called, to have faith that everything will improve, that God will surely make everything all right, etc., and then after a long while, when still no change has taken place, they will learn little by little to depend on the help of the eternal—that is, resign themselves and be strengthened in being satisfied with the eternal. —The person of deeper nature or one whom God has structured more eternally begins at once to understand that he must bear this as long as he lives, that he dare not ask God for such extraordinary, paradoxical aid. But God is still perfect love, and nothing is more certain to him than that. Consequently he resigns himself, and because the eternal is close to him he finds rest, continually and happily assured that God is love. But he must accept the suffering. Then after a while when he becomes more and more concrete in the actuality of life, comes more and more to himself *qua* finite being, when time and the movement of time exercise their power over him, when in spite of all effort it still becomes so difficult to live year after year with the aid only of the eternal, when in a more humble sense he becomes human or learns what it means to be a human being (since in his resignation he is still too ideal, too abstract, for which reason there is some despair in all resignation)—then for him faith's possibility means: whether

VIII¹
A 649
296

he will now believe by virtue of the absurd that God will help him temporally.* (Here lie all the paradoxes. Thus the forgiveness of sins means to be helped temporally; otherwise it is resignation, which can endure the punishment, still assured that God is love. But faith in the forgiveness of sin means to believe that in time God has forgotten the sin, that it is really true that God forgets.)

This is to say that most people never reach faith at all. They live a long time in immediacy, finally they advance to some reflection, and then they die. The exceptions begin the other way around; dialectical from childhood, that is, without immediacy, they begin with the dialectical, with reflection, and they go on living this way year after year (about as long as the others live in sheer immediacy) and then, at a more mature age, faith's possibility presents itself to them. For faith is immediacy after reflection.

Naturally the exceptions have a very unhappy childhood and youth, for to be essentially reflection at that age, which by nature is immediate, is the most profound melancholy. But there is a return. Most people drift on in such a way they never advance to spirit; all their many happy years of immediacy tend toward spiritual retardation and therefore they never become spirit. But the unhappy childhood and youth of the exceptions are transfigured into spirit.—*JP* II 1123 (*Pap.* VIII¹ A 649) May 11, 1848

Progress in My Life

However much I have been influenced by the Socratic, however much I was naturally predisposed to the category "the single individual" [*den Enkelte*] when I used it for the first time in the preface to the *Upbuilding Discourses*⁵⁵ in 1843, it nevertheless also had a purely personal meaning for me; the idea was not so clear to me that I would have used it immediately at that time

---

* *Note.* This is the inverse movement, which after all is "spirit." Spirit is the second movement. Humor is not mood but is found, with dialectical propriety, in a person who unhappily has been cheated out of his childhood and then later became spirit and simultaneously aware of childhood.

without this personal significance. When I used it the second time, that is, intensified, in the dedication to the *Upbuilding Discourses in Various Spirits*, I was clear that I was acting purely in the idea.[56] . . . —*Pap.* X³ A 308 *n.d.*, 1850

A Possible Preface to the Upbuilding Discourse

X⁵
B 117
312

"The Woman Who Was a Sinner"[57]

If neither "The Accounting"[58] nor *Two Discourses at the Communion on Fridays*[59] is published but only the upbuilding discourse, which is to be dedicated to my father,[60] the following preface could perhaps be used.

Preface

X⁵
B 117
313

What was first said in my first book of upbuilding discourses, in the Preface to *Two Upbuilding Discourses* in 1843, that this book "seeks that single individual [*hiin Enkelte*]";[61] what was repeated verbatim in the Preface to each new collection of upbuilding discourses;[62] what was pointed out, after I had exposed myself to the laughter and the insults of the crowd and thus, as well as I could, contributed to evoking awareness by dedicating the next large work, *Upbuilding Discourses in Various Spirits*, 1847, to "the single individual [*den Enkelte*]"; what the world revolution in 1848 certainly did not witness against or render untrue—emphasis upon the single individual—let me repeatedly remind [readers] of this. [*In margin:* If for the sake of recollection it is possible for a thinker to manage to concentrate all his thinking in one single idea, this has been granted to me, the upbuilding author, whose entire thinking is essentially contained in this one thought: the single individual.]

"The single individual"—of course, the single individual religiously understood, consequently understood in such a way that everyone, unconditionally everyone, yes, unconditionally everyone, just as much as everyone has or should have a conscience, can be this [*denne*] single individual and should be that, can stake his honor in willing to be that, but then also can find blessedness in being what is the expression for true fear of God, true love to one's neighbor, true humanity [*Menneskelighed*], and true human equality [*Menneske-Lighed*]. Oh, if only some might achieve it, if it is not, although the task for all, too high for all of us, yet not too high in such a way that it should be forgotten, forgotten as if it were not the task or as if this task did not exist [*deleted:* in November 1850], so that we may at least learn to forsake not only the mediocre but also the indifferent half measures that reject an established order, yet without driving through to become in an extraordinary sense the single individual, but rather schismatically organize parties and sects, which are neither the one nor the other.

November 1850

—*JP* II 2033 (*Pap.* X⁵ B 117) November 1850

EDITORIAL APPENDIX

ACKNOWLEDGMENTS

Preparation of manuscripts for *Kierkegaard's Writings* is supported by a genuinely enabling grant from the National Endowment for the Humanities. The grant includes gifts from the Dronning Margrethes og Prins Henriks Fond, the Danish Ministry of Cultural Affairs, The Augustinus Fond, the Carlsberg Fond, and the Lutheran Brotherhood Foundation.

The translators–editors are indebted to Grethe Kjær and Julia Watkin for their knowledgeable observations on crucial concepts and terminology and for their critical reading of the entire manuscript. Per Lønning, Wim R. Scholtens, and Sophia Scopetéa, members of the International Advisory Board for *Kierkegaard's Writings*, and Jack Schwandt have given valuable criticism of the manuscript on the whole and in detail. Kathryn Hong, associate editor for *KW*, scrutinized the manuscript. Regine Prenzel-Guthrie, associate editor for *KW*, scrutinized the manuscript and prepared the index.

Acknowledgment is made to Gyldendals Forlag for permission to absorb notes to *Søren Kierkegaards samlede Værker*.

Inclusion in the Supplement of entries from *Søren Kierkegaard's Journals and Papers* is by arrangement with Indiana University Press.

The book collection and the microfilm collection of the Kierkegaard Library, St. Olaf College, and Gregor Malantschuk's annotated set of *Kierkegaards samlede Værker* have been used in preparation of the text, Supplement, and Editorial Appendix.

The manuscript was typed by Dorothy Bolton. Francesca Lane Rasmus did the word processing of the final manuscript and prepared the composition tape. The volume has been guided through the press by Marta Nussbaum Steele.

COLLATION OF *UPBUILDING DISCOURSES IN VARIOUS SPIRITS* IN THE DANISH EDITIONS OF KIERKEGAARD'S COLLECTED WORKS

Vol. VIII Ed. 1 Pg.	Vol. VIII Ed. 2 Pg.	Vol. 11 Ed. 3 Pg.	Vol. VIII Ed. 1 Pg.	Vol. VIII Ed. 2 Pg.	Vol. 11 Ed. 3 Pg.
117	133	13	152	174	48
119	135	15	153	175	49
120	136	15	154	177	50
121	137	16	155	178	51
122	138	17	156	179	52
123	139	18	157	180	53
124	140	19	158	182	54
125	142	20	159	183	55
126	143	21	160	184	56
127	144	22	161	185	57
128	145	23	162	186	58
129	147	24	163	188	59
130	148	26	164	189	60
131	149	27	165	190	61
132	150	28	166	191	62
133	152	29	167	193	63
134	153	30	168	194	64
135	154	31	169	195	65
136	155	32	170	196	66
137	156	33	171	197	67
138	158	34	172	199	68
139	159	35	173	200	69
140	160	36	174	201	70
141	161	37	175	202	71
142	162	38	176	204	72
143	163	39	177	205	73
144	165	40	178	206	74
145	166	41	179	207	75
146	167	42	180	208	76
147	168	43	181	210	77
148	169	44	182	211	78
149	170	45	183	212	79
150	172	46	184	213	80
151	173	47	185	215	81

Vol. VIII	*Vol. VIII*	*Vol. 11*	*Vol. VIII*	*Vol. VIII*	*Vol. 11*
Ed. 1	*Ed. 2*	*Ed. 3*	*Ed. 1*	*Ed. 2*	*Ed. 3*
Pg.	*Pg.*	*Pg.*	*Pg.*	*Pg.*	*Pg.*
186	216	82	228	267	125
187	217	83	229	268	126
188	218	85	230	269	127
189	219	86	231	270	128
190	221	87	232	272	129
191	222	88	233	273	130
192	223	89	234	274	131
193	224	90	235	275	132
194	225	91	236	277	133
195	226	92	237	278	134
196	228	93	238	279	135
197	229	94	239	280	136
198	230	95	240	281	138
199	231	96	241	283	139
200	232	97	242	284	140
201	234	98	247	289	145
202	235	99	248	290	146
203	236	100	249	291	147
204	237	101	250	292	147
205	238	102	251	293	148
206	240	103	252	294	149
207	241	104	253	296	150
208	242	105	254	297	151
209	243	106	255	298	152
210	245	107	256	299	153
211	246	108	257	301	154
212	247	109	258	302	155
213	248	110	259	303	156
214	249	111	260	304	157
215	251	112	261	305	158
216	252	113	262	307	159
217	253	114	263	308	161
218	254	115	264	309	162
219	256	116	265	311	163
220	257	117	266	312	164
221	258	118	267	313	165
222	259	119	268	314	166
223	261	120	269	315	167
224	262	121	270	317	168
225	263	122	271	318	168
226	264	123	272	319	169
227	265	124	273	320	171

Vol. VIII Ed. 1 Pg.	*Vol. VIII* Ed. 2 Pg.	*Vol. 11* Ed. 3 Pg.	*Vol. VIII* Ed. 1 Pg.	*Vol. VIII* Ed. 2 Pg.	*Vol. 11* Ed. 3 Pg.
274	321	172	322	376	219
275	322	173	323	377	220
276	324	174	324	378	221
277	325	175	325	380	222
278	326	176	326	381	223
279	327	177	327	382	224
280	329	178	328	383	225
281	330	179	329	384	226
282	331	180	330	386	227
283	332	181	331	387	228
284	333	182	332	388	229
285	334	183	333	389	230
286	336	184	334	390	231
287	337	184	335	391	231
288	338	185	336	392	232
289	339	186	337	393	234
290	340	187	338	394	235
291	341	188	339	396	236
292	343	189	340	397	237
293	344	190	341	398	238
294	345	191	342	399	239
295	346	192	343	400	240
296	347	193	344	401	241
301	353	199	345	403	242
303	355	201	346	404	243
305	357	203	347	405	243
306	357	203	348	407	245
307	359	204	349	407	245
308	360	205	350	409	246
309	361	206	351	410	247
310	362	207	352	411	248
311	363	208	353	412	249
312	365	209	354	413	250
313	366	210	355	414	251
314	367	211	356	416	252
315	368	212	357	417	253
316	369	213	358	418	254
317	371	215	359	419	255
318	372	215	360	420	256
319	373	216	361	422	257
320	374	217	362	423	258
321	375	218	363	424	259

Vol. VIII Ed. 1 Pg.	Vol. VIII Ed. 2 Pg.	Vol. 11 Ed. 3 Pg.	Vol. VIII Ed. 1 Pg.	Vol. VIII Ed. 2 Pg.	Vol. 11 Ed. 3 Pg.
364	425	260	391	458	288
365	427	261	392	459	289
366	428	263	393	460	290
367	429	264	394	461	291
368	430	265	395	463	292
369	432	266	396	464	293
370	433	267	397	465	294
371	434	267	398	467	295
372	435	268	399	467	295
373	436	269	400	469	296
374	437	270	401	470	297
375	438	271	402	471	298
376	439	272	403	472	299
377	441	273	404	473	300
378	442	274	405	475	301
379	443	275	406	476	302
380	444	277	407	477	303
381	446	278	408	478	304
382	447	278	409	479	305
383	448	279	410	481	306
384	449	280	411	482	307
385	451	282	412	483	308
386	452	282	413	484	309
387	453	283	414	485	310
388	454	285	415	486	311
389	455	286	416	487	312
390	457	287			

NOTES

TITLE PAGE. *Upbuilding Discourses in Various Spirits.* See Supplement, pp. 363–64, 366 (*Pap.* VII¹ B 214, 217, 192:1–2) on proposed title; Historical Introduction, p. xii.

TABLE OF CONTENTS. See Supplement, p. 364 (*Pap.* VII¹ B 218); Historical Introduction, p. xii.

PART ONE
AN OCCASIONAL DISCOURSE

1. In the original publication, each of the three parts has its own full title page, and the volume has a common title page with the newly chosen title. "PART ONE" etc. are on separate pages, before the three separate title pages, and each of the three parts has separate pagination. See Historical Introduction, pp. xii.

2. See p. 5; Supplement, pp. 366–69, 388–90, 395–96 (*Pap.* VII¹ A 176; VIII¹ A 15; X³ A 308; X⁵ B 117).

3. See Supplement, p. 369 (*Pap.* VII¹ B 150).

4. With reference to the following paragraph, see Supplement, pp. 369–70 (*Pap.* VI A 25; VII¹ B 137, 138, 139).

5. See pp. 153–54. With reference to the following paragraph, see Supplement, pp. 370–71 (*Pap.* VII¹ B 140, 141, 145, 146).

6. Cf. Philippians 1:6.

7. See Ecclesiastes 3:1; Supplement, p. 371–72 (*Pap.* VII¹ B 147).

8. Ecclesiastes 3:2

9. See, for example, I Timothy 4:4.

10. See Matthew 23:23.

11. See Philippians 2:12.

12. Danish: "*Bedrøvelse efter Gud*" (p. 17: "*Sorg efter Gud*"). See II Corinthians 7:10. The Danish Bible of the time (Copenhagen: 1830; *ASKB* 7) has "*Bedrøvelse efter Gud*," and RSV has "godly grief." See also *Three Upbuilding Discourses* (1844), in *Eighteen Upbuilding Discourses*, p. 250, *KW* V (*SV* IV 138); *Christian Discourses, KW* XVII (*SV* X 263); *JP* I 443; IV 3915, p. 53 (*Pap.* II A 360; III C 1, p. 246).

13. Cf. Matthew 12:36.

14. Cf. II Corinthians 7:10; *JP* I 443 (*Pap.* II A 360).

15. With reference to the following two sentences, see Supplement, p. 372 (*Pap.* VII¹ B 192:8).

16. See Psalm 139:2

17. See Matthew 6:6.

18. See, for example, *JP* II 1348 (*Pap.* VII¹ A 143).

19. See Luke 10:42.

20. See Supplement, p. 372 (*Pap.* VII¹ B 192:9).

21. See Supplement, pp. 372–73 (*Pap.* VII¹ B 173, 174).

22. See Matthew 5:8.

23. For continuation of the sentence, see Supplement, pp. 373–74 (*Pap.* VII¹ B 192:10).

24. See Luke 16:19–26.

25. See I John 2:17.

26. See Supplement, p. 374 (*Pap.* VII¹ B 192:12).

27. The Danish words *Tvivl* [doubt], *Fortvivlelse* [despair], and *Tvesindethed* [double-mindedness] have a common root: *tve* (variant *tvi*), which means "two."

28. See James 3:5.

29. See James 3:15.

30. See Proverbs 14:34.

31. See Matthew 12:43–45.

32. See Matthew 12:45.

33. Cf. G. E. Lessing, *Nathan der Weise*, IV, 4; *Gotthold Ephraim Lessing's sämmtliche Schriften*, I–XXXII (Berlin, Stettin: 1825–28; *ASKB* 1747–62), XXII, p. 181; *Nathan the Wise*, tr. Patrick Maxwell (New York: Bloch, 1939), p. 295. See also *Stages on Life's Way*, p. 421, *KW* XI (*SV* VI 392).

34. See, for example, *JP* IV 4409 (*Pap.* II A 343): "Longing is the umbilical cord of the higher life."

35. With reference to the following paragraph, see Supplement, p. 374 (*Pap.* VII¹ A 22).

36. See p. 121 and Supplement, pp. 374–75 (*Pap.* VII¹ B 192:13).

37. See, for example, the discussion between Thrasymachus and Socrates in Plato, *Republic*, 336 b–354 b, especially 338 c; *Platonis quae exstant opera*, I–XI, ed. Friedrich Ast (Leipzig: 1819–32; *ASKB* 1144–54), IV, pp. 24–65, especially pp. 28–29; *The Collected Dialogues of Plato*, ed. Edith Hamilton and Huntington Cairns (Princeton: Princeton University Press, 1963), pp. 586–605, especially p. 588 (Thrasymachus speaking): "Hearken and hear then, said he. I affirm that the just is nothing else than the advantage of the stronger. Well, why don't you applaud? Nay, you'll do anything but that."

38. Socrates (469–399 B.C.). See note 37 above.

39. Cf. Romans 8:38–39.

40. See I John 5:19.

41. See Cicero, *De oratore*, II, 74, 299; *M. Tullii Ciceronis opera omnia*, I–IV and index, ed. Johann August Ernesti (Halle: 1756–57; *ASKB* 1224–29), I, p. 489; *Cicero De oratore*, I–II, tr. E. W. Sutton and H. Rackham (Loeb, Cambridge: Harvard University Press, 1976), I, pp. 426–27.

42. See James 1:8.

43. See James 1:7.

44. See Luke 18:13.

45. With reference to the following three sentences, see Supplement, p. 375 (*Pap.* VII¹ B 153:2).

46. With reference to the remainder of the paragraph and the following three paragraphs, see Supplement, pp. 375–76 (*Pap.* VII¹ B 153:4).

47. See James 2:19.

48. With reference to the remainder of the paragraph and the following paragraph, see Supplement, p. 376 (*Pap.* VII¹ B 162:2).

49. Cf., for example, Matthew 25:14–30; Revelation 21:8.

50. See, for example, Plato, *Republic*, 572 b; *Opera*, V, pp. 2–5; *Dialogues*, p. 799 (Socrates speaking): "This description has carried us too far, but the point that we have to notice is this, that in fact there exists in every one of us, even in some reputed most respectable, a terrible, fierce, and lawless brood of desires, which it seems are revealed in our sleep."

51. With reference to the following sentence, see Supplement, pp. 376–77 (*Pap.* VII¹ B 153:5).

52. Cf. Matthew 10:28.

53. See, for example, Galatians 5:16–21; I John 2:16.

54. See Genesis 2:18.

55. Cf. Ecclesiastes 4:10.

56. Cf. *The Sickness unto Death*, pp. 42–46, *KW* XIX (*SV* XI 155–58).

57. See Matthew 6:33.

58. With reference to the following paragraph, see Supplement, p. 377 (*Pap.* VII¹ B 163:3).

59. With reference to the following five paragraphs, see Supplement, p. 377 (*Pap.* VII¹ B 192:17).

60. See Luke 17:10.

61. See Matthew 11:12.

62. See I Samuel 15:22. See also *JP* II 2152; V 5893 (*Pap.* VIII¹ A 540; VII¹ A 106).

63. Attributed to Francis I of France. When he was imprisoned after the battle of Pavia (1525), he wrote to his mother a letter containing a line that in modified form became proverbial. See Jacques Antoine Dulaure, *Histoire physique, civile et morale de Paris*, I–VII (Paris: 1837), I, p. 209.

64. See Supplement, p. 377 (*Pap.* VII¹ B 194).

65. See Ephesians 4:14.

66. See II Timothy 3:7.

67. Cf. Ecclesiastes 1:9.

68. See *The Moment*, *KW* XXIII (*SV* XIV 245–46).

69. Cf. Matthew 12:36.

70. The source has not been located.

71. See Exodus 10.

72. Cf. Philippians 4:7.

73. See Matthew 10:29.

74. See Psalm 94:9.

75. Cf. Proverbs 4:23.

76. See Ecclesiastes 7:2.

77. Carl Søeborg, "*Om 100 Aar er Alting glemt,*" *Fader Evans Stambog*, ed. Andreas Peter Liunge (Copenhagen: 1824), p. 220. See also The Moment *and Late Writings*, *KW* XXIII (*SV* XIV 173).

78. Cf. Kierkegaard's letter to his nephew Hans Peter Kierkegaard, *Letters*, Letter 196, *KW* XXV.

79. See Mark 10:21.

80. See Luke 9:59.

81. See Matthew 25:21.

82. See Luke 17:10.

83. With reference to the following sentence, see Supplement, pp. 354–55 (*Pap.* VI A 93).

84. See Mark 12:41–44.

85. See I Corinthians 9:26.

86. With reference to the remainder of the paragraph, cf. Supplement, p. 354 (*Pap.* VI B 161).

87. See Mark 8:36.

88. See Matthew 27:41–42.

89. See John 19:30.

90. Cf. Shakespeare, *King Henry the Fifth*, II, 4, ll. 74–75; *The Complete Works of Shakespeare*, ed. George Lyman Kittredge (Boston: Ginn, 1936), p. 636 (Dauphin speaking): "Self-love, my liege, is not so vile a sin / As self-neglecting." The source of the translation of "self-neglect" as *Selvforagt* instead of *Selvforsømmelse* or *Selvtilsidesættelse* has not been located. Kierkegaard's editions of Danish and German translations of Shakespeare do not have *Selvforagt* [self-contempt]. It does appear, however, in a much later Danish version. See *William Shakspeare's Dramatiske Værker*, I–XVIII, tr. Peter Foersom and Edvard Lembcke (Copenhagen: 1861–71), IV, p. 41.

91. With reference to the remainder of the paragraph, see Supplement, p. 354 (*Pap.* VI B 161).

92. With reference to the remainder of the paragraph, see Supplement, p. 378 (*Pap.* VII¹ B 155:10).

93. Socrates conversing with Adimantus. See Plato, *Republic*, 492 b-c; *Opera*, IV, pp. 334–37; *Dialogues*, p. 728.

94. John the Baptizer. See Mark 1:4–6.

95. See Matthew 3:10.

96. See, for example, Plato, *Apology*, 19 d-20 c; *Opera*, VIII, pp. 104–05; *Dialogues*, p. 6 (Socrates speaking):

> The fact is that there is nothing in any of these charges, and if you have heard anyone say that I try to educate people and charge a fee, there is no truth in that either. I wish that there were, because I think that it is a fine thing if a man is qualified to teach, as in the case of Gorgias of Leontini and Prodicus of Ceos and Hippias of Elis. Each one of these is perfectly capable of going into any city and actually persuading the young men to leave the company of their fellow citizens, with any of whom they can associate for

nothing, and attach themselves to him, and pay money for the privilege, and be grateful into the bargain.

There is another expert too from Paros who I discovered was here on a visit; I happened to meet a man who has paid more in Sophists' fees than all the rest put together—I mean Callias, the son of Hipponicus. So I asked him—he has two sons, you see—Callias, I said, if your sons had been colts or calves, we should have had no difficulty in finding and engaging a trainer to perfect their natural qualities, and this trainer would have been some sort of horse dealer or agriculturalist. But seeing that they are human beings, whom do you intend to get as their instructor? Who is the expert in perfecting the human and social qualities? I assume from the fact of your having sons that you must have considered the question. Is there such a person or not?

Certainly, said he.

Who is he, and where does he come from? said I. And what does he charge?

Evenus of Paros, Socrates, said he, and his fee is five minas.

I felt that Evenus was to be congratulated if he really was a master of this art and taught it at such a moderate fee. I should certainly plume myself and give myself airs if I understood these things, but in fact, gentlemen, I do not.

97. See, for example, John 3:17–19.

98. For continuation of the text, see Supplement, p. 378 (*Pap.* VII¹ B 192:21).

99. See Karl Rosenkranz, *Erinnerungen an Karl Daub* (Berlin: 1837; *ASKB* 743), p. 24 (ed. tr.): "Like a sentry at his lonely post at night, one has thoughts that otherwise are altogether impossible." See also *Fear and Trembling*, p. 50, *KW* VI (*SV* III 100); *JP* I 899 (*Pap.* IV A 92).

100. With reference to the remainder of the paragraph and the following paragraph, see Supplement, pp. 378–79 (*Pap.* VII¹ B 157:2).

101. With reference to the remainder of the paragraph, see Supplement, p. 379 (*Pap.* VII¹ B 157:3).

102. Freely quoted from Johannes Climacus, *Postscript*, p. 84, *KW* XII.1 (*SV* VII 66).

103. See Genesis 12:1.

104. See Revelation 21:4.

105. See Johan Arndt, *Fire Bøger om den sande Christendom* (Christiania: 1829; *ASKB* 277). The line has not been located. See also *JP* V 5920 (*Pap.* VII¹ A 43).

106. For continuation of the text, see Supplement, p. 379 (*Pap.* VII¹ B 157:5).

107. With reference to the remainder of the paragraph and the following paragraph, see Supplement, pp. 355, 379 (*Pap.* VI A 106; VII¹ B 157:6).

108. See Supplement, pp. 379–80 (*Pap.* VII¹ B 164).

109. An allusion to Solon and Croesus. See Herodotus, *History*, I, 32, 34; *Die Geschichten des Herodotos*, I–II, tr. Friedrich Lange (Berlin: 1811–12; *ASKB*

1117), I, pp. 18–19, 20; *Herodotus*, I–IV, tr. A. D. Godley (Loeb, Cambridge: Harvard University Press, 1981–82), I, pp. 38–39, 40–41 (Solon speaking):

> Thus then, Croesus, the whole of man is but chance. Now if I am to speak of you, I say that I see you very rich and the king of many men. But I cannot yet answer your question, before I hear that you have ended your life well. . . . If then such a man besides all this shall also end his life well, then he is the man whom you seek, and is worthy to be called blest; but we must wait till he be dead, and call him not yet blest, but fortunate.

> But after Solon's departure, the divine anger fell heavily on Croesus: as I guess, because he supposed himself to be blest beyond all other men.

110. See Luke 15:7.

111. Epicurus. See Diogenes Laertius, *Lives of Eminent Philosophers*, X, 140; *Diogenis Laertii de vitis philosophorum*, I–II (Leipzig: 1833; *ASKB* 1109), II, p. 242; *Diogen Laërtses filosofiske Historie*, I–II, tr. Børge Riisbrigh (Copenhagen: 1812; *ASKB* 1110–11), I, p. 508; *Diogenes Laertius*, I–II, tr. R. D. Hicks (Loeb, Cambridge: Harvard University Press, 1979–80), II, pp. 664–65.

112. Cf. *Kierkegaard: Letters and Documents*, Letter 196, *KW* XXV.

113. See Romans 12:15.

114. See Mark 9:36.

115. See Ephesians 6:14–17.

116. See, for example, *JP* IV 4599 (*Pap.* VIII[1] A 161).

117. With reference to the following paragraph, see Supplement, pp. 378–79 (*Pap.* VII[1] B 157:2).

118. See Acts 5:40–41.

119. See Matthew 6:34.

120. With reference to the remainder of the paragraph, see Supplement, p. 380 (*Pap.* VII[1] B 160).

121. See Acts 22:27–30, 24:23.

122. Cf. John 4:24.

123. With reference to the remainder of the paragraph, see Supplement, pp. 374–75 (*Pap.* VII[1] B 192:12,13).

124. See Genesis 3:8.

125. See Plato, *Republic*, 518 a–b; *Opera*, IV, pp. 384–87; *Dialogues*, p. 750 (Socrates speaking):

> But a sensible man, I said, would remember that there are two distinct disturbances of the eyes arising from two causes, according as the shift is from light to darkness or from darkness to light, and, believing that the same thing happens to the soul too, whenever he saw a soul perturbed and unable to discern something, he would not laugh unthinkingly, but would observe whether coming from a brighter life its vision was obscured by the unfamiliar darkness, or whether the passage from the deeper dark of ignorance into a more luminous world and the greater brightness had dazzled its vision. And so he would deem the one happy in its experience and way of life and pity the

other, and if it pleased him to laugh at it, his laughter would be less laughable than that at the expense of the soul that had come down from the light above.

126. See Psalm 2:4.

127. See John 14:2.

128. Danish *Du*, the familiar second-person singular pronoun, used (as in German) only in addressing family members and close friends. In English, "thou" is a relic of the same form, but current ecclesiastical usage endows it with the distance and solemnity of the old formal second-person plural form. In the last three or four decades, the distinction has in practice almost disappeared in Denmark, and now almost everyone is addressed as *Du*.

129. See, for example, Proverbs 17:28.

130. With reference to the remainder of the paragraph, see Supplement, p. 380 (*Pap*. VII¹ B 158:8).

131. See Luke 17:10.

132. With reference to the following four paragraphs, see Supplement, p. 380 (*Pap*. VII¹ B 158:9).

133. See Proverbs 25:13.

134. With reference to the remainder of the sentence, see Supplement, p. 380 (*Pap*. VII¹ B 158:10).

135. See Hebrews 5:8.

136. Cf. Romans 5:3–4.

137. See Matthew 25:14–30; Luke 19:12–27.

138. For continuation of the sentence, see Supplement, p. 380 (*Pap*. VII¹ B 169:1).

139. With reference to the remainder of the paragraph and the following paragraph, see Supplement, p. 381 (*Pap*. VII¹ B 169:2).

140. With reference to the following sentence, see Supplement, p. 381 (*Pap*. VII¹ B 171).

141. See Matthew 7:14.

142. Cf. Philippians 2:13.

PART TWO
WHAT WE LEARN FROM THE LILIES IN THE FIELD
AND FROM THE BIRDS OF THE AIR

1. See Supplement, pp. 381, 387 (*Pap*. VII¹ B 175; VIII¹ A 1).

2. See Supplement, p. 381 (*Pap*. VII¹ B 192:25).

3. See p. 4 and note 2.

4. See *Christian Discourses*, *KW* XVII (*SV* X 14); *The Lily in the Field and the Bird of the Air*, in *Without Authority*, *KW* XVIII (*SV* XI 9).

5. With reference to the following paragraph, see Supplement, p. 381 (*Pap*. VII¹ B 192:26).

6. See Job 2:13.

7. The Danish *betragte* means both "to look at" and "to consider." Cf. *Practice in Christianity*, pp. 233–34, *KW* XX (*SV* XII 213–14).

8. See Supplement, p. 382 (*Pap.* VII¹ B 192:27).

9. See, for example, Klaus Gratz, *Kommentar über das Evangelium des Matthäus*, I–II (Tübingen: 1821), II, p. 384.

10. See Jeremiah 4:25. The Danish Bible of Kierkegaard's time had "*under Himlene*" [under the heavens]. The King James Bible has "of the heavens." RSV has "of the air."

11. See Psalm 145:16.

12. With reference to the remainder of the paragraph, see Supplement, p. 363 (*Pap.* VII¹ A 248).

13. James 1:27.

14. See Plato, *Phaedrus*, 236 d–237 a; *Platonis quae exstant opera*, I–XI, ed. Friedrich Ast (Leipzig: 1819–32; *ASKB* 1144–54), I, pp. 146–47; *The Collected Dialogues of Plato*, ed. Edith Hamilton and Huntington Cairns (Princeton: Princeton University Press, 1963), p. 484:

> SOCRATES: But, my dear good Phaedrus, it will be courting ridicule for an amateur like me to improvise on the same theme as an accomplished writer.
>
> PHAEDRUS: Look here, I'll have no more of this affectation, for I'm pretty sure I have something to say which will compel you to speak.
>
> SOCRATES: Then please don't say it.
>
> PHAEDRUS: Oh, but I shall, here and now, and what I say will be an oath. I swear to you by—but by whom, by what god? Or shall it be by this plane tree? I swear that unless you deliver your speech here in its very presence, I will assuredly never again declaim nor report any other speech by any author whatsoever.
>
> SOCRATES: Aha, you rogue! How clever of you to discover the means of compelling a lover of discourse to do your bidding!
>
> PHAEDRUS: Then why all this twisting?
>
> SOCRATES: I give it up, in view of what you've sworn. For how could I possibly do without such entertainment?
>
> PHAEDRUS: Then proceed.
>
> SOCRATES: Well, do you know what I'm going to do?
>
> PHAEDRUS: Do about what?
>
> SOCRATES: I shall cover my head before I begin; then I can rush through my speech at top speed without looking at you and breaking down for shame.

15. See I Peter 5:7.

16. With reference to the following sentence, see Supplement, p. 382 (*Pap.* VII¹ B 177:4).

17. With reference to the following sentence, cf. Supplement, p. 382 (*Pap.* VIII¹ A 75).

18. With reference to the following three sentences, see Supplement, pp. 355–56 (*Pap.* VI A 126).

19. See Matthew 22:5; Luke 14:18–20.

20. Cf. Ecclesiastes 3:18–19.

21. The reference is to Aristotle. See *Sickness unto Death*, p. 118, *KW* XIX

(*SV* XI 227). A clearly pertinent passage in Aristotle has not been located.

22. See Plato, *Phaedo*, 87 b–e; *Opera*, I, pp. 544–47; *Udvalgte Dialoger af Platon*, I–VIII, tr. Carl Johan Heise (Copenhagen: 1830–59; *ASKB* 1164–67, 1169 [I–VII]), I, pp. 61–63; *Dialogues*, pp. 69–70.

23. See, for example, *JP* II 2292 (*Pap.* VII¹ A 34).

24. See Genesis 1:26.

25. Ibid.

26. See, for example, *Sickness unto Death*, pp. 99, 117, 121, 126, 127, *KW* XIX (*SV* XI 209–210, 227, 231, 235, 237).

27. Matthew 8:20.

28. See John 5:17.

29. Cf. I Corinthians 3:9.

30. See II Thessalonians 3:10.

31. See Acts 18:3, 20:34; I Corinthians 4:12, 9:6–15.

32. With reference to the remainder of the paragraph, see Supplement, p. 383 (*Pap.* VII¹ B 178:2).

33. See, for example, Ephesians 3:13; Philippians 1:12–14; II Timothy 2:8–10.

34. See I Corinthians 9:18.

35. See Matthew 6:30.

36. See James 1:11.

37. Matthew 10:29.

38. With reference to the following sentence, see Supplement, p. 383 (*Pap.* VIII¹ A 462).

39. See Matthew 6:24.

40. Cf. Hebrews 10:39.

41. See Matthew 6:33.

42. See Luke 17:21.

43. Romans 14:17.

44. Cf. Luke 12:26.

45. With reference to the remainder of the paragraph, see Supplement, p. 384 (*Pap.* VII¹ B 178:4).

46. Cf. II Corinthians 3:11.

PART THREE
THE GOSPEL OF SUFFERINGS

1. With reference to the Preface, see Supplement, pp. 384, 388 (*Pap.* VII¹ B 190; VIII¹ A 6). The title "Christian Discourses" is used here for the first time in the authorship and can be understood as the central clue to the specific nature of what has been called Kierkegaard's second authorship.

2. For continuation of the Preface, see Supplement, pp. 384–85 (*Pap.* VII¹ A 224).

3. See Supplement, p. 385 (*Pap.* VII¹ B 193).

4. See John 14:6.

5. See Hebrews 11:13.

6. Cf. I Corinthians 14:33.

7. See Genesis 2:21.

8. Thomas Hansen Kingo, *"Gak under Jesus Kors at staa,"* 6, 2, *Psalmer og aandelige Sange af Thomas Kingo*, ed. Peter Andreas Fenger (Copenhagen: 1827; *ASKB* 203), p. 179.

9. Matthew 19:21.

10. See Luke 9:62.

11. Cf. Matthew 22:5; Luke 14:18–20.

12. Cf. Luke 14:26.

13. See Matthew 18:21–22.

14. See John 18:36.

15. See Matthew 27:28.

16. Nicodemus. See John 3:1–2.

17. See Philippians 2:7. See also, for example, *Philosophical Fragments, or A Fragment of Philosophy*, pp. 31–34, 55–56, 63–65, 93, *KW* VII (*SV* IV 199–201, 221–22, 228–29, 255–56).

18. See Matthew 26:53.

19. See Colossians 1:16–17.

20. See Matthew 27:51–55.

21. For continuation of the paragraph, see Supplement, p. 385 (*Pap.* VII¹ B 181:2).

22. See Philippians 2:9–10.

23. See Matthew 10:38, 16:24; Mark 8:34; I Corinthians 4:16, 11:1; Ephesians 5:1; Philippians 3:17; I Thessalonians 1:6, 2:14; II Thessalonians 3:7,9; Hebrews 6:10, 13:7. See also, for example, Luke 9:23. The Danish *efterfølge* and *Efterfølger* mean "to follow," "follower," and "to imitate," "imitator." The Danish translation of Thomas à Kempis, *De imitatione Christi* (Paris: 1702; *ASKB* 272) is *Om Christi Efterfølgelse*, tr. Jens Albrecht Leonhard Holm (Copenhagen: 1848; *ASKB* 273). On "imitation" and its correlative "prototype [*Forbillede*]," see *JP* II 1833–1940 and p. 591; VII, pp. 48, 77. Here "successor" and "follower" are the appropriate translations. Elsewhere the translations are used according to the context. See also *Practice*, p. 233, *KW* XX (*SV* XII 213).

24. Cf. John 14:2.

25. See Supplement, pp. 385–86 (*Pap.* VII¹ B 192:34).

26. See Acts 17:28.

27. Matthew 20:28.

28. Matthew 11:19; Luke 7:34.

29. See I Peter 2:22.

30. See Matthew 12:46–50.

31. See Matthew 9:18; Mark 5:22.

32. See Matthew 9:20–22.

33. See Maria Carolina v. Herder, *Erinnerungen aus dem Leben Joh. Gottfrieds von Herder, Johann Gottfried von Herder's sämmtliche Werke. Zur Philosophie und Geschichte*, I–XXII (Stuttgart, Tübingen: 1827–30; *ASKB* 1695–1705), XXII,

p. 237 (ed. tr.): "During the first week of his illness, he often said: 'Alas, if only a new, great, spiritual thought would come from anywhere that would grip and rejoice my soul through and through—I would recover right away.'"

34. See Hebrews 11:1.

35. See Matthew 17:20.

36. Archimedes. See Plutarch, "Marcellus," 14, *Lives*; *Plutark's Lev-netsbeskrivelser*, I–IV, tr. Stephan Tetens (Copenhagen: 1800–11; *ASKB* 1197–1200), III, p. 272; *Plutarch's Lives*, I–XI, tr. Bernadotte Perrin (Loeb, Cambridge: Harvard University Press, 1968–84), V, pp. 472–73: "Archimedes, who was a kinsman and friend of King Hiero, wrote to him that with any given force it was possible to move any given weight; and emboldened, as we are told, by the strength of his demonstration, he declared that, if there were another world, and he could go to it, he could move this."

37. See Matthew 25:1–13.

38. Cf. I Corinthians 9:26.

39. See James 2:19.

40. See Matthew 11:29.

41. See Matthew 12:20.

42. See Matthew 6:34.

43. See I Corinthians 7:21.

44. See Luke 23:34.

45. See Luke 22:61.

46. See Matthew 18:22.

47. See Luke 6:23.

48. See I Corinthians 6:20.

49. Cf. Galatians 3:24.

50. See I Corinthians 2:9.

51. See John 17:5.

52. See Galatians 4:4.

53. Cf. John 1:1–5; Colossians 1:16–17.

54. See John 1:10–11.

55. See Philippians 2:7.

56. See Mark 15:36.

57. See Luke 2:35.

58. See I Peter 2:8.

59. See Mark 14:66–72; Luke 22:54–62.

60. See John 19:5.

61. See Matthew 26:15.

62. See Matthew 26:39; Luke 22:42.

63. See Philippians 2:8.

64. See Luke 10:42.

65. Cf., for example, Thomas Hansen Kingo, "*Bryder frem, I hule Sukke*," st. 22, ll. 5–6, *Psalmer og aandelige Sange af Thomas Kingo*, ed. Peter Andreas Fenger (Copenhagen: 1827; *ASKB* 203), p. 176 (ed. tr.): "I would then in all my peril / Let God and Jesus rule."

66. See Psalm 111:10.

67. Cf. Job 7:4.
68. Cf. Philippians 2:13.
69. See Matthew 6:27.
70. See Genesis 3:24.
71. Cf. Isaiah 46:1–7.
72. Hermas, *Pastor*, I, "*Visiones*," 1–3, *Patrum apostolicorum opera*, ed. Carl Joseph Hefele (Tübingen: 1847; *ASKB* 152), pp. 326–45. See Supplement, p. 386 (*Pap.* VII¹ B 181:7).
73. Cf. Philippians 2:8.
74. See, for example, *Either/Or*, II, pp. 339–54, *KW* IV (*SV* II 307–18).
75. The Wisdom of Solomon, Apocrypha.
76. See Proverbs 25:11.
77. Job 1:21.
78. See Matthew 25:34.
79. See Luke 23:43.
80. Cf. *Stages*, p. 185, *KW* XI (*SV* VI 175).
81. I Timothy 1:19.
82. See Homer, *Odyssey*, XI, 582–92; *Homers Odyssee*, I–II, tr. Christian Wilster (Copenhagen: 1837), I, pp. 162–63; *Homer The Odyssey*, I–II, tr. A. T. Murray (Loeb, Cambridge: Harvard University Press, 1976–80), I, pp. 426–29 (Odysseus speaking):

> "Aye, and I saw Tantalus in violent torment, standing in a pool, and the water came nigh unto his chin. He seemed as one athirst, but could not take and drink; for as often as that old man stooped down, eager to drink, so often would the water be swallowed up and vanish away, and at his feet the black earth would appear, for some god made all dry. And trees, high and leafy, let stream their fruits above his head, pears, and pomegranates, and apple trees with their bright fruit, and sweet figs, and luxuriant olives. But as often as that old man would reach out toward these, to clutch them with his hands, the wind would toss them to the shadowy clouds."

83. Matthew 27:46; Mark 15:34.
84. See, for example, Luther, "*Predigt am Sonnabend vor Ostern*" (Matthew 27:46), *D. Martin Luthers Werke*, I–LXIII (Weimar: 1883–1987), XXIX, p. 249.
85. Solomon. See Ecclesiastes 1:1.
86. See Matthew 3:4.
87. See Matthew 3:1.
88. See Matthew 3:2.
89. Cf. John 1:21–27.
90. Luke 22:37.
91. See, for example, Isaiah 6:5–10.
92. See, for example, Jeremiah 23:1.
93. Luke 18:13.
94. See Lucius Firmianus Lactantius, *Institutiones divinae*, VI, 9; *Firmiani Lactantii opera*, I–II, ed. Otto Fridolin Fritzsche (Leipzig: 1842–44; *ASKB* 142–

43), II, p. 19; *The Divine Institutes, The Ante-Nicene Fathers*, I–X, ed. Alexander Roberts and James Donaldson (Buffalo: Christian Literature Publishing Co., 1885–97), VII, pp. 171–72. The idea is usually attributed to Augustine, although the expression is not his. Cf. *The City of God*, XIX, 25; *Sancti Aurelii Augustini . . . opera*, I–XVIII (Bassani: 1797–1807; *ASKB* 117–34), IX, p. 751; *Des heiligen Augustinus . . . Stadt Gottes*, I–II (Vienna: 1826), II, pp. 723–24; *The City of God, Basic Writings of Saint Augustine*, I–II, ed. Whitney J. Oates (New York: Random House, 1948), II, p. 504:

> For although some suppose that virtues which have a reference only to themselves, and are desired only on their own account, are yet true and genuine virtues, the fact is that even then they are inflated with pride, and are therefore to be reckoned vices rather than virtues. For as that which gives life to the flesh is not derived from flesh, but is above it, so that which gives blessed life to man is not derived from man, but is something above him; and what I say of man is true of every celestial power and virtue whatsoever.

95. Cf. Johann Hermann Schrader, "*Der Glaub' ist eine Zuversicht,*" tr. Hans Adolph Brorson, *Psalmer og aandelige Sange af Hans Adolph Brorson*, ed. Jens Albrecht Leonhard Holm (Copenhagen: 1838; *ASKB* 200), 126, st. 6, p. 395.

96. See Galatians 3:22.

97. See Romans 3:19.

98. See Job 9:3.

99. Cf. Philippians 4:4.

100. See, for example, *JP* III 3306 (*Pap.* VI A 145).

101. See Romans 12:11.

102. See Psalm 104:29.

103. See Luke 18:13.

104. See Matthew 27:46; Mark 15:34.

105. See Job 1:8.

106. See Luke 11:21.

107. See Matthew 7:14. *Trængsel* literally means "narrowness" and figuratively "adversity," "tribulation." Frequently there is tension between a familiar English version of a Biblical passage and Kierkegaard's Danish. For centuries the best-known English translation has been "strait is the gate and narrow is the way." *Trang* in Danish does mean "narrow," but it also means "hard," and the context sometimes requires the passage to be rendered as "narrow is the gate and hard is the way." See also, for example, *For Self-Examination*, pp. 57–70, *KW* XXI (*SV* XII 342–54). With reference to the remainder of the discourse, see Supplement, p. 386 (*Pap.* VIII¹ A 20).

108. See Luke 10:30–37.

109. Gerizim, the holy mountain of the Samaritans and the site of a temple; Moriah, a hill in Jerusalem, the site of Solomon's temple. Cf. II Maccabees 5:23; II Chronicles 3:1; John 4:21.

110. See Luke 17:34.

111. See Luke 18:10–14.

112. With reference to the following seven paragraphs, see Supplement, p. 386 (*Pap.* VIII¹ A 20).

113. A capacity attributed to Napoleon.

114. Cf. Matthew 7:14.

115. Cf. Romans 8:1–2. See also I John 5:4.

116. See Romans 8:37.

117. Cf. I Corinthians 10:13.

118. See Luke 21:28.

119. See Supplement, p. 386 (*Pap.* VIII¹ A 21).

120. See Luke 14:28. Cf. also *Four Upbuilding Discourses* (1844), in *Eighteen Discourses*, pp. 361–62, *KW* V (*SV* 136–37).

121. See Supplement, p. 386 (*Pap.* VIII¹ A 308). See also *JP* I 641 (*Pap.* VIII¹ A 293).

122. The Danish "*at holde Tungen lige i Munden*" literally means "to hold the tongue balanced in the middle of one's mouth," which in a more idiomatic formulation is "to watch one's tongue" and by extension "to mind one's p's and q's."

123. See Daniel 5:27.

124. See I Peter 2:22

125. Cf. I Corinthians 9:26.

126. Presumably "The Thorn in the Flesh," *Four Upbuilding Discourses* (1844), in *Eighteen Discourses*, pp. 327–46, *KW* V (*SV* V 106–23).

127. See Luther, "*Am Tag Nicolai des heiligen Bischoffs*" (Luke 12:35–40), *Werke*, XVII¹¹, p. 279.

128. See Philippians 2:12.

129. See Matthew 10:33.

130. In the early Church, Christians who were brought before a judge and tortured but were not martyred, were called "confessors." See, for example, Tertullian, *Apology*, II; *Qu. Sept. Flor. Tertulliani Opera*, I–IV, ed. E. F. Leopold (Leipzig: 1839; *ASKB* 147–50), I, pp. 56–59; *The Ante-Nicene Fathers*, III, pp. 18–20.

131. II Timothy 1:7. Cf. *Four Upbuilding Discourses* (1844), in *Eighteen Discourses*, pp. 347–75, *KW* V (*SV* V 124–48).

132. Cf. Romans 10:2.

133. With reference to the remainder of the paragraph and the following paragraph, see Supplement, p. 387 (*Pap.* VII¹ B 188:2).

134. Cf. Philippians 3:19.

135. See Romans 1:32.

136. See John 16:2.

137. Cf. Philippians 1:12–30.

138. Acts 5:41.

139. Cf. five sentences below and p. 328. The reversal in the last phrase is in the manuscript, in the first edition of *Opbyggelige Taler i forskjellig Aand*, and (without a footnote) in all three Danish editions of Kierkegaard's collected

works. The translators of the work in the German and French editions of the collected works consider the reversal to be a transcription error.

140. See I Corinthians 4:3.

141. See Philippians 3:8.

142. See I Corinthians 4:9,13.

143. See Acts 26:1–29.

144. See Plato, *Phaedo*, 118 a; *Platonis quae exstant opera*, I–XI, ed. Friedrich Ast (Leipzig: 1819–32; *ASKB* 1144–54), I, pp. 618–19; *Udvalgte Dialoger af Platon*, I–VIII, tr. Carl Johan Heise (Copenhagen: 1830–59; *ASKB* 1164–67, 1169 [I–VII]), I, pp. 124–25; *The Collected Dialogues of Plato*, ed. Edith Hamilton and Huntington Cairns (Princeton: Princeton University Press, 1963), p. 98:

> The coldness was spreading about as far as his waist when Socrates uncovered his face, for he had covered it up, and said—they were his last words— Crito, we ought to offer a cock to Asclepius. See to it, and don't forget.
>
> No, it shall be done, said Crito. Are you sure that there is nothing else? Socrates made no reply to this question, but after a little while he stirred, and when the man uncovered him, his eyes were fixed. When Crito saw this, he closed the mouth and eyes.

145. See Matthew 10:24.

146. Cf. Mark 9:49.

147. See Jeremiah 6:14; I Thessalonians 5:3.

148. Cf. John 5:44.

149. Danish: *Forundrings-Legen*. See, for example, *Early Polemical Writings*, p. 24, *KW* I (*SV* XIII 28); *Fragments*, pp. 52, 80, *KW* VII (*SV* IV 219, 244).

150. With reference to the following sentence, see Supplement, p. 387 (*Pap.* VII¹ B 188:4).

151. See Hebrews 10:39.

SUPPLEMENT

1. See, for example, *The Point of View for My Work as an Author*, in *The Point of View*, *KW* XXII (*SV* XIII 570); *JP* V 5887, 5947, 5966 (*Pap.* VII¹ A 98, 169, 229).

2. See, for example, Supplement, pp. 356–57 (*Pap.* VII¹ A 9, 107); *JP* V 5881, 5887, 5901, 5915, 5946, 5947 (*Pap.* VII¹ B 211, A 98, 114, 128, 164, 169).

3. *Two Ages: The Present Age and the Age of Revolution, A Literary Review*, *KW* XIV (*SV* VIII 2–105), published March 30, 1846.

4. See Historical Introduction, p. x and note 6.

5. See note 1 above.

6. Regine Olsen (1822–1904), to whom Kierkegaard had been engaged. See *JP* V 5477–83, 5501, 5502, 5505, 5509–11, 5513, 5515–21, 5523–26, 5528–30, 5532–35.

7. Jakob Peter Mynster (1775–1854), bishop of Sjælland.

8. One of Kierkegaard's favorite metaphors of the venture of faith. See, for example, *Stages*, pp. 444–45, 470–71, 476–77, *KW* XI (*SV* VI 415, 437–38, 443); *Postscript* pp. 140, 204, 232, 288, *KW* XII.1 (*SV* VII 114, 170–71, 195, 246); *JP* II 1142, 1402; IV 4937; V 5792, 5961 (*Pap.* X⁴ A 114; X² A 494; X⁴ A 290; VI B 18; VII¹ A 221).

9. See Matthew 19:26; Mark 10:27; Luke 18:27.

10. See I Corinthians 9:26.

11. Poul Martin Møller (1794–1838), professor of philosophy, University of Copenhagen, and Kierkegaard's favorite professor. See *JP* VI 6888 (*Pap.* XI¹ A 275).

12. See note 1 above.

13. See note 1 above.

14. See p. 117.

15. See pp. 155–212.

16. See *JP* I 630 (*Pap.* VI A 147).

17. See *JP* IV 4265 (*Pap.* VII¹ A 69).

18. See, for example, *JP* IV 3978, 3979 (*Pap.* IV A 28; V A 51).

19. See *JP* I 265 (*Pap.* II A 12).

20. See pp. 213–341.

21. See Acts 5:40–41.

22. Cf. Philippians 1:7–13.

23. See Acts 26:29.

24. See II Corinthians 6:10.

25. See Philippians 4:4.

26. See James 1:2.

27. See pp. 155–212.

28. See Matthew 6:24–33.

29. See Matthew 6:27.

30. Adolph Peter Adler, *Populaire Foredrag over Hegels objective Logik* (Copenhagen: 1842; *ASKB* 383); *Nogle Prædikener* (Copenhagen: 1843; *ASKB U* 9); *Skrivelser min Suspension og Entledigelse vedkommende* (Copenhagen: 1845; *ASKB U* 10); *Forsøg til en kort systematisk Fremstilling af Christendommen i dens Logik* (Copenhagen: 1846; *ASKB U* 13); *Nogle Digte* (Copenhagen: 1846; *ASKB* 1502); *Studier og Exempler* (Copenhagen: 1846; *ASKB U* 11); *Theologiske Studier* (Copenhagen: 1846; *ASKB U* 12). The proposed study, *The Book on Adler*, was published posthumously in the *Papirer*. See *KW* XXIV (*Pap.* VII² B 235).

31. The "four books" are the three works eventually published as the three parts of *Upbuilding Discourses in Various Spirits* and the posthumously published *Book on Adler*. See Supplement, p. 364 (*Pap.* VII¹ B 218).

32. See note 31 above.

33. The *Rigsbank Rigsdaler* [rix-dollar] was the basic monetary unit in Denmark until 1875. The *Daler* was divided into six marks of sixteen schillings each. The *Daler* was worth approximately $5 in 1973 U.S. money.

34. With reference to the following two paragraphs, cf. *Point of View*, *KW* XXII (*SV* XIII 591–98).

35. *Three Discourses on Imagined Occasions*, published April 29, 1845. The entry was not used in that work.

36. Cf., for example, Revelation 22:15.

37. Christian Molbech, *Dansk Ordbog indeholdende det danske Sprogs Stammeord, tilligemed afledede og sammensatte Ord, efter den nuværende Sprogbrug . . .*, I–II (Copenhagen: 1833; *ASKB* 1032), I, p. 41.

38. Socrates. See Plato, *Gorgias*, 464c–465b; *Platonis quae exstant opera*, I–XI, ed. Friedrich Ast (Leipzig, 1819–32; *ASKB* 1144–54), I, pp. 300–03; *Udvalgte Dialoger af Platon*, I–VIII, tr. Carl Johan Heise (Copenhagen: 1830–59; *ASKB* 1164–67, 1169 [I–VII]), III, pp. 44–46; *The Collected Dialogues of Plato*, ed. Edith Hamilton and Huntington Cairns (Princeton: Princeton University Press, 1963), p. 247 (Socrates speaking):

> There are then these four arts which always minister to what is best, one pair for the body, the other for the soul. But flattery perceiving this—I do not say by knowledge but by conjecture—has divided herself also into four branches, and insinuating herself into the guise of each of these parts, pretends to be that which she impersonates. And having no thought for what is best, she regularly uses pleasure as a bait to catch folly and deceives it into believing that she is of supreme worth. Thus it is that cookery has impersonated medicine and pretends to know the best foods for the body, so that, if a cook and a doctor had to contend in the presence of children or of men as senseless as children, which of the two, doctor or cook, was an expert in wholesome and bad food, the doctor would starve to death. This then I call a form of flattery, and I claim that this kind of thing is bad—I am now addressing you, Polus—because it aims at what is pleasant, ignoring the good, and I insist that it is not an art but a routine, because it can produce no principle in virtue of which it offers what it does, nor explain the nature thereof, and consequently is unable to point to the cause of each thing it offers. And I refuse the name of art to anything irrational. But if you have any objections to lodge, I am willing to submit to further examination.
>
> Cookery then, as I say, is a form of flattery that corresponds to medicine, and in the same way gymnastics is personated by beautification, a mischievous, deceitful, mean, and ignoble activity, which cheats us by shapes and colors, by smoothing and draping, thereby causing people to take on an alien charm to the neglect of the natural beauty produced by exercise.

39. See p. 115.

40. See Adler, *Nogle Prædikener*, p. ix.

41. See, for example, Genesis 4:25; I Kings 1:4.

42. See p. 87.

43. See p. 88.

44. See pp. 166–70.

45. See p. 187–89.

46. See Supplement, p. 387 (*Pap.* VIII¹ A 1).
47. See Supplement, p. 388 (*Pap.* VIII¹ A 6).
48. Acts 3:6
49. Pp. 213–341.
50. "The Gospel of Sufferings."
51. See note 52 below.
52. Johan Ludvig Heiberg (1791–1860), poet, literary critic, Hegelian philosopher, was also editor of a number of publications. Among them was *Urania*, an attractively designed almanac-type book for the New Year's gift book trade.
53. Knippelsbro is the bridge that connects the island Christianshavn, where J. L. Heiberg lived, with mainland Denmark.
54. Part Two of *Christian Discourses* (April 26, 1848), *KW* XVII (*SV* X 95–160).
55. *Two Upbuilding Discourses* (May 16, 1843), in *Eighteen Discourses*, pp. 1–48, *KW* V (*SV* III 7–52).
56. See *JP* VI 6388 (*Pap.* X¹ A 266).
57. *An Upbuilding Discourse* (December 20, 1850), in *Without Authority*, *KW* XVIII (*SV* XII 243–59). The Preface is not included.
58. *On My Work*, in *Point of View*, *KW* XXII (*SV* XIII 491–509).
59. *Two Discourses at the Communion on Fridays* (August 7, 1851), in *Without Authority*, *KW* XVIII (*SV* XII 263–90).
60. See note 57 above.
61. See note 55 above. The Preface is on p. 5, *Eighteen Discourses*, *KW* V (*SV* III 11). See also *JP* VI 6388 (*Pap.* X¹ A 266).
62. The two series of two, three, and four discourses published in 1843 and in 1844. See *Eighteen Discourses*, pp. 5, 53, 107, 179, 231, 295, *KW* V (*SV* III 11, 271; IV 7, 73, 121; V 79).

BIBLIOGRAPHICAL NOTE

For general bibliographies of Kierkegaard studies, see:

Jens Himmelstrup, *Søren Kierkegaard International Bibliografi*. Copenhagen: Nyt Nordisk Forlag Arnold Busck, 1962.

Aage Jørgensen, *Søren Kierkegaard-litteratur 1961–1970*. Aarhus: Akademisk Boghandel, 1971. *Søren Kierkegaard-litteratur 1971–1980*. Aarhus: privately published, 1983. *"Søren Kierkegaard-litteratur 1981–1990. Udkast til bibliografi,"* Uriasposten, VIII, 1989.

Bruce H. Kirmmse, *Kierkegaard in Golden Age Denmark*. Bloomington: Indiana University Press, 1990.

François H. Lapointe, *Sören Kierkegaard and His Critics: An International Bibliography of Criticism*. Westport, Connecticut: Greenwood Press, 1980.

International Kierkegaard Newsletter, ed. Julia Watkin. Copenhagen: 1979–.

Kierkegaard: A Collection of Critical Essays, ed. Josiah Thompson. New York: Doubleday (Anchor Books), 1972.

Kierkegaardiana, XII, 1982; XIII, 1984; XIV, 1988.

Søren Kierkegaard's Journals and Papers, I, ed. and tr. Howard V. Hong and Edna H. Hong, assisted by Gregor Malantschuk. Bloomington: Indiana University Press, 1967.

For topical bibliographies of Kierkegaard studies, see *Søren Kierkegaard's Journals and Papers*, I–IV (1967–75).

INDEX